Pali Text Society

THE MAHAVAMSA

Pali Text Society

THE MAHAVAMSA

OR

THE GREAT CHRONICLE OF CEYLON

TRANSLATED INTO ENGLISH

BY

WILHELM GEIGER Ph.D.
PROFESSOR OF INDOGERMANIC PHILOLOGY
AT ERLANGEN UNIVERSITY

ASSISTED BY MABEL HAYNES BODE, Ph.D.
LECTURER ON PALI AT
UNIVERSITY COLLEGE, LONDON

UNDER THE PATRONAGE OF THE
GOVERNMENT OF CEYLON

GYAN

Published by

Gyan Publishing House
5, Ansari Road
Daryaganj, New Delhi-110002
Phone: 011-47034999, 9811692060
E-mail: books@gyanbooks.com

Distribution Network
gyanbooks.com
India, USA, Canada, UK, Australia, France

ISBN : 978-81-212-3739-0 (PB)
First Published, 1912

2nd Impression 2020

Printed at: Gyan Press, Delhi.

The Mahavamsa
Translated into English by: Wilhelm Geiger

Pali Text Society

THE MAHĀVAṂSA

OR

THE GREAT CHRONICLE OF CEYLON

TRANSLATED INTO ENGLISH

BY

WILHELM GEIGER, PH.D.

PROFESSOR OF INDOGERMANIC PHILOLOGY
AT ERLANGEN UNIVERSITY

ASSISTED BY MABEL HAYNES BODE, PH.D.

LECTURER ON PALI AT
UNIVERSITY COLLEGE, LONDON

UNDER THE PATRONAGE OF THE GOVERNMENT OF CEYLON

London
PUBLISHED FOR THE PALI TEXT SOCIETY
BY
HENRY FROWDE
OXFORD UNIVERSITY PRESS, AMEN CORNER, E.C.
1912

EDITOR'S PREFACE

A FEW words are necessary to explain how the present work came to be written; and one or two points should be mentioned regarding the aims it is hoped to achieve. Early in 1908 the Government of Ceylon were contemplating a new and revised edition of Turnour's translation of the Mahāvaṃsa, published in 1837 and reprinted in L. C. Wijesinha's Mahāvaṃsa published in 1889, and were in correspondence on the subject with the Ceylon Branch of the Royal Asiatic Society. The Society appointed a numerous and influential Committee, and recommended myself as Editor for Europe.[1] By their letter of July 18, 1908, the Government of Ceylon requested me to undertake that post. I took the opportunity at the Congress of Orientalists held at Copenhagen in August, and again at the Congress on the History of Religions held in September at Oxford, to consult my colleagues on the best plan for carrying out the proposed revision. They agreed that the method most likely to lead to a satisfactory result within a reasonable time was to entrust the work to one competent critical scholar who could, if necessary, consult members of the Ceylon Committee, but who should be himself responsible for all the details of the work. I reported to Government accordingly, and recommended that Prof. Geiger, who had just completed his edition of the text, should be asked to undertake the task. The Government approved the plan, and asked me to make the necessary arrangements. Those arrangements have resulted in the publication of the present volume.

Professor Geiger has made a translation into German of his own revised critical edition published by the Pali Text Society

[1] See the *Journal of the Ceylon Branch of the Royal Asiatic Society*, vol. xxi, no. 61, pp. 40–42, 70, 86.

in 1908; and added the necessary introduction, appendices, and notes. Mrs. Bode has translated the German into English; and Professor Geiger has then revised the English translation.

The plan has been to produce a literal translation, as nearly as possible an absolutely correct reproduction of the statements recorded in the Chronicle. It is true there is considerable literary merit in the original poem, and that it may be possible hereafter to attempt a reproduction also, in English unrhymed verse, of the literary spirit of the poem. But a literal version would still be indispensable for historical purposes. For similar reasons it has been decided to retain in the translation certain technical terms used in the Buddhist Order. In a translation aiming at literary merit some English word more or less analogous in meaning might be used, regardless of the fact that such a word would involve implications not found in the original. Thus *bhikkhu* has often been rendered 'priest' or 'monk'. But a *bhikkhu* claims no such priestly powers as are implied by the former term, and would yield no such obedience as is implied in the other; and to discuss all the similarities and differences between these three ideas would require a small treatise. There are other technical terms of the same kind. It is sufficient here to explain that when such terms are left, in the present translation, untranslated, it is because an accurate translation is not considered possible. Most of them are, like *bhikkhu,* already intelligible to those who are likely to use this version. But they are shortly explained in foot-notes; and a list of them, with further interpretation, will be found at the end of the volume.

The Ceylon Government has defrayed the expense of this, as it did of the previously published translations of the Mahāvaṃsa.

T. W. RHYS DAVIDS.

TABLE OF CONTENTS

APPENDICES

INDEXES

MAPS

INTRODUCTION

§ 1. Literary questions concerning Dīpavaṃsa and Mahāvaṃsa.

THE LITERARY QUESTIONS connected with the Mahāvaṃsa and the development of the historical tradition in Ceylon have been thoroughly discussed in my book *Dīpavaṃsa and Mahāvaṃsa.*[1] I believe that I have there demonstrated that the two Ceylonese Chronicles are based upon older materials and for this reason should claim our attention as sources of history.

Now, however, R. O. FRANKE has taken a decided stand against my inferences.[2] He disputes the existence of an older historical work as foundation of Dīp. and Mah.

The former appears to him to be only a botched compilation of Pāli quotations from the Jātakas and other canonical works. But the author of the Mah. has merely copied the Dīp. and the same applies to Buddhaghosa and his historical introduction to the Samanta-Pāsādikā. I have however, I hope, succeeded in combating the doubts and objections raised by FRANKE.[3]

The defects of the Dīp., which naturally neither can nor should be disputed, concern the outer form, not the contents.

[1] *Dīp. und Mah. und die geschichtliche Überlieferung in Ceylon*, Leipzig, 1905. Translated into English by E. M. COOMARASWAMY, *Dīp. and Mah.*, Colombo, 1908. Quotations in the following pages follow the English edition. I may also refer here expressly to OLDENBERG's remarks, *Dīp.*, ed. Introd., p. 1 foll. (1879), as the starting-point for my own.

[2] *Dīp. und Mah.* in the *Wiener Zeitschr. f. d. Kunde des Morgenl.* 21, pp. 203 foll.; 317 foll.

[3] *Noch einmal Dīp. und Mah.; Zeitschr. d. D. morgenl. Gesellsch.* 63, p. 540 foll. I note that OLDENBERG in the *Archiv f. Religionswissensch.* 13. p. 614, agrees with my inferences against FRANKE.

But that the author of the Dīp. simply invented the contents of his chronicle is a thing impossible to believe.

Thus it is our task to trace the sources from which he drew his material. This is made possible for us by the Mahāvaṃsa-Ṭīkā, i. e. the native commentary on our chronicle which, under the title Vaṃsatthappakāsinī, was composed by an unknown author.

I will then here briefly sum up the principal results of my labours, referring, for confirmation in detail, to my earlier works.

1. In Ceylon there existed at the close of the fourth century A. D., that is, at the time in which the Dīpavaṃsa was composed, an older work, a sort of chronicle, of the history of the island from its legendary beginnings onwards. The work constituted part of the Aṭṭhakathā, i. e. the old commentary-literature on the canonical writings of the Buddhists which Buddhaghosa took as a basis for his illuminating works. It was, like the Aṭṭhakathā, composed in Old-Sinhalese prose, probably mingled with verse in the Pāli language.

2. This *Aṭṭhakathā-Mahāvaṃsa* existed, as did the Aṭṭhakathā generally, in different monasteries of the island, in various recensions which diverged only slightly from one another. Of particular importance for the further development of the tradition was the recension of the monks of the Mahavihara in Anuradhapura, upon which the author of the Mah. Ṭīkā drew for his material.

3. The chronicle must originally have come down only to the arrival of Mahinda in Ceylon. But it was continued later and indeed, to all appearance, down to the reign of Mahāsena (beginning of the fourth century A. D.), with which reign the Dīpavaṃsa as well as the Mahāvaṃsa comes to an end.

4. Of this work the DĪPAVAṂSA presents the first clumsy redaction in Pāli verses.[1] The MAHĀVAṂSA is then a new treatment of the same thing, distinguished from the Dīp.

[1] So far as language is concerned, the author's sources have been indicated, for numerous verses, by FRANKE; and herein lies the merit of his work, although I cannot consent to his conclusions.

by greater skill in the employment of the Pāli language, by more artistic composition and by a more liberal use of the material contained in the original work. While the authorship of the Dīp. is not known the author of the Mahāvaṃsa is known as Mahānāma.[1]

5. It is also on the Dīp. that BUDDHAGHOSA bases his historical introduction to the Samantapāsādikā;[2] but he completes and adds to its information with statements which could only have been drawn directly from the Aṭṭhakathā.

6. The MAHĀVAṂSA-ṬĪKĀ brings to the contents of the Dīp. and Mah. further additions, taken from the original work. It was certainly not composed till between 1000 and 1250 A.D. But there can be no doubt that the Aṭṭhakathā-Mahāvaṃsa lay before the author, as he also supposes it to be known to his readers and accessible to all.[3] For this reason his statements as to the original work, its form and its contents, naturally acquire particular importance.

These conclusions are not in any way altered if I am now inclined to consider the relation between Mah. and Dīp. as a closer one than in my first work. That the author of the former knew the latter and used it I have naturally never disputed. But I should now wish, in agreement with FLEET, to go much further and regard the Mah. as a conscious and intentional rearrangement of the Dīp., as a sort of commentary to this latter. I also think now that the quotation of the 'Mahavaṃsa of the ancients' in the prooemium of our Mah. refers precisely to the Dīp. I have besides already indicated the possibility of this view in my *Dīp. and Mah.*, p. 17. FLEET[4] then translates the well-known passage of the later Cūlavaṃsa (38. 59) datvā sahassaṃ dīpetuṃ Dīpavaṃsaṃ samādisi in very illuminating fashion: 'he (king Dhātusena) bestowed a thousand (pieces of gold) and gave orders to write a dīpikā on the Dīpavaṃsa.'

[1] See RHYS DAVIDS, *Journ. Roy. As. Soc.* 1905, p. 391.

[2] Edited by H. OLDENBERG, *The Vinaya Piṭakaṃ*, iii, p. 283 foll.

[3] I have indicated in *Z.D.M.G.* 63, p. 549 foll., passages in the *Mah. Ṭ.* which undoubtedly bear this out.

[4] *J.R.A.S.* 1909, p. 5, n. 1.

The interpretation hitherto given: that this is an allusion to a public recitation of the Dīp. must then be abandoned. But this dīpikā, which was composed by order of Dhātusena, is identified by FLEET with our Mahāvaṃsa. Thus, at the same time, the date of its origin is more precisely fixed. Dhātusena reigned, according to calculations which are to be confirmed further on, at the beginning of the sixth century after Christ. About this time the Mahāvaṃsa was composed.

§ 2. The Trustworthiness of the Ceylon Chronicles.

After these preliminary observations the Ceylonese Chronicles should now be judged particularly with respect to their value as HISTORICAL SOURCES, and the historical data drawn from them should be brought together.

In their character of historical sources the Dīp. and Mah. have been very differently appreciated.

FRANKE goes the furthest in scepticism. If he did in the beginning at least admit the POSSIBILITY [1] that the author of the Dīp. had some document or other before him, he has lately said most positively: 'in the absence of any sources, the last-named work (i.e. the Dīpavaṃsa) must be considered as standing unsupported on its own tottering feet.' [2] And therefore according to him no historical value can be conceded to the Dīp. nor to the Mah. nor finally to the Smp. FRANKE's scepticism, to which I shall return in discussing the history of the councils, ceases to be well founded as soon as we accept the thesis that the Ceylonese Chronicles are based on the Aṭṭhakathā. With this the tradition recedes several centuries, and the probability that it contains historical recollections is correspondingly reinforced, and that thesis must, as I have explained above, be considered as confirmed.

KERN [3] too expresses himself with great caution on the historical value of Dīp. and Mah. He indeed says in his *Manual of Indian Buddhism*, p. 9, '. . . the chronicles

[1] *Literarisches Centralblatt*, 1906, No. 37, column 1275, l. 2.

[2] *Journal of the Pali Text Soc.* 1908, p. 1.

[3] *Buddhismus*, German translation by Jacobi, ii, p. 283.

Dīpavaṃsa, Mahāvaṃsa, and Sāsanavaṃsa deserve a special notice on account of their being so highly important for the ecclesiastical history of Ceylon.' But here, however, it is only admitted that the chronicles can be utilized as of value for the period from Devānampiyatissa onwards or perhaps only for a yet later time. For the most ancient times, when the history of continental India is also to be taken into consideration, KERN is hardly inclined to accept them as authentic sources.

A very trenchant verdict is pronounced by V. A. SMITH in his *Asoka* on the Ceylonese Chronicles. He says in the plainest fashion: 'in this work (i.e. in the *Asoka*) the Ceylonese chronology prior to B.C. 160 is absolutely and completely rejected, as being not merely of doubtful authority but positively false in its principal propositions.'[1]

Perhaps V. A. SMITH has since modified his judgement. For he says now:[2] 'These Sinhalese stories the value of which has been sometimes overestimated, demand cautious criticism at least as much as do other records of popular and ecclesiastical tradition.' This sounds less cutting. The warning to handle critically, which the excellent historian considers necessary with regard to the Ceylonese Chronicles, is certainly justified. It applies to all historical documents, and I have no intention at all of disputing the justice of it.

The judgement pronounced by RHYS DAVIDS[3] on Dīp. and Mah. sounds much more favourable. He says: 'The Ceylon Chronicles would not suffer in comparison with the best of the Chronicles, even though so considerably later in date, written in England or in France.' He also lays stress on the fact that, as is self-evident, those Chronicles contain no pure history. But they represent the traditions of their time and permit us to draw retrospective conclusions as to earlier periods.

Lately H. C. NORMAN[4] has defended the Ceylonese Chronicles, with complete justice as it seems to me, against

[1] *Asoka, the Buddhist Emperor of India*, p. 57.

[2] *Early History of India* (2nd ed., 1908), p. 9.

[3] *Buddhist India*, 1903, p. 274.

[4] *A Defense of the Chronicles of the Southern Buddhists*, *J.R.A.S.* 1908, p. 1 foll.

undeserved distrust and exaggerated scepticism. I draw attention expressly to this essay because it naturally has many points of contact with my own researches.

If we next consider the two chronicles as a whole, without any prepossessions, it is not easy to understand whence this widespread doubt of their trustworthiness. The presentation of the subject, taken as a whole, may be called modest and simple, indeed dry. True, there is no lack of fables and marvellous tales. But they appear as outward decoration which can be easily omitted. Besides, we always meet with such stories of miracles in connexion with events of a quite clearly defined category, namely, when it is a question of celebrating the splendour and majesty of the Buddhist Order.

Mahinda arrives in Ceylon in marvellous fashion, flying through the air; miraculous phenomena accompany the 'Establishment of the Doctrine', the arrival of the relics, the planting of the Bodhi-tree, and so forth. None of this can appear strange to us. The ornament with which tradition here decks out the victory of the Order and the true faith enfolds a deeper meaning. The facts in themselves are extraordinarily simple; but to the pious sentiment of the believer they seemed great; and fantasy glorifies them with the many-coloured lights of miracle and legend.

I do not conceal from myself that this judgement of the situation lays itself open to the reproach that our method is simply to eliminate from the tradition all the miraculous stories and consider what is left over as authentic history.[1] But I think WINDISCH[2] has shown admirably how, in fact, in the Buddhist tradition, around a relative small nucleus all kinds of additions have collected in time, by which events, originally simple, are withdrawn gradually into the region

[1] V. A. SMITH, *Asoka*, pp. 45–46: 'Most writers have been content to lop off the miracles and to accept the residuum of the story as authentic history. Such a method of interpreting a legend does not seem to be consistent with sound principles of historical criticism.

[2] *Māra und Buddha* (*Abhandl. d. phil.-hist. Cl. der K. Sächs. Gesellsch. d. Wiss.*, xv, 4, 1895), *Buddha's Geburt* (*ib.*, xxvi, 2, 1907), *Die Komposition des Mahāvastu* (*ib.*, xxvii, 14, 1909).

of the marvellous. 'But we must not therefore pour away the child with the bath. Here, too, the task of Science is to lay bare the grain of truth; not only this, but she must seek the meaning and significance of the mythical crown of rays that has gathered round the nucleus. For the mythical is often the covering of deep thoughts.'[1]

We shall, of course, be obliged to begin by removing the mythical additions. But we need by no means take the residue as current coin. Here we are concerned to examine how far the tradition is established as trustworthy, by internal or external evidence, and how far shaken as being untrustworthy.

If we pause first at internal evidence then the Ceylonese Chronicles will assuredly at once win approval in that they at least WISHED to write the truth. Certainly the writers could not go beyond the ideas determined by their age and their social position, and beheld the events of a past time in the mirror of a one-sided tradition. But they certainly did not intend to deceive hearers or readers. This is clear from the remarkably objective standpoint from which they judge even the mortal foes of the Aryan race. That certainly deserves to be emphasized. It is true not only of dominating personalities (such as, to all appearance, Eḷāra was) but also of the two usurpers Sena and Guttika it is said, Dīp. 18. 47 and Mah. 21. 11: rajjaṃ dhammena kārayuṃ.

Besides, the obvious endeavour to make out a systematic chronology is such as to inspire confidence at the outset. Indeed, whole sections of the Dīp. consist entirely of synchronistic connexions of the ecclesiastical tradition with profane history and of the history of India with that of Ceylon.

§ 3. External support of the Chronicles.

The above certainly are, in the first place, only general considerations, the value of which I myself would by no means estimate too highly. Meanwhile it is more important that the Ceylonese tradition has after all found support to a considerable extent from external testimony.

[1] WINDISCH, *Buddha's Geburt*, p. 4.

1. First as to the LIST OF INDIAN KINGS BEFORE ASOKA,[1] the statements concerning Bimbisāra and Ajātasattu as contemporaries of the Buddha agree with the canonical writings and, in respect of the names, with those of the Brahmanic tradition.

The Jaina-tradition has other names; this, however, does not affect the actual agreement. There can be no doubt that the nine Nandas as well as the two forerunners of Asoka: Candagutta and Bindusāra, were altogether historical personages. Here also, in the number of years of Candagutta's reign the Ceylonese tradition agrees completely with the Indian. V. A. SMITH,[2] too, does not hesitate to accept the number 24 as historical.

Besides the renowned counsellor of Candagutta, the brahman Cāṇakka (Skt. Cāṇakya) is known to the Ceylonese Chronicles. In respect of the length of Bindusāra's reign their statements differ from those of the Purāṇas by three years, in respect of that of Asoka by only one year. The Ceylonese tradition concerning Indian history since the Buddha is, therefore, not unsupported.

2. The CONVERSION OF CEYLON is, according to Dīp. and Mah., and finally, according to the unanimous tradition of the country itself, the work of Mahinda, a son of Asoka, and his sister Saṃghamittā. V. A. SMITH calls the stories relating to this in the Chronicles 'a tissue of absurdities'.[3] Asoka himself mentions Ceylon, as he explains, twice in his Inscriptions: in the Rock-Edict XIII, among the countries to which he despatched missionaries, and in Rock-Edict II, among those in which he provides for distribution of medicines.[4] Since these Edicts belong to the thirteenth year

[1] Cf. the tables to § 9.

[2] *Early History of India*, pp. 115–118. Cf. also *Asoka*, p. 95.

[3] *Asoka*, p. 45. OLDENBERG also (*ibid.*, p. 46) considers the tradition a pure invention.

[4] Cf. the translations in V. A. SMITH's *Asoka*, pp. 129-133 and pp. 115–116. The expression cikisakā (=Skt. cikitsā, p. tikicchā), which SENART translates *remèdes*, is rendered by BÜHLER (see *Z.D.M.G.* 48, 1894, p. 50) 'hospitals'.

of Asoka's reign there appears to be an error in the Ceylonese tradition which puts the conversion of Ceylon as far on as the eighteenth year. On the other hand Asoka, in the opinion of SMITH, would, if he had really handed over his son Mahinda and his daughter Saṃghamittā to the Church, and had brought about the conversion of the king of Ceylon, certainly not have neglected to bring it into notice. The name 'Saṃghamittā' is, he thinks, from its very meaning, suspicious.

I discuss the arguments in the reverse order. The name Saṃghamittā is of course that which she herself assumed on entering the Order. That, beside this name, under which she became a renowned saint of the Buddhist Church, the lay-name fell into complete oblivion can certainly not cause any surprise.

That Asoka makes no mention of Mahinda and Saṃghamittā in his Edicts is an *argumentum e silentio.* That there is any cogency in such an argument V. A. SMITH will surely not maintain. It is indeed very difficult to say in what connexion the king would be obliged to speak of the matter. It can be perhaps expected chiefly in the so-called Minor Rock-Edict I, the Edict of Rūpnāth, Sahasrām and Brahmagiri. But here the reason would again disappear if with FLEET[1] we date this edict in the year 256 A.D. In this case, the sending of Mahinda would be about twenty years earlier than the edict, and would belong to past times.

I certainly do not wish to decide here for or against FLEET's theory. But it is clear that we are standing on too uncertain ground to allow ourselves to proceed without hesitation from an *argumentum e silentio.*

Now, finally, what as to the mention of Missions to Ceylon in the Asoka Inscriptions earlier than the thirteenth year of the king's reign?

I may observe that, at the outset, it is not absolutely certain whether by the Tambapaṇṇi of the Inscriptions Ceylon is really meant. Possibly the name may designate the

[1] 'The Conversion of Asoka,' *J.R.A.S.* 1908, p. 486 foll.; 'The Last Edict of Asoka,' *ib.*, p. 811 foll.; 'The Last Words of Asoka,' *ib.*, 1910, p. 1301 foll.

Tinnevelli district at the southern extremity of India, where the river Tāmraparṇī flows into the sea.[1] But, at the same time, if Taṃbapaṇṇi should be understood to mean Ceylon the authenticity of Dīp. and Mah. is not affected in the ESSENTIAL points.

Let us look at the positive contents of the tradition. We are certain of: (1) the name Mahinda as the apostle of Ceylon. Nor is that disputed by V. A. SMITH. Here the Ceylonese narrative finds gratifying support from Hiuen-thsang[2] who mentions Mahendra by name expressly as the man by whom the true doctrine was spread abroad in the kingdom of Siṃhala. It is certain: (2) that this Mahendra was a near relative of king Asoka. The Chinese pilgrims call him the younger brother[3] of this latter, the Ceylon Chronicles call him his son. Here we have two conflicting reports, and it would be simply arbitrary to prefer the statement of the Chinese pilgrims to the Ceylonese tradition.

But at what result do we arrive if we put together these established facts and the mention of Ceylon in the earlier Asoka Inscriptions? Simply and solely that which is self-evident, namely, that before Mahinda relations existed between continental India and Ceylon and efforts were made to transplant the Buddhist doctrine to Ceylon.

But with Mahinda this process comes to a successful end. We can understand therefore that all the interest became concentrated in his person, and that tradition wrought together in dramatic fashion that which was a thing of slow continuous development. I consider that this would always and in all circumstances have been the critical judgment on the

[1] *Imp. Gazetteer of India*, s.v. Cf. on this subject HULTSZCH, *J.R.A.S.* 1910, p. 1310, n. 4.

[2] ST. JULIEN, *Mémoires sur les contrées occidentales, par Hiouen-thsang*, ii, p. 140; BEAL, Si-yu-ki, *Buddhist Records of the Western World*, transl. from the Chinese of Hiuen-thsang, ii, pp. 246–247; T. WATTERS, *On Yuan Chwang*, ii. 93, 230, 234.

[3] Besides Hiuen-thsang we have mention by Fā-hian (see LEGGE, *A Record of Buddhistic Kingdoms by Fâ-hien*, p. 77) of a younger brother of Asoka, who became a monk, without, however, mention of his name or allusion to the mission to Ceylon.

reports of our Chronicles as to the conversion of Ceylon. The fact, in essential respects, holds good, but it is a question of putting it in the right light.

Besides, a hint that Mahinda's mission was preceded by similar missions to Ceylon is to be found even in Dīp. and Mah., when they relate that Asoka, sending to Devānampiyatissa, with presents for his second consecration as king, exhorted him to adhere to the doctrine of the Buddha.[1]

Certainly on chronological grounds this cannot be immediately connected with the notices of the conversion of Ceylon to be found in the inscriptions. But it shows us that, even from the point of view of the Chronicles of Ceylon, Buddhism was not quite unknown in that country already before Mahinda's time.

3. The History of the Missions as related in Dīp. and Mah.[2] receives most striking confirmation in the inscriptions discovered. On the inner lid of the relic-urn which was found in Tope no. 2 of the Sānchi group there is this inscription: Sapurisa(sa) Majhimasa '(relics) of the pious man Majjhima'. On the outer lid is Sapurisa(sa) Kāsapagotasa Hemāvatācariyasa '(relics) of the pious man Kassapagotta (i.e. of the Kassapa clan), the teacher of the Himalaya'.[3] Now Majjhima is, in fact, named in the Mah. as the teacher who converted the Himalaya region and Kassapagotto thero appears as his companion in the Dīp.[4]

Again in the superscription of a relic-casket from Tope no. 2 of the Sonāri group the same Majjhima is mentioned.

On another urn from the same Tope we again find the name of Kassapagotta, this time with the epithet Kotiputta and again with the designation 'Teacher of the whole Himalaya'.

In a third urn-inscription Gotiputta (i.e. Kotiputta Kassapa-

[1] Dīp. 12. 5–6; Mah. 11. 34–35; Smp. 323$^{5-8}$.

[2] Dīp. 8. 1–13; Mah. 12. 1–54. Cf. also Smp. 314^{17}–318^{25}.

[3] See Cunningham, *The Bhilsa Topes*, p. 287. Cf. Rhys Davids, *Buddhist India*, pp. 299–301.

[4] Mah. 12. 6, 41; Dīp. 8. 10. Cf. Smp. 317^{19}; *Mahābodhivaṃsa* (ed. Strong) 115^{5}, where also Kassapagotta is mentioned together with Majjhima. Cf. also *Mah. Ṭīkā*, 222^{7}.

gotta) appears in connexion with Dadabhisāra. This is evidently the Dundubhissara of the Dīp. and the Mahābodhivaṃsa who was also among those theras who won the Himalaya countries to the Buddha's doctrine.[1]

Finally the name of the thera who, according to tradition, presided over the third council under Asoka's rule, is also shown to be authentic by an inscription in a relic-casket from Tope no. 2 of the Sānchi group.[2] There is no doubt that by the Sapurisasa Mogaliputasa is meant the Moggaliputta Tissa of the Ceylonese Chronicles.

4. Moreover, the narrative of the transplanting of a branch of the sacred Bodhi-tree from Uruvelā to Ceylon finds interesting confirmation in the monuments.

At least GRÜNWEDEL, in an ingenious and, to me, convincing way,[3] points out that the sculptures of the lower and middle architraves of the East Gate of the Sānchi Tope are representations of that event. Since the Sānchi-sculptures belong to the second century B.C. the representation is distant from the event by roughly speaking, only 100 or at most 150 years.

§ 4. Errors in the Chronology of the Earliest Historical Period.

I consider that such objective confirmation of the Chronicles proves at the very least this much: that their statements are not absolutely untenable and are at least worthy of being tested. Naturally they are not infallible and the longer the interval between the time of the events and the time when they are related, the greater the possibility of an objective error, and so much the more will the influence of legend be noticeable.

As regards the oldest period from Vijaya to Devanampiyatissa we feel a certain distrust of the tradition and traditional

[1] CUNNINGHAM, *l. l.*, pp. 316-317.

[2] CUNNINGHAM, *l. l.*, p. 289.

[3] GRÜNWEDEL, *Buddhist. Kunst in Indien*, pp. 72–73. Cf. also RHYS DAVIDS, *Buddhist India*, p. 302.

chronology from the very fact that Vijaya's arrival in Ceylon is dated on the day of the Buddha's death.[1] This seems to be a biassed account. Besides, there are the round numbers for the length of the single reigns which have in themselves the appearance of a set scheme and involve, moreover, a positive impossibility in respect of the last two kings of that period, PAṆḌUKĀBHAYA and MUṬASIVA.

According to our Chronicles[2] Paṇḍukābhaya was born shortly before the death of Paṇḍuvāsudeva. Then followed the reign of Abhaya, twenty years, and an interregnum of seventeen years. Then Paṇḍukābhaya ascends the throne at the age of thirty-seven years. He reigns seventy years. That would bring his age to 107 years!

This, however, is not enough. Paṇḍukābhaya's successor is his son Muṭasiva. He is born of Suvaṇṇapāli whom Paṇḍukābhaya had already married before the beginning of his reign. Muṭasiva must then have been past the prime of manhood when he succeeded to the throne. In spite of this a reign of sixty years is attributed to him.

It seems to me that certain names and events in the tradition may indeed be maintained, but that the last reigns were lengthened in order to make Vijaya and the Buddha contemporaries.

That in respect of certain facts, the tradition is by no means without value for that first period of Ceylonese history, is shown, for instance, by the account of Paṇḍukābhaya's campaigns,[3] which decidedly gives an impression of trustworthiness.

Also after Devānampiyatissa's reign we find matter for doubt.[4] A reign of forty years is attributed to the king

[1] Mah. 6. 47. In the Dīp. 9. 21–22 it is stated, in a somewhat more general way, that *at the time* of the death of the Buddha (parinibbāṇasamaye, not precisely on the day of the death) Vijaya landed in Ceylon. The same in Smp. 320[20].

[2] Dīp. 11. 1, 4; Mah. 9. 28; 10. 106. See previously TURNOUR, *Mahâwanso*, Introd., p. li.

[3] Mah. 10. 26 foll. See below, Appendix C, p. 288 foll.

[4] Cf. also on this subject FLEET, *J.R.A.S.* 1909, p. 340.

mentioned, who is said to have been Muṭasiva's second son, although he was no longer young when he ascended the throne. But to him succeeded three younger brothers, Uttiya,[1] Mahāsiva and Sūratissa, each of whom reigned ten (= thirty) years. Nay, after the intervening rule of the two Damiḷas, Sena and Guttika, which lasted twelve years, a fourth brother, Asela, ascends the throne and also reigns ten years.

The reigns of the sons of Muṭasiva, who himself occupied the throne for sixty years, would then cover a period of ninety-two years!

We see clearly that also in the period between Devānampiyatissa and Duṭṭhagāmaṇi there were still gaps in the tradition which were filled in with fictitious construction. For the line of Devānampiyatissa we have again the remarkable round numbers 40 + 10 + 10 + 10 + 10.

In the later periods we encounter no such difficulties and impossibilities. The chronology is credible, the numbers appear less artificial and more trustworthy.

But even in that first historical period one fact stands out clearly and distinctly from the wavering traditions concerning the times immediately before and after. That is the reign of Devānampiyatissa and the arrival of Mahinda in Ceylon. And with this we approach the general standpoint from which we have to judge the historical tradition as to the earliest and earlier times in our Chronicles.

§ 5. The Year of the Buddha's Death.

We have to do with a monkish tradition. The starting-point of its chronological statements is the year of the Buddha's death. For this tradition naturally not every event nor every historical personage is important to an equal degree, but chiefly in so far as they were of importance for the development of the Buddhist community. There are isolated occurrences and personalities connected, even in early times,

[1] The name of Uttiya and his consort is confirmed by an inscription in Periya-Puliyankulam (Northern Province). See *Archaeological Survey of Ceylon, Annual Report*, 1905 (xx. 1909), p. 45.

with a certain date which announced the time that had passed since the Buddha's death.[1] As for the intervening period the traditions concerning it were far less well established and precise, especially from the chronological point of view.

Here fictions were made, building up and completing the tradition from which subsequently, with those fixed points as framework, the chronological system was developed that we find in the Dīp. and Mah., as also in the Introduction to the Smp., and again in the later historical literature of Ceylon. In the Dīp., the oldest source accessible to us, this system appears already complete. It is most certainly not a creation of the author of the Chronicle but only taken over, in all probability, from the Aṭṭhakathā.

One of the fixed dates, which was established at a specially early period, and which evidently forms the corner-stone of the whole system, is the number 218 for the consecration (abhiseka) of Asoka. The Dīp. 6. 1, says:—

> dve satāni ca vassāni aṭṭhārasa vassāni ca ।
> saṃbuddhe parinibbute abhisitto Piyadassano ॥

'218 years after the Saṃbuddha had passed into Nirvāṇa Piyadassano (Asoka) was consecrated.'

And the Mah. 5. 21:—

> Jinanibbāṇato pacchā purā tassābhisekato
> Saṭṭhārasaṃ vassasatadvayaṃ evaṃ vijāniyaṃ.

'After the Nirvāṇa of the Conqueror and before his (Asoka's) consecration there were 218 years; this should be known.'

[1] In the same way, to date the Mahāvīra in the Jaina tradition the number 155 is evidently decisive as being the sum total of the years between his death and the beginning of Candragupta's reign. See Hemacandra's *Pariśiṣṭaparvan*, ed. JACOBI, viii. 339; Pref., p. 6. If we accept the year 321 B.C. for this last event we have as result 476 B.C. as the year of Mahāvīra's death. Certainly this is in contradiction with the Buddhist reckoning in so far as, according to Majjh. Nik. II. 243[18] foll., the 'Nigaṇṭha Nātaputta' (i.e. the Mahāvīra) must have died BEFORE the Buddha. OLDENBERG, *Z.D.M.G.* 34, p. 749

THAT IS TO SAY, THAT AFTER A LAPSE OF 218 YEARS, i.e. SOMETIME IN THE YEAR 219 AFTER THE BUDDHA'S DEATH, THE CONSECRATION OF ASOKA TOOK PLACE.[1]

Since Asoka had already reigned four years before he performed the abhiseka ceremony[2] his accession falls 214 years after the Nirvāṇa. According to the Ceylonese tradition the reign of Asoka was preceded by that of Bindusāra, lasting twenty-eight, and that of Candagutta lasting twenty-four years (Mah. 5. 18; Dīp. 5. 100). Thus Candagutta would have ascended the throne 214 – (28 + 24 years), i.e. 162 years after the Nirvāṇa.[3] Now this event is one of the few in the earlier Indian history which we can date with some approach to certainty. It falls in the year 321 B.C. or within two years of this date,[4] allowing for error.

THUS THERE RESULTS AS THE PROBABLE YEAR OF THE BUDDHA'S DEATH (321 + 162) = 483 B.C. As he died at the age of eighty years the year of his birth should be put at 563 B.C.

But we must emphatically state that this calculation too is hypothetical, that we are only able to give an approximate and not a perfectly exact result. Moreover, we shall see below that, in the Ceylon Chronicles themselves, there is a contradiction which we can hardly pass by.

First of all the whole calculation, as OLDENBERG[5] has quite justly insisted, rests on the supposition that the date

[1] Slightly different in the Smp., p. 299[20], which puts the abhiseka in the year 218 (dvinnaṃ vassasatānaṃ upari aṭṭhārasame vasse). On the tradition on Asoka's age of the Northern Buddhists see § 11.

[2] Dīp. 6. 21–22; cf. Smp. *l.l.* Moreover, Mah. 5. 22 contains the same statement. NORMAN, *J.R.A.S.* 1908, p. 10, is mistaken when he says that, according to the Mah., accession should be put at the year 218 A.B. and the abhiseka at 222.

[3] With this calculation cf. FLEET, *J.R.A.S.* 1906, pp. 984–986 and 1909, p. 1 foll., and particularly p. 28 foll. See also WICKREMASINGHE, *Epigraphia Zeylanica*, i, p. 142, n. 7.

[4] V. A. SMITH, *J.R.A.S.* 1901, pp. 831–834; *Early History of India*, pp. 38–39.

[5] *Archiv für Religionswissenschaft*, 1910, p. 611.

218 for Asoka's abhiseka is authentic. It really seems to me that it is just on this very point that scepticism is least necessary. The date is supported by the best testimony and has nothing in it to call for suspicion. The interval of time is certainly not so great that the preserving, within the ecclesiastical world, of a definite tradition as to an event of such great importance should be improbable or indeed impossible.

On the other hand we must not forget that the date 321 for Candragupta's accession, which forms a point of support for the hypothesis, is only approximately correct. A little shifting back or forward is therefore quite possible.

Finally, there is the supposition that the length of Candagutta's reign (twenty-four years) and Bindusāra's (twenty-eight) is established with certainty. Now it seems indeed that, with regard to the former, scepticism is quite out of place. Here the northern tradition is in agreement with the southern,[1] which is certainly an important point. On the other hand there is a difference of three years in respect of Bindusāra's reign. Here again there is a possibility that the date may be shifted.

Nevertheless it does seem that on the much-disputed question of the year of the Buddha's death there is a tendency toward unison. Marked differences of view are disappearing, the accepted dates are less far removed one from another.[2]

The chronology current in Ceylon, Burma, Siam starts out from the middle of the year 544 B.C.[3] as the date of the Nirvāṇa. That this date is wrong and contains an error of, roughly speaking, sixty years, is now, we may say, generally admitted. Moreover, FLEET[4] has pointed out that this reckoning is by no means based on a continuous tradition

[1] Cf. below the tables to § 9.

[2] For earlier views see FLEET, *J.R.A.S.* 1909, pp. 4–5; MABEL DUFF, *Chronology of India*, p. 7; KERN, *Manual of Indian Buddhism*, p. 107, n. 6.

[3] Not 543! See WICKREMASINGHE, *Epigraphia Zeylanica*, i, p. 122, n. 7. The year of Buddha, 2444, began on May 13, 1900.

[4] 'The Origin of the Buddhavarsha, the Ceylonese Reckoning from the Death of Buddha,' *J.R.A.S.* 1909, p. 323 foll., esp. 332.

from early times. It is rather a relatively late fabrication, which probably does not go back further than the twelfth century A.D.[1] How the error of sixty years came into the era certainly still needs explanation.

Again, the date 477 B.C. as the year of the Buddha's death, which was accepted by MAX MÜLLER and CUNNINGHAM, must be given up. It rests on the erroneous premise that the year of Candragupta's accession was 315 B.C.[2]

V. A. SMITH[3] accepts 487 or 486 B.C. as the year of the Nirvāṇa, GOPALA AIYER,[4] who starts from 269 as the year of Asoka's coronation, the year 486 B.C. Both attach some importance, it would seem, to the so-called 'dotted Record',[5] which was continued in Canton up to the year 489 A.D. and marks each year, from the date of the Buddha onwards, with a dot. In the year 489 A.D. the number of dots amounted to 975, which would bring us to the year 486 B.C. as the starting-point.

I would not for my part attach too much importance to this 'dotted Record'. It is singularly improbable that in the course of time—it is a question of nearly a thousand years!—not a single error or oversight should have occurred. The essential, to my thinking, is that the difference between the various reckonings is already reduced by now to three or four years. But if V. A. SMITH, from his own standpoint, arrives at a result so closely approaching that to which the corrected Ceylon-Tradition brings us, he might well have been led to a somewhat milder judgment as to their trustworthiness and their value.

Finally, the whole difference comes down to this: whether, agreeing with the Purāṇas, we allow Bindusāra a reign of twenty-five years, or, in agreement with the Mahāvaṃsa, allow him twenty-eight years. In the former case we come to the

[1] As it now appears (see below) in the eleventh century.

[2] *S.B.E.*, x, 2nd ed., 1908, pp. 43–47.

[3] *Early History of India*, pp. 41–43.

[4] 'The Date of Buddha,' *Ind. Ant.* xxxvii, 1908, p. 341 foll.

[5] See TAKAKUSU, *J.R.A.S.* 1896, p. 436 foll.; 1897, p. 113; FLEET, *ib.*, 1909, p. 9.

year 486 as the year of the Nirvāṇa, in the latter case to 483 B.C. If we then take the 219th year after the Nirvāṇa as the year of Asoka's abhiseka, there results in the former case 268/67 B.C., in the latter 265/64 B.C.

It would be of great importance to us if we might refer the date 256 at the end of the so-called 'Minor Rock-Edict I'[1] to the years elapsed from the Nirvāṇa to the publication of the Edict. This opinion was formerly held, represented particularly by BÜHLER and FLEET.[2]

But recently the interpretation of that Edict was cleared up to a certain extent. The merit belongs to F. W. THOMAS.[3] He was the first to point out that the expressions vivuṭhena and vivāsā (vivuthā), which appear in connexion with the number 256, should be derived from vi-vas in the sense 'to be absent from home, to dwell far away'. Then in his second article he has ingeniously demonstrated that the number 256 does not denote years but nights, i.e. nights and days. In the Sahasrām text he first discovered the word lāti=rātri in duve sapaṃnālātisatā = Skt. dve ṣaṭpañcāsarātriśate.

These discoveries were acknowledged both by FLEET and HULTZSCH.[4] But now opinions diverge. F. W. THOMAS takes it to mean that Asoka published the Edict when on a religious journey. The number would refer to the 256 changes of camp in the course of this tour of inspection.

But FLEET interprets vivutha and vivāsa in another way. According to him the allusion is to the renunciation of the household life, to the life far from house and family. He takes it to mean that Asoka after a reign of thirty-seven years had renounced the throne and the world to spend the rest of his life in religious retreat. His dwelling was the mountain

[1] The Edict is to be found in Rūpnāth, Sahasrām, in Brahmagiri and elsewhere. V. A. SMITH, *Asoka*, p. 138, n. 3.

[2] Cf. BÜHLER, *Epigraphia Indica*, iii. 138; FLEET, 'The last Edict of Asoka,' *J.R.A.S.* 1908, p. 811 foll.

[3] *Ind. Ant.* xxxvii, 1908, pp. 22-23, and especially 'Les vivāsāḥ d'Aśoka', *Journal Asiatique*, May–June, 1910, p. 507 foll.

[4] FLEET, 'The Last Words of Asoka,' *J.R.A.S.* 1910, p. 1302 foll.; HULTZSCH, 'A Third Note on the Rūpnāth Edict,' *ib.*, p. 1308 foll.

Suvarṇagiri near Girivraja in Magadha.[1] Hence in the passage which is preamble to the Edict in the Mysore versions Suvarṇagiri is named, and not the capital Pāṭaliputra, as the place where the Edict, the 'last word of Asoka', was published.

Moreover, the number 256 has, according to FLEET, a special significance. It was not by chance that Asoka published the Edict on the 256th day of his life in retreat. At this very time the 256th year since the Nirvāṇa came to an end. Asoka would thus have spent, for each year elapsed since the Buddha's death, one day in religious contemplation as a brahmacārī.

This is a very ingenious idea. But it would be hazardous for the present time to base further conclusions on this bold and seductive combination.

§ 6. Traces of an era in Ceylon reckoned from 483 B.C.

Recently, however, the date 483 seems to have found further support. Here we must take into consideration an important observation of WICKREMASINGHE,[2] which completes the proof adduced by FLEET and discussed above, of the late origin of the Ceylonese era, that starts from the year 544. Indications are to be found that in earlier times, and indeed down to the beginning of the eleventh century, an era persisted even in Ceylon which was reckoned from 483 B.C., as the year of the Buddha's death. From the middle of the eleventh century the new era took its rise, being reckoned from the year 544, and this is still in use.

In dealing with the question we have to date the immediate predecessors of king Parākramabāhu I, beginning with Udaya III (1507 A.B.).[3]

As to Parākramabāhu I, we have information from inscrip-

[1] Cf. also on this, FLEET, 'The Conversion of Asoka,' *J.R.A.S.* 1908, p. 486 *foll.*

[2] See *Epigraphia Zeylanica*, i, p. 155 foll.

[3] The names are given in WIJESIṈHA, The Mahávaṇsa, Part II, translated, pp. xxii-xxiii.

tions, confirmed and completed by literary data, according to which he was crowned when 1696 years had elapsed since the Buddha's death, that is, in the year 1697 A.B. Eight years later, 1705 A.B., a second coronation apparently took place. In the fourth year afterwards, when 1708 years had gone by since the Nirvāṇa, that is, in 1709 A.B., he held a Buddhist Synod.[1] According to the Ceylonese era those are the years 1153, 1161, 1165 A.D. But this date for Parākramabāhu is supported by an entirely independent source, namely a South-Indian inscription at the Temple of Tiruvālīśvara in Ārpākkama. Thus for the second half of the twelfth century the existence of the Ceylon era, reckoned from 544, is established with certainty.

Now according to the Cūlavaṃsa[2] (56. 16 foll.) the six predecessors of Parākramabāhu, from Parākrama Pāṇḍu onwards, reigned 107 years. Thus the accession of the last-named prince falls at 1590 A.B. or, according to the Ceylonese era, 1046 A.D. Moreover, this date is confirmed by the South-Indian Maṇimaṅgalam inscription, which is dated in the same year.[3]

According to the latter, Parākrama Pāṇḍu was conquered and killed in this year by the Coḷa king Rājādhirāja I. It is true the Cūlavaṃsa gives Parākrama Pāṇḍu a reign of two years, but we must rather take the accession and death of the king as falling in one and the same year, 1590 A.B. = 1046 A.D. Thus it is proved, at the same time, that the Ceylon-era also existed in the middle of the eleventh century.

But from a South-Indian inscription we can also fix a date for Udaya III among the predecessors of Parākrama Paṇḍu, a date which throws a completely new light on the whole reckoning of eras.

[1] See the Galvihāra-Insc. of Poḷonnaruwa, ll. 1–4 (ED. MÜLLER, *Ancient Inscr. of Ceylon*, pp. 87, 120); *Nikāya-sangraha*, ed. WICKREMASINGHE, pp. 20^{26}, 22^{6}. Cf. *Epigr. Zeyl.* i, p. 123.

[2] I designate thus the later continuation of the Mahāvaṃsa from 37. 51 onwards.

[3] HULTZSCH, *South Indian Inscriptions*, iii, no. 28, p. 53; *Epigr. Zeyl.* pp. 80, 155.

Since, according to the Cūlavaṃsa,[1] the time between the accession of Udaya III and that of Parākrama Pāṇḍu amounts to ninety-three years eight days, and, as we saw above, the latter ascended the throne in 1590 A. B., we have consequently for the accession of this former king the date 1497 A. B. But this year, according to the Tanjore inscription of king Rājendra Coḷadeva, must be about the year 1015 A. D.

The inscription[2] gives an account of a military expedition to Ceylon. This invasion by Coḷa corresponds as to its details with one which, according to the Cūlavaṃsa 53. 40 foll., occurred under Udaya III at the beginning of his reign. KIELHORN has calculated the time of Coḷadeva's accession as between the end of 1011 and the middle of 1012 A. D.; the expedition falls between the fourth and sixth year of the reign, that is, between 1015 and 1018. These years must coincide with the years 1497 and 1498 A. B. Of the 1497 years (–1015) remain 482, which fall within pre-Christian times. In other words: THE BUDDHA DIED 483 B. C.

So, with WICKREMASINGHE (*l. l.*, p. 157) we must state the matter thus. The author of that part of the Cūlavaṃsa which deals with the kings from Udaya III to Parākramabāhu I lived at a time when the present era, reckoned from 544 B. C., was in use. He was acquainted with three well-established dates, 1497, 1590, and 1692 A. B., for the accession of Udaya III, Parākrama Pāṇḍu, and Parākramabāhu I. But he did not know that the first of the three dates was based on quite a different era, reckoned from 483 B. C. The interval between Udaya III and Parākrama Pāṇḍu amounted, in his view, to ninety-three years, but was in reality only thirty-one years (1015–1046 A. D.).

Certainly, considering the detail in which the events of the period from Udaya III to Parākrama Pāṇḍu are described by the Cūlavaṃsa, it is difficult to say at what point we should undertake to strike out the surplus of sixty-two years. The

[1] See WIJESIṆHA, *l. l.*, p. xxii.

[2] HULTZSCH, *South Indian Inscr.* ii, no. 9, pp. 90–93; KIELHORN, *Epigraphia Indica*, vii, p. 7; *Epigr. Zeyl.* i, p. 79.

principal part must perhaps fall within the reign of Mahinda V and the interregnum that followed, for which thirty-six years and twelve years are set down. But that the tradition regarding the period in question is not well established is easily explained by the unrest and confusion which prevailed at that time.

§ 7. The dates of Devānampiyatissa and Duṭṭhagāmaṇi.

The tradition according to which Asoka was consecrated king 218 years after the Nirvāṇa certainly arose in India. The first envoys of Buddhism brought it to Ceylon with them, and here A CHRONOLOGICAL CONNEXION WAS ESTABLISHED BETWEEN THE REIGN OF ASOKA AND THAT OF DEVĀNAṂPIYATISSA, under whom Buddhism made its entry into Ceylon.

That Devānaṃpiyatissa and Asoka were really contemporaries we have no reason to doubt. On the one hand the Ceylonese tradition concerning the missions is supported by the discoveries in the Bhilsa-topes. On the other hand we know from Asoka's inscriptions that as a matter of fact an eager missionary-activity prevailed in his time.

According to the Dīpavaṃsa DEVĀNAṂPIYATISSA was consecrated king 236 years after the Buddha's death,[1] i.e. in the 237th year. According to the Mah. 11. 40 the consecrating of Devānaṃpiyatissa took place on the first day of the bright half of the ninth month, Maggasira (October–November).

Now since, according to Dīp. 11. 14, the consecration of Tissa was later by a certain number of years—I shall discuss the passage further on—AND SIX MONTHS later—than the abhiseka of Asoka, this latter event must have taken place

[1] Dīp. 17. 78:
dve satāni ca vassāni chattiṃsa ca saṃvacchare
saṃbuddhe parinibbute abhisitto Devānaṃpiyo.
Observe that the formula used is the same as in 6. 1 for dating Asoka's abhiseka. See above, p. xxiii. The date 236 is also to be found in the *Nikāya-saṃgraha*, ed. WICKREMASINGHE, p. 10[3], and it results in Dīp. and Mah. as the sum total of the reigns of all the kings from Vijaya to Devānaṃpiyatissa.

in the third month Jeṭṭha (April–May),[1] and in fact, as we know, in the 219th year after the Nirvāṇa.

According to the tradition prevailing in Ceylon[2] the Buddha died on the full-moon day of the second month of the year Vesākha (March–April), according to our reckoning: of the year 483 B.C. Thus on the same day 265 B.C. the year 218 A.B. would have come to an end. A month later, roughly speaking, Asoka would be consecrated. In the month Vesākha, 247 B.C. the year 236 A.B. came to an end. In the autumn of the same year the first coronation of Devānampiyatissa took place. A second coronation[3] of this king was celebrated in the following Vesākha (March–April), 246 B.C.

But there are certain statements which are not in agreement with this reckoning. In a passage in the Dīp.[4] it is said that Mahinda came to Ceylon 236 years after the Nirvāṇa. And it is said expressly that this arrival took place on the full-moon day of the third month Jeṭṭha (April–May).[5] But a new Buddha-year had begun in the preceding month. Thus if Tissa's first consecration falls in the 237th year A.B., then Mahinda's arrival falls in the 238th, that is, not 236 but 237 years had elapsed since the Nirvāṇa.

This contradiction was discovered by FLEET[6] who made an ingenious attempt to explain it.

The full-moon day of Vesākha as the day of the Buddha's death is open to doubt. This day recurs only too frequently in the Buddha's life. On the other hand FLEET points out

[1] On the names of the months in the Indian calendar see our transl., note to 1. 12.

[2] Mah. 3. 2; Buddhaghosa in Sum. I. 6^{10} and Smp. $283^{3,4}$. Cf. Dīp. 5. 1 foll. for the same results.

[3] Dīp. 11. 39; Mah. 11. 42.

[4] Dīp. 15. 71:

dve vassasatā honti chattiṃsa ca vassā tathā
Mahindo nāma nāmena jotayissati sāsanaṃ.

[5] Dīp. 12. 44; 17. 88 (thirty days after the second consecration!); Mah. 13. 18. At Dīp. 11. 40 read tato māsaṃ atikkamma. See OLDENBERG, note on this passage.

[6] 'The Day on which Buddha died.' *J.R.A.S.* 1909, p. 1 foll.; particularly 6, 11, 31.

that according to a notice in Hiuen-thsang the sect of the Sarvāstivādins puts the date of the Nirvāṇa, contrary to the usual statement, at the eighth day of the second half of the eighth month of the year, Kattika (Sept.–Oct.).[1] Following this FLEET reckons the day of the Buddha's death as falling on October 13, 483 B.C.

If we take this day as our point of departure the above-mentioned contradiction disappears. The year 218 A.B. came then to an end on October 13, 265, and Asoka was not crowned in this year, but in the year 264 B.C. in the third month.[2] The year 236 A.B. ends on October 13, 247 B.C., a month later in the year 237 A.B. Tissa was consecrated king;[3] in the same year, five months later, there followed the second[4] coronation, and yet one month later the arrival of Mahinda in Ceylon.

We have then the following dates:—

1. October 13, 265, end of the year 218 A.B.
2. April 25, 264, Asoka's abhiseka.
3. October 13, 247, end of the year 236 A.B.
4. November 6, 247, Tissa's first coronation.
5. April 16, 246, Tissa's second coronation.
6. May 16, 246, Mahinda comes to Ceylon.

But here I must point out a difficulty which shows, to say the least, that our sources are not always exact in their calculation of time supposing we do not accept a variation by even one year. The death of Muṭasiva, and therefore also the first crowning of Devānampiyatissa, we find transferred to the seventeenth year of Asoka, in Smp. 321[1], and, as it appears, also in Dīp. 11. 14.[5]

[1] See BEAL, *Buddhist Records of the Western World*, ii, p. 33; STANISLAS JULIEN, *Mémoires*, i, pp. 334–335.

[2] The day, according to FLEET, is April 25. *J.R.A.S.* 1909, pp. 26 and 31.

[3] According to FLEET, *l. l.*, p. 32, on November 6.

[4] According to FLEET, *l.l.*, on April 16.

[5] The phrasing in the Smp. Asokadhammarājassa sattarasame vasse idha Muṭasivarājā kālaṃ akāsi Devānampiyatisso rajjaṃ pāpuṇi is not at all ambiguous. The Dīp. expresses

But now even if we set out from April 25, 264 (not 265) B C. as the date of Asoka's abhiseka, the seventeenth year is already ended on the same day of 247. Then Tissa's coronation, as the dates 218 and 236 have already shown, falls, without any doubt, in the eighteenth (not seventeenth) year of Asoka.

But that notice in the Smp. is not an isolated example. At Mah. 20. 1 the planting of the Bodhi-tree in Anurādhapura is transferred to the eighteenth year of Asoka. This, too, does not agree with the reckoning elsewhere. There can be no doubt that that event falls in the nineteenth year of Asoka.[1] Naturally, together with that chronological statement, other dates based upon it and given by the Mahāvaṃsa 20. 2 foll. are shifted also.

It suffices to point out these discrepancies. They are merely to show that caution is after all not out of place.

2. Further, there is an interesting date connected with the time of VAṬṬAGĀMAṆI. We have, namely, according to Mah. 33. 80–81, an interval of 217 years 10 months and 10 days between the founding of the Mahāvihāra by Devānampiyatissa and that of the Abhayagiri-vihāra by Vaṭṭagāmaṇi.[2]

The date of the consecration of the Mahāvihāra can be exactly ascertained by the Ceylon chronology. On the full-moon day of the month Jeṭṭha Mahinda came to Ceylon. This was, according to FLEET's calculation,[3] May 16 (246 B.C.). A day later, on May 17, Mahinda came to the capital and

itself less clearly; however, by the words tamhi sattarase vasse chamāse ca anāgate I can only understand that there were six months still to come to complete the seventeenth year.

[1] We can hardly use the passage Dīp. 12. 42–43 for chronology. But it seems to give the correct reckoning, the nineteenth year of Asoka, for Mahinda's arrival in Ceylon.

[2] The same date, possibly taken from the Mah., is to be found in the Nik. Saṃgr., p. 11[16]. The Mah. Ṭīkā, p. 115 (on Mah. 5. 11–13), gives as the date of the schism of the Dhammarucikā of the Abhayagiri the round number of 217 years after the founding of the faith in Ceylon.

[3] *J.R.A.S.* 1909, p. 28. For the following cf. Mah. 14. 42; 15. 11, 24.

spent the night in the Mahāmeghavana. This the king presented to Mahinda and his companions as an ārāma on the following day, May 18, 246 B.C. This then is the day of the founding of the Mahāvihāra. We are brought then to the end of March 28 B.C. for the founding of the Abhayagiri-vihāra.

I now believe that we ought to attach special importance precisely to those dates which state generally the interval between two important events. The date number 218 in connexion with Vaṭṭagāmaṇi was also known in later times.

It is implied in the number 454 of Vaṭṭagāmaṇi in the Galvihāra-Inscription of Poḷonnaruwa.[1] For this has evidently arisen from the addition of 236 (the date of Devānampiyatissa) to 218.

Moreover, there can be no doubt as to the statement in Mah. 33. 78 foll. that the founding of the Abhayagiri-vihāra took place in the second half of the reign of Vaṭṭagāmaṇi. Therefore I do not hesitate to place the beginning of this second half of Vaṭṭagāmaṇi's reign at the end of the year 29 or the beginning of the year 28 B.C.

Of course this leads us into certain difficulties when we add up the figures of the individual reigns between Devānampiyatissa and Vaṭṭagāmaṇi according to the readings accepted in my edition. From these figures it results that Vaṭṭagāmaṇi ascended the throne for the second time in the year 39 B.C. We have then a difference, in round numbers, of about ten years.

This difficulty disappears if we read[2] Mah. 21. 11, with the Singhalese MSS. (duve) dvāvīsavassāni, not with the Burmese duve dvādasa vassāni, to give thus to the Damiḷas Sena and Guttika twenty-two and not twelve years' reign. To be sure the Dīp. (18. 47) has dvādasa vassāni, which certainly must be taken into account. On the other hand the later Ceylonese literature (Thūpavaṃsa, Pūjāvaliya, Rājā-

[1] Ed. Müller, *Ancient Inscriptions of Ceylon*, p. 87 (Sāra siya supænæs hawuruddak). See Fleet, *J.R.A.S.* 1909, p. 330.

[2] In my edition I originally accepted the former reading, however in the 'Corrections' (p. 368) I have given the preference to dvādasa.

valiya [1]) only gives the number 22. In any case at the time the Thūp. was composed, according to it, the date stood so in the Mah.

Naturally, to be consequent, we must also read Mah. 27. 6 in the prophecy concerning Duṭṭhagāmaṇi, with the Sinhalese MSS. cha cattālīsa sataṃ '146' or cattālīsa sataṃ '140'. From the point of view of textual criticism the latter reading seems to me to be the safer; also I should be inclined to believe that in this connexion a round number would be more appropriate.

I confess that I only brought myself unwillingly to depart from the reading of the Burmese MSS. They contain elsewhere, without doubt, the better text. Perhaps we must conclude that, in regard to Sena and Guttika, the Burmese recension adopted the reading of the Dīp. and that, in accordance with this, in Mah. 27. 6, also the number was altered to chattiṃsasatavassāni to do away with the mistake thus caused in the addition total.

Taking as a basis the date 483 B.C. we can provisionally draw up a list of the kings according to Dīp. and Mah.[2]

§ 8. List of the Ancient Kings of Ceylon.

No.	Name	Dīp.	Mah.	Length of Reign		Buddh. Era 483 B.C.	Christian Era
				Dīp.	Mah.		
				Y. M. D.	Y. M. D.		
1	Vijaya	9.42	7.74	38 — —	38 — —	*1-38*	*483-445*
	Interregnum . .	11.9	8.5	1 — —	1 — —	*38-39*	*445-444*
2	Paṇḍuvāsudeva .	10.5	9.25	30 — —	30 — —	*39-69*	*444-414*
3	Abhaya	10.7	10.52	20 — —	20 — —	*69-89*	*414-394*
	Interregnum . .	11.11	10.105	17 — —	17 — —	*89-106*	*394-377*
4	Paṇḍukābhaya . .	11.4	10.106	70 — —	70 — —	*106-176*	*377-307*
5	Muṭasiva	11.5 (17.78)	11.4	60 — —	60 — —	*176-236*	*307-247*
				236 — —	236 — —		

[1] For the passages see Dīp. and Mah., p. 120.

[2] See FLEET's list, *J.R.A.S.* 1909, p. 350. The particular aim of this Introduction obliges me, on my side, to draw up a table to enable the reader of the translation to take a rapid survey.

No.	Name	Dīp.	Mah.	Length of Reign		Buddh. Era 483 B.C.	Christian Era
				Dīp.	Mah.		
				Y. M. D.	Y. M. D.		
							B.C.
6	Devānampiyatissa.	17.92	20.28	40 — —	40 — —	236-276	247-207
7	Uttiya	17.93	20.57	10 — —	10 — —	276-286	207-197
8	Mahāsiva	18.45	21.1	10 — —	10 — —	286-296	197-187
9	Sūratissa	18.46	21.3	10 — —	10 — —	296-306	187-177
10	Sena . } . . .	18.47	21.11	12 — —	22[1] — —	306-328	177-155
11	Guttika }						
12	Asela	18.48	21.12	10 — —	10 — —	328-338	155-145
13	Eḷāra	18.49	21.14 (27.6)	44 — —	44 — —	338-382	145-101
				136 — —	146 — —		
14	Duṭṭhagāmaṇi . .	18.54	32.35, 57	24 — —	24 — —	382-406	101-77
15	Saddhātissa . . .	20.7	33.4	18 — —	18 — —	406-424	77-59
16	Thūlathana . . .	20.8	33.19	— 1 10	— 1 10	424	59
17	Lañjatissa . . .	20.9	33.28	9 6 —	9 — 15	424-433	59-50
18	Khallāṭanāga . .	20.12	33.29	6 — —	6 — —	433-439	50-44
	(Mahārattaka) .	20.13	—	— — 1	— — —	—	—
				57 7 11	57 1 25		
19	Vaṭṭagāmaṇi . .	20.14	33.37	— 5 —	— 5 —	439[2]	44
	Five Damiḷas . .	20.15-17	33.56-61	14 7 —	14 7 —	439-454	44-29
20	Pulahattha (3 y.)						
21	Bāhiya (2 y.) . .						
22	Panayamāva (7 y.)						
23	Piḷayamāva (7 m.)						
24	Dāṭhika (2 y.) . .						
(19)	Vaṭṭagāmaṇi . .	20.19	33.102	12 — —	12 — —	454-466	29-17
25	MahācūlīMahātissa	20.22	34.1	14 — —	14 — —	466-480	17-3
26	Coranāga	20.24	34.13	12 — —	12 — —	480-492	3 B.C.-9 A.D.
27	Tissa	20 25	34.15	3 — —	3 — —	492-495	9 A.D.-12 A.D.
28	Siva . . . . }			1 2 —	1 2 — }		A.D.
29	Vaṭuka . . . }			1 2 —	1 2 — }		
30	Dārubhatikatissa }	20.26–30	34.18–27	1 1 —	1 1 — }	495-499	12-16
31	Niliya . . . . }			— 3 —	— 6 — }		
32	Anulā . . . . }			— 4 —	— 4 —		
				60 — —	60 3 —		
33	Kuṭakaṇṇatissa . .	20.35	34.30	22 — —	22 — —	499-521	16-38
34	Bhātikābhaya . .	21.30	34.37	28 — —	28 — —	521-549	38-66
35	Mahādāthikamahā-nāga	21.33	34.69	12 — —	12 — —	549-561	66-78
36	Āmaṇḍagāmaṇi .	21.37	35.1	9 8 —	9 8 —	561-571	78-88
37	Kaṇirajānutissa .	21.38	35.9	3 — —	3 — —	571-574	88-91
38	Cūlābhaya . . .	21.40	35.12	1 — —	1 — —	574-575	91-92
39	Sīvalī	21.41	35.14	— 4 —	— 4 —	575	92
	Interregnum . .	—	35.27	— — —	3 — —	575-578	92-95

[1] According to the Burmese MSS. only 12 years. See p. xxxv.

[2] See the same figure Nik. saṃgr. 10[14].

No.	Name	Dīp.	Mah.	Length of Reign Dīp. Y. M. D.	Length of Reign Mah. Y. M. D.	Buddh. Era 483 B. C.	Christian Era
40	Iḷanāga	21.43	35.45	6 — —	6 — —	578–584	95–101
41	Candamukhasiva .	21.45	35.46	8 7 —	8 7 —	584–593	101–110
42	Yasalālakatissa . .	21.46	35.50	8 7 —	7 8 —	593–601	110–118
43	Subharāja . . .	21.48	35.56	6 — —	6 — —	601–607	118–124
44	Vasabha	22.11	35.100	44 — —	44 — —	607–651	124–168
45	Vaṅkanāsikatissa .	22.12, 27	35.112	3 — —	3 — —	651–654	168–171
46	Gajabāhukagāmaṇi	22.14, 28	35 115	22 — —	22 — —	654–676	171–193
47	Mahallanāga . .	22.17, 29	35.123	6 — —	6 — —	676–682	193–199
				180 2 —	182 3 —		
48	Bhātikatissa . . .	22.22, 30	36.1	24 — —	24 — —	682–706	199–223
49	Kaniṭṭhatissa . .	22.25, 31	36.6	18 — —	18 — —	706–724	223–241
50	Khujjanāga . . .	22.32	36.18	2 — —	2 — —	724–726	241–243
51	Kuñcanāga . . .	22.33	36.19	1 — —	1 — —	726–727	243–244
52	Sirināga I . . .	22.36	36.23	19 — —	19 — —	727–746	244–263
53	Vohārikatissa[1] . .	22.45	36.27	22 — —	22 — —	746–768	263–285
54	Abhayanāga[1] . .	22.38	36.51	22 — —	8 — —	768–776	285–293
55	Sirināga II . . .	22.46	36.54	2 — —	2 — —	776–778	293–295
56	Vijayakumāra . .	22.51	36.57	1 — —	1 — —	778–779	295–296
57	Saṃghatissa . . .	22.52	36.64	4 — —	4 — —	779–783	296–300
58	Saṃghabodhi . .	22.53	36.73	2 — —	2 — —	783–785	300–302
59	Goṭhakābhaya . .	22.60	36.98	13 — —	13 — —	785–798	302–315
60	Jeṭṭhatissa . . .	22.65	36.132	10 — —	10 — —	798–808	315–325
61	Mahāsena	22.66	37.1	27 — —	27 — —	808–835	325–352
				167 — —	153 — —		
		Total sum . .		836 9 11	834 7 25		

Of course the dates set down can only be regarded as having an approximate value. For the Chronicles, mostly, give the reign of each individual king rounded off in whole years. Rājāvali and Pūjāvali reckon the sum total at 844 years, 9 months 25 days, the Nikāyasaṃgraha reckons the time up to Mahāsena's accession at 818, and thus the time up to his death at 845 years.[2]

[1] The Dīp. places Abhayanāga before Vohārikatissa. This appears to be the cause of the mistake in the figures. The same length of reign is ascribed to Vohārikatissa as to his predecessor, who is really his successor. According to Nik. saṃgr. 12^{9} Vohārikatissa ascended the throne 752 years, 4 months 10 days after the Buddha's death.

[2] Rājāvali, ed. B. GUṆASEKARA, p. 42^{22}; Pūjāv., ed. *idem*, p. 23^{30}; Nik. S., ed. WICKREMASINGHE, p. 14^{10}.

From Devānampiyatissa to Mahāsena's death 609 years elapsed, according to the later sources.[1] But this only proves that the accession of the former should be dated 236 A.B. (609 + 236 = 845), but naturally nothing can be deduced from this statement to aid us in dating the Nirvāṇa itself.

I will now supplement my list with the names and dates of the immediate successors of Mahāsena:—[2]

62.	Siri-Meghavaṇṇa	27 years	352–379 A.D.
63.	Jeṭṭhatissa	9 ,,	379–388 ,,
64.	Buddhadāsa	28 ,,	388–416 ,,
65.	Upatissa	42 ,,	416–458 ,,
66.	Mahānāma	22 ,,	458–480 ,,
67–75.	Soṭṭhisena to Pīṭhiya	29 ,,	480–509 ,,
76.	Dhātusena	18 ,,	509–527 ,,
77.	Kassapa	17 ,,	527–544 ,,

For this later period we now have an interesting Indian-Ceylonese synchronism which appears to confirm the reckoning having as point of departure 483 B.C.

SYLVAIN LÉVI[3] has communicated the following passage from the account of the Chinese Wang Hiuen ts'e. The king of Cheu-tzeu (i.e. Ceylon), by name Chi-mi-kia-po-mo (i.e. Śrī-Meghavarman[4]), sent two bhikṣus to India to the monastery erected by Asoka near the sacred tree of the Buddha in Bodh Gayā. They found no lodging here and subsequently told their king. He sent an embassy to the king then ruling over India, San-meou-to-lo-kiu-to (i.e. Samudragupta), and sought permission to build on the sacred spot a monastery for Ceylonese pilgrims. Thus the synchronism of king Siri-Meghavaṇṇa, the successor of Mahāsena, with Samudragupta is confirmed. The latter, according to

[1] See *Epigr. Zeyl.* i, p. 143.

[2] Cf. Cūlav. 37. 99, 104, 178, 208, 247 (according to the numbering of the Colombo edition of 1877: Mah. 37. 49, 54, 128, 158, 197); 38. 1, 112; 39. 58. As to numbers 62, 64, 77, it is said that they died in the twenty-eighth (or twenty-ninth or eighteenth) year. So it is possible that the dates have again been made later by one year.

[3] *Journ. As.* 1900, pp. 316 foll., 401 foll.

[4] The form of this name, as given by the Chinese narrator, results from a confusion between varṇa and varman.

V. SMITH,[1] reigned from 326 to (about) 375, the former, according to our reckoning, from 483 as the year of the Nirvāṇa 352–379 A.D.

According to Chinese sources [2] another embassy came from Ceylon to China, sent by king Kia-che, i. e. Kāśyapa, in the year 527 A.D. Evidently this is a reference to Kassapa I whose reign, according to my list, did in fact begin about 527.

§ 9. The Indian Kings from Bimbisāra to Asoka.

In the table on the next page I have brought together the names of the kings from Bimbisāra, the contemporary of the Buddha, to Asoka, according to the Ceylonese, the Burmese, the Nepalese, and the Jaina tradition. On this I will first make the following observations.

The BURMESE TRADITION [3] is undoubtedly dependent on the CEYLONESE, as represented by Dīp. and Mah. Buddhaghosa [4] is also in complete agreement with the Mah. He certainly ascribes a reign of eighteen instead of eight years to Anuruddha and Muṇḍa, but the sum total of the reigns of all the kings reckoned up by him at the conclusion is only correct if we alter that eighteen to eight.

The NEPALESE list of the Aśokāvadāna [5] comes perhaps midway between the Ceylonese and the Jaina tradition. It is specially remarkable that in this too appears the name of

[1] *Early History of India*, p. 266 foll. (cf. *Ind. Ant.* 1902, p. 257). See also FLEET, *J.R.A.S.* 1909, p. 343.

[2] SYLVAIN LÉVI, *l. l.*, p. 423 foll. Cf. now also E. R. AYRTON, *J.R.A.S.* 1911, p. 1142, on a new fact which speaks in favour of the reckoning from 483 B.C. On the other hand a difficulty presents itself with respect to the embassy of Mo-ho-nan (i.e. Mahānāma) to China in the year 428 A.D. (SYLV. LÉVI, pp. 412, 421). At the time there reigned in Ceylon not Mahānāma but his elder brother Upatissa II. The former did not ascend the throne till 458 A.D.

[3] See on this BIGANDET, *The Life or Legend of Gaudama the Buddha* (1866), pp. 347, 361–363, 371–372, 374–375.

[4] Smp. 321^3 foll. Cf. also Sum. 153^{22} foll., where the kings from Bimbisāra to Nāgadāsa are enumerated.

[5] Cf. BURNOUF, *Introduction à l'histoire du Bouddhisme Indien*, pp. 358–359. It is noteworthy that the name of Candragupta is missing.

TABLE OF INDIAN KINGS

Dīpavaṃsa	Years	Mahāvaṃsa	Years	Burmese trad.	Years	Aśokāvadāna	Years	Jaina trad.	Years	Purāṇas	Years
Bimbisāra (3.56 59)	52	Bimbisāra (2.29-30)	52	Bimbisāra		Bimbisāra		Śreṇika		Śiśunāga	40
Ajātasattu[1] (3.60-61)	32	Ajātassattu[1] (2.31-32)	32	Ajātassattu	35	Ajātaśatru		Kūṇika		Kākavarṇa	36
Udayabhadda (5.97)	16	Udayabhadda (4.1)	16	Udayabhadda	15	Ujāyin or Udayibhadda		Udāyin	60	Kṣemadharman	20
— —		Anuruddha } Muṇḍa } (4.2-3)	8	Anuruddha } Muṇḍa }	9	Muṇḍa				Kṣatraujas Bimbisāra	40 28
Nāgadāsa (11.11)	24	Nāgadāsaka (4.4)	24	Nāgadāsaka	4					Ajātaśatru	25
Susunāga (5.98)	10	Susunāga (4.6)	18	Susunāga	32						
Kālāsoka (4.44; 5.25,80)	!	Kālāsoka (4.7)	28	Kālāsoka	28	Kākavarṇin Sahālin Tulakuci				Darbhaka or Darśaka or Harṣaka	25
Ten Sons of Kālāsoka (5.99)	22	Ten Sons of Kālāsoka (5.14)	22	Bhaddasena and 8 Brothers	33	Mahamaṇḍala Prasenajit				Udāyin Nandivardhana Mahānandin	33 42 43
—		Nine Nandas (5.15)	22	Uggasenananda and 8 Brothers	21	Nanda		Nine Nandas		Mahāpadma and 8 Sons	100
Candagutta (5.100)	24	Candagutta (5.16-18)	24	Candagutta	24			Candragupta		Candragupta	24
Bindusāra (5.101)	?	Bindusāra (5.18)	28	Bindusāra	27	Bindusāra		Bindusāra		Bindusāra	25
Asoka (5.101)	37	Asoka (20.1-6)	37	Asoka		Aśoka		Aśoka		Aśoka	36

[1] The Tibetan tradition appears to be very similar to the Ceylonese. According to it Ajātaśatru reigned thirty-two years and Dharmāśoka fifty-four years, from the first to the latter were ten generations of kings. Rockhill, *Life of the Buddha* (1907), p. 233.

Muṇḍa whom the Jainas do not know but who is mentioned in the Aṅguttara-Nikāya.[1] Thus the Ceylonese tradition is in this point confirmed by the Northern tradition.

The JAINA list is based on the Pariśiṣṭaparvan of Hemacandra.[2] It is, I think, generally admitted[3] that in this list Śreṇika and Kūṇika correspond to the Bimbisāra and Ajātasattu of the Pāli sources. On the other hand the names from Anuruddha–Muṇḍa downwards to the Nandas are missing. But among these names those of both Muṇḍa and Kālāsoka are well established by other testimony, as we shall see presently.

The PURĀṆIC list has the series Bimbisāra–Ajātaśatru–Udāyin (=Udayabhadda) in common with the Ceylonese. But the Purāṇas insert yet another king before the last-named, and the Ceylonese Chronicles place those three kings at the head of the whole list; the Purāṇas range the corresponding four kings in the second half of the list. Moreover, I cannot say that the Purāṇa list inspires me with much confidence. The tradition as to individual names is very unstable in the different Purāṇas. The same is the case with the dates of the individual reigns, although the totals agree fairly well.[4]

The question then arises: which list merits the most confidence, the Ceylonese, the Jaina, or that of the Purāṇas? JACOBI[5] is disposed to give the preference to the Jaina list. He adheres to the view that Kālāsoka, 'the black Asoka,' and Kākavarṇin (Kākavarṇa), 'the crow-coloured,' are one and the same person. That is certainly correct and is confirmed by the fact that Kālāsoka in the Pāli sources is named

[1] A. III. 57[23] foll. OLDENBERG has already, *Z.D.M.G.* 34 (1880), p. 752, stated this fact.

[2] Ed. JACOBI (*Bibl. Ind.*), I. 22 foll.; VI. 22 foll., 231 foll.; VIII. 1 foll., 297 foll.; IX. 14 foll.

[3] JACOBI, *The Kalpasūtra of Bhadrabāhu* (*Abhandl. für die Kunde des Morgenl.* vii. 1), Introduction, p. 2. The combination Śreṇika = Bimbisāra occurs ROCKHILL, *Life of Buddha* (1907), p. 67.

[4] See MABEL DUFF, *The Chronology of India*, Table to p. 322.

[5] *The Kalpasūtra*, Introd.; also *Z. D. M. G.* 34, pp. 185–186. Cf. OLDENBERG, *Z. D. M. G.* 34, p. 750 foll.; and further, JACOBI, *Z. D. M. G.* 35, p. 667 foll.

as the successor of Susunāga and Kākavarṇa in the Purāṇas as the successor of Śiśunāga.[1] Here at least the Southern and the Northern tradition are in agreement.

JACOBI moreover believes Kākavarṇin = Kālāsoka to be identical with the Udāyin of the Jaina tradition, the Udayabhadda[2] of the Southern Buddhist sources. The ground for his belief is that it is said of both Udāyin and Kālāsoka that they removed the royal residence from Rājagṛha to Pāṭaliputra. He believes that the Ceylonese tradition has made two kings out of one person, has inserted various new kings between them and has thus artificially filled up the gap of 100 years which, according to the Ceylonese view, had elapsed between the Nirvāṇa and the Second Council. The list of kings as finally drawn up by JACOBI is this :—

Bimbisāra (Śreṇika).
Ajātaśatru (Kūṇika).
Muṇḍa (= Darśaka, Harṣaka, &c.).
Udāyin (Kālāsoka, Kākavarṇin).
Nanda dynasty.

I confess that, in agreement with OLDENBERG,[3] I do not feel convinced by JACOBI's grounds for identifying Kālāsoka with Udāyin. The removal of the residence from Rājagṛha to Pāṭaliputra is attributed to Udāyin by the Jainas,[4] and by the Brahmans (in the Purāṇas), to Kālāsoka in the Burmese tradition[5] which, beyond a doubt, comes from Ceylon. Hiuenthsang attributes it to king Aśoka whose lifetime he places a hundred years after the Nirvāṇa. He does in fact know only ONE Aśoka whom he names Wu-yau, or, as rendered once phonetically, 'O-shu-kia.[6] But to all appearance he combined

[1] The identification of Kālāsoka with Kākavarṇa has not been taken into account by V. A. SMITH (*J.R.A.S.* 1901, p. 839 foll.), who completely denies the existence of Kālāsoka.

[2] The name is written Udāyibhadda, Mah. 4. 1, 2 in the Sinhalese MSS. The same in D. I. 50[25] foll.

[3] *Z.D.M.G.* 34, p. 751 foll.

[4] Pariśiṣṭaparvan, VI. 33 foll., 175 foll.

[5] See RHYS DAVIDS, *Buddhist Suttas* (*S. B. E.* xi), Introd., p. xiii.

[6] BEAL, *Buddhist Records*, ii, p. 85 foll.; ST. JULIEN, *Mémoires*, i, p. 414 foll.

two different kings in one person. For if he attributes the founding of Pāṭaliputra to an Aśoka, this cannot possibly fit in with the historical Dharmāśoka of the third century B.C. For we know that Pāṭaliputra was already, under Candragupta, the capital of the country. Thus when Hiuen-thsang says that 'O-shu-kia[1] or Wu-yau founded the city of Pāṭaliputra he repeated a tradition which originally referred not to the Aśoka of the third century but to an earlier king, who must have lived before Candragupta.

I shall return once more to this subject. Here I will only observe that Hiuen-thsang, in any case with respect to the removal of the royal residence, is against the tradition of the Jainas and nearer to the Burmese. We can say then that the removal is attributed by the Jainas and Brahmans to Udāyin, by the Buddhists to Kālāsoka.

Is really the only solution to conclude that the two names were one and the same person? May it not be conjectured with equal or yet more probability that we have here simply a difference in the tradition among the Jainas and Brahmans on the one hand and the Buddhists on the other? Besides even in the Brahmanic tradition Kākavarṇa = Kālāsoka and Udāyin are again two different personages. Here then the same duplication must have occurred as in the Southern Buddhist tradition. It becomes therefore the more difficult to accept JACOBI's hypothesis. It seems greatly preferable to conclude that the Jaina list is defective. In this list Muṇḍa too is missing, who seems to be sufficiently established by the Aśokāvadāna and the mention in the Aṅguttara-Nikāya.

If finally the choice lies between the list of the Purāṇas and that of the Ceylonese Chronicles, which seems to be more probable and trustworthy, I do not hesitate to give the preference wholly and unreservedly to the latter.

In the Purāṇas, Nandivardhana and Mahānandin[2] must

[1] The former in BEAL, p. 90, the latter p. 85. Both names are thus used indifferently in connexion with the same event. This proves that we ought not to conclude, with OLDENBERG (*Vin. Piṭ.* i, Introd., p. xxxiii, n. 1), that the two names represent a remembrance of two different Asokas.

[2] It seems that Nandivardhana is to represent the ten sons of Kālā-

fill up some gap or other in the chronology. The reigns of these two together are put down at eighty-five years! But no deeds whatever are recorded.[1]

Again, in the Purāṇas yet another king, called Darśaka, &c., is inserted between Ajātaśatru and Udāyin. That is certainly an error. The Pāli canon indubitably asserts,[2] that Udāyibhadda was the son of Ajātasattu and probably also his successor. Otherwise the reign of the father and son would extend over eighty-three years.

Moreover that the two generations of the Nanda, namely Mahāpadma and his eight sons, together reigned for a century is a statement that does not bear the stamp of probability.

The chief difference between the Purāṇas and the Ceylonese sources lies in the place taken by Kālāsoka (Kākavarṇa) and his father. In the former they are placed at the head of the whole dynasty, in the latter they are ranged after Bimbisāra and Ajātasattu and their immediate successors. Thus, before all, the question is which of the two traditions we decide to accept and whether any reasons can be adduced for our decision.

Now we see that the tradition of Ceylon in its details always finds support from without. Its greater fullness of detail, generally speaking, as against the Jaina list finds a parallel in the Purāṇas.[3] In this respect the Southern Buddhist and Brahmanic traditions support each other.

In all forms the tradition as to the series is well established: nine Nandas—Candragupta—Bindusāra—Aśoka. The succession Bimbisāra—Ajātasattu—Udayabhadda is confirmed by the Jaina list and the Aśokāvadāna. Muṇḍa, entirely absent from the Jaina list and the Purāṇas, is named in the

śoka. At least the *Mahābodhivaṃsa* (ed. STRONG, p. 98) includes a prince of this name among them. Mahānandin looks like a duplicate of Nandivardhana.

[1] Even V. A. SMITH, *Early History of India*, p. 36, has to admit that they are mere 'nominis umbrae'.

[2] In the *Sāmaññaphala-suttanta*, D. I. 50^{25} foll. The same according to the Tibetan tradition. ROCKHILL, *Life of Buddha* (1907), p. 91.

[3] Also in Tibetan sources. See note to the Table.

Buddhistic canon and in the Aśokāvadāna. And in the same way the Aśokāvadāna puts Kākavarṇin AFTER Udāyin and Muṇḍa as the Ceylon Chronicles place their Kālāsoka, not BEFORE them as the Purāṇas place their Kākavarṇa.

Thus the greater probability seems to be in favour of placing Kākavarṇa and with him naturally his father Śiśunāga in the second half of the series of kings, not in the first.

I believe then that with respect also to the series of Indian kings before Asoka, the Ceylonese tradition is more valuable than that of the Brahmans and Jainas. The last-named is certainly defective. But as to the Purāṇas I am compelled to think that when the dynasty before Candragupta had once received the name Śaiśunāga, then in order to exalt its greatness and antiquity, the eponymos and his immediate successors, including Bimbisāra and his successors, were placed at the head of the whole series of kings. This would end in a reversal in the order of the first and second half.

At the present time greater stress is laid, and with justice, on the importance of research in Northern Buddhism.[1] It is most important for the understanding of the development of Buddhism. Still I believe that if we wish to learn the origins of Buddhism, and especially the history of those origins, we shall have to draw chiefly upon the Pāli sources.

The dates of the Indian kings according to the Southern Buddhist tradition are the following:—

(1) Bimbisāra[2]	B.B 60—B.B. 8	B.C. 543—B.C. 491
2. Ajātasattu	,, 8 —A.B. 24	,, 491— ,, 459
3. Udayabhadda	A.B. 24—A.B. 40	,, 459— ,, 443
4. Anuruddha } 5. Muṇḍa }	,, 40— ,, 48	,, 443— ,, 435
6. Nāgadāsaka	,, 48— ,, 72	,, 435— ,, 411
7. Susunāga	,, 72— ,, 90	,, 411— ,, 393
8. Kālāsoka	,, 90— ,, 118	,, 393— ,, 365
9. Ten sons of Kālāsoka	,, 118— ,, 140	,, 365— ,, 343
11. Nine Nandas	,, 140— ,, 162	,, 343— ,, 321
12. Candagutta	,, 162— ,, 186	,, 321— ,, 297
13. Bindusāra	,, 186— ,, 214	,, 297— ,, 269
14. Asoka (*a*) before and	,, 214— ,, 219	,, 269— ,, 264
(*b*) after the abhiseka	,, 219— ,, 256	,, 264— ,, 227

[1] Cf. e.g. WALLESER, *Z.D.M.G.* 1910, p. 238, in a discussion of DE LA VALLÉE POUSSIN'S *Bouddhisme*.

[2] As to the chronological relation between Bimbisāra and the

§ 10. The Ācariyaparamparā and Indian-Ceylonese synchronisms.

In the chronological system on which the Dīp. and Mah. are based the succession of the great teachers from Upāli down to Mahinda plays an important part. This ācariya-paramparā is of interest because in it there is a continuous synchronological connexion between the history of Ceylon and that of India. Here the system appears carried out in detail and completed.[1]

Of course the dates must not be considered altogether authentic. Besides, for the most part they fall within the most uncertain period of Indian-Ceylonese history, before the accession of Devānampiyatissa. They only show how in Ceylon the several names and events of tradition were fitted into the framework of the few well-established leading dates.

It seems doubtful too that the theras mentioned, with the exception of Upāli and Moggaliputtatissa, were Vinaya-pāmokkhā if indeed this should be taken to mean one having recognized authority in the Church.

Soṇaka did not even take part in the Second Council which took place in his time. The leading personages in this were Revata, Sabbakāmī, Sambhūta Sāṇavāsī and Yasa. Evidently it was only a question of proving that the 'Succession of Teachers' of Mahinda could be traced back to Upāli, the great authority in the Vinaya at the time of the Buddha.

The list is as follows :—

Buddha more precise statements are furnished by Dīp. 3. 56 foll. and Mah. 2. 28 foll. According to these the two met for the first time when the Buddha was thirty-five and Bimbisāra thirty years of age, i.e. 528 B.C. This was the year 15 of Bimbisāra's reign. After that Bimbisāra reigned yet another thirty-seven years (till 491 B.C.). He was succeeded by Ajātasattu. Eight years after his accession the Buddha died.

[1] See NORMAN, *J.R.A.S.* 1908, pp. 5-6. The list of the patriarchs according to the Northern tradition is quite different. In this the succession is: (1) Kāśyapa, who presided over the First Council; (2) Ānanda; (3) Sāṇakavāsa; (4) Upagupta, the president of the Second Council; (5) Daitika or Dhītika; (6) Kāla, who was principally concerned in the conversion of Ceylon. See BEAL, 'Succession of Buddhist Patriarchs' (*Ind. Ant.* ix, 1880, p. 148 foll.).

1. UPĀLI.[1] (*a*) At the time of the Buddha's death (483 B.C.) he had completed forty-four years from his upasampadā. So we should have for this last the date 527 B.C. Buddha's death, according to tradition, coincides in time with the coming of Vijaya to Ceylon and with the 8th year of Ajātasattu. Vijaya dies in the 14th year of Udayabhadda, i.e. 446 B.C., in the 16th year of the same king, i.e. 444 B.C., Paṇḍuvāsudeva is crowned king in Ceylon.[2]

(*b*) Upāli after the Buddha's death becomes Chief of the Vinaya and remains so for thirty years. The sum total of his years, reckoned from the upasampadā, amounts to seventy-four. He dies therefore 453 B.C. after, as Dīp. 4. 38 says, Udaya had reigned six years.

2. DĀSAKA.[3] (*a*) He is ordained by Upāli, when the latter has completed sixty years of his priesthood, or sixteen years after the Buddha's death, i.e. 467 B.C. This agrees with the statement that it happened in the year 24 of Ajātasattu and in the year 16 of Vijaya. According to Mah. 5. 106 he was then twelve years old, thus the year of his birth was 479 B. C.

(*b*) Dāsaka is (after Upāli) for fifty years Chief of the Vinaya, i. e. he dies 403 B. C., or according to the Dīp., in the year 8 of Susunāga. In Ceylon meanwhile (Dīp. 11. 10) Paṇḍuvāsudeva has died in the year 21 of Nāgadāsaka, i.e. 414 B. C., and Abhaya has been crowned king.

3. SOṆAKA.[4] (*a*) He is ordained a priest by Dāsaka when the latter has completed forty-five years from his upasampadā, therefore 422 B. C. Thus according to Dīp. 4. 41. But according to Dīp. 5. 78 Dāsaka had only been forty years a priest when Soṇaka was ordained by him. This brings us to 427 B. C. Here therefore the tradition is uncertain. It also points to the year 10 of Nāgadāsa or the year 20 of Paṇḍuvāsudeva as the year of Soṇaka's ordination, i. e. 425 or 424 B.C.

[1] Dīp. 4. 34, 38; 5. 76, 95, 103.

[2] Dīp. 11. 8. The number of years of Vijaya's reign (38) brings us to 445 as the year of his death. The length of the interregnum is given Dīp. 11. 9, Mah. 8. 5, as one year.

[3] Dīp. 4. 27–28, 43; 5. 91, 95, 96, 98, 104.

[4] Dīp. 4. 41; 5. 78, 79, 92, 95, 96, 99, 105.

(*b*) Soṇaka is Chief of the Vinaya for forty-four years and a priest for sixty-six years. Since Dāsaka died 403 B.C. Soṇaka's death would fall in 359 B.C. This would bring us again to 425 as the year of ordination. The statement that Soṇaka died in the year 6 of the reign of Asoka's sons points also to 359 B.C. as the year of his death. The most probable date of Soṇaka's ordination is, however, 423 or 422 B.C., as we shall see from Siggava's chronology. According to Mah. 5. 115 Soṇaka was fifteen years old when he met Dāsaka. He was therefore born in 438 or 437 B.C. In Ceylon [1] the year 11 of the interregnum between Abhaya and Paṇḍukābhaya corresponds to the year 10 of Kālāsoka (=383 B.C.) and the year 58 of Paṇḍukābhaya to the year 2 of Candagutta (= 319 B.C.).

4. SIGGAVA.[2] (*a*) Soṇaka confers ordination on Siggava forty years after his own upasaṃpadā. At that time Kālāsoka had reigned ten years and half a month. In Ceylon eleven and a half years of the interregnum after Abhaya had elapsed. Thus we come to the year 383 (or 382) B.C. and to the year 423 (or 422) as the year of Soṇaka's upasaṃpadā.

(*b*) Siggava is a priest for seventy-six years and dies in the year 14 of Candagutta. This coincides with the year 307 B.C. There must be an error in the statement that he was head of the Church for fifty-five years. Since Soṇaka's death may be reckoned with all probability as occurring in the year 359, Siggava, if he died in 307, can only have held this office fifty-two years.

The year of Siggava's birth, since he was eighteen years old at the time of his meeting with Soṇaka (Mah. 5. 120), falls in the year 401 B.C.

5. (*a*) MOGGALIPUTTATISSA.[3] He is ordained by Siggava sixty-four years after the latter's upasaṃpadā, in the year 2

[1] Dīp. 5. 69, 81; 5. 80.

[2] Dīp. 4. 44–46 (cf. with this the note in OLDENBERG'S edition); 5. 73, 95, 96, 106.

[3] Dīp. 5. 69, 81, 95, 96, 101, 107. Relics of (Moggaliputta)tissa, attested by an inscription, have been found in the Sānchi-tope no. 2. See CUNNINGHAM, *Bhilsa Topes*, p. 289.

of Candagutta and 58 of Pakuṇḍaka (i.e. Paṇḍukābhaya), therefore 319 B.C.

(*b*) He is Chief of the Vinaya for sixty-eight years after Siggava and dies eighty years after ordination, twenty-six years after Asoka's abhiseka (=264 B.C.). The first two statements accord with 239 B.C., the last with 238 B.C. However, if we place the consecration of Asoka as early as the year 265, which results (see above, p. xxxii) from dating the Buddha's death on the full-moon day of Vesākha, then even according to this reckoning Moggaliputta's death should be placed at 239 B.C.

6. MAHINDA.[1] (*a*) Moggaliputta ordains Mahinda in the year 6 of Asoka, (reckoned from the abhiseka) or the year 48 of Muṭasiva. This brings us, in both cases, if we take the spring of 265 as that of Asoka's abhiseka, to the time between the spring of 259 and 258. Mahinda was born[2] 204 A.B. i.e. 279 B.C., thus he was ordained at the age of twenty.

Mahinda comes to Ceylon twelve and a half years after his ordination and eighteen years after Asoka's abhiseka,[3] as we have already seen, in the spring 246 B.C.

(*b*) He dies in the year 8 of Uttiya's reign and on the 8th day of the bright half of the month Assayuja.[4] The year of his death is therefore 199 B.C.

I. ĀCARIYAPARAMPARĀ

	Priest	Chief of Vinaya
1. Upāli . . .	44 B.B.—30 A.B. = 527 B.C.—453 B.C.	from 1 A.B.
2. Dāsaka . .	30 A.B.—94 „ = 467 „ —403 „	„ 30 „
3. Soṇaka . .	60 „ —124 „ = 423 „ —359 „	„ 94 „
4. Siggava . .	100 „ —176 „ = 383 „ —307 „	„ 124 „
5. Moggaliputta	164 „ —244 „ = 319 „ —239 „	„ 176 „
6. Mahinda . .	224 „ —284 „ = 259 „ —199 „	

[1] Dīp. 5. 82. The time between the ordination of Moggaliputta and that of Mahinda is here stated to be sixty-six years. It would be correct to say sixty, as OLDENBERG has already observed.

[2] Dīp. 6. 20 foll.; 7. 21–22; Mah. 5. 209.

[3] Dīp. 12. 42; Mah. 13. 1, 5.

[4] Dīp. 17. 93, 95; Mah. 20. 32–33.

II. Ceylonese and Indian Synchronisms

Year of Ceylon King		Year of Indian King		Year of Christian Era
Vijaya	1 =	Ajātasattu	8	483 B.C.
"	16 =	"	24	467 "
"	37 =	Udayabhadda	14	446 "
Paṇḍuvāsudeva	1 =	"	16	444 "
"	20 =	Nāgadāsaka	10	425/4 "
Abhaya	1 =	"	21	414 "
Interregnum	11 =	Kālāsoka	10	383 "
Paṇḍukābhaya	58 =	Candagutta	2	319 "
Muṭasiva	1 =	"	14	307 "
"	48 =	Asoka	6	259 "

§ 11. The Buddhist Councils.

According to the Southern Buddhist tradition three Councils, as is known, took place, the first immediately after the death of the Buddha, the second a hundred years later under Kālāsoka, the third 236 years after the Nirvāṇa in the reign of Dhammāsoka.

There has been repeated discussion, especially in recent times, as to the authenticity or non-authenticity of the history of the Councils.[1] I am not able, within the limits of this introduction, to go into all the details. I will rather restrict myself, in the first place, to a résumé of that which is recorded in the Pāli sources as to the Councils. By way of comparison I will then indicate the most important statements of the Northern Buddhist tradition. Finally, I will endeavour to extract the historical kernel which, in my opinion, is contained in the Ceylonese tradition concerning those events.

[1] I would refer chiefly to MINAYEFF, *Recherches sur le Bouddhisme*, p. 13 foll.; OLDENBERG, 'Buddhistische Studien,' *Z.D.M.G.* 52, p. 613 foll.; KERN, *Manual of Indian Buddhism*, p. 101 foll.; V. A. SMITH *J.R.A.S.* 1901, p. 842 foll.; L. DE LA VALLÉE POUSSIN, 'Les premiers Conciles (bouddhiques),' *Le Muséon*, N.S. 6. 1905, p. 213 foll. (cf. 'The Buddhist Councils,' *Ind. Ant.* 1908, pp. 1 foll., 81 foll.); R. O. FRANKE, 'The Buddhist Councils at Rājagaha and Vesālī,' *J.P.T.S.* 1908, p. 1 foll.; RHYS DAVIDS, *Dialogues of the Buddha*, ii. 76, 77. The Chinese accounts of the First Council have been brought together by SUZUKI, 'The first Buddhist Council,' in *the Monist*, xiv. 2, 1904, p. 253 foll.

I can only incidentally, where it appears to me to be absolutely necessary, take up a position with regard to views of other inquirers, and must avoid many explanations which suggest themselves, in order not to overstep the space allotted to me.

First, with regard to the SOUTHERN BUDDHIST SOURCES for the history of the Councils, the principal, both in age and importance, are Khandhaka XI and XII of the Cullavagga in the Vinaya-Piṭaka [1] which deal with the First and Second Council.

Then follow the Dīp. and Mah. with accounts of the three Councils [2] and also the historical Introduction to Buddhaghosa's Samantapāsādikā.[3] Moreover, Buddhaghosa treats of the First Council, frequently with the same wording, in the Introduction to his Sumaṅgalavilāsinī.[4] As secondary sources we may mention the Mahābodhivaṃsa [5] and Sāsanavaṃsa,[6] and also in the Sinhalese language principally the Nikāya-Saṃgraha.[7]

The NORTHERN BUDDHIST ACCOUNTS will be mentioned in treating of the several Councils.

The First Council.

The account in C.V. is this:

Mahākassapa, travelling with his disciples from Pāvā to Kusinārā, hears of the death of the Buddha. The monks are profoundly grieved, but Subhadda comforts them with the frivolous utterance that they can now do what they will, and that they are freed from an irksome control.

Thereupon Mahākassapa proposes to undertake a saṃgīti of the Dhamma and the Vinaya, that the doctrine may thus

[1] OLDENBERG, *Vin. Piṭ.* ii, p. 284 foll. Cf. *S.B.E.* xx, p. 370 foll.

[2] GEIGER, *Dīp. and Mah.* p. 108 foll. In the Dīp. there is a double account of each Council.

[3] See OLDENBERG, *Vin. Piṭ.* iii, p. 283 foll.

[4] Ed. RHYS DAVIDS and CARPENTER, i. (*P.T.S.* 1886), p. 2 foll.

[5] Ed. STRONG (*P.T.S.* 1891), p. 85 foll.

[6] Ed. M. BODE (*P.T.S.* 1897), p. 3 foll.

[7] Ed. WICKREMASINGHE, 1890, pp. 3, 4, 8.

be kept pure. To this end 500 monks are chosen, among whom, by the wish of the assembly, is Ānanda, though he is not yet an Arahant.

The Council takes place in Rājagaha and passes off in the manner described in the Mah.

Some points are to be added from the C.V. namely:

(1) Ānanda relates that the Buddha had, in his presence, declared the community of monks empowered after his death to do away with the less important precepts,[1] if they wished. Since they are not able to agree in deciding what is to be understood by this expression, they resolve not to do away with any precept.

(2) Certain reproaches are cast upon Ānanda. Although he is not conscious of any fault he acknowledges himself guilty from respect for the Assembly.

(3) The thera Purāṇa enters Rājagaha. He is called upon to take part in the work of the Assembly. He renders due acknowledgment to this work but prefers to hold by that which he himself has heard from the Master's lips.

(4) Ānanda further relates how the Buddha, before his death, had also pronounced the monk Channa liable to the brahmadaṇḍa penance. The fulfilling of this duty is entrusted to Ānanda. Channa is deeply troubled. With zealous endeavour he attains to arahantship, upon which the penance is remitted.[2]

As regards the time at which the First Council was held, the Dīp. 1. 24; 5. 4 mentions the fourth month after the Master's death. This was the second Vassa-month, i.e. Sāvaṇa, the fifth month of the year.[3]

This reckoning is based on the tradition according to which the Buddha died on the full-moon day of the month Vesākha.

Buddhaghosa and the Mah. agree with this statement.[4] The latter certainly mentions the bright half of Āsāḷha the

[1] Khuddānukhuddakāni sikkhāpadāni. See Mahāparinibbāṇasutta, D. II. 154.

[2] I omit the episode of Udena, C.V. XI. 13–14.

[3] See M.V. III. 2. 2 (Oldenberg, *Vin. Piṭ.* i, p. 137).

[4] Smp. $285^{32\cdot 35}$, 286^{34}; Sum. 6^{10-20}, 8^{14-15}; Mah. 3. 14–16.

fourth month of the year[1] as the beginning of the Council, but adds that the first month was spent in preparations, thus the proceeding did not begin till the month Sāvaṇa.

It is an obviously later addition which we find in the Sum., that not only the Vinaya and the Dhamma, in all their details, but also the Abhidhamma are established at the First Council.

The same is found in the later tradition.

Among the Northern Buddhist Sources dealing with the First Council I mention the Mahāvastu.[2] Here, in agreement with the Southern tradition Kāśyapa is given as the originator of the Council, the number of the bhikṣus taking part in it is stated to be 500 and the place the Saptaparṇa grotto near Rājagṛha.

There is, besides, an account in the second volume of the Dulva, the Tibetan Vinaya of the Sarvāstivādin sect.[3] The fixing of the Canon took place, according to this source, in the following order: (1) Dharma, by Ānanda ; (2) Vinaya, by Upāli; (3) Mātṛkā (i.e. Abhidharma) by Mahākāśyapa himself. It is worthy of remark that the Dulva puts the accusations brought against Ānanda in the time before the beginning of the proceedings, thus before his attainment of arahantship.

Fā-hian and Hiuen-thsang[4] also mention the First Council. The former gives the number of the bhikṣus as 500, the latter as 1,000; the former speaks in a general way of 'a collection of sacred books', the latter expressly mentions also the redaction of the Abhidharma by Mahākāśyapa.

The Second Council.

According to C.V. XII. the Second Council takes place 100 years after the Buddha's death, and is brought about by the dasa vatthūni[5] of the Vajji monks of Vesālī, which

[1] The full moon of Āsāḷha of the year 483 fell, according to Jacobi's reckoning (see Fleet, *J.R.A.S.* 1909, p. 20) on June 24.

[2] Ed. Senart, i, p. 69 foll.

[3] See Rockhill, *Life of the Buddha* (1907), p. 148 foll.

[4] Beal, *Buddhist Records*, i, pp. lx–lxi; ii, pp. 162–164; Legge, *Records of Buddhistic Kingdoms*, p. 85.

[5] On these ten points, according to the Pāli-tradition, see below in

signified a relaxing of monastic discipline. In the further course of its narrative, too, the C.V. agrees with the Mah. and the rest of the SOUTHERN BUDDHIST SOURCES. The contrast comes out distinctly between the city-dwelling monks of Vesālī and the Arahants living in solitary retreat (āraññakā, Vin. II. 299[5]) and of strict tendencies.

Yasa's speech in presence of the Vesālian upāsakas is given in full extent. The disciple of Revata, whom the Vajji monks bring over to their side (Mah. 4. 30) is called Uttara. It is also characteristic that the orthodox monks before they undertake the refutation of the heresies first assure themselves of the consent of Sabbakāmī, the Saṃghathera at that time.[1]

The number of those taking part in the Council is given unanimously as 700.[2] The Dīp. and the Mah. set the time of the Council in the eleventh year of the reign of Kālāsoka (=383–382 B.C.), later documents put it in the tenth year.[3] The locality is generally considered to be the Vālikārāma.[4] Only the Dīp, (5. 29) mentions the Kūṭāgārasālā of the Mahāvana monastery, I do not think we need attach any importance to this discrepancy, which probably takes its rise in some misunderstanding.

Still it is of importance that the Dīp. 5. 30 foll. states, to complete the narrative, that the heretical monks held a separate Council, called Mahāsaṃgīti, and that they here

the Translation, note to 4. 9. See for further observations L. DE LA VALLÉE POUSSIN, *Le Muséon*, N.S. vi (1905), p. 276 foll.; *Ind. Ant.* 37 (1908), p. 88 foll.

[1] C.V. XII. 2. 4–6 = Vin. II, p. 303[19] foll.

[2] C.V. XII. 2. 9 (= Vin. II. 307[35]); Dīp. 4. 52; Mah. 4. 62; Smp. 294[7]. But when the Dīp. 5. 20 speaks of 1,200,000 who took part in the Council it does not contradict itself in this. By this naturally exaggerated number the Dīp. means those who took part in the General Assembly. Mah. 4. 60 and Smp. 294[9] give for this the same number.

[3] Dīp. 4. 44, 47; Mah. 4. 8. Cf. Mahābodhiv. 96[6]; Sāsanav. 7[1-3]; Nik. Saṃgr. 4[21].

[4] Mah. 4. 50, 63; Smp. 94[15]; Mahābodhiv. 96[20]; Sāsanav. 6[13]; Nik. Saṃgr. 6[4].

made out a different redaction of the Canonical Scriptures. With this may be compared the brief notice in Mah. 5. 3–4, according to which the heretical monks of the Second Council, under the name Mahāsaṃghika, formed a separate sect, as the first branching-off from the orthodox doctrine.

In the NORTHERN TRADITION we have accounts of the second Council in the Dulva,[1] from the Tibetan historian Tāranātha[2], from Fā-hian and Hiuen-thsang.[3]

As according to the Southern sources so according to these accounts the ten points of the Vajji monks form the starting-point of the movement.

As to the date there is great uncertainty. In the same way, with respect to the place, the tradition wavers between Vaiśālī and Pāṭaliputra.[4] Of the famous theras of the Second Council mentioned in the Southern scriptures we meet the following in the Northern:—Sarvakāma = Sabbakāmī, Yaśa = Yasa, Sāḷha = Sāḷha, Saṃbhūta = Saṃbhūta Sāṇavāsī, Revata = Revata, Kuyyasobhita (?) = Khujjasobhita and Ajita = Ajita.

The Third Council.

With respect to the Third Council we must, in the first place, depend on SOUTHERN BUDDHIST SOURCES since it has up to this time been accepted that the Northern Buddhist took no account of this Assembly of the Church. Our oldest source is the Dīp. 7. 34–43, 44–59; then comes Smp. 306[27] foll., then Mah. 5. 228 foll. Respecting the course of events we may refer to the translation following below, since no essential differences exist.

The president of the Council was Tissa Moggaliputta, the place Pāṭaliputta, also called Kusumapura 'the city of flowers'. As date, the year 236 A. B. = 247 B. C. is given, Dīp. 7. 37, 44.[5]

[1] See ROCKHILL, *Life of the Buddha*, pp. 171–180.

[2] *Tāranātha's Geschichte des Buddhismus in Indien*, übersetzt von SCHIEFNER, p. 41 foll. Cf. WASSILJEW, *Der Buddhismus*, p. 61 foll.

[3] BEAL, *l. l.*, i, p. liv; ii, pp. 74–75; LEGGE, *l. l.*, p. 75.

[4] On these wavering traditions see below.

[5] Cf. Sāsanav. i, p. 8[1, 3]; Nik. Saṃgr. 9[4]. When Dīp. 1. 24, 25 says

The Mah. 5. 280 says that the Council was concluded in the seventeenth year of the reign of Asoka. It lasted, according to both chronicles, nine months. Thus, according to FLEET'S[1] reckoning, the Council began in the middle of January 247 B.C. and came to an end at the end of October in the same year.

Now with respect to the trustworthiness of the Southern Buddhist accounts of the Councils I have arrived at the following conclusion. Here, as elsewhere, a genuine historical reminiscence underlies the tradition. This holds good of all three Councils. A general framework of facts is given with some few data deeply engraved in memory. But within this framework, even in the oldest form of the tradition, all kinds of details were introduced which correspond to the opinions and circumstances of later times. We must keep to the most general statements if we would come near the historical truth. Everything special and particular should be looked upon with a certain scepticism.

For the FIRST COUNCIL we need not hesitate to extract as the historical kernel of the tradition, the fact that, after the Buddha's death, his nearest disciples assembled in the capital of the country to establish the most important rules of the Order as, according to their recollection, the Master himself had laid them down. This may then have formed the groundwork of the later Vinaya. That the Buddhist canon was established then and there in the form in which we now have it, a form that can only be the fruit of centuries of development,[2] is naturally out of the question. We see indeed how

that the First Council took place four months after the Nirvāṇa and the Third Council 118 years later there is here a manifest error, for which the clumsiness of the author of the Dīp. is responsible. The date 118 is evidently reckoned from the Second Council, mention of which has dropped out, and it refers, as in Mah. 5. 100, not to the beginning of the Third Council, but to the birth of Moggaliputta Tissa. See Dīp. 5. 55.

[1] *J.R.A.S.* 1910, p. 426.

[2] See RHYS DAVIDS, *Dialogues*, i, x-xx; *Buddhist India*, p. 161 foll.; OLDENBERG, *Vin. Piṭ.* i, p. x foll.

the tradition itself adds new details. Speaking at first only of Vinaya and Dhamma it then, in a later form, makes the Abhidhamma also take its rise in the First Council.

In my interpretation I attach special importance to the episode of Purāṇa (see p. liii). It gives the impression of a genuine historical reminiscence, the more so since it is just of such a nature as to diminish the authority of the theras of the First Council. There was therefore certainly no reason to invent this story. As a statement of fact, however, it has no meaning unless there had really been beforehand some proposal to establish the teachings of the Buddha.

Certainly not very much more than this can be proved to be historical in the account of the First Council. The narrator in the C.V. adheres in his narrative to the Mahāparinibbāṇa-sutta (D. Sutta XVI = D. II, p. 72 foll.). This has been convincingly demonstrated by OLDENBERG [1] and in greater detail by FRANKE.[2] I should not therefore like to attach most importance, as does L. DE LA VALLÉE POUSSIN,[3] precisely to the episode of Ānanda's failings and the punishment of Channa. They may very well have been incorporated in the account only because they exist in the Sutta D. XVI.[4] It is not even certain whether it was just the frivolous words of Subhadda that brought about the holding of the Council, here too it may be that the narrator has only followed the Sutta in making this fact a motive for the Council.

In that case OLDENBERG's [5] objection to the historical character

[1] *Vin. Piṭ.* i, p. xxvi foll. [2] *J.P.T.S.* 1908, p. 8 foll.

[3] *Ind. Ant.* 1908, pp. 15–16, 18.

[4] FRANKE, *l.l.*, p. 18, foll., observes very aptly that in C.V. XI and XII the precept of D. XVI. 6. 2 (= D. II, p. 154) concerning the use of bhante and āvuso, has been strictly retained. Here, again, the narrator's dependence, as to form, on the Mahāparinibbāna-sutta is evident. Because he found the precept in the sutta, he retains it in his account. But when FRANKE then goes so far as to argue that the accounts of the Council in C.V. were only invented to illustrate that question of etiquette, that they were therefore 'more or less readings in "good form" for bhikkhus in all events and circumstances', there are assuredly few who will follow him. I am quite unable to do so.

[5] *L. l.* Cf. also RHYS DAVIDS, *Buddhist Suttas* (*S.B.E.* xi), General

of the First Council disappears. He is of opinion that, since Subhadda's words are mentioned, in the Mahāparinibbāṇa-sutta, there must also have been some allusion to the Council if it really was brought about by those words. According to my view the Council—or whatever this assembly of monks in Rājagaha may be called—is the established fact (see above). If the introduction of the narrative in the C.V. really should not be in agreement with the Sutta D. XVI, which I will only assume but without yielding the point, then the fact of the Council itself is not put aside. In that case the narrator, looking for a motive or means of introducing the Council, found it in that passage of the Sutta, a connexion which did not correspond to the reality.[1]

The SECOND and THIRD COUNCIL must be discussed together.

It is historically confirmed, I think, that the first schism in the Church proceeded from Vesālī and that the dasa vatthūni of the Vajji-monks brought it about. But it is doubtful when this separation resulted, where it took place, and whether after this Second Council yet a third took place and at what time.

According to the Southern Buddhist tradition, as we saw, the Second Council was held in Vesālī itself under king Kālāsoka in the year 383/2 B.C., the third under Dhammāsoka in Pāṭaliputta in the year 247 B.C. The first led to the separation of the Mahāsaṃghikas from the Theravāda. The second led to the expulsion from the community of certain elements wrongfully intruded there.

My opinion now is that this distinction between two separate Councils is in fact correct. The Northern Buddhists have mistakenly fused the two into one as they confounded the kings Kālāsoka and Dhammāsoka one with another. But traces of the right tradition are still preserved

Introduction, p. xi foll. JACOBI, *Z.D.M.G.* 34, p. 185, is, however, not inclined to give such great weight to the *argumentum e silentio*.

[1] RHYS DAVIDS, *Dialogues*, ii. 76, 77, has discussed the value of the evidence as to the First Council, and arrived at a somewhat similar conclusion.

in the wavering uncertain statements as to the time and place of the Council.

According to the Tibetan tradition in the Dulva[1] the first schism occurred 160 years after the death of the Buddha, when king Dharmāśoka reigned in Kusumapura. But the same source (ROCKHILL, p. 186) also records an assembly which took place in Pāṭaliputra 137 years after the Nirvāṇa, under Mahāpadma and Nanda.

In Chinese sources[2] we find the same uncertainty. The Council that led to the first schism is in these placed now 100, now 116, now 160 years after the Buddha's death.

As the place of the Council Fā-hian and Hiuen-thsang[3] mention Vaiśālī. But according to the Dulva (R., p. 182) the schism arose in Kusumapura (i.e. Pāṭaliputra). Tāranātha (p. 41) speaks of the ten points taught by the heretical monks of Vaiśālī and which gave occasion for a Council that took place in Kusumapura. The Chinese sources too (see St. J., *l. l.*) mention Pāṭaliputra.

Evidently, as has been said, the failure to distinguish between the two Aśokas was the cause of the whole confusion. This is plain from the fact that with respect to this king's date we find the same contradictions in the Northern sources. Hiuen-thsang knows only one Aśoka, Dharmāśoka, the historical king of the third century B.C. But he puts him 100 years after the Nirvāṇa, that is, he gives him the period of the earlier Aśoka. For hardly any scholar will admit now, I believe, that Buddha died in the fourth century B.C.; moreover, Hiuen-thsang, as we saw (see above, p. xliv), names also Dharmāśoka as the founder of Pāṭaliputra, although we know beyond dispute that Pāṭaliputra was the capital of the country before his time. He has thus transferred to Dharmāśoka, the son of Candragupta, a tradition which related to an earlier king.

[1] According to Bhavya, in ROCKHILL, *Life of the Buddha*, p. 182.

[2] ST. JULIEN, *Journ. As.*, V. Série, t. xiv, pp. 343, 333, 336. Cf. below, Appendix B.

[3] See above, p. lvi, n. 3. Fā-hian, however, does not express himself so definitely as Hiuen-thsang.

In the Tibetan sources Aśoka is generally dated 100–160 years after the Nirvāṇa. But there is beside this an allusion which, in agreement with the Southern tradition, places him 234 years after the Buddha.[1]

Tāranātha says[2] that in the Tibetan Vinaya the date 110 A.B. is given for Aśoka, but that in the other sources the dates are 210 and 220.

Lastly, in the Chinese Tripiṭaka there are, according to TAKAKUSU, four dates for Aśoka: 116 A.B., 118 A.B., 130 A.B., and 218 A.B. The last-mentioned date, however, is found apparently only in the Chinese Sudarśana-vibhāṣā Vinaya, which is a translation of Buddhaghosa's Samantapāsādikā.[3]

But there is something more. The Northern writings are very familiar with the ten points raised by the monks of Vaiśālī and the schism produced by them. But they also know of another division[4] associated with the names of the monks Mahādeva and Bhadra. These latter set up five dogmas which were also expressed in brief aphorisms and which led to a schism. In Vasumitra's account[5] the confusion is complete when he relates that somewhat more than 100 years after the Nirvāṇa, under king Aśoka in Pāṭaliputra the schism of the Mahāsaṃghikas resulted from the five dogmas, which are then described. Here then, finally, the five dogmas of Mahādeva are confounded with the ten points of the Vajji-monks.

It is perhaps not too daring to conjecture that in this division associated with the name of Mahādeva there is a reminiscence of the proceedings that brought about the Third Council. But this conjecture is now also confirmed by an acute observation of L. DE LA VALLÉE POUSSIN. He

[1] See ROCKHILL, *l. l.*, p. 233.

[2] Transl. by Schiefner, p. 42.

[3] *A Record of the Buddhist Religion* by I-TSING, transl. by TAKAKUSU, p. 14, n. 1, p. 217.

[4] See esp. *Tāranātha*, p. 51; Bhavya in ROCKHILL, *l. l.*, p. 186; WASSILJEW, *Der Buddhismus*, i, pp. 62–63.

[5] See ROCKHILL, *l. l.*, p. 187, n. 1.

establishes the fact [1] that the five dogmas of Mahādeva belong to those which are combated in the Kathāvatthu. But the Kathāvatthu was composed (see Mah. 5. 278) by Moggaliputta Tissa on the occasion of the Council of Pāṭaliputta.

Thus a new link has been found between the Northern and Southern tradition of the Third Council.[2] I adhere, therefore, to the assumption that a second Council took place under Kālāsoka and a third under Dhammāsoka.

The course of events at the Second Council may, taken as a whole, be as the Southern and Northern sources relate. The '10 points' are historical, and we must also regard as historical the names of the theras concerned in refuting them.[3] Moreover, the division of the community, till then united, into two schools is, as I believe, a fact. But we must not exaggerate our notion of the harshness of this separation.

With the toleration peculiar to the Indians the different sects have always mutually recognized each other and kept up relations with each other. I may refer to the beautiful utterance attributed by Vasumitra to the Buddha concerning the

[1] Buddhist notes. The five Points of Mahādeva and the Kathāvatthu, *J.R.A.S.* 1910, p. 413 foll.

[2] V. A. SMITH, *J.R.A.S.* 1901, p. 827 foll. and particularly p. 839 foll., argues thus: As there are two different traditions concerning the time of the Second Council the Southern tradition has invented a second Aśoka in addition to the historical one, and out of one Council has made two. It will be seen that my argument follows the exactly opposite course: as there were two Aśokas the Northern tradition has confounded the two Councils which took place in their time. SMITH'S argument has the defect of not explaining how the different tradition regarding the Second Council arose.

[3] That an extraordinarily great age is attributed of certain theras need hardly be brought forward as testimony against the general trustworthiness of the account (KERN, *Manual*, p. 105). These are the embellishments by which it was intended to exalt the authority of the theras. In like manner an age of 150 years is attributed to the first Patriarch of the Dhyāna Sect in China, Bodhidharma. (SUZUKI, *J.P.T.S.* 1906-7, pp. 11, 13.) Besides, the Yasa of the Second Council was certainly not the Yasa who in M.V. I. 7 foll. appears as a contemporary of the Buddha. He is distinguished from this latter by the epithet *Kākaṇḍakatrajo*.

twelve future schools: 'These schools will be the repositories of the diversified fruits of my scriptures without priority or inferiority—just as the taste of sea-water is everywhere the same—or as the twelve sons of one man all honest and true, so will be the exposition of my doctrine advocated by these schools.'[1]

We may conjecture that the Second Council contributed to the completion of the Vinaya and the Dhamma, though C.V. XII does not expressly speak of it. That may have been taken as a matter of course. Besides, in the concluding words (C.V. XII. 2. 9) the second Council, like the first, is designated Vinayasaṃgīti.

At the time of the Third Council the canonical literature of the Dhamma and Vinaya, as we now have it in the Pāli recension, was evidently completed in essentials. This is proved by mention of portions of the canon in the inscription of Bairāt. Here Aśoka recommends seven scriptures for particular study. Of these scriptures six can be pointed out with more or less certainty in the Pāli canon.[2]

And now, besides, the literary movement is proceeding which leads to the compilation of the Abhidhamma. We see this from the allusion, already mentioned above, in Mah. 5. 278, according to which Moggaliputta Tissa in order to refute the errors which brought about the Third Council, composed his Kathāvatthuppakaraṇa. But this work belongs to the Abhidhamma.

The importance of the Councils, from the standpoint of the orthodox, lay in the elimination of tendencies which could no longer be regarded as consistent with the faith. But of higher importance was the resolve formed in Pāṭaliputra to bear Buddhism beyond the borders of its narrower home. With this Buddhism entered on its victorious progress through the Eastern World.

[1] See Beal, *Ind. Ant.* ix, 1880, p. 300.

[2] Oldenberg, *Vin. Piṭ.* i, p. xl; *Z.D.M.G.* 52, p. 634 foll., against Minayeff, *Recherches sur le Bouddhisme*, pp. 83–92; Rhys Davids, *Dialogues*, i, p. xiii.

LIST OF ABBREVIATIONS

A. = Aṅguttara-Nikāya (ed. MORRIS and HARDY, 5 vols., Pali Text Soc. 1885–1900). Vol. vi, Indexes by Miss HUNT, 1910.

Asl. = Atthasālinī (ed. E. MÜLLER, P.T.S., 1897).

B.R. = Sanskrit-Wörterbuch von BÖHTLINGK und ROTH, 7 vols., St. Petersburg, 1855–1875.

C.V. = Cullavagga (the Vinaya Piṭaka, ed. OLDENBERG, vol. ii, 1880).

D. = Dīgha-Nikāya (ed. RHYS DAVIDS and CARPENTER, 3 vols., P.T.S. 1890–1911).

Dīp. = Dīpavaṃsa (ed. and transl. OLDENBERG, 1879).

I.A. = Indian Antiquary.

J.As. = Journal Asiatique.

Jāt. = Jātaka (ed. FAUSBÖLL, 7 vols., 1877–1897).

J.P.T.S. = Journal of the Pali Text Society.

J.R.A.S. = Journal of the Royal Asiatic Society.

Kamb. Mah. = Kambodja Mahāvaṃsa (s. HARDY, J.P.T.S. 1902–3, p. 61 foll.).

M. = Majjhima-Nikāya (ed. TRENCKNER and CHALMERS, 3 vols., P.T.S. 1888–1899).

Mah. ed. = Mahāvaṃsa (ed. W. GEIGER, P.T.S. 1908).

M.Bv. = Mahābodhivaṃsa (ed. STRONG, P.T.S. 1901).

M.V. = Mahāvagga (The Vinaya Piṭaka, ed. OLDENBERG, vol. i, 1879).

P.D. = Dictionary of the Pāli Language, by CHILDERS, 1875.

Vin. Piṭ. = The Vinaya Piṭaka, ed. OLDENBERG, 5 vols., 1879–1883.

S. = Saṃyutta Nikāya (ed. FEER, 5 vols., P.T.S. 1884–1898 ; vol. 6 ; Indexes by Mrs. RHYS DAVIDS, 1904).

S.B.B. = Sacred Books of the Buddhists.

S.B.E. = Sacred Books of the East.

Smp. = Samanta-Pāsādikā (Introd. to S. in Vin. Piṭ. ii, p. 283 foll.).

Sum. = Sumaṅgala-Vilāsinī (ed. RHYS DAVIDS and CARPENTER, vol. i, P.T.S. 1886).

Z.D.M.G. = Zeitschrift der Deutschen Morgenländischen Gesellschaft.

Map of ANCIENT CEYLON

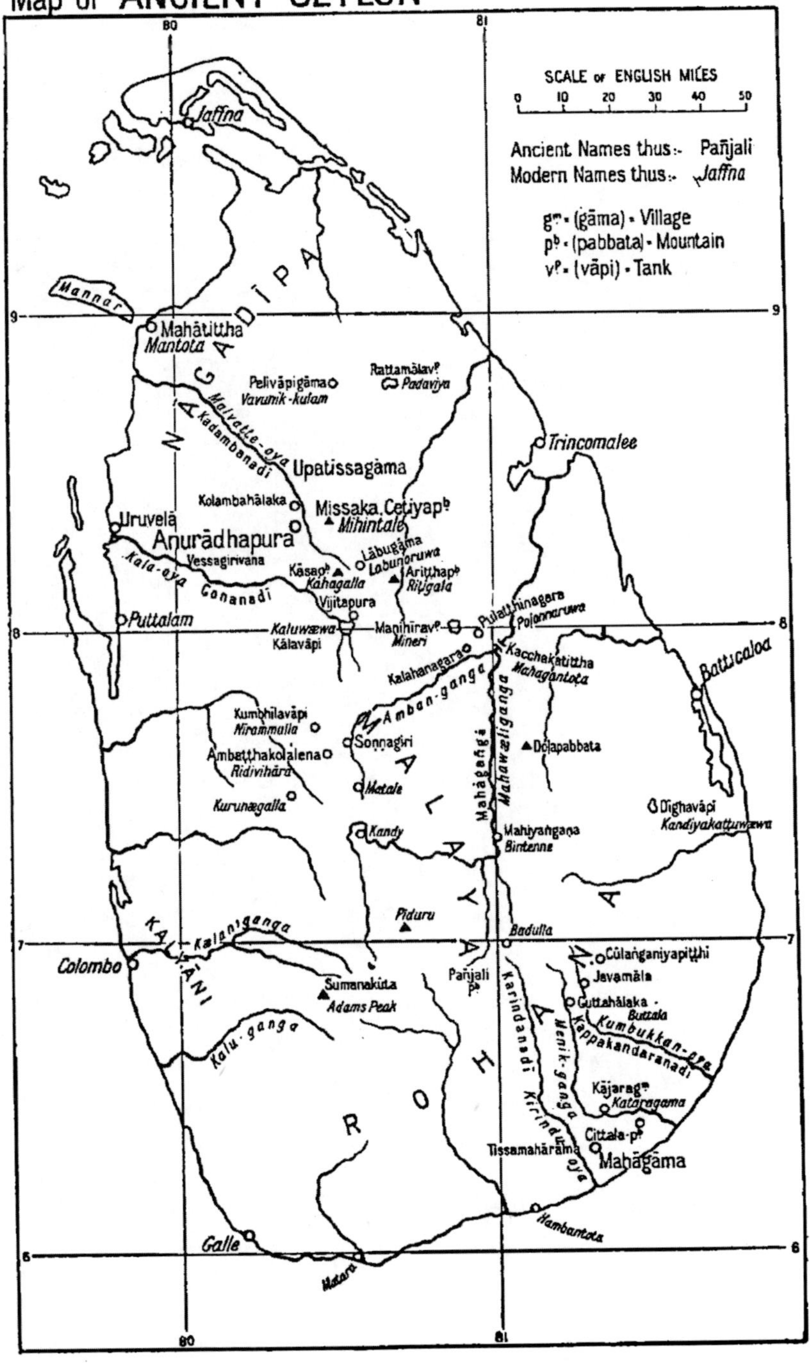

THE MAHĀVAṂSA

CHAPTER I

THE VISIT OF THE TATHĀGATA

HAVING made obeisance to the Saṃbuddha the pure, sprung 1
of a pure race, I will recite the Mahāvaṃsa, of varied content
and lacking nothing. That (Mahāvaṃsa) which was compiled 2
by the ancient (sages) was here too long drawn out and there
too closely knit; and contained many repetitions. Attend ye 3
now to this (Mahāvaṃsa) that is free from such faults, easy
to understand and remember, arousing serene joy and
emotion and handed down (to us) by tradition,—(attend ye to 4
it) while that ye call up serene joy and emotion (in you) [1]
at passages that awaken serene joy and emotion.

On seeing the Saṃbuddha Dīpaṃkara, in olden times, our 5
Conqueror resolved to become a Buddha, that he might release
the world from evil. When he had offered homage to that 6
Saṃbuddha and likewise to Koṇḍañña and to the sage
Maṅgala, to Sumana, to the Buddha Revata and likewise to
the great sage Sobhita, to the Saṃbuddha Anomadassi, to 7
Paduma and to the Conqueror Nārada, to the Saṃbuddha
Padumuttara and to the Tathāgata Sumedha, and to Sujāta, 8
to Piyadassi and to the Master Atthadassi, to Dham-
madassi and Siddhattha, to Tissa and the Conqueror Phussa, 9
to Vipassi and the Saṃbuddha Sikhi, and the Saṃ-
buddha Vessabhu, the mighty one, to the Saṃbuddha

[1] Read janayantā, referring the participle to the subject implied in suṇotha. The terms pasāda 'serene joy' and saṃvega 'emotion' occur also in the postscripts of the single chapters of the Mah. Pasāda signifies the feeling of blissfulness, joy and satisfaction in the doctrine of the Buddha, saṃvega the feeling of horror and recoil from the world and its misery. See also 23. 62 with note.

10 Kakusandha, and likewise to Koṇāgamana, as also to the
blessed Kassapa,—having offered homage to these twenty-four
Sambuddhas and having received from them the prophecy of
11 his (future) buddhahood he, the great hero, when he had ful-
filled all perfections [1] and reached the highest enlightenment,
the sublime Buddha Gotama, delivered the world from
suffering.

12 At Uruvelā,[2] in the Magadha country, the great sage, sitting
at the foot of the Bodhi-tree, reached the supreme enlighten-
13 ment on the full-moon day of the month Vesākha.[3] Seven
weeks he tarried there, mastering his senses,[4] while that he
himself knew the high bliss of deliverance and let (others)
14 behold its felicity.[5] Then he went to Bārāṇasī and set rolling
the wheel of the law; and while he dwelt there through the
rain-months, he brought sixty (hearers) to arahantship.[6]
15 When he had sent forth these bhikkhus to preach the doctrine,
and when he had converted the thirty companions of the

[1] The ten pāramī. Cf. *Jāt.* i, p. 20 foll. The idea is late and not found in the four Nikāyas. See Rhys Davids, *Buddhist India*, p. 177; Kern, *Manual of Indian Buddhism*, p. 66.

[2] Buddh Gayā or Bodh Gayā in Gayā district, Bengal.

[3] The second month in the ordinary Indian lunar year, answering in the time of Buddha to part of March and part of April. The names of the Indian lunar months are as follows:—

(1) Citta	= February: March or March: April.
(2) Vesākha	= March: April or April: May.
(3) Jeṭṭha	= April: May or May: June.
(4) Āsāḷha	= May: June or June: July.
(5) Sāvaṇa	= June: July or July: August.
(6) Poṭṭhapāda	= July: August or August: September.
(7) Assayuja	= August: September or September: October.
(8) Kattika	= September: October or October: November.
(9) Maggasira	= October: November or November: December.
(10) Phussa	= November: December or December: January.
(11) Māgha	= December: January or January: February.
(12) Phagguṇa	= January: February or February: March.

See Fleet, *J.R.A.S.* 1909, p. 6.

[4] Vasī. A play on this word and vasi 'he tarried'.

[5] With the whole passage cf. Mah. ed., p. iii.

[6] Saṭṭhiṃ arahataṃ akā. Arahataṃ as a gen. plural is dependent on the numeral. Literally: he made sixty arahants.

company of Bhadda[1] then did the Master dwell at Uruvelā 16
the winter through, for the sake of converting the thou-
sand jaṭilas[2] led by Kassapa, making them ripe (for
deliverance).

Now since a great sacrifice by Kassapa of Uruvelā was near 17
at hand, and since he saw that this latter would fain have him
away,[3] he, the victorious over enemies, went to seek alms 18
among the Northern Kurus;[4] and when he had eaten his
meal at evening time near the lake Anotatta,[5] the Conqueror, 19
in the ninth month of his buddhahood, at the full moon of
Phussa,[6] himself set forth for the isle of Laṅkā, to win Laṅkā
for the faith.[7] For Laṅkā was known to the Conqueror as 20
a place where his doctrine should (thereafter) shine in glory;
and (he knew that) from Laṅkā, filled with the yakkhas, the
yakkhas must (first) be driven forth.[8]

And he knew also that in the midst of Laṅkā, on the fair 21
river bank, in the delightful Mahānāga garden, three yojanas
long and a yojana wide, the (customary) meeting-place for 22
the yakkhas, there was a great gathering of (all) the
yakkhas dwelling in the island. To this great gathering of 23
that yakkhas went the Blessed One, and there, in the midst of
that assembly, hovering in the air over their heads, at the 24
place of the (future) Mahiyaṅgaṇa-thūpa,[9] he struck terror

[1] For the conversion of the Tiṃsa Bhaddavaggiyā see M.V. I. 14.

[2] Jaṭilā, ascetics wearing the hair long and matted. See M.V. I. 15 ff.

[3] Lit. after he had known this latter's wish that he should not come.

[4] The Uttarā Kurū are a half-mythological people, dwelling in the north of India.

[5] One of the seven great lakes, situated in the Himalaya mountains.

[6] The tenth month of the lunar year. See note on 1. 12.

[7] Lit. to purify, to cleanse (visodhetuṃ). Laṅkā = Ceylon.

[8] From the ñātā (N. Si. F.) in the first line another ñātā (N. Pl. M.) must be understood with yakkhā nibbāsiyā (Part. Fut. Pass., Skr. nir-vas, Caus.) in the second line of the verse, to complete the sentence.

[9] According to tradition the Bintenne-dāgaba (TENNENT, *Ceylon*, ii, pp. 420–421), on the right bank of the Mahawæliganga, which is called mahāgaṅgā or simply gaṅgā in the Mah.

25 to their hearts by rain, storm, darkness and so forth.[1] The
yakkhas, overwhelmed by fear, besought the fearless Vanquisher to release them from terrors, and the Vanquisher,
26 destroyer of fear,[2] spoke thus to the terrified yakkhas: 'I will banish this your fear and your distress, O yakkhas, give ye here
27 to me with one accord a place where I may sit down.' The
yakkhas thus answered the Blessed One: 'We all, O Lord, give you even the whole of our island. Give us release from
28 our fear.' Then, when he had destroyed their terror, cold
and darkness, and had spread his rug of skin[3] on the ground
29 that they bestowed on him, the Conqueror, sitting there, made
the rug to spread wide, while burning flame surrounded it. Daunted by the burning heat thereof and terrified, they stood
30 around on the border. Then did the Saviour cause the pleasant
Giridīpa[4] to come here near to them, and when they had settled
31 there, he made it return to its former place. Then did the
Saviour fold his rug of skin; the devas assembled, and in
32 their assembly the Master preached them the doctrine. The
conversion of many koṭis of living beings took place,[5] and countless were those who came unto the (three) refuges and the precepts of duty.[6]

[1] Lit. he made for them a means of terror, consisting of rain, storm, darkness and so forth.

[2] Lit. who confers fearlessness (or freedom from peril), a play on the words abhaya and bhaya. See 37. 30.

[3] Lit. piece of hide.

[4] It would be a mistake to look for a clear geographical statement. The underlying notion here expressed is simply that the yakkhas were driven back to the highlands (giri) in the interior of the island. They are still to be found in Ceylon in later times. The meaning of dīpa was formerly a wider one; a later tradition has brought it to mean 'island' in our sense. Cf. also Nāgadīpa as name of a part of Ceylon itself (1. 47 with note).

[5] The term dhammābhisamaya (see CHILDERS, *P. D.*, s. v.) means 'the attainment by an unconverted man of one of the four paths' (of sanctification). Koṭi is an indefinite great number, according to the Indian system equal to ten millions.

[6] Saraṇesu ca sīlesu ṭhita is the expression for the adherence of the laity. They take their refuge (saraṇa) in the Buddha, his doctrine and his community, and undertake to keep certain binding commandments. See notes to 1. 62.

The prince of devas, Mahāsumana of the Sumanakūṭa- 33
mountain,[1] who had attained to the fruit of entering into
the path of salvation,[2] craved of him who should be worshipped,
something to worship. The Conqueror, the (giver of) good to 34
living beings, he who had pure and blue-black locks, passing his
hand over his (own) head, bestowed on him a handful of hairs.
And he, receiving this in a splendid golden urn, when he had 35
laid the hairs upon a heap of many-coloured gems, seven cubits
round, piled up at the place where the Master had sat, covered 36
them over with a thūpa of sapphire and worshipped them.

When the Saṃbuddha had died, the thera named Sarabhu, 37
disciple of the thera Sāriputta, by his miraculous power received,
even from the funeral pyre, the collar-bone of the Conqueror and 38
brought it hither (to Laṅkā), and, with the bhikkhus all around
him, he there laid it in that same cetiya, covered it over with 39
golden-coloured stones,[3] and (then he), the worker of miracles,
having made the thūpa twelve cubits[4] high, departed again from
thence. The son of king Devānampiyatissa's brother, named 40
Uddhacūḷābhaya, saw the wondrous cetiya and (again) covered 41
it over and made it thirty cubits high. The king Duṭṭhagā-
maṇi, dwelling there while he made war upon the Damiḷas,
built a mantle cetiya over it eighty cubits high. Thus was 42
the Mahiyaṅgaṇa-thūpa completed. When he had thus made 43
our island a fit dwelling-place for men, the mighty ruler,
valiant as are great heroes, departed for Uruvelā.

Here ends the Visit to Mahiyaṅgaṇa.

Now the most compassionate Teacher, the Conqueror, 44
rejoicing in the salvation of the whole world, when dwelling

[1] Sumanakūṭa is the Adam's Peak.

[2] Sotāpatti is the stage of a sotāpanna 'who has entered the stream', who has attained to the first grade of sanctification, a converted man. As to the second and third grade see the notes to 15. 18 and 13. 17.

[3] On medavaṇṇapāsāṇā, stones of the (golden, or cream) colour of fat, fat-coloured, see Mah. ed., p. 355.

[4] See note to 15. 167.

45 at Jetavana[1] in the fifth year of his buddhahood, saw that a
war, caused by a gem-set throne, was like to come to pass
46 between the nāgas Mahodara and Cūlodara, uncle and nephew,
and their followers; and he, the Sambuddha, on the uposatha-
47 day of the dark half of the month Citta, in the early morning,
took his sacred alms-bowl and his robes, and, from compassion
for the nāgas, sought the Nāgadīpa.[2]

48 That same nāga Mahodara was then a king, gifted with
miraculous power, in a nāga-kingdom in the ocean, that
49 covered half a thousand yojanas. His younger sister had been
given (in marriage) to the nāga-king on the Kaṇṇāvaḍḍhamāna-
50 mountain; her son was Cūlodara. His mother's father had
given to his mother a splendid throne of jewels, then the nāga
51 had died and therefore this war of nephew with uncle was
threatening; and also the nāgas of the mountains were armed
with miraculous power.

52 The deva named Samiddhisumana took a rājāyatana-tree
53 standing in Jetavana, his own fair habitation, and, holding it
like a parasol over the Conqueror, he, with the Teacher's leave,
54 attended him to that spot where he had formerly dwelt.[3] That
very deva had been, in his latest birth, a man in Nāgadīpa.
On the spot where thereafter the rājāyatana-tree stood, he
55 saw paccekabuddhas taking their meal. And at the sight his
heart was glad and he offered branches to cleanse the alms-
56 bowl. Therefore he was reborn in that tree in the pleasant
Jetavana-garden, and it (the tree) stood afterwards outside at
57 the side of the gate-rampart.[4] The God of all gods saw (in
this) an advantage for that deva, and, for the sake of the
good which should spring (therefrom) for our land, he brought
him hither (to Laṅkā) together with his tree.

58 Hovering there in mid-air above the battlefield the Master,

[1] A park and monastery near Sāvatthī in the Kosala country (see Vogel, *J.R.A.S.* 1908, p. 971 foll.), presented to the Master by Anāthapiṇḍika. *Jāt.* i. 92 foll.

[2] Apparently the north-western part of Ceylon. See 20. 25, with the note.

[3] I. e. to Nāgadīpa.

[4] Koṭṭhaka 'battlemented dwelling or gateway'. See M.V. VIII. 15. 5; C.V. IV. 4. 6; *S.B.E.* xvii, p. 219, n. 1; xx, p. 11, n. 1.

who drives away (spiritual) darkness, called forth dread darkness
over the nāgas. Then comforting those who were distressed 59
by terror he once again spread light abroad. When they
saw the Blessed One they joyfully did reverence to the
Master's feet. Then preached the Vanquisher to them the 60
doctrine that begets concord, and both [nāgas] gladly gave
up the throne to the Sage.[1] When the Master, having 61
alighted on the earth, had taken his place on a seat there,
and had been refreshed with celestial food and drink by the
nāga-kings, he, the Lord, established in the (three) refuges[2] 62
and in the moral precepts[3] eighty koṭis of snake-spirits,
dwellers in the ocean and on the mainland.

The nāga-king Maṇiakkhika of Kalyāṇī,[4] mother's brother 63
to the nāga Mahodara, who had come thither to take part in
the battle, and who, aforetime, at the Buddha's first coming, 64
having heard the true doctrine preached, had become estab-
lished in the refuges and in the moral duties, prayed now to
the Tathāgata: 'Great is the compassion that thou hast 65
shown us here, O Master! Hadst thou not appeared we had
all been consumed to ashes. May thy compassion yet light also 66
especially on me, O thou who art rich in loving-kindness, in
that thou shalt come yet again hither to my dwelling-country,
O thou peerless one.' When the Lord had consented by his 67
silence to come thither, he planted the rājāyatana-tree on that
very spot as a sacred memorial, and the Lord of the Worlds 68
gave over the rājāyatana-tree and the precious throne-seat to
the nāga-kings to do homage thereto. 'In remembrance that 69
I have used these do homage to them,[5] ye nāga-kings!

[1] I. e. the Buddha.

[2] I. e. buddha, dhamma, saṃgha 'the Buddha, his doctrine and his community'. The Buddhist confession of faith consists in the words buddhaṃ saraṇam gacchāmi, dhammaṃ s. g., saṃghaṃ s. g. 'I take my refuge in the B. &c.'

[3] The pañca sīlāni, which are binding on all Buddhists, are abstention from destruction of life, theft, adultery, lying, and from the use of intoxicating liquors. Cf. note to 18. 10.

[4] Now Kælani, name of a river which falls into the sea near Colombo.

[5] Lit. 'Do homage to them as to a memorial consisting in objects used by me.'

This, well beloved, will bring to pass blessing and happiness
70 for you.' When the Blessed One had uttered this and other
exhortation to the nāgas, he, the compassionate saviour of all
the world, returned to Jetavana.

Here ends the Visit to Nāgadīpa.

71 In the third year after this, the nāga-king Maṇiakkhika
sought out the Sambuddha and invited him, together with the
72 brotherhood. In the eighth year after he had attained to
buddhahood, when the Vanquisher was dwelling in Jetavana,
73 the Master, set forth surrounded by five hundred bhikkhus, on
the second day of the beautiful month of Vesākha, at the full-
moon, and when the hour of the meal was announced the
74 Vanquisher, prince of the wise, forthwith putting on his robe
and taking his alms-bowl went to the Kalyāṇī country, the
75 habitation of Maṇiakkhika. Under a canopy decked with
gems, raised upon the spot where (afterwards) the Kalyāṇī-
cetiya was built, he took his place, together with the brother-
76 hood of bhikkhus, upon a precious throne-seat. And, greatly
rejoicing, the nāga-king with his following served celestial
food, both hard and soft, to the king of truth, the Con-
queror, with his followers.

77 When the Teacher, compassionate to the whole world, had
preached the doctrine there, he rose, the Master, and left the
78 traces of his footsteps plain to sight on Sumanakūṭa. And after
he had spent the day as it pleased him at the foot of this
mountain, with the brotherhood, he set forth for Dīghavāpi.[1]
79 And there the Master seated himself with the brotherhood at
the place where the cetiya (thereafter) stood, and gave himself
80 up to meditation, to consecrate the spot. Then arose the Great
Sage from that place, and knowing well which places were fit
and which unfit he went to the place of the (later) Mahāmegha-
81 vanārāma.[2] After he had seated himself with his disciples at

[1] The Dīghavāpi is probably the Kandiya-kaṭṭu tank in the Eastern Province, about 30 miles SSW. from Batticaloa. A large dāgaba is said to be in the neighbourhood of the tank. PARKER, *Ancient Ceylon*, pp. 318, 396.

[2] The Mahāmeghavana was a park south of the capital Anurādha-

the place, where the sacred Bodhi-tree came afterwards to be, the Master gave himself up to meditation; and likewise there
where the Great Thūpa [1] stood (in later days) and there also 82
where (afterwards) the thūpa in the Thūpārāma [2] stood. Then when he rose up from meditation he went to the place of the
(later) Silācetiya,[3] and after the Leader of the assembly (of 83
bhikkhus) had uttered exhortation to the assembly of devas, he, the Enlightened, who has trodden all the paths of enlightenment, returned thence to Jetavana.

Thus the Master of boundless wisdom, looking to the 84
salvation of Laṅkā in time to come, and knowing in that time the highest good for the hosts of asuras and nāgas and so forth in Laṅkā, visited this fair island three times,—he, the compassionate Enlightener of the world;—therefore this isle, radiant with the light of truth, came to high honour among faithful believers.

Here ends the Visit to Kalyāṇī.

Here ends the first chapter, called 'The Visit of the Tathāgata', in the Mahāvaṃsa, compiled for the serene joy and emotion of the pious.

pura and was presented to the priesthood as an ārāma or monastery by the king Devānaṃpiyatissa. See 15. 8 foll. and note to 11. 2.

[1] The Ruwanwæli-dāgaba of Anurādhapura. SMITHER, *Architectural Remains, Anurádhapura*, p. 23 foll.; PARKER, *Ancient Ceylon*, p. 279 foll.

[2] A monastery in Anurādhapura. SMITHER, *l. c.*, p. 1 foll.; PARKER, *l. c.*, p. 263 foll. Cf. note to 17. 30.

[3] I.e. 'Stone-cetiya,' now Selacaitya in Anurādhapura. SMITHER, *l. c.*, p. 55; PARKER, *l. c.*, p. 297 foll.

CHAPTER II

THE RACE OF MAHĀSAṂMATA

1 SPRUNG of the race of king Mahāsaṃmata was the Great
Sage. For in the beginning of this age of the world there
2 was a king named Mahāsaṃmata, and (the kings) Roja and
Vararoja, and the two Kalyāṇakas,[1] Uposatha and Mandhātar
3 and the two, Caraka and Upacara, and Cetiya and Mucala and
he who bore the name Mahāmucala, Mucalinda and Sāgara
4 and he who bore the name Sāgaradeva; Bharata and
Aṅgīrasa and Ruci and also Suruci, Patāpa and Mahāpatāpa
5 and the two Panādas likewise, Sudassana and Neru, two
6 and two;[2] also Accimā. His sons and grandsons, these
twenty-eight princes whose lifetime was immeasurably (long),
7 dwelt in Kusāvatī, Rājagaha, and Mithilā.[3] Then followed
a hundred kings,[4] and (then) fifty-six, and (then) sixty,

[1] I. e. Kalyāṇa and Varakalyāṇa. Dīp. 3. 6.

[2] Panāda and Mahāpanāda, Sudassana and Mahāsudassana, Neru and Mahāneru.

[3] Kusāvatī is the later Kusinārā. See note on 3. 2. Rājagaha, now Rājgir, was the capital of Magadha, and Mithilā, situated in the Bengal district Tirhut, that of Videha.

[4] The dynasties from Accimā to Kalārajanaka are dealt with in detail in Dīp. 3. 14-37. Besides (i) the number of the princes sprung of each dynasty, the (ii) capital cities of each period, and (iii) the last king of each line are mentioned. The numbers and names are these:

100	at Pakula (?)	the last being		Arimdana.
56	„ Ayujjha	„	„	Duppasaha.
60	„ Bārāṇasī	„	„	Ajitajana.
84,000	„ Kapilanagara	„	„	Brahmadatta.
36	„ Hatthipura	„	„	Kambalavasabha.
32	„ Ekacakkhu	„	„	Purindadadeva.
28	„ Vajirā	„	„	Sādhina.
22	„ Madhurā	„	„	Dhammagutta.

eighty-four thousand, and then further thirty-six, thirty-two, 8
twenty-eight, then further twenty-eight, eighteen, seventeen,
fifteen, fourteen; nine, seven, twelve, then further twenty- 9
five; and (again) twenty-five, twelve and (again) twelve, and
yet again nine and eighty-four thousand with Makhādeva 10
coming at the head, and (once more) eighty-four thousand
with Kalārajanaka at the head; and sixteen even unto 11
Okkāka; these descendants (of Mahāsammata) reigned in
groups in their due order, each one in his capital.

The prince Okkāmukha was Okkāka's eldest son; Nipuṇa, 12
Candimā, Candamukha and Sivisaṃjaya, the great king 13
Vessantara, Jāli, and Sīhavāhana and Sīhassara: these were
his sons and grandsons. Eighty-two thousand in number were 14
the royal sons and grandsons of king Sīhassara; Jayasena
was the last of them. They are known as the Sakya kings 15
of Kapilavatthu.[1] The great king Sīhahanu was Jayasena's

18	at Ariṭṭhapura	the last being	Siṭṭhi.
17	„ Indapatta	„ „	Brahmadeva.
15	„ Ekacakkhu	„ „	Baladatta.
14	„ Kosambī	„ „	Bhaddadeva.
9	„ Kaṇṇagoccha	„ „	Naradeva.
7	„ Rojānanagara	„ „	Mahinda.
12	„ Campā	„ „	Nāgadeva.
25	„ Mithilā	„ „	Buddhadatta.
25	„ Rājagaha	„ „	Dīpaṃkara.
12	„ Takkasilā	„ „	Tālissara.
12	„ Kusinārā	„ „	Purinda.
9	„ Malitthiya	„ „	Sāgaradeva.

The son of Sāgaradeva was Makhādeva; the dynasty of Makhādeva (84,000) reigned in Mithilā. The last prince was Nemiya, father of Kalārajanaka. These were followed by Samaṃkura, then by Asoka; this was followed by a dynasty of 84,000 princes reigning in Bārāṇasī. The last was Vijaya. He was followed by Vijitasena, Dhammasena, Nāgasena, Samatha, Disaṃpati, Reṇu, Kusa, Mahākusa, Navaratha, Dasaratha, Rāma, Biḷāratha, Cittadassi, Atthadassi, Sujāta, Okkāka, and so on. The same in Aṭṭhakathā, Mah. T. 81^{11}–83^{33}. The Kamb. Mah., v. 729–789, follows the Ṭīkā.

[1] The site of Kapilavatthu, the capital of the Sakya tribe and Gotama Buddha's birthplace, is probably the present Tilaura Kot in Nepal. See RHYS DAVIDS, *Buddhist India*, p. 18 n.

16 son, and Jayasena's daughter was named Yasodharā. In
17 Devadaha there was a prince named Devadahasakka, Añjana
and Kaccānā were his two children. Kaccānā was the first
18 consort of Sīhahanu, but the Sakka Añjana's queen was
Yasodharā. Añjana had two daughters, Māyā and Pajāpatī,
19 and also two sons, Daṇḍapāṇi and the Sākiya Suppa-
20 buddha. But Sīhahanu had five sons and two daughters:
Suddhodana, Dhotodana, Sakka-, Sukka-,[1] and Amitodana,
and Amitā and Pamitā; these were the five sons and two
daughters.

21 The royal consort of the Sakka Suppabuddha was Amitā;
22 she had two children: Bhaddakaccānā and Devadatta. Māyā
and Pajāpatī were Suddhodana's queens, and the son of the
great king Suddhodana and of Māyā was our Conqueror.

23 Of this race of Mahāsammata, thus succeeding, was born,
in unbroken line, the Great Sage, he who stands at the head
24 of all men of lordly birth. The consort of the prince
Siddhattha, the Bodhisatta, was Bhaddakaccānā; her son was
Rāhula.

25 Bimbisāra and the prince Siddhattha were friends, and
26 friends likewise were the fathers of both. The Bodhisatta
was five years older than Bimbisāra; twenty-nine years old
27 was he when he left (his father's) house. When he had
striven six years and thereafter had attained to wisdom, he,
28 being thirty-five years old, visited Bimbisāra. The virtuous
Bimbisāra was fifteen years old when he was anointed king
29 by his own father, and when sixteen years had gone by since
his coming to the throne, the Master preached his doctrine.
30 Two and fifty years he reigned; fifteen years of his reign
passed before the meeting with the Conqueror, and yet thirty-
seven years (of his reign) followed in the lifetime of the
Tathāgata.

31 Bimbisāra's son, the foolish Ajātasattu, reigned thirty-two
32 years after he, the traitor, had slain (his father). In the
eighth year of Ajātasattu the Sage entered into nibbāṇa and
thereafter did he, Ajātasattu, reign yet twenty-four years.

[1] I. e. Sakkodana and Sukkodana.

The Tathāgata, who has reached the summit of all virtue, 33
yielded himself up, albeit free, into the power of imperma-
nence. He who shall contemplate this (same) dread-begetting impermanence shall attain unto the end of suffering.

Here ends the second chapter, called 'The Race of Mahāsaṃmata', in the Mahāvaṃsa, compiled for the serene joy and emotion of the pious.

CHAPTER III

THE FIRST COUNCIL

1 WHEN the Conqueror the incomparable, he who has the
five eyes,[1] had lived eighty-four years and had fulfilled all his
2 duties in the world, in all ways, then at Kusinārā[2] in the
holy place between the two sāla-trees,[3] on the full-moon day
of the month Vesākha, was the light of the world extinguished.
3 Beyond all reckoning in numbers, did bhikkhus assemble
there and khattiyas and brahmans, vessas and suddas, and
4 gods likewise. Seven hundred thousand leading bhikkhus
were among them, the thera Mahākassapa was at that time
the saṃghatthera.
5 When he had performed all rites due to the (dead) body of
the Master and the bodily relics, the great thera, desiring that
6 the doctrine of the Master might long endure, did, seven days
after the Lord of the World, gifted with the ten powers,[4] had
passed into nibbāṇa, bethinking him of the evil words of the
7 aged Subhadda[5] and also bethinking him that he (the Master)

[1] The five eyes possessed by the Buddha are the bodily eyes (maṃsacakkhu), the heavenly eye (dibba°) by which he sees everything that comes to pass in the universe, the eye of understanding (knowledge), the eye of omniscience, and finally the Buddha-eye by means of which he beholds the saving truth.

[2] A town of the clan of the Mallas, in the territory of the present Nepal.

[3] *Shorea Robusta.*

[4] On the dasa balāni, ten kinds of knowledge, peculiar to a Buddha, see KERN, *Manual of Indian Buddhism*, p. 62; CHILDERS, *P.D.*, s.v. balaṃ.

[5] Vuḍḍha = vuḍḍhapabbajita 'who had not become a monk till he was old'. On the speech of Subhadda, see C.V. XI. 1.1 = *Vin. Piṭ.* ii. 284. KERN, *l. l.*, pp. 101–102.

had given him his garment,[1] and had (thereby) made him equal
with himself, and (bethinking him) that the Sage had com-
manded the establishing of the holy truth, and (lastly) that 8
the Saṃbuddha's consent existed to make a compilation of the
holy dhamma[2] appointed to this end five hundred eminent 9
bhikkhus, who had overcome the āsavas,[3] repeaters of the nine-
fold doctrine and versed in all its separate parts; but there was
one less (than five hundred) because of the thera Ānanda.[4]
And the thera Ānanda also, again and again entreated by 10
the bhikkhus, resolved to (join with them in) that compilation
of the dhamma, for it was not possible without him.

When these theras, pitiful toward the whole world, had 11
passed half a month—seven days in the funeral ceremonies
and seven in homage of the relics—and had resolved thus: 12
'Spending the rainy season in Rājagaha, we will make a com-
pilation of the dhamma, no other (monks) must be permitted
to dwell there'; and when they had made their pilgrimage 13
over Jambudīpa,[5] consoling here and there the sorrowing
people, they, moved with desire that the good might long 14
endure,[6] betook them in the bright half of the month Āsāḷha
to Rājagaha, (the city) richly provided with the four things
needful.[7]

After the theras, with Mahākassapa at the head, unwavering 15
in virtue, familiar with the thought of the Saṃbuddha,

[1] The Buddha gave his garment to Kassapa. On the second saraṃ depend cīvaradānaṃ 'the giving of the robe', and samattethapanaṃ 'putting on a footing of equality', and then further anuggahaṃ kataṃ and anumatiṃ satiṃ (Acc. Si. F. of Part. Pres. of atthi). Cf. Mah. ed., pp. xxx and li.

[2] Kātuṃ saddhammasaṃgītiṃ. Cf. the note on 3. 17.

[3] Khīṇāsava 'one in whom the four āsavas are extinct' is the epithet of an arahant. On āsava, see RHYS DAVIDS, *Dialogues of the Buddha*, i. 92; ii. 28.

[4] A place must be kept for Ānanda.

[5] The continent of India.

[6] A play upon the word sukkapakkha, used in the sense, 'bright half of the month,' and also 'pure, holy side or party'.

[7] The four paccayā of a bhikkhu are clothing, food given as alms, a dwelling-place, and medicines.

16 had arrived at that place to spend the rainy season there, they
busied themselves during the first of the rain-months with
repairing all the dwellings, when they had announced this to
Ajātasattu.

17 When the repair of the vihāra was finished they said to the
18 king: 'Now we will hold the council.'[1] To the question,
'What should be done?' they answered: 'A place (should be provided) for the meetings.' When the king had asked: 'Where
(these were to be)?' and the place had been pointed out by them,
19 he with all speed had a splendid hall built by the side of the
Vebhāra Rock by the entrance of the Sattapaṇṇi grotto, (and
20 it was) like to the assembly-hall of the gods. When it was
adorned in every way he caused precious mats to be spread
21 according to the number of the bhikkhus. Placed on the south
side and facing the north a lofty and noble seat was prepared
22 for the thera, and in the middle of the hall a high seat was
prepared for the preacher,[2] facing the east and worthy of the
blessed (Buddha) himself.

23 So the king bade them tell the theras: 'My work is finished,'
and the theras addressed the thera Ānanda, the joy-bringer:
24 'To-morrow, Ānanda, the assembly (comes together); it behoves thee not to take part in it since thou art still preparing
thee (for the highest state),[3] therefore strive thou, unwearied
25 in good.' Thus spurred on, the thera put forth due effort

[1] Dhammasaṃgīti is the term for assembly of the church, council. The original meaning is general recitation of the canonical texts which, indeed, takes place in an assembly of the church and in the following manner: an eminent thera recites the texts sentence by sentence and the assembly repeats them after him in chorus. In this way dhammasaṃgīti is connected with dhammasaṃgaha, by which we understand a *settling* or *redaction of the canonical texts*, which also can only be carried out in the manner stated. Comp. *J.P.T.S.* 1909, pp. 31, 32.

[2] Therāsana is the seat for the president, who directs the assembly; dhammāsana the same for the monk who recites, the word uttama is to be taken literally.

[3] Still a sekha, i.e. not an arahant, who has reached the highest degree. This is preceded by seven grades of preparation; he who is still at one of these is sekha 'a learner'. See *J.P.T.S.* 1909, p. 217.

and reached the state of an arahant without being confined
to any one of the four postures.[1]

On the second day of the second month of the rainy season 26
the bhikkhus met together in that splendid hall. Leaving a 27
fitting place vacant for Ānanda, the arahants seated themselves
on chairs, according to their rank. The thera Ānanda, to make 28
known to them that he had reached the state of an arahant,
went not with them thither. But when some asked: Where
is the thera Ānanda? he took the seat prepared for him, 29
rising out of the ground or passing through the air.[2]

Together the theras chose the thera Upāli to speak for[3] the 30
vinaya, for the rest of the dhamma[4] they chose Ānanda.
The great thera (Mahākassapa) laid on himself (the task) of 31
asking questions touching the vinaya and the thera Upāli
(was ready) to explain it.

Sitting in the thera's chair, the former asked the latter the 32
questions touching the vinaya; and Upāli, seated in the
preacher's chair, expounded (the matter). And as this best 33
master of the vinaya expounded each (clause) in turn all (the
bhikkhus) knowing the custom, repeated the vinaya after him.

Then the thera (Mahākassapa) taking (the task) upon himself 34
questioned concerning the dhamma, him[5] the chief of those
who had most often heard (the word), him the treasure-
keeper[6] of the Great Seer (the Buddha); and the thera 35
Ānanda, taking (the task) upon himself, taking his seat in
the preacher's chair, expounded the whole dhamma. And 36

[1] Lit. free from the iriyāpatha; the four postures of an ascetic are understood here. They are described as: standing, sitting, walking, lying down. Ānanda became an arahant at the moment when he was on the point of lying down.

[2] Lit. 'the path of the light.' Ānanda shows that he can use the miraculous powers particular to an arahant.

[3] Lit. 'as burden bearer for.' Cf. B.R., *Skt. Wtb.*, s.v. dhuraṃdhara (4).

[4] The vinaya contains the rules of monastic discipline, the dhamma the dogmatic teaching.

[5] I.e. Ānanda.

[6] Kosārakkha, according to the Ṭīkā = dhammabhaṇḍāgārika, i.e. treasurer of the truth or the true doctrine.

all the (theras) knowing all that was contained in the doctrine repeated the dhamma in turn after the sage of the Videha country.

37 Thus in seven months was that compiling of the dhamma
to save the whole world completed by those (theras) bent on
38 the whole world's salvation. 'The thera Mahākassapa has
made the blessed Buddha's message to endure five hundred
39 years,' rejoicing in this thought, at the end of the council,
40 the earth encircled by the ocean trembled six times and many
wondrous signs were shown in the world in many ways. Now
since the canon was compiled by the theras it was called the
41 Thera tradition.[1] The theras who had held the First Council
and had (thereby) brought great blessing to the world, having
lived their allotted span of life, entered, all, into nibbāṇa.

42 Also the theras who have overcome darkness with the light of insight, those great shining lights in the conquest of the world's darkness, have been extinguished by the dread tempest of death. Therefore will the wise man renounce the joy of life.

Here ends the third chapter, called 'The First Council', in the Mahāvaṃsa, compiled for the serene joy and emotion of the pious.

[1] The oldest account of the First Council is contained in the C.V. XI (OLDENBERG, *the Vin. Piṭ.* ii, p. 284 foll.); *Vinaya Texts*, iii (*S.B.E.* xx), p. 370 foll.

CHAPTER IV

THE SECOND COUNCIL

WHEN Ajātasattu's son Udayabhaddaka[1] had slain him he, 1
the traitor, reigned sixteen years. Udayabhaddaka's son 2
Anuruddhaka slew (his father) and Anuruddha's son named
Muṇḍa did likewise. Traitors and fools, these (sons) reigned 3
over the kingdom; in the reign of these two (kings) eight
years elapsed.

Muṇḍa's son Nāgadāsaka slew his father and then did the 4
evildoer reign twenty-four years.

Then were the citizens wroth, saying: 'This is a dynasty 5
of parricides,' and when they had banished the king Nāgadā-
saka they met together and (since) the minister known by the 6
name Susunāga was proved to be worthy, they anointed him
king, mindful of the good of all. He reigned as king eighteen 7
years. His son Kālāsoka reigned twenty-eight years. At the 8
end of the tenth year of Kālāsoka's reign a century had gone
by since the parinibbāṇa of the Sambuddha.

At that time in Vesālī many bhikkhus of the Vajji-clan[2] 9
did shamelessly teach that the Ten Points[3] were lawful,
namely 'Salt in the horn', 'Two fingers' breadth', 'Visiting 10

[1] In the Sinhalese MSS. this name appears in the form 'Udāyibhaddaka'. Cf. D. 1. 50^{25} Udāyibh° or Udāyabh° (E. MÜLLER, *J.P.T.S.* 1888, p. 14). The Dīp. 4. 38, 5. 97, 11. 8 has Udaya(bhadda).

[2] On the confederacy of the Vajjis see RHYS DAVIDS, *Buddhist India*, pp. 25–26. On Vesālī, *ibid.*, p. 40. According to V. SMITH (*Early History of India*, p. 27, n. 1; *J.R.A.S.* 1902, p. 267 foll.) its site is the modern Basāṛ (N. lat. 25° 58′ 20″, E. long. 85° 11′ 30″) in the District Muzaffarpur, north of Patna.

[3] The history of the Second Council is also given in the C.V. XII. Cf. *Vinaya Texts*, iii (*S.B.E.* xx), pp. 386 foll. Here C.V. XII. 1. 9; 2. 8) the single points are explained:

(i) Siṅgiloṇakappa, the custom of putting salt in a horn vessel, in order to season unsalted foods, when received.

(ii) Dvaṅgulakappa, the custom of taking the midday meal,

the village', 'Dwelling', 'Consent', 'Example', 'Unchurned
11 milk', 'Unfermented palm-wine', 'Seat without fringe', 'Gold and so forth'.

When this came to the ears of the thera Yasa, the son of
12 the brahman Kākaṇḍaka, gifted with the six supernormal powers,[1] who was wandering about in the Vajji country, he betook himself to the Mahāvana (vihāra)[2] with the resolve to
13 settle the matter. In the uposatha-hall those (monks) had placed a vessel made of metal and filled with water and had said to the lay-folk: 'Bestow on the brotherhood kahāpaṇas[3]
14 and so on.' The thera forbade them with the words 'This is unlawful; give nothing!' Then did they threaten the thera

even after the prescribed time, as long as the sun's shadow had not passed the meridian by more than two-fingers' breadth.

(iii) Gāmantarakappa, the custom of going into the village, after the meal, and there eating again, if invited.

(iv) Āvāsakappa, the custom of holding the uposatha-feast separately by bhikkhus dwelling in the same district.

(v) Anumatikappa, the carrying out of official acts by an incomplete chapter, on the supposition that the consent of absent bhikkhus was obtained afterwards.

(vi) Āciṇṇakappa, the custom of doing something because of the preceptor's practice.

(vii) Āmathitakappa, taking unchurned milk, even after the mealtime.

(viii) Jalogikappa, drinking unfermented palm-wine.

(ix) Adasakaṃ nisīdanaṃ, the use of mats to sit on which were not of the prescribed size, if they were without fringe.

(x) Jātarūparajataṃ, accepting gold and silver.

[1] Chaḷabhiññā. The six abhiññā are (i) the power of iddhi, (ii) the heavenly ear, i. e. supranormal power of hearing, (iii) the power to read the thoughts of others, (iv) the knowledge of former existences, (v) the heavenly eye, i. e. supranormal power of seeing, (vi) the abandonment of the āsavas. The last of these abhiññā is one of the signs of an arahant. See Rhys Davids, *Dialogues of the Buddha*, i. 62; Aung, *Compendium of Philosophy*, pp. 60-63; 224 foll.

[2] The Mahāvana-monastery is mentioned by Fā-Hian. See Beal, *Buddhist Records of the Western World*, i, p. 52.

[3] Kahāpaṇa (Skr. kārṣāpaṇa) is a square copper coin, weighing 146·4 grains = 9·48 grams. See Rapson, *Indian Coins*, p. 2; Rhys Davids, *Buddhist India*, p. 100.

Yasa with the penance called the Craving of pardon from lay-
folk.[1] He asked for one to bear him company and went 15
with him into the city proclaiming to the citizens, that his
teaching was according to the dhamma.

When the bhikkhus heard what (Yasa's) companion had to 16
tell, they came to thrust him out and surrounded the thera's
house. The thera left it, rising up and passing through the 17
air, and halting at Kosambī, he forthwith sent messengers to
the bhikkhus of Pāvā and Avanti;[2] he himself went to the 18
Ahogaṅga-mountain and related all to the thera Saṃbhūta
Sāṇavāsi.[3]

Sixty great theras from Pāvā and eighty from Avanti, all 19
free from the āsavas,[4] came together on the Ahogaṅga. The
bhikkhus who met together here from this and that region 20
were in all ninety thousand. When they had all conferred
together they, knowing that the deeply learned thera Revata 21
of Soreyya[5] who was free from the āsavas, was the chief
among them at that time, went thence to seek him out.

When the thera heard this resolution (by his divine ear) he 22
set out at once, wishing to travel easily,[6] upon the way to
Vesālī. Arriving day by day in the evening at the spot 23
whence the sage had departed in the morning (the theras)
met him (at last) at Sahajāti.

There the thera Yasa, as the thera Saṃbhūta had 24
charged him to do, at the end of the recital of the sacred
word, addressing himself to the great thera Revata, ques-
tioned him on the Ten Points. The thera rejected them, and 25

[1] Paṭisāraṇiyakamma, see KERN, *Manual*, p. 87, note 8.

[2] Kosambī on the Yamunā was the capital of the Vatsas or Vaṃsas, Pāvā that of the Mallas; Avanti was the region of Ujjenī; RHYS DAVIDS, *Buddhist India*, pp. 36, 26, 28. Instead of Pāveyyakā some of the Sinhalese MSS. read Pāṭheyyakā. But also at M.V. VII. 1. 1 (= *Vin. Piṭ.* i. 253[5]) the Burmese MSS. have Pāveyyakā.

[3] See *Vin. Texts*, iii (*S.B.E.* xx), p. 394, note 2.

[4] Anāsava, see p. 15, n. 3.

[5] Not far from Takkasilā in W. India, see Pārājika, 1. 4 (*Vin. Piṭ.* iii, p. 11); KERN, *Manual*, p. 36.

[6] Cf. for the detailed description, C.V. XII. 1. 9 = *Vin. Texts*, iii (*S.B.E.* xx), p. 396.

when he had heard the matter, he said: 'Let us make an end (of this dispute).'

26 The heretical bhikkhus, too, in order to win support, sought the thera Revata. Preparing in abundance the things needful
27 for ascetics,[1] they took ship with all speed and went to Sahajāti, bestowing food sumptuously when the mealtime came.[2]
28 The thera Sāḷha, free from the āsavas, who lived at Sahajāti, having thought on the matter, perceived: 'Those of Pāvā
29 hold the true doctrine.' And the great god Brahmā drew near to him and said: 'Stand thou firm in the doctrine,' and he replied that he would ever stand firm in the doctrine.

30 They[3] took those needful things (that they had brought as gifts) and sought the thera Revata, but the thera did not take their part and dismissed (the pupil) who took their part.[4]
31 They went thence to Vesālī, shameless they went from there
32 to Pupphapura,[5] and told king Kālāsoka: 'Guarding our Master's perfumed chamber we dwell in the Mahāvana-vihāra
33 in the Vajji territory; but bhikkhus dwelling in the country are coming, great king, with the thought: We will take the vihāra for ourselves. Forbid them!'

34 When they had thus misled the king they went (back) to Vesālī. Here in Sahajāti eleven hundred and ninety thou-
35 sand bhikkhus were come together under the thera Revata,
36 to bring the dispute to a peaceful end. And the thera would not end the dispute save in the presence of those with whom

[1] Sāmaṇaka parikkhāra (as a gift to Revata) is that which a monk is allowed to call his own, such as robes, the alms-bowl, &c. Cf. CHILDERS, s. v. parikkhāro.

[2] The underlying meaning is that they indulged in riotous living on their journey. Vissagga has the implied sense of something rich and luxuriant. The Ṭīkā paraphrases bhattavissaggaṃ with bhattaparivesanaṃ, bhattaparibhogaṃ.

[3] I. e. the Vajjian monks.

[4] On this passage see Mah. ed., pp. xxv–xxvi. However, I now prefer the reading pakkhagāhiṃ, since the passage evidently refers to Revata's disciple Uttara (C.V. XII. 2. 3), who allowed himself to be won over by the Vajjian monks.

[5] Pupphapura, the City of Flowers, a name of Pāṭaliputta (now Patna), capital at that time of the kingdom of Magadha.

it had begun;[1] therefore all the bhikkhus went thence to Vesālī.

The misguided king likewise sent his ministers thither, but 37
led astray by the design of the devas they went elsewhere.
And the monarch, when he had sent them, saw himself 38
in a dream, that night, hurled into the hell called Loha-
kumbhī. The king was sorely terrified and, to calm his fears, 39
his sister, Nandā, the therī free from the āsavas, came to
him, passing through the air.

'An ill deed is this that thou hast done! Reconcile thee 40
with these venerable bhikkhus, the true believers. Placing
thyself on their side, protect thou their faith. If thou dost 41
so, blessed art thou!' she said, and thereon vanished. And
forthwith in the morning the king set out to go to Vesālī.
He went to the Mahāvana (monastery), assembled the con- 42
gregation of the bhikkhus there, and when he had heard what
was said by both of the (opposing) sides, and had decided,
himself, for the true faith, when moreover this prince was 43
reconciled with all the rightly believing bhikkhus and had
declared that he was for the right belief, he said: 'Do what 44
ye think well to further the doctrine,' and when he had pro-
mised to be their protector, he returned to his capital.

Thereafter the brotherhood came together to decide upon 45
those points; then, in the congregation (of monks), aimless[2]
words were spent. Then the thera Revata, who went into the 46
midst of the brotherhood, resolved to settle the matter by
means of an ubbāhikā.[3] He appointed four bhikkhus from 47
the East, and four from Pāvā, for the ubbāhikā to set the
dispute to rest. Sabbakāmi and Sāḷha, one named Khujjaso- 48
bhita, and Vāsabhagāmika, these were the theras from the

[1] Mūlaṭṭhehi vinā, lit. 'without those who were at the root.'

[2] Anaggāni bhassāni 'aimless' or 'inexact' speeches. The reading anaggāni bhassāni (Ed. Col. nantāni bh°) is confirmed by C.V. IV. 14. 19 and XII. 2. 7.

[3] Ubbāhikāya 'by means of a *Referat*', the settlement of a dispute being laid in the hands of certain chosen brethren. For the rule on this, see C.V. IV. 14. 19 ff.; *Vin. Texts*, iii (*S.B.E.* xx), p. 49 ff.

49 East; Revata, Sāṇasambhūta, Yasa, the son of Kākaṇḍaka,
and Sumana, these were the four theras from Pāvā.
50 Now to decide on those points the eight theras who were
free from the āsavas betook them to the quiet and solitary
51 Vālikārāma. There, in the beautiful spot prepared for them by
the young Ajita,[1] the great theras took up their abode, they who
52 knew the thoughts of the Greatest of Sages. And the great
thera Revata, skilled in questioning, questioned the thera
53 Sabbakāmi successively on each one of those points. Questioned
by him the great thera Sabbakāmi thus gave judgment: 'All
54 these points are unlawful, according to tradition.' And when,
in due order, they had ended (their task) in this place, they
did all again, in like manner, with question and answer, in the
55 presence of the brotherhood. And thus did the great theras
refute the teaching of those ten thousand heretical bhikkhus
who maintained the Ten Points.

56 Sabbakāmi was then the saṃghatthera on the earth, one
hundred and twenty years did he number since his upasaṃpadā.

57 Sabbakāmi and Sāḷha, Revata, Khujjasobhita, Yasa, the
son of Kākaṇḍaka, and Sambhūta Sāṇavāsika, the six theras,
58 were pupils of the thera Ānanda; but Vāsabhagāmika and
59 Sumana, the two theras, were pupils of the thera Anuruddha.
These eight fortunate theras had beheld the Tathāgata in
60 time past. One hundred and twelve thousand bhikkhus had
come together, and of all these bhikkhus the thera Revata
then was the chief.

61 At that time the thera Revata, in order to hold a council,
that the true faith might long endure, chose seven hundred
62 out of all that troop of bhikkhus; (those chosen were)
arahants endowed with the four special sciences, understanding of meanings and so forth,[2] knowing the tipiṭaka.

[1] The reading daharenājitenettha is confirmed by C.V. XII. 2. 7: atha kho saṃgho āyasmantaṃ pi Ajitaṃ sammanni therānaṃ bhikkhūnaṃ āsanapaññāpakaṃ (*Vin. Piṭ.* ii. 305[34]).

[2] Pabhinnatthādiñāṇānaṃ is explained in the Ṭīkā as atthapaṭisambhidādipabhedagatañāṇānaṃ; atthādippabhedagatehi paṭisambhidāñāṇehi samannāgatānaṃ t

All these (theras met) in the Vālikārāma protected by 63
Kālāsoka, under the leadership of the thera Revata, (and)
compiled the dhamma.[1] Since they accepted the dhamma 64
already established in time past and proclaimed afterward,
they completed their work in eight months.

When these theras of high renown had held the Second 65
Council, they, since in them all evil had perished, attained in
course of time unto nibbāṇa.

When we bethink us of the death of the sons of the 66
Universal Teacher, who were gifted with perfect insight, who
had attained all that is to attain, who had conferred blessings
on (the beings of) the three forms of existence,[2] then may
we lay to heart the entire vanity of all that comes into being [3]
and vigilantly strive (after deliverance).

Here ends the fourth chapter, called 'The Second Council', in the Mahāvaṃsa, compiled for the serene joy and emotion of the pious.

attho; ādiggahaṇenettha dhammapaṭisaṃbhidādīni ñāṇāni gahitāni. The compound means therefore literally, 'who possess the specialized knowledge of the attha and so forth,' that is, the four paṭisaṃbhidā. By this term is understood 'a transcendent faculty in grasping the meaning of a text or subject (attha); in grasping the Law of all things as taught by the Buddha (dhamma); in exegesis (nirutti); readiness in expounding and discussion (paṭibhāna)'. See Paṭisambhidā-magga 1. 88.

[1] Akaruṃ dhammasaṃgahaṃ. See note to 3. 17.

[2] The three forms of existence are kāmabhava, rūpabhava, arūpabhava 'sensual existence, corporeal existence, formless existence' (CHILDERS, *P.D.* s. vv.), that is, existences in the three worlds so named, which together form that part of the universe called the sattaloka, 'world of beings.' In this the kāmaloka includes the eleven lowest worlds, the rūpaloka the sixteen higher, and the arūpaloka the four highest, celestial worlds.

[3] Saṃkhatāsārakattaṃ: saṃkhata is a synonym of saṃkhārā, and means in the widest sense the material and transitory world. See CHILDERS, s. v. saṃkhāro.

CHAPTER V

THE THIRD COUNCIL

1 THAT redaction of the true dhamma, which was arranged at
the beginning by the great theras Mahākassapa and others,
2 is called that of the theras. One and united was the school
of the theras in the first hundred years. But afterwards
3 arose other schools of doctrine.[1] The heretical bhikkhus,
subdued by the theras who had held the Second Council,[2] in
4 all ten thousand, founded the school which bears the name
Mahāsaṃghika.[3]

From this arose the Gokulika and Ekavyohārika (schools).
5 From the Gokulikā arose the Paṇṇatti sect and the Bahulikā,
from these the Cetiya sect. (Thus) there are six, with
6 the Mahāsaṃghikā, and yet two more (groups) parted from
the followers of the Thera-doctrine: the Mahiṃsāsakā and
7 the Vajjiputtaka bhikkhus. And there parted from them
likewise the Dhammuttariyā and the Bhadrayānika bhikkhus,
the Chandāgārikā, the Saṃmitī and the Vajjiputtiya bhikkhus.
8 From the Mahiṃsāsaka bhikkhus two (groups) parted, the
bhikkhus who held by the Sabbattha-school and the Dhamma-
9 guttika bhikkhus. From the Sabbattha sect arose the Kassa-
piyā, from these arose the Saṃkantika bhikkhus, from these
10 last the Sutta sect. These are twelve together with (those
of) the Thera-doctrine; thereto are added the six schools
named and these together are eighteen.
11 Thus in the second century arose seventeen schools, and
12 other schools arose afterwards. The Hemavatā and the

[1] Ācariyavāda stands in contrast to theravāda. This latter is the true and orthodox church community, the other expresses collectively the various sects which arose in the course of time.

[2] Tehi saṃgītikārehi therehi dutiyehi, lit. 'by those the second council-holding theras'.

[3] I.e. the 'Great Community'.

Rājagiriyā and likewise the Siddhatthakā, the first Seliya
bhikkhus, the other Seliyā, and the Vājiriyā: these six 13
separated (from the rest) in Jambudīpa, the Dhammarucī and
the Sāgaliyā separated (from the rest) in the island of Laṅkā.[1]

Here ends the Story of the Ācariya-schools.

The sons of Kālāsoka were ten brothers, twenty-two years 14
did they reign. Afterwards, the nine Nandas[2] were kings in 15
succession; they too reigned twenty-two years.

Then did the brahman Cāṇakka[3] anoint a glorious youth, 16
known by the name Candagutta, as king over all Jambudīpa, 17
born of a noble clan, the Moriyas, when, filled with bitter hate,
he had slain the ninth (Nanda) Dhanananda.

Twenty-four years he reigned, and his son Bindusāra reigned 18
twenty-eight. A hundred glorious sons and one had Bindu-
sāra;[4] Asoka[5] stood high above them all in valour, splendour, 19
might, and wondrous powers. He, when he had slain his 20
ninety-nine brothers born of different mothers, won the
undivided sovereignty over all Jambudīpa. Be it known, 21
that two hundred and eighteen years had passed from the
nibbāṇa of the Master unto Asoka's consecration.

[1] The Nikāya-saṃgraha (ed. WICKREMASINGHE, pp. 11[32] and 13[9]) informs us that the Dhammarucī branched off from the Theravādins 454 years A. B., and the Sāgaliyā from the former 795 years A. B. The former event took place under Vaḷa-gam-bā (Vaṭṭagāmaṇi Abhaya, see Mah. 33. 95 ff.), and the latter under Goṭhābhaya (see Mah. 36. 110 ff.).

[2] The Mah. Ṭīkā, pp. 117–119, gives a detailed account of the Nanda dynasty; also Kamb. Mah. V. 953–994.

[3] On the Moriya dynasty and on Cāṇakka and Candagutta see Mah. Ṭīkā, pp. 119–123; Kamb. Mah. V. 995–1090. Candragupta's minister, Cāṇakya, is also known to play an important part in the Mudrārākṣasa. See SYLVAIN LÉVI, *Le Théâtre Indien*, pp. 226 ff. A work on politics, ascribed to him, the Kauṭilīyaśāstra, still exists. HILLEBRANDT, *Über das Kauṭilīyaśāstra und Verwandtes*. Cp. also *I.A.* 38, 1909, pp. 257 ff.

[4] On Bindusāra and on Candagutta's death see Mah. Ṭīkā, pp. 124, 125; Kamb. Mah. V. 1092–1128.

[5] On Asoka's birth and early youth, see Mah. Ṭīkā, pp. 125-128; Kamb. Mah. V. 1129-1198.

22 Four years after the famous (Asoka) had won for himself
the undivided sovereignty he consecrated himself as king in
23 the city Pāṭaliputta. Straightway after his consecration his
command spread so far as a yojana (upward) into the air and
downward into the (depths of the) earth.[1]
24 Day by day did the devas bring eight men's loads of water
of (the lake) Anotatta; the king dealt it out to his people.
25 From the Himalaya did the devas bring for cleansing the
teeth twigs of nāga-creeper, enough for many thousands,
26 healthful fruits, myrobalan and terminalia and mango-
fruits from the same place, perfect in colour, smell, and
27 taste. The spirits of the air [2] brought garments of five
colours, and yellow stuff for napkins, and also celestial drink
28 from the Chaddanta-lake.[3] Out of the nāga-kingdom the
nāgas (brought) stuff, coloured like the jasmine-blossom and
without a seam, and celestial lotus-flowers and collyrium and
29 unguents; parrots brought daily from the Chaddanta-lake
30 ninety thousand waggon-loads of rice.[4] Mice converted this
rice, unbroken, into grains without husk or powder, and
31 therewith was meal provided for the royal family. Perpetually
did honey-bees prepare honey for him, and in the forges bears
32 swung the hammers. Karavīka-birds, graceful and sweet
33 of voice, came and made delightful music for the king. And
being consecrated king, Asoka raised his youngest brother
Tissa, son of his own mother, to the office of vice-regent.

Here ends the Consecration of the pious Asoka.

34 (Asoka's) father had shown hospitality to sixty thousand

[1] The sense of this passage, not rightly understood up to the present time, is evidently this: not only men upon the earth but also the spirits of the air and the earth heard and obeyed Asoka's command.

[2] The marū (Skt. marut) in contrast to the devā in 24.

[3] Here follow two spurious verses, 'To die (?) in this city there came gazelles, boars, birds into the kitchens and willingly perished. Leopards were used to take the herds to pasture and lead them to their stalls, gazelles and boars were used to watch over fields, plots, and ponds and so forth.'

[4] On parrots furnishing hill paddy, see *Jāt.* i, pp. 325^{1-3}, 327^{6} foll.; MORRIS, *J.P.T.S.* 1884, p. 107.

brahmans, versed in the Brahma-doctrine, and in like manner
he himself nourished them for three years. But when he 35
saw their want of self-control at the distribution of food he
commanded his ministers saying: '(Hereafter) I will give
according to my choice.' The shrewd (king) bade (them) 36
bring the followers of the different schools into his presence,
tested them in an assembly, and gave them to eat, and sent
them thence when he had entertained them.

As he once, standing at the window, saw a peaceful ascetic, 37
the sāmaṇera Nigrodha, passing along the street, he felt
kindly toward him. The youth was the son of prince 38
Sumana, the eldest brother of all the sons of Bindusāra.

When Bindusāra had fallen sick Asoka left the govern- 39
ment of Ujjenī conferred on him by his father, and came
to Pupphapura,[1] and when he had made himself master of 40
the city, after his father's death, he caused his eldest brother
to be slain and took on himself the sovereignty in the
splendid city.

The consort of prince Sumana, who bore the same name 41
(Sumanā), being with child, fled straightway by the east
gate and went to a caṇḍāla village, and there the guardian 42
god of a nigrodha-tree[2] called her by her name, built a hut
and gave it to her. And as, that very day, she bore a 43
beautiful boy, she gave to her son the name Nigrodha,
enjoying the protection of the guardian god. When the 44
headman of the caṇḍālas saw (the mother), he looked on her
as his own wife, and kept her seven years with honour. Then, 45
as the thera Mahāvaruṇa saw that the boy bore the signs of
his destiny,[3] the arahant questioned his mother and ordained 46
him, and even in the room where they shaved him[4] he

[1] See note to 4. 31. UJJENĪ, Skr. Ujjayinī, now Ujjain in the Gwalior State, Central India, was the old capital of Avanti. RHYS DAVIDS, *Buddhist India*, p. 3 foll.

[2] Nigrodha = *Ficus Indica*, banyan-tree.

[3] Upanissaya includes all those qualities, aptitudes and marks of an individual, which show that he is qualified to attain arahantship.

[4] The shaving of the hair is one of the ceremonies at the reception of a novice into the order.

attained to the state of arahant. Going thence to visit his
47 royal mother, he entered the splendid city by the south gate,
and following the road that led to that village, he passed
48 (on his way) the king's court. Well pleased was the king by
his grave bearing, but kindly feeling arose in him also by
reason of a former life lived together.

49 Now once, in time past, there were three brothers, traders
in honey; one was used to sell the honey, two to get the
50 honey. A certain paccekabuddha was sick of a wound; and
another paccekabuddha, who, for his sake, wished for honey,
51 came even then to the city on his usual way for seeking alms.
A maiden, who was going for water to the river-bank, saw
52 him. When she knew, from questioning him, that he wished
for honey, she pointed with hand outstretched and said:
'Yonder is a honey-store, sir, go thither.'

53 The trader, with believing heart, gave to the buddha who
came there a bowlful of honey, so that it ran over the edge.
54 As he saw the honey filling (the bowl) and flowing over the
edge, and streaming down to the ground, he, full of faith,
55 wished: 'May I, for this gift, come by the undivided sove-
reignty of Jambudīpa, and may my command reach forth
a yojana (upward) into the air and (downward) under the earth.
56 To his brothers as they came, he said: 'To a man of such
and such a kind have I given honey; agree thereto since the
57 honey is yours also.' The eldest brother said grudgingly:
'It was surely a caṇḍāla, for the caṇḍālas ever clothe them-
58 selves in yellow garments.' The second said: 'Away with
thy paccekabuddha over the sea!' But when they heard his
promise to let them participate of the reward, they gave their
59 sanction. Then the (maid who) had pointed out the store
wished that she might become the royal spouse of the (first),
and (desired) a lovely form with limbs of perfect outline.[1]

60 Asoka was he who gave the honey, the queen Asaṃdhi-
mittā was the maid, Nigrodha he who uttered the word
'caṇḍāla', Tissa he who had wished him away over the sea.[2]
61 He who had uttered the word 'caṇḍāla' lived (in expiation

[1] Adissamānasaṃdhi means literally 'with invisible joints'.
[2] Pāravādī, lit. 'who had spoken of the further shore.'

thereof) in a caṇḍāla village, but because he had desired deliverance, he also, even in the seventh year, attained unto deliverance.[1]

The king, in whom kindly feelings had arisen towards that 62
same (Nigrodha), summoned him in all haste into his presence;
but he came staidly and calmly thither. And the king said 63
to him: 'Sit, my dear, upon a fitting seat.' Since he saw no
other bhikkhu there he approached the royal throne. Then, 64
as he stepped toward the throne, the king thought: 'To-day,
this sāmaṇera will be lord in my house!' Leaning on the 65
king's hand he (the monk) mounted the throne and took his
seat on the royal throne under the white canopy. And seeing 66
him seated there king Asoka rejoiced greatly that he had
honoured him according to his rank.[2] When he had refreshed 67
him with hard and soft foods prepared for himself he questioned
the sāmaṇera concerning the doctrine taught by the Sambuddha.
Then the sāmaṇera preached to him the 'Appamādavagga'.[3] 68

And when the lord of the earth had heard him he was won
to the doctrine of the Conqueror, and he said to (Nigrodha): 69
'My dear, I bestow on thee eight perpetual supplies of food.'
And he answered: 'These will I bestow on my master.'[4]

[1] The stop should be put after āsi. Patthesi refers to the existence as madhuvāṇija. When the eldest brother had transferred the patti ('reward') to his younger brothers each one of them uttered a patthanā, that of the third was mokkha, i.e. the attainment of arahantship.

[2] Sambhāvetvāna guṇato is an allusion to 63. The king leaves it to Nigrodha to choose his own place since he does not know his rank. From the fact of Nigrodha's seating himself on the throne Asoka perceives that a monk of the highest rank is before him, and he rejoices that he did not assign a lower place to him.

[3] I.e. the section entitled 'unwearying zeal'. There are eleven minor vaggas in the Saṃyutta-Nikāya, bearing this title, and nine Appamādasuttas.

[4] Upajjhāyassa. Every novice on his entrance into the order chooses an upajjhāya 'a master', and an ācariya 'teacher'. It appears from M.V. I. 25. 6 ff., 32. 1 ff., that there is no difference between the functions of the two. The ācariya seems, according to M.V. I. 32. 1, to be only the deputy or substitute of the upajjhāya.

70 When again eight (supplies) were bestowed on him he allotted
these to his teacher; and when yet eight more were bestowed
71 he gave them to the community of bhikkhus. And when
yet again eight were bestowed, he, full of understanding,
consented to accept them. Together with thirty-two bhik-
72 khus, he went on the following day, and when he had been
served by the king with his own hands, and had preached the
doctrine to the ruler, he confirmed him with many of his
train in the refuges and precepts of duty.[1]

Here ends the Visit of the sāmaṇera Nigrodha.

73 Thereon the king, with glad faith, doubled day by day
(the number) of bhikkhus (receiving bounty), till they were
74 sixty thousand. Putting aside the sixty thousand teachers of
false doctrine,[2] he bestowed alms perpetually on sixty thousand
bhikkhus in his house.

75 Having commanded costly foods, hard and soft, to be
prepared speedily, in order to feast the sixty thousand bhik-
76 khus, and having caused the town to be gaily decked, he
went to the brotherhood and bade them to his house; and
after he had brought them thither, had bestowed hospitality
on them and largely provided them with the things needful
77 for ascetics,[3] he questioned them thus: 'How great is (the
content of) the dhamma taught by the Master?' And the
thera Moggaliputta-Tissa answered him upon this matter.
78 When he heard: 'There are eighty-four (thousand) sections of
the dhamma,' the king said: 'Each one of them will I honour
with a vihāra.'

79 Then bestowing ninety-six koṭis (of money) in eighty-four
80 thousand towns, the ruler bade the kings all over the earth

[1] See note to 1. 32.

[2] Titthiyānaṃ. Those whom his father (according to v. 34) had already supported and whom Asoka did in fact entertain, with certain changes. He now gradually substituted Buddhist monks. Verses 73 and 74 are suspicious, since the Ṭīkā does not comment on them.

[3] Sāmaṇaka, see note to 4. 26.

begin (to build) vihāras and he himself began to build the
Asokārāma.[1]

With the grant for the three gems,[2] for Nigrodha and for 81
the sick, he bestowed in (support of) the faith for each of
them a hundred thousand (pieces of money) each day. With the 82
treasure spent for the Buddha the (priests) held thūpa-offerings[3]
of many kinds continually in many vihāras. With the treasure 83
spent for the dhamma the people continually prepared the
four things needful for the use of bhikkhus who were learned
in the doctrine. Of the loads of water borne from the 84
Anotatta-lake he bestowed four on the brotherhood, one every
day to sixty theras who knew the tipiṭaka; but one he had 85
commanded to be given to the queen Asaṃdhimittā, while
the king himself had but two for his own use. To the sixty 86
thousand bhikkhus and to sixteen thousand women (of the
palace), he gave day by day those tooth-sticks called nāga-
latā.[4]

When, one day, the monarch heard of the nāga-king 87
Mahākāla of wondrous might, who had beheld four Buddhas,
who had lived through one age of the world, he sent for him 88
to be brought (into his presence) fettered with a chain of
gold; and when he had brought him and made him sit upon
the throne under the white canopy, when he had done homage 89
to him with (gifts of) various flowers, and had bidden the
sixteen thousand women (of the palace) to surround him, he
(the king) spoke thus: 'Let us behold the (bodily) form of the 90
omniscient Great Sage, of Him who hath boundless know-
ledge, who hath set rolling the wheel of the true doctrine.'
The nāga-king created a beauteous figure of the Buddha, 91
endowed with the thirty-two greater signs and brilliant
with the eighty lesser signs (of a Buddha), surrounded by the 92

[1] The Asoka monastery in the capital Pāṭaliputta.

[2] Ratanattayaṃ. The three gems are Buddha, dhamma, saṃgha: Buddha, his doctrine and community, see note on 1. 32.

[3] Thūpapūjā. The tope (thūpa) is never missing from a Buddhist monastery. Festivals of which a tope is the centre are frequently mentioned in the Mahāvaṃsa.

[4] The nāga-creeper. See 5. 25.

fathom-long rays of glory and adorned with the crown of flames.[1]

At the sight thereof the king was filled with joy and amaze-
93 ment and thought: 'Even such is the image created by this
(Mahākāla), nay then, what (must) the (real) form of the
Tathāgata have been!' And he was more and more uplifted
94 with joy, and for seven days without ceasing did he, the great
king of wondrous power, keep the great festival called the
'Feast of the eyes'.[2]

Here ends the Entrance (of Asoka) into the doctrine.

95 Now the mighty and believing king and thera Moggaliputta
had already in former times been seen by the holy ones.[3]
96 At the time of the Second Council, the theras, looking into
the future, saw the downfall of the faith in the time of that
97 king. Looking around in the whole world for one who should
be able to stay that downfall, they saw the Brahmā Tissa[4]
98 who had not long to live (in the Brahmā heaven). To him
they went and prayed him, the mighty in wisdom, to bring
this downfall to nought by being reborn himself among men.
99 And he granted their prayer, desiring that the doctrine should
shine forth in brightness. But to the youthful Siggava and
100 Caṇḍavajji the sages spoke thus: 'When a hundred and
eighteen years are passed the downfall of the religion will
101 begin. We shall not live to see that (time). You, bhikkhus,

[1] On the signs of a Buddha, see the Lakkhaṇa Suttanta in D. III, p. 142 foll., and GRÜNWEDEL, *Buddhistische Kunst in Indien*, p. 138 foll.

[2] Akkhipūjā. It corresponds to our 'consecration'. See *Vin.* iii. 300.

[3] Vasīhi = 'by those who have the senses under control'. In the Kamb. Mahāv. follows here (vv. 1276–1338) an episode relating to Asaṃdhimittā. Asoka puts his consort to the test, she having boasted of merit acquired. He requires of her that she shall provide, between one day and another, robes for the 60,000 monks. With the help of the god Kubera, who remembers the kindness shown by her to the paccekabuddha (see above, vv. 51 foll.), she accomplishes what the king demands of her.

[4] Tissa, a dweller in the Brahmā heaven.

have had no part in this matter[1] therefore you merit punish-
ment, and your punishment shall be this: that the doctrine 102
may shine forth in brightness, the Brahmā Tissa, mighty in
wisdom, will be reborn in the house of the brahman Moggali.
As time passes on one of you shall receive the boy into the 103
order, another shall carefully instruct him in the word of the
Sambuddha.

There was a thera Dāsaka—disciple of the thera Upāli. 104
Soṇaka was his (Dāsaka's) disciple, and both those theras
were disciples of Soṇaka.

In former times there lived in Vesālī a learned brahman 105
named Dāsaka. As the eldest of three hundred disciples he 106
dwelt with his teacher, and at the end of twelve years having
come to the end of (studying) the vedas, he, going about
with the (other) disciples, met the thera Upāli, dwelling
at the Vālika-monastery, after he had established the sacred 107
word (in council), and sitting down near him he questioned
him concerning hard passages in the vedas, and the other
expounded them to him. 'A doctrine is come after all the 108
doctrines, O brahman, yet all doctrines end in the one
doctrine; which is that one?'

Thus spoke the thera concerning the name (of the true 109
doctrine), but the young brahman knew it not. He asked:
'What manta is this?' and when the answer was given: 'The
manta of the Buddha,' he said: 'Impart it to me,' and the 110
other answered: 'We impart it (only) unto one who wears
our robe.'

And he (Dāsaka) asked his teacher and also his father and
mother on behalf of that manta.[2] When he with three 111
hundred young brahmans had received from the thera the
pabbajjā the brahman in time received the upasampadā.
Then to a thousand (disciples) who had overcome the āsavas,[3] 112

[1] Imaṃ adhikaraṇaṃ, that is, in the work of the Second Council.

[2] That is, he asked if he might be permitted to learn it under the condition mentioned.

[3] By khīṇāsavā in v. 112 (see note on 3. 9) are understood the arahants; by ariyā in v. 113, all the Buddha's hearers (Vibhaṅga

among whom was the thera Dāsaka, did the thera Upāli teach
113 the whole tipiṭaka. Past reckoning is the number of the
other Ariyas, and of those who yet stood outside (the religion),
by whom the piṭakas were learned from the thera.
114 In the land of the Kāsi[1] lived the son of a caravan-guide,
named Soṇaka. With his father and mother he had come
115 trading, to Giribbaja.[2] He went, youth as he was, fifteen
years old, into the Veḷuvana[3] (monastery); fifty-five young
brahmans, his companions, came with him.
116 When he saw the thera Dāsaka there with his disciples
around him, faith came to him and he asked him for the
pabbajjā-ordination. (The thera) said: 'Ask thy teacher.'
117 Afterwards, the young Soṇaka, having fasted three meal-times
and won his parents' leave to enter the order, came again,
118 and then, when he had received from the thera Dāsaka
the pabbajjā and the upasampadā, together with those other
119 youths, he learned the three piṭakas. Amid the company of
the thousand disciples of the thera, who had overcome the
āsavas, who were versed in the piṭakas, the ascetic Soṇaka
was the foremost.
120 In the city that bears the name of the pāṭali flower[4] there
lived the wise Siggava, son of a minister. He, when eighteen
121 years old and dwelling in three palaces fitted for the three
seasons of the year, went, in company with his friend
122 Caṇḍavajji, a minister's son, and surrounded by five hundred
followers, to the Kukkuṭārāma,[5] and visited the thera Soṇaka.
123 And when he perceived that (the thera) sat sunk in a trance

372), by puthujjanā the remaining multitude who still stand outside the way leading to perfection.

[1] The Kāsis (Skr. kāśi) are one of the sixteen tribes of northern India, settled in the district round Benares. Kāsi is also the old name of Benares. Rhys Davids, *Buddhist India*, p. 24.

[2] The old capital of Magadha, Skr. girivraja 'Mountain Stronghold'. It was situated on the top of a hill, at the foot of which afterwards Rājagaha was built. Rhys Davids, *l. c.*, p. 37.

[3] I. e. Bamboo-grove.

[4] I. e. Pāṭaliputta. See note to 4. 31. Pāṭali *Bignonia suaveolens*.

[5] A monastery in Pāṭaliputta. V. A. Smith, *Asoka*, pp. 183, 193, 194.

with senses restrained[1] and did not answer his greeting, he
asked the brotherhood about this matter. They said: 'Those 124
who are deep in a trance give no reply.' (So he asked) 'How
come they forth from (the trance)?' And the bhikkhus said:
'At a call from the master, or a call from the brotherhood, or 125
when the allotted time is ended, or at the approach of death
they come forth (from the trance).' 126

As they saw, speaking thus, that these (youths) were
destined for holiness,[2] they caused the call from the brother-
hood to be given; and (the thera) awoke from the trance and
went to them. The youth asked: 'Wherefore didst thou not 127
speak to me, venerable one?' The (thera) answered: 'We
were enjoying that which is for us to enjoy.' The (young
man) said: 'Let us also enjoy this.' He answered: 'Those 128
only can we cause to enjoy it who are like unto us.'

Then, with their parents' leave, the young Siggava and 129
Caṇḍavajji and their five hundred followers likewise received
the pabbajjā and (afterwards) the upasampadā-ordination from
the thera Soṇaka. With him as their master the two eagerly 130
studied the three piṭakas and attained to the six supernormal
powers.[3]

Thereafter when Siggava knew that Tissa had been born 131
into this world, the thera, from that time, frequented his
house for seven years. And not for seven years did it befall 132
him to hear the words 'Go further on' (said to him). But in
the eighth year did he hear those words 'Go further on', in
that house. As he went forth the brahman Moggali, who was 133
even then coming in, saw him and asked him: 'Hast thou
received aught in our house?' And he answered: 'Yes.'
When (Moggali) went into his house he heard (what had 134
befallen) and when the thera came to the house again, on the
second day afterwards, he reproached him with the lie. And 135

[1] Samāpattisamāpannaṃ. 'There are eight samāpattis, attainments or endowments, which are eight successive states induced by the ecstatic meditation,' CHILDERS, *P.D.* s.v. See SPENCE HARDY, *Manual of Buddhism*, p. 170, and *J.P.T.S.*, 1909, p. 61.

[2] See note to 5. 45.

[3] On the six abhiññā, see note to 4. 12.

when he had heard the thera's words the brahman, full of
136 faith, gave him continual alms of his own food, and little by
little did all of his household become believers, and the
brahman continually offered hospitality (to the thera), giving
him a seat in his house.

137 So as time passed the young Tissa gradually came to the
age of sixteen years and reached the further shore of the
138 ocean of the three vedas. The thera, thinking that he might
have speech with him in this way, made all the seats in his
139 house to vanish, save the seat of the young brahman. Being
come from the Brahmā-world (this latter) loved cleanliness,
and therefore were they used to keep his chair hung up for
better care thereof.[1]

140 Then the people in the house, finding no other seat, full of
confusion, since the thera had to stand, prepared the seat
141 of the young Tissa for him. When the young brahman re-
turned from his teacher's house and saw (the thera) sitting
there he fell into anger and spoke to him in unfriendly wise.
142 The thera said to him: 'Young man, dost thou know the
manta?' And the young brahman (for answer) asked him the
143 same question again. Since the thera replied: 'I know it,' he
asked him concerning hard passages in the vedas. The thera
144 expounded them to him; for, when leading the lay life, he
had already studied the vedas even to the end. How should
he not be able to expound them since he had mastered the
four special sciences?[2]

145 'For him whose thought arises and does not perish, thought
shall perish and not arise (again); but for him whose thought
shall perish and not arise, thought shall arise (again) and not
perish.'[3]

[1] This verse is suspicious; the Ṭīkā makes no comment on it.

[2] Pabhinnapatisaṃbhida, see note to 4. 62.

[3] A play on the double meaning of cittaṃ and nirujjhati. Whosoever thinks aright and whose thought does not go astray, i. e. whosoever knows the truth, his intellect comes unto nibbāṇa never to return again. But on the other hand, he who does not think aright and does not follow the true doctrine will enter into a new existence and will not reach deliverance.

The wise thera asked this question from the (chapter called) 146
Cittayamaka.[1] And it was as the (darkness of) night to the
other, and he said to him: 'What kind of manta is that, 147
O bhikkhu?' 'The manta of the Buddha,' answered (the
thera); and when the other said: 'Impart it to me,' he said:
'I impart it (only) to one who wears our robe.'[2]

So with the leave of his father and mother (the young man) 148
received the pabbajjā-ordination, for the sake of the manta,
and the thera, when he had ordained him, imparted to him
duly the (method of the) kammaṭṭhānas.[3] By practice of 149
meditation this highly gifted man soon won the fruit of sotā-
patti,[4] and when the thera was aware of this he sent him to 150
the thera Caṇḍavajji that he might learn the suttapiṭaka
and abhidhammapiṭaka of him. And this he learned (from
Caṇḍavajji).

And thereafter the monk Siggava, having conferred on him 151
the upasampadā, taught him the vinaya and again instructed
him in the two other (piṭakas). When, afterwards, the young 152
Tissa had gained the true insight,[5] he attained in time to the
mastery of the six supernormal powers and reached the rank
of a thera. Far and wide shone his renown like the sun and 153
moon. The world paid heed to his word even as to the word
of the Sambuddha.

Here ends the Story of the thera Tissa, the son of Moggali.

One day the prince[6] (Tissa) when hunting saw gazelles 154
sporting joyously in the wild. And at this sight he thought:
'Even the gazelles sport thus joyously, who feed on grass in 155

[1] I. e. 'The double thought.' The reference is to the Yamakappakaraṇa of the abhidhamma.

[2] Cf. 5. 109, 110.

[3] Kammaṭṭhāna 'The foundations of (right) acting'. By this is meant the right method for the practice of meditation. See CHILDERS, *P.D.* s. v.

[4] I. e. the first stage of sanctification. See note to 1. 33.

[5] The vipassanā is one of the signs of the arahant. It is tenfold. See the details in AUNG, *Compendium of Philosophy*, pp. 65 foll., 180.

[6] Uparājā, viceregent.

the wild. Wherefore are not the bhikkhus joyous and gay, who have their food and dwelling in comfort?'
156 Returned home he told the king his thought. To teach
him the king handed over to him the government of the
157 kingdom for one week, saying: 'Enjoy, prince, for one week, my royal state; then will I put thee to death.' Thus said the ruler.
158 And when the week was gone by he asked: 'Wherefore art
thou thus wasted away?' And when (Tissa) answered: 'By
reason of the fear of death,' the king spoke again to him
159 and said: 'Thinking that thou must die when the week was gone by, thou wast no longer joyous and gay; how then can ascetics be joyous and gay, my dear, who think ever upon death?'
160 And (Tissa) when his brother spoke thus, was turned toward
faith in the doctrine (of the Buddha). And afterwards when
161 he once went forth hunting, he saw the thera Mahādham-
marakkhita, the self-controlled, sitting at the foot of a tree,
162 and fanned by a cobra with a branch of a sāla-tree. And that wise (prince) thought: 'When shall I, like this thera, be ordained in the religion of the Conqueror, and live in the forest-wilderness?'
163 When the thera, to convert him, had come thither flying
through the air, standing on the water of the pond in the
164 Asokārāma, he, leaving his goodly garments behind him in the
165 air, plunged into the water and bathed his limbs. And when
the prince saw this marvel he was filled with joyful faith, and
the wise man made this wise resolve: 'This very day will
166 I receive the pabbajjā-ordination.' He went to the king and
respectfully besought him to let him receive the pabbajjā.
Since the king could not turn him from (his resolve) he took
167 him with him and went with a great retinue to the vihāra.
There (the prince) received the pabbajjā from the thera
168 Mahādhammarakkhita and with him four hundred thousand
persons, but the number of those who afterwards were ordained
169 is not known. A nephew of the monarch known by the
name Aggibrahmā was the consort of the king's daughter
170 Saṃghamittā and the son of these two (was) named

Sumana.[1] He (Aggibrahmā) also craved the king's leave and was ordained together with the prince.

The prince's ordination, whence flowed blessing to many 171
folk, was in the fourth year of (the reign of) king Asoka. In 172
the same year he received the upasampadā-ordination, and
since his destiny was holiness[2] the prince, zealously striv-
ing, became an arahant, gifted with the six supernormal
powers.

All those beautiful vihāras (then) begun they duly finished 173
in all the cities within three years; but, by the miraculous 174
power of the thera Indagutta, who watched over the work,
the ārāma named after Asoka was likewise quickly brought
to completion. On those spots which the Conqueror himself 175
had visited the monarch built beautiful cetiyas here and there.
On every side from the eighty-four thousand cities came letters 176
on one day with the news: 'The vihāras are completed.'

When the great king, great in majesty, in wondrous power 177
and valour, received the letters, he, desiring to hold high
festival in all the ārāmas at once, proclaimed in the town 178
with beat of drum: 'On the seventh day from this day shall
a festival of all the ārāmas be kept, in every way, in all the
provinces. Yojana by yojana on the earth shall great largess 179
be given; the ārāmas in the villages and the streets shall be
adorned. In all the vihāras let lavish gifts of every kind be 180
bestowed upon the brotherhood, according to the time and the
means (of givers), and adornments, such as garlands of lamps 181
and garlands of flowers, here and there, and all that is meet
for festivals,[3] with music of every kind, in manifold ways.
And all are to take upon themselves the duties of the 182
uposatha-day and hear religious discourse, and offerings of

[1] In my edition of the text the stop should be deleted after sāmiko and put after nāmato. So pi in v. 170 refers to Aggibrahmā.

[2] He was sampannaupanissayo. Cf. note to 5. 45.

[3] Upahāra. The Ṭīkā explains this word thus: sabbe gandhabbā sakasakaturiyabhaṇḍaṃ gahetvā tattha tattha vihāresu gandhabbaṃ va karontū ti attho 'Let all the minstrels taking each his own instrument of music play in the vihāras everywhere'.

183 many kinds must they make on the same day.' And all the
people everywhere held religious festivals of every kind,
glorious as the world of gods,[1] even as had been commanded
and (did) yet more.
184 On that day the great king wearing all his adornments
with the women of his household, with his ministers and sur-
185 rounded by the multitude of his troops, went to his own ārāma,
as if cleaving the earth. In the midst of the brotherhood he
186 stood, bowing down to the venerable brotherhood. In the
assembly were eighty koṭis of bhikkhus, and among these
187 were a hundred thousand ascetics who had overcome the
āsavas. Moreover there were ninety times one hundred thou-
188 sand bhikkhunīs, and among these a thousand had overcome
the āsavas. These (monks and nuns) wrought the miracle
called the 'unveiling of the world' to the end that the king
189 Dhammāsoka might be converted.—Caṇḍāsoka (the wicked
Asoka) was he called in earlier times, by reason of his evil
deeds; he was known as Dhammāsoka (the pious Asoka) after-
190 wards because of his pious deeds.—He looked around over the
(whole) Jambudīpa bounded by the ocean and over all the
191 vihāras adorned with the manifold (beauties of) the festival—
and with exceeding joy, as he saw them, he asked the brethren,
while taking his seat: 'Whose generosity toward the doctrine
of the Blessed One was ever (so) great (as mine), venerable
sirs?'
192 The thera Moggaliputta answered the king's question:
'Even in the lifetime of the Blessed One there was no generous
giver like to thee.'
193 When the king heard this he rejoiced yet more and asked:
'Nay then, is there a kinsman of Buddha's religion[2] like
unto me?'
194 But the thera perceived the destiny of the king's son

[1] The Ṭīkā understands the word devalokamanoramā thus, and adds: nakkhattaghuṭṭhe devanagare devagaṇā viya manussā manoramā mahāpūjā paṭiyādesuṃ ti attho 'As the multitudes of gods in the celestial city, where festival has been proclaimed, so did men arrange splendid offerings'.

[2] Sāsanadāyāda: evidently the term is a title of honour.

Mahinda[1] and of his daughter Saṃghamittā, and foresaw the 195
progress of the doctrine that was to arise from (them), and
he, on whom lay the charge of the doctrine, replied thus to
the king: 'Even a lavish giver of gifts like to thee is not 196
a kinsman of the religion; giver of wealth[2] is he called, O 197
ruler of men. But he who lets son or daughter enter the
religious order is a kinsman of the religion and withal a giver
of gifts.'

Since the monarch would fain become a kinsman of the 198
religion he asked Mahinda and Saṃghamittā, who stood near:
'Do you wish to receive the pabbajjā, dear ones? The 199
pabbajjā is held to be a great (good).' Then, when they heard
their father's words, they said to him: 'This very day we 200
would fain enter the order, if thou, O king, dost wish it; for
us, even as for thee, will blessing come of our pabbajjā.'

For already since the time of the prince's (Tissa's) pabbajjā 201
had he resolved to enter the order, and she since (the ordina-
tion) of Aggibrahmā.[3] Although the monarch wished to confer 202
on Mahinda the dignity of prince-regent, yet did he consent
to his ordination with the thought: 'This (last) is the greater
dignity.' So he permitted his dear son Mahinda, distin- 203
guished (above all others) by intelligence, beauty and strength,
and his daughter Saṃghamittā, to be ordained with all
solemnity.[4]

At that time Mahinda, the king's son, was twenty years 204
old, and the king's daughter Saṃghamittā was then eighteen
years old. On the very same day did he receive the pabbajjā- 205
and also the upasampadā-ordination, and for her the pabbajjā-
ordination and the placing under a teacher[5] took place on the
same day.

The prince's master[6] was the thera named after Moggali;[7] 206

[1] See note to 5. 45.

[2] Paccayadāyaka. On paccaya see note to 3. 14.

[3] Cf. 5. 167, 170.

[4] The Ṭīkā explains samahaṃ by sapūjāsakkāraṃ.

[5] This was necessary as Saṃghamittā was not of the prescribed age.

[6] Upajjhāya, see note to 5. 69.

[7] That is, Moggaliputtatissa, 'Tissa, the son of Moggali.'

the pabbajjā-ordination was conferred on him by the thera
207 Mahādeva, but Majjhantika pronounced the ceremonial words,[1]
and even in the very place where he (received) the upasaṃ-
padā-ordination this great man reached the state of an arahant
together with the special kinds of knowledge.[2]
208 The directress of Saṃghamittā was the renowned Dhamma-
pālā, and her teacher was Ayupālā; in time she became free
209 from the āsavas. Those two lights of the doctrine, who
brought great blessing to the island of Laṅkā, received the
pabbajjā in the sixth year of king Dhammāsoka. The great
210 Mahinda, the converter of the island (of Laṅkā), learned the
three piṭakas with his master in three years. This bhikkhuṇī,
211 even like the new moon, and the bhikkhu Mahinda, like the
sun, illumined always the sky, the doctrine of the Sambuddha.
212 Once in time past, a dweller in the forest, who went forth
into the forest from Pāṭaliputta, loved a wood-nymph named
213 Kuntī. Owing to the union with him she bore two sons, the
elder was Tissa and the younger was named Sumitta. After-
214 wards both received the pabbajjā-ordination from the thera
Mahāvaruṇa and attained to arahantship and the possession
of the six supernormal powers.
215 (Once) the elder suffered pains in the foot from the poison
of a venomous insect, and when his younger brother asked
(what he needed) he told him that a handful of ghee was the
216 remedy. But the thera set himself against pointing out to
the king what things needful in sickness,[3] and against going
217 in search of the ghee after the midday meal.[4] 'If, on thy
begging-round, thou receivest ghee, bring it to me,' said the
218 thera Tissa to the excellent thera Sumitta. When he went

[1] Kammavācaṃ akā: i. e. he was president of the chapter when Mahinda was ordained. Kammavācā 'is the name of the proceedings at a kamma or ecclesiastical act, by which some question is decided by vote'. CHILDERS, *P.D.* s. v.

[2] See note to 5. 144.

[3] Gilānapaccaye is a 'locative of aim', which concurs with the 'final dative' (SPEYER, *Ved. and Skr. Syntax*, para. 81 b), and refers to nivedanaṃ 'informing, announcement'.

[4] The begging-round of the mendicants must be carried out in the forenoon, according to the rules of the order.

forth on his begging-round he received not one handful of
ghee, and (in the meanwhile) the pain had come to such a pass
that even a hundred vessels of ghee could not have cured it.
And because of that malady the thera was near to death, 219
and when he had exhorted (the other) to strive unceasingly he
formed the resolve to pass into nibbāṇa.

Lifted up in the air as he sat, and winning mastery of his 220
own body by the fire-meditation,[1] according to his own free
resolve, he passed into nibbāṇa. Flames that broke forth 221
from his body consumed the flesh and skin of the thera's whole
body,[2] the bones they did not consume.

When the monarch heard that the thera had died in this 222
wise he went to his own ārāma surrounded by the multitude
of his troops. Mounted on an elephant the king brought 223
down the bones,[3] and when he had caused due honour to be
paid to the relics, he questioned the brotherhood as to (the
thera's) illness. Hearing about it he was greatly moved, 224
and had tanks made at the city gates and filled them with
remedies for the sick, and day by day he had remedies be- 225
stowed on the congregation of the bhikkhus, thinking: might
the bhikkhus never find remedies hard to obtain.

The thera Sumitta passed into nibbāṇa even when he was 226
walking (in meditation) in the caṅkama-hall,[4] and by this
also was a great multitude of people converted to the doctrine
(of the Buddha). Both these theras, the sons of Kuntī, who 227
had wrought a great good in the world, passed into nibbāṇa
in the eighth year of Asoka.

From that time onwards the revenues of the brotherhood 228

[1] Tejojhānavasena. The meditating ascetic concentrates all his thoughts on the concept 'fire' (tejo) which is one of the ten kasiṇāni or divisions of kammaṭṭhāna (see CHILDERS, s.v. kasiṇo, and note to 5. 148); the effect is that a fire arises within his body which consumes him.

[2] Nimmaṃsacchārikaṃ ḍahi sakalaṃ kāyaṃ, literally, 'burned the whole body into a fleshless and skinless one.'

[3] Which were still floating in the air.

[4] A caṅkama belongs to each vihāra. It is 'a straight piece of ground cleared and levelled for the purpose of walking up and down upon for exercise and meditation'. See *S.B.E.* xx, p. 103, n. 1.

were exceeding great, and since those who were converted
229 later caused the revenues to increase, heretics who had (thereby)
lost revenue and honour took likewise the yellow robe, for the
230 sake of revenue, and dwelt together with the bhikkhus. They
proclaimed their own doctrines as the doctrine of the Buddha
and carried out their own practices even as they wished.

231 And when the thera Moggaliputta, great in firmness of
soul, saw the coming-out of this exceedingly evil plague-boil
232 on the doctrine, he, far-seeing, deliberated upon the right time
to do away with it. And when he had committed his great
company of bhikkhus to (the direction of) the thera Mahinda,
233 he took up his abode, all alone, further up the Ganges on the
Ahogaṅga-mountain, and for seven years he gave himself up
to solitary retreat.

234 By reason of the great number of the heretics and their
unruliness, the bhikkhus could not restrain them by the law;
235 and therefore the bhikkhus in Jambudīpa for seven years held
no uposatha-ceremony nor the ceremony of pavāraṇā in all
the ārāmas.

236 When the great king, the famed Dhammāsoka, was aware
of this, he sent a minister to the splendid Asokārāma, laying
237 on him this command: 'Go, settle this matter and let the
uposatha-festival be carried out by the community of bhikkhus
238 in my ārāma.' This fool went thither, and when he had
called the community of bhikkhus together he announced the
king's command: 'Carry out the uposatha-festival.'

239 'We hold not the uposatha-festival with heretics,' the
community of bhikkhus replied to that misguided minister.
240 The minister struck off the head of several theras, one by one,
with his sword, saying, 'I will force you to hold the uposatha-
241 festival.' When the king's brother, Tissa, saw that crime he
came speedily and sat on the seat nearest to the minister.
242 When the minister saw the thera he went to the king and told
him (the whole matter).

243 When the monarch heard it he was troubled and went with
all speed and asked the community of bhikkhus, greatly
disturbed in mind: 'Who, in truth, is guilty of this deed that
has been done?'

And certain of them answered in their ignorance: 'The guilt 244
is thine,' and others said: 'Both of you are guilty'; but those
who were wise answered: 'Thou art not guilty.'
When the king heard this he said: 'Is there a bhikkhu who 245
is able to set my doubts to rest and to befriend religion?'
'There is the thera Tissa, the son of Moggali, O king,' 246
answered the brethren to the king. Then was the king filled
with zeal.
He sent four theras, each attended by a thousand bhikkhus 247
and four ministers, each with a thousand followers, that same 248
day, with the charge laid on them by (the king) himself to
bring the thera thither; but though they prayed him he
came not.
When the king heard this he sent again eight theras and 249
eight ministers each with a thousand followers, but even as
before he came not.
The king asked: 'Nay then, how shall the thera come?' 250
The bhikkhus told him how the thera could be moved to
come: 'O great king, if they shall say to him, "be our helper, 251
venerable sir, to befriend religion," then will the thera
come.'
Again the king sent (messengers) sixteen theras and sixteen 252
ministers, each with a thousand followers, laying that (same)
charge upon them, and he said to them: 'Aged as he is, the 253
thera will not enter any wheeled vehicle; bring the thera by
ship on the Ganges.'
So they went to him and told him, and hardly had he heard 254
(their message) but he rose up. And they brought the thera
in a ship and the king went to meet him. Going down even 255
knee-deep into the water the king respectfully gave his right
hand to the thera, as he came down from the ship.[1] The 256

[1] According to Smp. 310, 12 foll. the king had dreamed a dream, the night before, which the soothsayers interpreted thus, that a samaṇanāga, a great ascetic, would touch his right hand. As the thera now laid hold of the king's hand the attendants were about to kill him. For to touch the king's hand was a crime punishable by death. However, the king restrained them. But the thera laid hold of the king's hand as a sign that he accepted him as his pupil.

venerable thera took the king's right hand [1] from compassion toward him, and came down from the ship.

257 The king led the thera to the pleasure-garden called Rati-
vaḍḍhana, and when he had washed and anointed his feet and
258 had seated himself the monarch spoke thus, to test the thera's
259 faculty: 'Sir, I would fain see a miracle.' And to the ques-
tion which (miracle he desired) he answered: 'An earthquake.'
And again the other said to him: 'Which wouldst thou see,
260 of the whole (earth shaken) or only of a single region?' Then
when he had asked: 'Which is the more difficult?' and heard
(the reply): 'The shaking of a single region is the more diffi-
cult,' he declared that he desired to see this last.

261 Then within the boundary of a yojana (in extent) did the
thera place a waggon, a horse and a man, and a vessel full of
262 water at the four cardinal points, and over this yojana by
his miraculous power he caused the earth to tremble, together
with the half of (each of) these (things) and let the king
seated there behold this.[2]

263 Then the monarch asked the thera whether or not he him-
self shared the guilt of the murder of the bhikkhus by the
264 minister. The thera taught the king: 'There is no resulting
guilt [3] without evil intent,' and he recited the Tittira-jātaka.[4]

265 Abiding a week there in the pleasant royal park he in-
266 structed the ruler in the lovely religion of the Sambuddha. In

[1] Here there is a play on the words dakkhiṇa 'right' and dakkhiṇeyya 'venerable'.

[2] The expressions are difficult to render but the sense is clear. On the boundaries of a space measuring a mile in diameter, there were placed at N., S., E., and W. a waggon, a horse, a man, and a vessel full of water. The earthquake was so strictly limited in its action that these objects were affected by the quaking only as to the half on the inner side, the other half remained unmoved.

[3] In paṭiccakamma the term kamma is employed in the technical sense as the sum of all good and evil deeds that bring of necessity reward or punishment as their result, and if not balanced lead inevitably to a new existence after death. Paṭicca means 'following on something, conditioned by something'. The formation of the compound is the same as in paṭiccasamuppāda, paccayākāra.

[4] FAUSBÖLL, *Jātaka* III. 64 foll. The Kambodian Mah. inserts here a metrical version of the story.

this same week the monarch sent out two yakkhas and
assembled together all the bhikkhus on the earth. On the 267
seventh day he went to his own splendid ārāma and arranged an
assembly of the community of bhikkhus in its full numbers.

Then seated with the thera on one side behind a curtain the 268
ruler called to him in turn the bhikkhus of the several con-
fessions and asked them: 'Sir, what did the Blessed One 269
teach?' And they each expounded their wrong doctrine, the
Sassata-doctrine and so forth.[1] And all these adherents of 270
false doctrine did the king cause to be expelled from the order;
those who were expelled were in all sixty thousand. And now 271
he asked the rightly-believing bhikkhus: 'What does the
Blessed One teach?' And they answered: 'He teaches the
Vibhajja-doctrine.'[2]

And the monarch asked the thera: 'Sir, does the Saṃ- 272
buddha (really) teach the Vibhajja-doctrine?' The thera
answered: 'Yes.' And when the king knew this he was glad
at heart and said: 'Since the community is (henceforth) puri- 273
fied, sir, therefore should the brotherhood hold the uposatha-
festival,' and he made the thera guardian of the order and 274
returned to his fair capital; the brotherhood held thenceforth
the uposatha-festival in concord.

Out of the great number of the brotherhood of bhikkhus 275
the thera chose a thousand learned bhikkhus, endowed with
the six supernormal powers, knowing the three piṭakas and
versed in the special sciences,[3] to make a compilation of the 276
true doctrine. Together with them did he, in the Asokārāma,
make a compilation of the true dhamma.[4] Even as the thera 277
Mahākassapa and the thera Yasa had held a council so did the
thera Tissa. In the midst of this council the thera Tissa set 278

[1] The different diṭṭhiyo or heretical doctrines, reckoned as sixty-two in all, are frequently mentioned in the canonical books, thus in the Brahmajālasuttanta of the Dīghanikāya (D. 1, 13 foll.).

[2] CHILDERS (*P. D.* s. v. vibhajati) renders the sense appropriately with 'religion of Logic or Reason'. Vibhajjavāda is identical with theravāda. KERN, *Manual*, p. 110.

[3] See the notes to 4. 62 and 4. 12.

[4] Kātuṃ saddhammasaṃgahaṃ. See note to 3. 17.

forth the Kathāvatthuppakaraṇa,[1] refuting the other doc-
279 trines. Thus was this council under the protection of king
Asoka ended by the thousand bhikkhus in nine months.

280 In the seventeenth year of the king's reign the wise (thera)
who was seventy-two years old, closed the council with a great
281 pavāraṇā-ceremony.[2] And, as if to shout applause to the re-
establishment of doctrine, the great earth shook at the close
of the council.

282 Nay, abandoning the high, the glorious Brahma-heaven and coming down for the sake of the doctrine to the loathsome world of men, he, who had fulfilled his own duty, fulfilled the duties toward the doctrine. Who else verily may neglect duties toward the doctrine?

Here ends the fifth chapter, called 'The Third Council', in the Mahāvaṃsa, compiled for the serene joy and emotion of the pious.

[1] A work of the Abhidhamma. *Kathāvatthu*, ed. by A. C. Taylor, vol. i, ii, *P.T.S.* 1894, 1897.

[2] See note to 12. 2.

CHAPTER VI

THE COMING OF VIJAYA

In the country of the Vaṅgas[1] in the Vaṅga capital there 1
lived once a king of the Vaṅgas. The daughter of the king
of the Kaliṅgas was that king's consort. By his spouse the 2
king had a daughter, the soothsayers prophesied her union
with the king of beasts. Very fair was she and very amorous 3
and for shame the king and queen could not suffer her.

Alone she went forth from the house, desiring the joy of 4
independent life; unrecognized she joined a caravan travelling
to the Magadha country. In the Lāḷa country a lion attacked 5
the caravan in the forest, the other folk fled this way and that,
but she fled along the way by which the lion had come.

When the lion had taken his prey and was leaving the spot 6
he beheld her from afar, love (for her) laid hold on him, and
he came towards her with waving tail and ears laid back.
Seeing him she bethought her of that prophecy of the sooth- 7
sayers which she had heard, and without fear she caressed him
stroking his limbs.

The lion, roused to fiercest passion by her touch, took her 8
upon his back and bore her with all speed to his cave, and
there he was united with her, and from this union with 9
him the princess in time bore twin-children, a son and a
daughter.

The son's hands and feet were formed like a lion's and there- 10
fore she named him Sīhabāhu, but the daughter (she named)
Sīhasīvalī. When he was sixteen years old the son questioned 11
his mother on the doubt (that had arisen in him): 'Where-
fore are you and our father so different, dear mother?' She 12
told him all. Then he asked: 'Why do we not go forth (from
here)?' And she answered: 'Thy father has closed the cave
up with a rock.' Then he took that barrier before the great 13

[1] I.e. Bengal.

cave upon his shoulder and went (a distance of) fifty yojanas going and coming in one day.

14 Then (once), when the lion had gone forth in search of prey,
(Sīhabāhu) took his mother on his right shoulder and his
15 young sister on his left, and went away with speed. They
clothed themselves with branches of trees, and so came to a
border-village and there, even at that time, was a son of the
16 princess's uncle, a commander in the army of the Vaṅga king,
to whom was given the rule over the border-country; and he
was just then sitting under a banyan-tree overseeing the work
that was done.

17 When he saw them he asked them (who they were) and
they said: 'We are forest-folk'; the commander bade (his
18 people) give them clothing; and this turned into splendid
(garments). He had food offered to them on leaves and by
reason of their merit these were turned into dishes of gold.
19 Then, amazed, the commander asked them, 'Who are you?'
20 The princess told him her family and clan. Then the commander
took his uncle's daughter with him and went to the
capital of the Vaṅgas and married her.

21 When the lion, returning in haste to his cave, missed
those three (persons), he was sorrowful, and grieving after his
22 son he neither ate nor drank. Seeking for his children he
went to the border-village, and every village where he came
was deserted by the dwellers therein.

23 And the border-folk came to the king and told him this:
'A lion ravages thy country; ward off (this danger) O king!'

24 Since he found none who could ward off (this danger) he
had a thousand (pieces of money) led about the city on
an elephant's back and this proclamation made: 'Let him
25 who brings the lion receive these!' And in like manner the
monarch (offered) two thousand and three thousand. Twice
26 did Sīhabāhu's[1] mother restrain him. The third time without
asking his mother's leave, Sīhabāhu took the three thousand
gold-pieces (as reward) for slaying his own father.

27 They presented the youth to the king, and the king spoke

[1] Sīhabhuja in the text (*metri causa!*) which means the same as Sīhabāhu 'Lion-arm'.

thus to him: 'If thou shalt take the lion I will give thee
at once the kingdom.' And he went to the opening of the 28
cave, and as soon as he saw from afar the lion who came
forward, for love toward his son, he shot an arrow to
slay him.

The arrow struck the lion's forehead but because of his 29
tenderness (toward his son) it rebounded and fell on the
earth at the youth's feet. And so it fell out three times, then 30
did the king of beasts grow wrathful and the arrow sent at
him struck him and pierced his body.

(Sīhabāhu) took the head of the lion with the mane and 31
returned to his city. And just seven days had passed then
since the death of the king of the Vaṅgas. Since the king 32
had no son the ministers, who rejoiced over his deed on
hearing that he was the king's grandson and on recognizing 33
his mother, met all together and said of one accord to the
prince Sīhabāhu 'Be thou (our) king'.

And he accepted the kingship but handed it over then to 34
his mother's husband and he himself went with Sīhasīvalī to
the land of his birth. There he built a city, and they called 35
it Sīhapura, and in the forest stretching a hundred yojanas
around he founded villages. In the kingdom of Lāḷa, in that 36
city did Sīhabāhu, ruler of men, hold sway when he had made
Sīhasīvalī his queen. As time passed on his consort bore twin 37
sons sixteen times, the eldest was named Vijaya, the second 38
Sumitta; together there were thirty-two sons. In time the
king consecrated Vijaya as prince-regent.

Vijaya was of evil conduct and his followers were even (like 39
himself), and many intolerable deeds of violence were done by
them. Angered by this the people told the matter to the 40
king; the king, speaking persuasively to them, severely
blamed his son. But all fell out again as before, the second 41
and yet the third time; and the angered people said to the
king: 'Kill thy son.'

Then did the king cause Vijaya and his followers, seven 42
hundred men, to be shaven over half the head[1] and put them 43

[1] The shaving of the hair signifies loss of freedom. In Sinhalese **miḍi** (= Skr. **muṇḍita** 'shaven') means 'slave'.

on a ship and sent them forth upon the sea, and their wives
44 and children also. The men, women, and children sent
forth separately landed separately, each (company) upon an
45 island, and they dwelt even there. The island where the
children landed was called Naggadīpa[1] and the island where
46 the women landed Mahilādīpaka.[2] But Vijaya landed at the
haven called Suppāraka,[3] but being there in danger by reason
of the violence of his followers he embarked again.
47 The prince named VIJAYA, the valiant, landed in Laṅkā, in
the region called Tambapaṇṇi on the day that the Tathāgata
lay down between the two twinlike sāla-trees to pass into
nibbāṇa.

Here ends the sixth chapter, called 'The Coming of Vijaya', in the Mahāvaṃsa, compiled for the serene joy and emotion of the pious.

[1] That is, 'Island of children,' from nagga 'naked'.

[2] That is, 'Island of women.'

[3] Skt. Śūrpāraka, situated on the west coast of India, now Sopāra in the Thāna District, north of Bombay. See *Imp. Gazetteer of India*, s.v.

CHAPTER VII

THE CONSECRATING OF VIJAYA

WHEN the Guide of the World, having accomplished the 1
salvation of the whole world and having reached the utmost
stage of blissful rest, was lying on the bed of his nibbāṇa,
in the midst of the great assembly of gods, he, the great sage, 2
the greatest of those who have speech, spoke to Sakka [1] who
stood there near him: 'Vijaya, son of king Sīhabāhu, is come 3
to Laṅkā from the country of Lāḷa, together with seven
hundred followers. In Laṅkā, O lord of gods, will my 4
religion be established, therefore carefully protect him with
his followers and Laṅkā.'

When the lord of gods heard the words of the Tathāgata 5
he from respect handed over the guardianship of Laṅkā to
the god who is in colour like the lotus.[2]

And no sooner had the god received the charge from 6
Sakka than he came speedily to Laṅkā and sat down at the
foot of a tree in the guise of a wandering ascetic. And all 7
the followers of Vijaya came to him and asked him: 'What
island is this, sir?' 'The island of Laṅkā,' he answered.
'There are no men here, and here no dangers will arise.' 8
And when he had spoken so and sprinkled water on them from
his water-vessel, and had wound a thread about their hands [3] 9
he vanished through the air. And there appeared, in the form
of a bitch, a yakkhiṇī who was an attendant (of Kuvaṇṇā).[4]

[1] A name of Indra, king of the gods.

[2] Devass' uppalavaṇṇassa, that is Viṣṇu. The allusion is to the colour of the BLUE lotus (uppala).

[3] As a paritta, that is as a protecting charm against the influence of demons.

[4] The Ṭīkā says: Kuvaṇṇāya Sīsapāti-nāmikā paricārikayakkhiṇī. The Kambodian Mah. also gives the same name Sīsapātika.

10 One (of Vijaya's men) went after her, although he was
forbidden by the prince (for he thought), 'Only where there
11 is a village are dogs to be found.' Her mistress, a yakkhiṇī
named Kuvaṇṇā, sat there[1] at the foot of a tree spinning, as
a woman-hermit might.

12 When the man saw the pond and the woman-hermit sitting
there, he bathed there and drank and taking young shoots of
13 lotuses and water in lotus-leaves he came forth again. And
she said to him: 'Stay! thou art my prey!' Then the man
14 stood there as if fast bound. But because of the power of
the magic thread she could not devour him, and though he
was entreated by the yakkhiṇī, the man would not yield up
15 the thread. Then the yakkhiṇī seized him, and hurled him
who cried aloud into a chasm. And there in like manner she
hurled (all) the seven hundred one by one after him.

16 And when they all did not return fear came on Vijaya;
armed with the five weapons[2] he set out, and when he beheld
17 the beautiful pond, where he saw no footstep of any man
coming forth, but saw that woman-hermit there, he thought:
18 'Surely my men have been seized by this woman.' And he
said to her, 'Lady, hast thou not seen my men?' 'What
dost thou want with thy people, prince?' she answered.
'Drink thou and bathe.'

19 Then was it clear to him: 'This is surely a yakkhiṇī, she
knows my rank,' and swiftly, uttering his name, he came at
20 her drawing his bow. He caught the yakkhiṇī in the noose
about the neck, and seizing her hair with his left hand he
21 lifted his sword in the right and cried: 'Slave! give me
back my men, or I slay thee!' Then, tormented with fear
22 the yakkhiṇī prayed him for her life. 'Spare my life, sir,
I will give thee a kingdom and do thee a woman's service and
other service as thou wilt.'

23 And that he might not be betrayed he made the yakkhiṇī
swear an oath, and so soon as the charge was laid on her,
'Bring hither my men with all speed,' she brought them to

[1] There, that is where Vijaya's man followed the bitch.

[2] Naddhapañcāyudho. The five weapons are, according to CLOUGH, sword, bow, battle-axe, spear, and shield.

that place. When he said, 'These men are hungry,' she 24
showed them rice and other (foods) and goods of every kind
that had been in the ships of those traders whom she had
devoured.

(Vijaya's) men prepared the rice and the condiments, and 25
when they had first set them before the prince they all ate
of them.

[1] When the yakkhiṇī had taken the first portions (of the 26
meal) that Vijaya handed to her, she was well pleased, and
assuming the lovely form of a sixteen-year-old maiden she 27
approached the prince adorned with all the ornaments. At
the foot of a tree she made a splendid bed, well-covered 28
around with a tent, and adorned with a canopy. And seeing
this, the king's son, looking forward to the time to come,
took her to him as his spouse and lay (with her) blissfully on 29
that bed; and all his men encamped around the tent.

As the night went on he heard the sounds of music and 30
singing, and asked the yakkhiṇī, who was lying near him:
'What means this noise?' And the yakkhiṇī thought: 'I 31
will bestow kingship on my lord and all the yakkhas must be
slain, for (else) the yakkhas will slay me, for it was through
me that men have taken up their dwelling (in Laṅkā).' [2]

And she said to the prince: 'Here there is a yakkha-city 32
called Sirīsavatthu; the daughter of the chief of the yakkhas [3] 33
who dwells in the city of Laṅkā has been brought hither,
and her mother too is come.[4] And for the wedding there is 34
high festival, lasting seven days; therefore there is this
noise, for a great multitude is gathered together. Even to-day 35

[1] Instead of verses 26–84 the later (Sinhalese) recension has a somewhat divergent reading, the text of which is printed in my edition, p. 326 foll. Appendix A. Cf. *ibid.*, Introd., p. xxxiv.

[2] To manussāvāsakāraṇā 'because of (my) bringing about a settlement of men', the Ṭīkā adds the words imasmiṃ dīpe 'in this island'.

[3] Lit. 'of the eldest yakkha.'

[4] The Ṭīkā calls the bride's father Mahākālasena, the bride Polamittā, the mother Goṇḍā. The names Kālasena and Polamittā occur also in the Kamb. Mah.

do thou destroy the yakkhas, for afterwards it will no longer
be possible.'

He replied: 'How can I slay the yakkhas who are in-
36 visible?' 'Wheresoever they may be,' she said, 'I will utter
cries, and where thou shalt hear that sound, strike! and by
my magic power shall thy weapon fall upon their bodies.'
37 Since he listened to her and did even (as she said) he slew
all the yakkhas, and when he had fought victoriously he
38 himself put on the garments of the yakkha-king and bestowed
the other raiment on one and another of his followers.

When he had spent some days at that spot he went to
39 Tambapaṇṇi. There Vijaya founded the city of Tambapaṇṇi
and dwelt there, together with the yakkhiṇī, surrounded by
his ministers.

40 When those who were commanded by Vijaya landed from
their ship, they sat down wearied, resting their hands upon the
41 ground—and since their hands were reddened by touching the
dust of the red earth[1] that region and also the island were
42 (named) Tambapaṇṇi.[2] But the king Sīhabāhu, since he had
slain the lion (was called) Sīhala and, by reason of the ties
between him and them, all those (followers of Vijaya) were
also (called) Sīhala.

43 Here and there did Vijaya's ministers found villages.
Anurādhagāma was built by a man of that name near the
44 Kadamba river;[3] the chaplain Upatissa built Upatissagāma[4]
on the bank of the Gambhīra river, to the north of Anu-
45 rādhagāma. Three other ministers built, each for himself,
Ujjenī, Uruvelā, and the city of Vijita.[5]

[1] The soil of Ceylon is composed of laterit which crumbles into a red dust.

[2] A play on the word tambapāṇi, red hand.

[3] Now Malwaṭṭe-oya which flows by the ruins of Anurādhapura.

[4] This is probably to be sought on one of the right-bank tributaries of the lower Malwaṭṭe-oya. According to Mah. 28. 7 the Gambhīra-nadī flows 1 yojana (i. e. 7–8 miles) north of Anurādhapura.

[5] According to tradition the remains of the city of Vijita exist as those ruins which lie not far from the Kalu-wæwa (Kālavāpi) about 24 miles south of Anurādhapura in the jungle. TENNENT, *Ceylon*, ii, p. 602 foll. I think the tradition is right, although PARKER,

When they had founded settlements in the land the ministers 46
all came together and spoke thus to the prince: 'Sire, consent
to be consecrated as king.' But, in spite of their demand, 47
the prince refused the consecration, unless a maiden of a noble
house were consecrated as queen (at the same time).

But the ministers, whose minds were eagerly bent upon the 48
consecrating of their lord, and who, although the means
were difficult, had overcome all anxious fears about the matter, 49
sent people, entrusted with many precious gifts, jewels, pearls,
and so forth, to the city of Madhurā[1] in southern (India), to 50
woo the daughter of the Paṇḍu king for their lord, devoted
(as they were) to their ruler; and they also (sent to woo)
the daughters of others for the ministers and retainers.

When the messengers were quickly come by ship to the 51
city of Madhurā they laid the gifts and letter before the king.
The king took counsel with his ministers, and since he was 52
minded to send his daughter (to Laṅkā) he, having first
received also daughters of others for the ministers (of Vijaya), 53
nigh upon a hundred maidens, proclaimed with beat of drum:
'Those men here who are willing to let a daughter depart for
Laṅkā shall provide their daughters with a double store of 54
clothing and place them at the doors of their houses. By this
sign shall we (know that we may) take them to ourselves.'

When he had thus obtained many maidens and had given 55
compensation to their families, he sent his daughter, bedecked
with all her ornaments, and all that was needful for the
journey,[2] and all the maidens whom he had fitted out, accord- 56
ing to their rank, elephants withal and horses and waggons,
worthy of a king, and craftsmen and a thousand families of 57
the eighteen guilds, entrusted with a letter to the con-
queror Vijaya. All this multitude of men disembarked at 58

Ancient Ceylon, p. 237 foll., identifies Vijitapura with a suburb of Polannaruwa mentioned in the twelfth century A.D. As to the site of Uruvelā see 28. 36 and note.

[1] Now Madura, in the south of the Madras Presidency.

[2] The Ṭīkā explains saparicchadaṃ by paribhogabhaṇḍikaṃ samakuṭappāsādhanikaṃ vā. Cf. Skt. paricchada.

Mahātittha; for that very reason is that landing-place known as Mahātittha.[1]

59 Vijaya had one son and one daughter by the yakkhiṇī; when he now heard that the princess had arrived he said to
60 the yakkhiṇī: 'Go thou now, dear one, leaving the two children behind; men are ever in fear of superhuman beings.'
61 But when she heard this she was seized with fear of the yakkhas; then he said (again) to the yakkhiṇī: 'Delay not! I will bestow on thee an offering[2] by (spending)
62 a thousand (pieces of money).' When she had again and again besought him (in vain) she took her two children and departed for Laṅkāpura, though fearing that evil should come of it.

63 She set the children down outside and went, herself, into that city. When the yakkhas in the city recognized the
64 yakkhiṇī, in their terror they took her for a spy and there was great stir among them; but one who was violent killed the yakkhiṇī with a single blow of his fist.

65 But her uncle, on the mother's side, a yakkha, went forth from the city and when he saw the children he asked them:
66 'Whose children are you?' and hearing that they were Kuvaṇṇā's he said: 'Here has your mother been slain, and they will slay you also if they see you: (therefore) flee swiftly!'

67 Fleeing with speed they went from thence to the Sumanakūṭa.[3] The brother, the elder of the two, when he grew up
68 took his sister, the younger, for his wife, and multiplying with sons and daughters, they dwelt, with the king's leave, there in Malaya.[4] From these are sprung the Pulindā.[5]

[1] I. e. 'the great landing-place'; now Mantoṭa opposite the island Manaar.

[2] Since Kuvaṇṇā is a yakkhiṇī, she must receive like the devatās a bali or religious offering, oblation.

[3] I. e. Adam's Peak.

[4] The central mountain-region in the interior of Ceylon.

[5] Pulindā, a designation of barbarous tribes, is here evidently a name of the Wæddās. The tract of country inland between Colombo, Kalutara, Galle and the mountains is now called Sabaragamuwa from Skt. śabara; p. savara, a synonym of pulinda.

The envoys of the Paṇḍu king delivered up to the prince 69
Vijaya the gifts and the (maidens) with the king's daughter at
their head. When Vijaya had offered hospitality and bestowed 70
honours on the envoys he bestowed the maidens, according to
their rank, upon his ministers and retainers. According to 71
custom the ministers in full assembly consecrated Vijaya king
and appointed a great festival.

Then king Vijaya consecrated the daughter of the Paṇḍu 72
king with solemn ceremony as his queen; he bestowed wealth 73
on his ministers, and every year he sent to his wife's father a
shell-pearl worth twice a hundred thousand (pieces of money).

When he had forsaken his former evil way of life, Vijaya, 74
the lord of men, ruling over all Laṅkā in peace and righteousness reigned, as is known, in the city of Tambapaṇṇi, thirty-eight years.

Here ends the seventh chapter, called 'The Consecrating of Vijaya', in the Mahāvaṃsa, compiled for the serene joy and emotion of the pious.

CHAPTER VIII

THE CONSECRATING OF PAṆḌUVĀSUDEVA

1 THE great king Vijaya, being in the last year (of his life),
bethought him: 'I am old and there lives no son of mine.
2 The kingdom peopled with (such great) difficulty may come
to naught after my death; therefore would I fain have my
brother Sumitta brought here (that I may give) the govern-
3 ment (into his hands).' When he had taken counsel with his
ministers he sent a letter to him, and within a short time
after Vijaya had sent the letter he passed away to the
celestial world.

4 When he was dead the ministers ruled, dwelling in Upatissa-
5 gāma while they awaited the coming of the prince. After
the death of king Vijaya and before the coming of the prince
was our island of Laṅkā kingless for a year.

6 In Sīhapura, after the death of king Sīhabāhu, his son
7 Sumitta was king; he had three sons by the daughter of the
Madda[1] king. The messengers coming to Sīhapura handed
8 the letter to the king. When he had heard the letter the king
spoke thus to his three sons: 'I am old, dear ones; one
9 of you must depart for the greatly favoured and beauteous
Laṅkā belonging to my brother, and there, after his death,
assume (the sovereignty of) that fair kingdom.'

10 The king's youngest son, the prince Paṇḍuvāsudeva,
thought: 'I will go thither.' And when he had assured himself
11 of the success of his journey[2] and empowered by his father, he
took with him thirty-two sons of ministers and embarked
12 (with them) in the disguise of mendicant monks. They landed

[1] Madda = Skt. Madra, now Madras.

[2] Ñatvā sotthiṃ gatimhi ca (by asking the soothsayers). Ṭīkā: nemittikavacaneneva jānitvā 'knowing from the word of the soothsayers'.

at the mouth of the Mahākandara[1] river; when the people saw these mendicant monks they received them with due respect.
When they had inquired about the capital, they arrived 13
gradually approaching (the city), at Upatissagāma, protected
by the devatās. Now a minister there, charged by the 14
(other) ministers, had questioned a soothsayer concerning the
coming of the prince, and he had furthermore[2] foretold him:
'Just on the seventh day will the prince come and one who 15
shall spring of his house shall establish (here) the religion of the
Buddha.' Now when the ministers saw the mendicant monks 16
arrive there, just on the seventh day, and inquiring into the
matter recognized them, they entrusted Paṇḍuvāsudeva with 17
the sovereignty of Laṅkā; but since he lacked a consort he
did not yet receive the solemn consecration.

A son of the Sakka Amitodana was the Sakka Paṇḍu. 18
Since he heard that the Sakyas would (shortly) be destroyed[3]
he took his followers with him and went to another tract of 19
land on the further side of the Ganges and founded a city
there and ruled there as king. He had seven sons.

His youngest daughter was called Bhaddakaccānā. She 20
was (even as) a woman made of gold,[4] fair of form and eagerly
wooed. For (love of) her did seven kings send precious gifts 21
to the king (Paṇḍu), but for fear of the kings, and since he
was told (by soothsayers) that an auspicious journey would 22

[1] Not identified. Probably one of the rivers falling into the sea north of Manaar.

[2] That is, besides the fact of Paṇḍuvāsudeva's coming he had foretold the details that follow.

[3] The Sakyas were annihilated in war by the Kosala king Viḍūḍabha, shortly before the death of the Buddha; see RHYS DAVIDS, *Buddhist India*, p. 11. This catastrophe is foretold to Paṇḍu by soothsayers. Ṭīkā: Viḍūḍhabhayuddhato puretaraṃ eva nemittikavacaneneva Sakyānaṃ bhavitabbaṃ vināsaṃ jānitvā ti attho 'Since he knew, even before the war with Viḍūḍabha, by the word of the soothsayers the future destruction of the Sakyas'.

[4] The golden colour of the skin always, in Sinhalese poems, counts for a mark of particular beauty. Kusajāt. 172: ran-ruwak karageṇa. As a designation of beautiful women ran-liya 'golden creeper' is employed at Sælalihiṇisandesa 55; Kusajāt. 557.

come to pass, nay, one with the result of royal consecration,
he placed his daughter speedily upon a ship, together with
23 thirty-two women-friends, and launched the ship upon the
Ganges, saying: 'Whosoever can, let him take my daughter.'
And they could not overtake her, but the ship fared swiftly
thence.

24 Already on the second day they reached the haven called
25 Goṇagāmaka [1] and there they landed robed like nuns. When
they had inquired about the capital, they arrived gradually
approaching (the city), at Upatissagāma, protected by the
devatās.[2]

26 One of the ministers who had heard the saying of a
soothsayer, saw the women come, and inquiring into the
27 matter recognized them and brought them to the king. So
his ministers, full of pious understanding, consecrated as their
king PAṆḌUVĀSUDEVA, whose every wish was fulfilled.

28 When he had consecrated Subhaddakaccānā, of noble stature,
as his own queen, and had given those (maidens) who had
arrived with her to the followers who had come with him, the
monarch lived happily.

Here ends the eighth chapter, called 'The Consecrating of Paṇḍuvāsudeva', in the Mahāvaṃsa, compiled for the serene joy and emotion of the pious.

[1] At the mouth of the Mahākandara-nadī. Cf. 8. 12.

[2] The wording is exactly like v. 13, in order to lay stress on the parallel in the proceedings. In the same way v. 26 is based on vv. 14 and 16.

CHAPTER IX

THE CONSECRATING OF ABHAYA

THE queen bore ten sons and one daughter: the eldest of 1
all was named Abhaya, the youngest (child, the) daughter was
named Cittā. When the brahmans skilled in sacred texts saw 2
her they foretold: 'For the sake of sovereignty will her son
slay his uncles.' When the brothers resolved: 'let us kill our 3
young sister,' Abhaya restrained them.

In due time they lodged her in a chamber having but
one pillar, and the entry thereto they made through the 4
king's sleeping-chamber; and within they placed a serving-
woman, and a hundred soldiers without. But since she 5
(Cittā) drove men mad by the mere sight of her beauty, the
name given to her was lengthened by an epithet 'Ummā-
dacittā'.[1]

When they heard of the coming of the princess Bhadda- 6
kaccānā to Lankā her brothers also,[2] except one, urged by
their mother, departed thither.

When on arriving they had visited the ruler of Lankā, 7
Paṇḍuvāsudeva and their youngest sister too and had lamented
with her,[3] they, hospitably received by the king and having 8
the king's leave, went about the island of Lankā and took up
their abode wheresoever it pleased them.[4]

The place where Rāma settled is called Rāmagoṇa, the 9
settlements of Uruvela and Anurādha (are called) by their
names, and the settlements of Vijita, Dīghāyu, and Rohaṇa 10
are named Vijitagāma, Dīghāyu, and Rohaṇa.[5] Anurādha 11

[1] The allusion is to ummādeti 'makes mad'.

[2] Puttā, literally: 'the sons,' that is, of the Sakya Paṇḍu.

[3] Probably over the fate of Ummādacittā.

[4] Cariṃsu belongs to cārikaṃ and nivāsaṃ both.

[5] Cf. 7. 43 foll. where the names Anurādha, Uruvela, and Vijita also appear. Evidently we have to do with a different tradition as to the foundation of the same cities.

built a tank and when he had built a palace to the south of
12 this, he took up his abode there. Afterwards the great king
Paṇḍuvāsudeva consecrated his eldest son Abhaya as vice-
regent.

13 When the son of prince Dīghāyu, Dīghagāmaṇi, heard of
14 Ummādacittā he went, driven by longing for her, to Upatissa-
gāma, and there sought out the ruler of the land. And this
(latter) appointed him together with the vice-regent, to
service at the royal court.

15 Now (once) Cittā saw Gāmaṇi in the place where he stood
opposite her window, and, her heart on fire with love, she
16 asked her serving-woman: 'Who is that?' When she heard:
'He is the son of thy uncle,' she trusted the matter to her
17 attendant and he, being in league with her, fastened a hook-
ladder to the window in the night,[1] climbed up, broke the
window and so came in.

18 So he had intercourse with her and did not go forth till
break of day. And he returned there constantly, nor was he
discovered, for there was no entry (to the chamber).

19 And she became with child by him, and when the fruit of
her womb was ripe the serving-woman told her mother, and
20 the mother, having questioned her daughter, told the king.
The king took counsel with his sons and said: 'He too [2] must
be received among us; let us give her (in marriage) to him.'
21 And saying: 'If it is a son we will slay him' they gave
her to him.

But she, when the time of her delivery was come near,
22 went to the lying-in-chamber. And thinking: 'These were
accomplices in the matter,' the princes, from fear, did to death
23 the herdsman Cittā and the slave Kāḷavela, attendants on
Gāmaṇi, since they would make no promise.[3] They were

[1] Gavakkhamhi ḍasāpetvā rattiṃ kakkaṭayantakaṃ, lit. 'making a crab-machine to bite on to the window'. For explanation of this passage see Mah. ed., Introd., p. xxvi.

[2] So pi, namely, Dīghagāmaṇi.

[3] Patiññaṃ adente, that is, they would not fall in with the design of the brothers to kill the boy who might perhaps come into the world. Cf. Mah. ed., Introd., p. xvi.

reborn as yakkhas and both kept guard over the child in the
mother's womb. And Cittā made her attendant find another 24
woman who was near her delivery. And Cittā bore a son but
this woman bore a daughter. Cittā caused a thousand (pieces 25
of money) to be handed over to (the other) together with her
own son, and the latter's daughter to be then brought to her
and laid beside her. When the king's sons heard 'a daughter 26
is born', they were well pleased; but the two, mother and
grandmother, joining the names of the grandfather and the 27
eldest uncle gave the boy the name Paṇḍukābhaya.

The ruler of Laṅkā, Paṇḍuvāsudeva, reigned thirty years. 28
When Paṇḍukābhaya was born, he died.

When the ruler was dead, the king's sons all assembled 29
together and held the great festival of consecration of their
brother, the safety-giving ABHAYA.[1]

Here ends the ninth chapter, called 'The Consecrating of Abhaya', in the Mahāvaṃsa, compiled for the serene joy and emotion of the pious.

[1] A play on the word abhaya 'the fearless', and abhayada 'bestowing fearlessness, freedom from danger, or security'.

CHAPTER X

THE CONSECRATING OF PAṆḌUKĀBHAYA

1 (As) commanded by Ummādacittā the serving-woman took
the boy, laid him in a basket and went with him to Dvāra-
maṇḍalaka.[1]
2 When the princes, who had gone a-hunting in the Tumbara
forest saw the serving-woman they asked her: 'Where art
3 thou going? What is that?' She answered: 'I am going
to Dvāramaṇḍalaka; that is a sweet cake for my daughter.'
4 The princes said to her: 'Take it out.' Then Citta and
Kāḷavela who had come forth to protect (the boy) caused a
5 great boar to appear at that moment. The princes pursued
him; but she took (the boy) and went thither and gave the
boy and a thousand (pieces of money) secretly to a certain
6 man who was entrusted (with the matter). On that very day
his wife bore a son, and he, declaring: 'My wife has borne
twin sons,' reared that boy (with his own).
7 The (boy) was already seven years old when his uncles found
out (where he was) and charged followers of theirs to kill (with
8 him) the boys playing in a certain pond. Now the boy was
used to hide, by diving, in a certain hollow tree standing in
the water and having the mouth of the hollow hidden under
9 water, entering by the hollow, and when he had stayed long
within he would come forth in the same way, and being again
among the other boys, however much they questioned him, he
would mislead them with evasive words.
10 On the day the (princes') people came[2] the boy with
his clothes on dived into the water and stayed hidden in
11 the hollow tree. When those men had counted the clothes and

[1] According to Mah. 23. 23 the village is situated near the Cetiya-mountain (Mihintale), east of Anurādhapura.

[2] See Mah. ed., Introd., p. liii.

killed the other boys they went away and declared: 'The boys
have all been killed!' When they were gone that (boy) went 12
to his foster-father's[1] house, and comforted by him he lived
on there to the age of twelve years.

When his uncles again heard that the boy was alive they 13
charged (their followers) to kill all the herdsmen. Just on 14
that day the herdsmen had taken a deer and sent the boy into
the village to bring fire. He went home, but sent his foster- 15
father's son out saying: 'I am footsore, take thou fire for the
herdsmen; then thou too wilt have some of the roast to eat.' 16
Hearing those words he took fire to the herdsmen: and at 17
that moment those (men) despatched to do it surrounded the
herdsmen and killed them all, and when they had killed them
they (went and) told (the boy's) uncles.

Then, when he was sixteen years old, his uncles discovered 18
him; his mother sent him a thousand (pieces of money) and
a command to bring him to (a place of) safety.[2] His foster- 19
father told him all his mother's message, and giving him a
slave and the thousand (pieces of money) he sent him to Paṇ-
ḍula. The brahman named Paṇḍula, a rich man and learned 20
in the vedas, dwelt in the southern district in (the village)
Paṇḍulagāmaka. The prince went thither and sought out the 21
brahman Paṇḍula. When this latter had asked him: 'Art
thou Paṇḍukābhaya, my dear?' and was answered 'Yes', he 22
paid him honour (as a guest) and said: 'Thou wilt be king,
and full seventy years wilt thou rule; learn the art,[3] my dear!' 23
and he instructed him, and by his son Canda[4] also that art
was mastered in a short time.

He gave him a hundred thousand (pieces of money) to enrol 24
soldiers and when five hundred men had been enrolled by him
(he said): 'The (woman) at whose touch leaves turn to gold 25

[1] Āyutta or āyuttaka 'the man entrusted (with the bringing-up)'.

[2] Tassa rakkhaṃ cādisi, lit. 'and disposed (or commanded) his protection'.

[3] Sippaṃ uggaṇha, in this case 'the art' is the knowledge needed by a reigning prince.

[4] Candena cassa puttena belongs, according to the Ṭīkā, to sippaṃ samāpitaṃ.

26 make thou thy queen, and my son Canda thy chaplain.' When
he had thus said and given him money he sent him forth from
thence with his soldiers. Proclaiming his name he, the
27 virtuous prince, fared forth and when in the city of Paṇa near
the Kāsa-mountain[1] he had gathered together seven hundred
28 followers and provision for all, he went thence, followed by
one thousand two hundred men to the mountain called Giri-
kaṇḍa.

29 An uncle of Paṇḍukābhaya, named Girikaṇḍasiva, drew his
revenues from this district that Paṇḍuvāsudeva had handed
30 over to him. This prince was even then on the point of reap-
ing (a field) measuring a hundred karīsas; his daughter was
31 the beautiful princess named Pālī. And she, with a great
retinue, had mounted her splendid waggon, and came bring-
32 ing food for her father and for the reapers. The prince's
men, who saw the princess there, told the prince (about
33 her); the prince coming thither in haste and dividing her
followers into two bands, drove his own waggon, followed
by his men, near her and asked: 'Where art thou going?'
34 And when she had told him all the prince, whose heart was
fired with love, asked for a share of the food.

35 She stepped down from the waggon and, at the foot of a
banyan-tree, she offered the prince food in a golden bowl.
36 Then she took banyan-leaves to entertain the rest of the people
(with food) and in an instant the leaves were changed into
37 golden vessels. When the prince saw this and remembered the
brahman's words he was glad (thinking): 'I have found the
38 maiden who is worthy to be made queen.' So she entertained
them all, but yet the food became not less; it seemed that but
39 one man's portion had been taken away. Thus from that
time onward that youthful princess who was so rich in virtues
and merit was called by the name Suvaṇṇapālī.

40 And the prince took the maiden and mounted his waggon
and fared onward, fearless and surrounded by a mighty army.

[1] Probably near the modern Kahagalagama 'village of the Kaha mountain', about 18 miles SE. from Anurādhapura, and 10 miles WNW. from the mountain Riṭigala. See also 25. 50, and the Appendix C on Paṇḍukābhaya's campaigns.

When her father heard this he despatched all his soldiers, and 41
they came and gave battle and returned, defeated by the 42
others; at that place (afterwards) a village was built called
Kalahanagara.[1] When her five brothers heard this they (also)
departed to make war. And all those did Canda the son of 43
Paṇḍula slay; Lohitavāhakhaṇḍa [2] was their battle-field.

With a great host Paṇḍukābhaya marched from thence to 44
the further shore of the Gaṅgā [3] toward the Doḷa-mountain.
Here he sojourned four years. When his uncles heard that he 45
was there they marched thither, leaving the king behind, to
do battle with him. When they had made a fortified camp 46
near the Dhūmarakkha-mountain they fought a battle with
their nephew. But the nephew pursued the uncles to this side 47
of the river, and having defeated them in flight he held their
fortified camp for two years.

And they went to Upatissagāma and told all this to the 48
king. And the king sent the prince a letter together with a
thousand (pieces of money) saying: 'Keep thou possession of 49
the land on the further shore, but come not over to this shore.
When the nine brothers heard of this they were wroth with
the king and said: 'Long hast thou been, in truth, a helper 50
to him! Now dost thou give him the kingdom. For that we
will put thee to death.' He yielded up the government to 51
them, and with one accord they appointed their brother named
Tissa to be regent.

This safety-giving Abhaya [4] had reigned as king in Upatis- 52
sagāma twenty years.

Now a yakkhiṇī named Cetiyā, who dwelt on the Dhūma- 53

[1] I. e. Battle-town. A Kalahagala lies to the south of Mineri-Tank (Maṇihīra), not far from the left bank of the Ambanganga, which flows into the Mahawæliganga lower down. *Census of Ceylon*, 1901, iv, pp. 468–469.

[2] Lit. perhaps 'Field of the stream of blood'.

[3] I. e. Mahāgaṅgā, now Mahawæliganga. Pāragaṅgā means, from the standpoint of the narrator (at Anurādhapura), the right, oragaṅgā 'this side', the left bank of the Mahawæliganga. As to the Doḷapabbata (now Dolagal-wela), see Appendix C.

[4] See note to 9. 29.

rakkha-mountain [1] near the pond (called) Tumbariyaṅgaṇa, used to wander about in the form of a mare.

54 And once a certain man saw this beautiful (mare) with her white body and red feet and told the prince: 'Here is a mare whose appearance is thus and so—'

55 The prince took a noose and came to capture her. When she
saw him coming up behind her she fled for fear of his majestic
56 aspect. She fled without rendering herself invisible and he
pursued her swiftly as she fled. Seven times in her flight she
57 circled round the pond, and plunging into the Mahāgaṅgā and
climbing forth again to the shore she fled seven times around
58 the Dhūmarakkha-mountain; and yet three times more she
circled round the pond and plunged yet again in the Gaṅgā
59 near the Kacchaka-ford,[2] but there he seized her by the mane
and (grasped) a palm-leaf that was floating down the stream;
60 by the effect of his merit this turned into a great sword. He
thrust at her with the sword, crying: 'I will slay thee.' And
she said to him: 'I will conquer the kingdom and give it to
61 thee, lord! Slay me not!' Then he seized her by the neck
and boring her nostrils with the point of his sword he secured
her thus with a rope; but she followed wheresoever he would.

62 When the mighty (hero) had gone to the Dhūmarakkha-
mountain, bestriding the mare, he dwelt there on the Dhūma-
63 rakkha-mountain four years. And having marched thence
with his force and come to the Ariṭṭha-mountain [3] he sojourned
there seven years awaiting a fit time to make war.

64 Eight of his uncles, leaving two behind,[4] drew near to the
65 Ariṭṭha-mountain in battle array, and when they had laid out
a fortified camp near a small city and had placed a commander
at the head they surrounded the Arittha-mountain on every
side.

[1] According to v. 62 foll. not far from the Kacchakatittha (see note to v. 58), on the left bank of the Mahawæliganga. The Dhūmarakkhapabbata is also mentioned, Mah. 37.203 (=163 of the Colombo edition ii).

[2] Cf. 23. 17 and 25. 12. Now Mahagantoṭa, a ford below the place where Ambanganga and Mahawæliganga join. See note to 35. 58.

[3] Now Riṭigala, North-Central Province, north of Habarana.

[4] Namely, Abhaya and Girikaṇḍasiva.

After speech with the yakkhiṇī, the prince, according to 66
her cunning counsel, sent in advance a company of his soldiers
taking with them kingly apparel and weapons as presents and
the message: 'Take all this; I will make peace with you.' 67
But as they were lulled to security thinking: 'We will take 68
him prisoner if he comes,' he mounted the yakkha-mare and
went forth to battle at the head of a great host. The 69
yakkhiṇī neighed full loudly and his army, inside and outside
(the camp)[1] raised a mighty battle-cry. The prince's men 70
killed all the soldiers of the enemy's army and the eight
uncles with them, and they raised a pyramid of skulls. The 71
commander escaped and fled (for safety) to a thicket; that
(same thicket) is therefore called Senāpatigumbaka. When 72
the prince saw the pyramid of skulls, where the skulls of his
uncles lay uppermost, he said: ''Tis like a heap of gourds';
and therefore they named (the place) Lābugāmaka.[2]

When he was thus left victor in battle, Paṇḍukābhaya 73
went thence to the dwelling-place of his great-uncle Anurādha.
The great-uncle handed over his palace to him and built 74
himself a dwelling elsewhere; but he dwelt in his house.
When he had inquired of a soothsayer who was versed in the 75
knowledge of (fitting) sites, he founded the capital, even near
that village. Since it had served as dwelling to two Anurādhas, 76
it was called Anurādhapura, and also because it was founded
under the constellation Anurādha. When he had caused the 77
(state) parasol of his uncles to be brought and purified in
a natural pond that is here,[3] PAṆḌUKĀBHAYA kept it for
himself and with the water of that same pond he solemnized 78
his own consecration; and Suvaṇṇapālī, his spouse, he con-
secrated queen. On the young Canda, even as he had agreed, 79

[1] I. e. the soldiers he had sent in advance into the enemy's camp and the army approaching now with him.

[2] I. e. 'Village of Gourds.' Even now we find on the map, to the north-west of the Riṭigala, a place called Labunoruwa = p. lābunagaraka. Cf. *Return of Architectural and Archaeological Remains ... existing in Ceylon*, 1890, p. 76; *Census of Ceylon*, 1901, vol. iv, p. 464.

[3] Idha, i. e. in Anurādhapura, the residence of the chronicler.

he conferred the office of his chaplain and other appointments on his other followers according to their merits.

80 Because his mother and he himself had been befriended by
him, he did not slay the king Abhaya, his eldest uncle, but
81 handed over the government to him for the night-time: he
became the 'Nagaraguttika' (Guardian of the City). From that
82 time onward there were nagaraguttikas in the capital. His
father-in-law also, Girikaṇḍasiva, he did not slay but handed
83 over to this uncle the district of Girikaṇḍa. He had the
pond[1] deepened and abundantly filled with water, and since
he had taken water therefrom, when victorious (for his
consecration), they called it Jayavāpi.[2]

84 He settled the yakkha Kāḷavela on the east side of the
city, the yakkha Cittarāja at the lower end of the Abhaya-
85 tank.[3] The slave-woman who had helped him in time past
and was re-born of a yakkhiṇī, the thankful (king) settled at
86 the south gate of the City. Within the royal precincts he
housed the yakkhiṇī in the form of a mare. Year by year he
87 had sacrificial offerings made to them and to other (yakkhas);
but on festival-days he sat with Cittarāja beside him on a
seat of equal height, and having gods and men to dance before
88 him, the king took his pleasure, in joyous and merry wise.

He laid out also four suburbs as well as the Abhaya-tank,
89 the common cemetery, the place of execution, and the chapel
of the Queens of the West, the banyan-tree of Vessavaṇa[4] and
90 the Palmyra-palm of the Demon of Maladies,[5] the ground set
apart for the Yonas and the house of the Great Sacrifice; all
these he laid out near the west gate.[6]

[1] I. e. the pond in Anurādhapura, mentioned in v. 77. Since the old name has been changed, it is impossible to identify the Jayavāpi.

[2] I. e. the tank of victory.

[3] See v. 88. The Abhaya-vāpi which was laid out by the king Paṇḍukābhaya himself, is the tank now called Basawak-kulam. PARKER, *Ancient Ceylon*, p. 360 foll.

[4] I. e. of Kubera, god of wealth (Skt. Vaiśravaṇa), who perhaps is here considered as a chthonian god.

[5] Or the God of the Huntsmen, according to the reading vyādhadevassa.

[6] On the various buildings and foundations mentioned in 89 and 90,

He set five hundred caṇḍālas to the work of cleaning the 91
(streets of the) town, two hundred caṇḍālas to the work of
cleaning the sewers, one hundred and fifty caṇḍālas he em- 92
ployed to bear the dead and as many caṇḍālas to be watchers
in the cemetery. For these he built a village north-west 93
of the cemetery and they continually carried out their duty
as it was appointed.

Toward the north-east of the caṇḍāla-village he made the 94
cemetery, called the Lower Cemetery, for the caṇḍāla folk.
North of this cemetery, between (it and) the Pāsāṇa-mountain, 95
the line of huts for the huntsmen were built thenceforth.
Northward from thence, as far as the Gāmaṇi-tank,[1] a her- 96
mitage was made for many ascetics; eastward of that same 97
cemetery the ruler built a house for the nigaṇṭha[2] Jotiya.
In that same region dwelt the nigaṇṭha named Giri and 98
many ascetics of various heretical sects. And there the lord 99
of the land built also a chapel for the nigaṇṭha Kumbhaṇḍa;
it was named after him. Toward the west from thence and 100
eastward of the street of the huntsmen lived five hundred
families of heretical beliefs. On the further side of Jotiya's 101
house and on this side of the Gāmaṇi-tank he likewise built
a monastery for wandering mendicant monks, and a dwelling 102
for the ājīvakas and a residence for the brahmans, and in
this place and that he built a lying-in shelter and a hall[3] for
those recovering from sickness.

Ten years after his consecration did Paṇḍukābhaya the 103
ruler of Laṅkā establish the village-boundaries over the
whole of the island of Laṅkā. With Kāḷavela and Cittarāja, 104

see Mah. ed., Introd., p. liv. Since the Ṭīkā leaves us in the lurch it will be difficult to add anything further.

[1] The Gāmaṇivāpi is perhaps the Karambǟwa-tank which lies somewhat more than a mile north from the Bulan-kulam. PARKER, however, identifies it with the Peramiyan-kulam. *Ancient Ceylon*, p. 364.

[2] Name of a sect of ascetics (the Jaina) who went about naked.

[3] According to the Ṭīkā we have to take sivikā-sotthisālaṃ as sivikāsālaṃ ca sotthisālaṃ ca. The former word is explained by vijāyanaghara 'house of delivery', the latter by gilānasālā 'hall for the sick'.

who were visible (in bodily form) the prince enjoyed his good
105 fortune, he who had yakkhas and bhūtas [1] for friends. Be-
tween the king Paṇḍukābhaya and Abhaya were seventeen
years without a king.

106 When the ruler of the earth, Paṇḍukābhaya, the intelligent, being thirty-seven years old, had assumed the rule over the kingdom, he reigned full seventy years in fair and wealthy [2] Anurādhapura.

Here ends the tenth chapter, called 'The Consecrating of Paṇḍukābhaya' in the Mahāvaṃsa, compiled for the serene joy and emotion of the pious.

[1] That is, ghosts; but the expression is ambiguous. It could also mean 'he who had those that had become yakkhas (namely Kāḷavela and Citta) for friends'.

[2] Ṭīkā: samiddhe ti, sampattiyā pūrite aḍḍhe vā 'filled with prosperity or wealthy'.

CHAPTER XI

THE CONSECRATING OF DEVĀNAṂPIYATISSA

AFTER his death his son, known by the name of MUṬASIVA, 1
the son of Suvaṇṇapālī, succeeded him in the government,
which was (then) in a peaceful state. The king laid out the 2
beautiful Mahāmeghavana-garden, rich in all the good
qualities that its name promises [1] and provided with fruit-
trees and flowering-trees. At the time that the place was 3
chosen for the garden, a great cloud, gathering at an unwonted
season, poured forth rain; therefore they called the garden
Mahāmeghavana.

Sixty years king Muṭasiva reigned in splendid Anurādha- 4
pura, the fair face of the land of Laṅkā. He had ten sons, 5
each thoughtful of the other's welfare, and two daughters
equal [2] (in beauty), worthy of their family. The second son, 6
known by the name Devānaṃpiyatissa, was foremost among
all his brothers in virtue and intelligence.

This DEVĀNAṂPIYATISSA became king after his father's 7
death. Even at the time of his consecration many wonders
came to pass. In the whole isle of Laṅkā treasures and 8

[1] Following the reading of the Burmese MSS. and the Ṭīkā nāmānugaguṇodito 'eminent in the qualities corresponding to the name'. Mahāmeghavana means 'grove of the great cloud'. The qualities which it possesses are such as accompany abundant rainfall: streams, trees with thick foliage, shade, coolness and so forth. Cf. the explanation of the Ṭīkā, Mah. ed., note on this passage. The Mahāmeghavana was situated south of the city of Anurādhapura, where now the Mahāvihāra stands. Between it and the southern wall of the city was another park, called Nandana or Jotivana. See 15. 1, 8; PARKER, *Ancient Ceylon*, pp. 272–274.

[2] Ṭīkā: anukūlā ti, samānavaṇṇā; ayaṃ surūpā ayaṃ virūpā ti vacanapacchinditum anarahā samānarūpā; aññamañña-anukūlarūpasampattiyā samannāgatā ti adhippāyo. The sense is: they were of equal beauty.

jewels that had been buried deep rose up to the surface of the
9 earth. Jewels which had been in ships wrecked near Laṅkā and
those which were naturally formed there (in the ocean) issued
10 forth upon the land. At the foot of the Chāta-mountain
there grew up three bamboo-stems, in girth even as a waggon-
11 pole.[1] One of them, 'the creeper-stem,' shone like silver; on
this might be seen delightful creepers gleaming with a golden
12 colour. But one was the 'flower-stem', on this again might
be seen flowers of many kinds, of manifold colours, in full
13 bloom. And last, one was the 'bird-stem' whereon might be
seen numbers of birds and beasts of many (kinds) and of
14 many colours, as if living. Pearls of the eight kinds, namely
horse-pearl, elephant-pearl, waggon-pearl, myrobalan-pearl,
bracelet-pearl, ring-pearl, kakudha fruit-pearl, and common
15 (pearls) came forth out of the ocean and lay upon the shore
in heaps.

16 All this was the effect of Devānampiyatissa's merit. Sap-
phire, beryl, ruby, these gems and many jewels and those
17 pearls and those bamboo-stems they brought, all in the same
week, to the king.

When the king saw them he was glad at heart and thought:
18 'My friend Dhammāsoka and nobody else is worthy to have
these priceless treasures; I will send them to him as a gift.'
19 For the two monarchs, Devānampiyatissa and Dhammāsoka
already had been friends a long time, though they had never
seen each other.

20 The king sent four persons appointed as his envoys: his
nephew Mahāriṭṭha, who was the chief of his ministers, then
21 his chaplain, a minister and his treasurer,[2] attended by a body
of retainers, and he bade them take with them those priceless
22 jewels, the three kinds of precious stones, and the three stems
(like) waggon-poles, and a spiral shell winding to the right, and

[1] This must be the meaning of rathapatoda, although patodà properly means 'goad, whip'.

[2] The Ṭīkā also tells us the names of Ariṭṭha's three companions, namely Tālipabbata (in Kamb. Mah. Hāḷi°), Tela and Tissa. These names are, we may conjecture, taken from the original source of the Mah., the old Aṭṭhakathā.

the eight kinds of pearls. When they had embarked at Jambu- 23
kola[1] and in seven days had reached the haven[2] in safety,
and from thence in seven days more had come to Pāṭaliputta, 24
they gave those gifts into the hands of king Dhammāsoka.
When he saw them he rejoiced greatly. Thinking: 'Here 25
I have no such precious things,' the monarch, in his joy,
bestowed on Ariṭṭha the rank of a commander in his army,
on the brahman the dignity of chaplain, to the minister he 26
gave the rank of staff-bearer, and to the treasurer that of
a guild-lord.[3]

When he had allotted to the (envoys) abundance of (all) 27
things for their entertainment and dwelling-houses, he took
counsel with his ministers considering (what should be sent
as) a return-gift; and he took[4] a fan,[5] a diadem, a sword, 28
a parasol, shoes, a turban, ear-ornaments,[6] chains,[7] a pitcher,
yellow sandalwood, a set of garments that had no need of 29
cleansing, a costly napkin, unguent brought by the nāgas,
red-coloured earth, water from the lake Anotatta and 30
also water from the Ganges, a (spiral) shell winding in

[1] A landing-place in northern Ceylon. See chiefly 19. 25.

[2] The haven of Tāmalittī. See note to 11. 38.

[3] Very characteristic, and throwing light on court-life in India, chiefly in the fifth century A.D. The complimentary bestowing of titles and dignities was then the custom, just as at the present day.

[4] The accusatives in the text are all dependent on v. 33. From this point the things enumerated are merely either the insignia of a royal prince or such as are used for the ceremony of consecrating a king.

[5] Vālavījanī is a fly-whisk (Skt. cāmara) made of the hair of a yak's tail.

[6] The Ṭīkā explains vataṃsa (Skt. avataṃsa) by kaṇṇapilandhana. See *Vinaya Texts*, ii, p. 347, note on C.V. I. 13. 1. In Thūpav., p. 17^{23} pupphavataṃsaka is rendered in Sinhalese malkaḍa.

[7] That pāmaṅga must be a band or chain is clear from the simile in Thūpav. 3^{17-19}. The Buddha Dīpaṃkara winds the girdle round his red garment as one might wind a golden pāmaṅga about a bunch of flowers. The same simile occurs Mahābodhiv., ed. STRONG, p. 62^{10}; cf. also C.V. 5. 2. 1; Sum. Vil. I. 80^{12} on D. 1. 1. 10. (To be read thus, Mah. ed., p. 355, line 29.)

31 auspicious wise,[1] a maiden in the flower of her youth, utensils
as golden platters, a costly litter, yellow and emblic myro-
32 balans and precious ambrosial healing herbs, sixty times one
hundred waggon loads of mountain-rice brought thither by
parrots, nay, all that was needful for consecrating a king,
33 marvellous in splendour; and sending these (things) in due
time as a gift to his friend the lord of men sent envoys also
34 with the gift of the true doctrine, saying: 'I have taken
refuge in the Buddha, his Doctrine and his Order, I have
declared myself a lay-disciple in the religion of the Sakya son;[2]
35 seek then even thou, O best of men converting thy mind with
36 believing heart refuge in these best of gems!' and saying
moreover: 'Consecrate my friend yet again as king,' he
dismissed his friend's ministers, with many marks of honour.

37 When the ministers had stayed five months, highly honoured
they set forth with the envoys, on the first day of the bright
38 half of the month Vesākha.[3] Having embarked at Tāmalittī[4]
and landed at Jambukola they sought out the king, when
39 they arrived here on the twelfth day. The envoys handed the
gifts to the ruler of Laṅkā; the ruler of Laṅkā made them
welcome with great hospitality.

40 But the envoys most faithful to their king consecrated the
ruler of Laṅkā, whose (first) consecration had been held in the
month Maggasira[5] on the day when the moon first shows
41 itself, fulfilling the charge of Dhammāsoka, yet again as king,
they rejoicing in the salvation of their king (consecrated) him
who rejoiced in the good fortune of Laṅkā.

[1] Winding towards the right, dakkhiṇāvaṭṭo; cf. v. 22.

[2] I. e. of Buddha, sprung from the tribe of the Sakyas. See 2. 15 foll.

[3] See note to 1. 12.

[4] Skt. Tāmraliptī, a harbour in the region at the mouth of the Ganges, now Tamluk. At Tāmraliptī the Chinese pilgrim Fā-hien embarked for Ceylon in the beginning of the fifth century A. D. See LEGGE, *Record of Buddhistic Kingdoms*, p. 100.

[5] According to the Dīp. 11. 14 and 38, the first coronation of D. was held in the second winter month under the Nakkhatta Āsāḷha, and the second coronation on the twelfth day of the bright half of the Vesākha month. Cf. Introduction, para. 7.

Thus on the full-moon day of the month Vesākha the ruler 42
of men, in whose name was contained the words 'friend of the gods',[1] bestowing good upon his people, held his consecration (as king) in Laṅkā, where in every place they held high festival.

Here ends the eleventh chapter, called 'The Consecrating of Devānaṃpiyatissa' in the Mahāvaṃsa, compiled for the serene joy and emotion of the pious.

[1] Devānaṃpiyatissa means 'Tissa, friend of the gods'.

CHAPTER XII

THE CONVERTING OF DIFFERENT COUNTRIES

1 WHEN the thera Moggaliputta, the illuminator of the religion of the Conqueror, had brought the (third) council to an
2 end and when, looking into the future, he had beheld the founding of the religion in adjacent countries, (then) in the
3 month Kattika[1] he sent forth theras, one here and one there. The thera Majjhantika he sent to Kasmīra and Gandhāra, the
4 thera Mahādeva he sent to Mahisamaṇḍala. To Vanavāsa he sent the thera named Rakkhita, and to Aparantaka the Yona
5 named Dhammarakkhita; to Mahāraṭṭha (he sent) the thera named Mahādhammarakkhita, but the thera Mahārakkhita he
6 sent into the country of the Yona. He sent the thera Majjhima to the Himalaya country, and to Suvaṇṇabhūmi he sent the
7 two theras Soṇa and Uttara. The great thera Mahinda, the theras Iṭṭhiya, Uttiya, Sambala and Bhaddasāla his dis-
8 ciples, these five theras he sent forth with the charge: 'Ye shall found in the lovely island of Laṅkā the lovely religion of the Conqueror.'

9 At that time in Kasmīra and Gandhāra[2] did the nāga-king of wondrous power, Aravāḷa, cause the rain called 'Hail' to
10 pour down upon the ripe crops, and cruelly did he overwhelm everything with a flood. The thera Majjhantika went thither
11 with all speed, passing through the air, and wrought (miracles such as) walking on the surface of the water in Aravāḷa's lake and so forth. When the nāgas beheld it they told their king with fury about this thing.

12 Then full of fury the nāga-king brought divers terrors to

[1] See note to 1. 12. As to the time of the third council, cf. the Introduction.

[2] Gandhāra comprises the districts of Peshāwar and Rāwal Piṇḍī in the northern Punjab. Kasmīra is the modern Kashmīr.

pass; fierce winds blew, a cloud gave forth thunder and rain,
thunder strokes crashed, and lightning flashed here and there, 13
trees and mountain-tops were hurled down. Nāgas in grisly 14
forms terrified (beholders) on every side, he himself spat forth
smoke and fire threatening in different ways.

When the thera by his wondrous power had brought all 15
these terrors to naught, he said to the nāga-king, showing his
eminent might: 'Even if the world together with the gods 16
came seeking to terrify me, they would not be equal to me (in
strength) whatever fears and dread (they may arouse) in this
place.[1] Nay, if thou shouldst raise the whole earth with the 17
ocean and the mountains, thou mighty nāga, and shouldst
hurl them upon me, thou couldst in no wise arouse fear and 18
dread in me. It were surely but thy own destruction, thou
lord of serpents.'

Then to him, humbled by these words the thera preached 19
the doctrine, and thereupon the nāga-king came unto the
(three) refuges and the precepts of duty,[2] and this likewise 20
did eighty-four thousand serpents and many gandhabbas,
yakkhas and kumbhaṇḍakas[3] in the Himalaya. But a yak- 21
kha named Paṇḍaka with (his wife) the yakkhiṇī Hāritā and his
five hundred sons obtained the first fruit (of sanctification).[4]

'Henceforth let no anger arise as of old; work no more 22
harm to the harvest, for living beings love their happiness;
cherish love for beings, let men live in happiness.' Thus 23
were they taught by him and they did according to (this
teaching). Then the lord of serpents made the thera sit upon 24
a jewel-throne and he stood near, fanning him. But the 25
dwellers in Kasmīra and Gandhāra who had come to worship

[1] The right reading appears to be yaṃ ettha bhayabheravaṃ. The construction of the sentence is, however, very difficult. For the explanation of the Ṭīkā see Mah. ed., note on the passage.

[2] See note to 1. 32 and 62.

[3] Skt. kumbhāṇḍa, name of a class of supernatural beings under the rule of Virūḷhaka. The gandhabbas (= Skr. gandharva) are a class of demigods who are the attendants of Dhataraṭṭha. Virūḷhaka, and Dhataraṭṭha are two of the four great kings of the world (lokapālā), the regents of the south and north.

[4] I. e. the sotāpattiphala. Cf. note to 1. 33.

the nāga-king acknowledged the thera as the mightier in
26 working wonders,[1] and when they had paid the thera reverence
they seated themselves on one side near him. The thera
expounded to them the dhamma, (namely) the Āsīvisūpamā.[2]
27 The conversion of eighty thousand persons took place[3] and
a hundred thousand persons received the pabbajjā from the
28 thera. Since then Kasmīra and Gandhāra shine with yellow
robes and prize above all the three things.[4]
29 The thera Mahādeva who had gone to the Mahisamaṇḍala[5]
country preached in the midst of the people the Devadūta-
30 suttanta.[6] Forty thousand (persons) made pure (in themselves)
the eye of the truth and yet forty thousand received from
him the pabbajjā-ordination.
31 The thera Rakkhita, who had gone to Vanavāsa,[7] preached,
floating in the air in the midst of the people, the Anamatagga-
32 saṃyutta.[8] The conversion of sixty thousand persons took
place, thirty-seven thousand in number received the pabbajjā
33 from him. Five hundred vihāras were founded in the

[1] Cf. Mah. ed., note on this passage, also 14. 20 with note. The positive mahiddhika stands for the comparative.

[2] The āsīvisa-sutta of S. IV, pp. 172–175, or the āsīvisopamā 'simile of the serpent' of A. II, pp. 110–111.

[3] See note to 1. 32.

[4] Namely buddha, dhamma, saṃgha, the Buddha, his doctrine and his order. See note to 1. 62.

[5] Mahisamaṇḍala is generally taken as the modern Mysore. But Fleet, *J.R.A.S.* 1910, p. 429 foll., has shown that this identification is hardly correct. He himself takes Mahisamaṇḍala as 'territory of the Māhisha' of which the capital was Māhishmatī. Agreeing with Pargiter he places this capital on the island of the Narbadā river, now called Mandhāta. See *Imperial Gazetteer of India*, s.v. Mahisamaṇḍala is, therefore, a district south of the Vindhyan mountains.

[6] I.e. 'Discourse on the Messengers of God.' See M. III, pp. 178-187; A. I, pp. 138-142. The suttanta deals with old age, disease, and death as messengers of Yama the god of death.

[7] The Vanavāsaka or Vanavāsin are mentioned in the Mahābhārata, 6. 366, and Harivaṃśa, 5232, as a people dwelling in southern India. See B.R., *Skt. Wtb.* s.vv. There is also a modern town Banavāsi in North Kānara which seems to have preserved the old name. *Imp. Gaz. of India*, s.v.

[8] S. II, pp. 178–193.

country. Thus did the thera establish there the religion of the Conqueror.

The thera Dhammarakkhita the Yona, being gone to 34
Aparantaka[1] and having preached in the midst of the people
the Aggikkhandhopamā-sutta,[2] gave to drink of the nectar of 35
truth to thirty-seven thousand living beings who had come
together there, he who perfectly understood truth and untruth. 36
A thousand men and yet more women went forth from noble
families and received the pabbajjā.

The wise Mahādhammarakkhita, who had gone to Mahā- 37
raṭṭha,[3] related there the jātaka called Mahānāradakassapa.[4]
Eighty-four thousand persons attained to the reward of the 38
path (of salvation), thirteen thousand received from him the
pabbajjā.

The wise Mahārakkhita who went to the country of the 39
Yona[5] delivered in the midst of the people the Kālakārāma-
suttanta.[6] A hundred and seventy thousand living beings 40
attained to the reward of the path (of salvation); ten thousand
received the pabbajjā.

The wise Majjhima[7] preached in the Himalaya region whither 41

[1] Skr. Aparānta 'the western ends', comprising the territory of northern Gujarāt, Kāthiāwār, Kachchh, and Sind. FLEET, *J.R.A.S.* 1910, p. 427.

[2] I. e. 'The discourse on the parable of the flames of fire.' A. IV, pp. 128–135.

[3] Skr. Mahārāṣṭra, the country of the Marāṭhī.

[4] FAUSBÖLL, *Jāt.* vi, pp. 219–255.

[5] The Yonas (Skt. Yavana) are also mentioned, together with the Kambojas, in the Rock Edicts V and XIII of Aśoka. They 'must mean the clans of foreign race (not necessarily Greek) on the north-western frontier, included in the empire (of Aśoka)'. V. A. SMITH, *Asoka*, p. 132, n. 2. It is remarkable that just at that time (246 B.C.) the Greco-Bactrian kingdom was founded by Diodotos. See SPIEGEL, *Eran. Alterthumsk.*, III, p. 49 foll.

[6] Probably by this title is meant the suttanta 24 of the Catukkanipāta in A. II, pp. 24–26. The Kālakārāma is supposed to be the place where Buddha delivered this discourse.

[7] The companions of Majjhima, according to Dīp. 8. 10, Smp. 317[19], MBv. 115[5], and Ṭīkā 222[5], were the theras Kassapagotta, Mūladeva (Alakadeva), Sahadeva, and Dundubhissara. See the Introduction.

he had gone with four theras, the Dhammacakkappavattana-
42 suttanta.[1] Eighty koṭis of living beings attained to the reward
of the path (of salvation). The five theras separately con-
43 verted five kingdoms; from each of them a hundred thousand
persons received the pabbajjā, believing in the doctrine of
the Sammāsambuddha.

44 Together with the thera Uttara the thera Soṇa of wondrous
45 might went to Suvaṇṇabhūmi.[2] Now at this time, when-
ever a boy was born in the king's palace, a fearsome female
demon who came forth out of the sea, was wont to devour (the
46 child) and vanish again. And at that very moment a prince
was born in the king's palace. When the people saw the
theras they thought: 'These are companions of the demons,'
47 and they came armed to kill them. And the theras
asked: 'What does this mean?' and said to them: 'We
48 are pious ascetics, in no wise companions of the demon.'
Then the demon came forth from the ocean with her follow-
49 ing, and when the people saw them they raised a great outcry.
50 But the thera created twice as many terrifying demons and
therewith surrounded the demon and her following on every
side. She thought: 'This (country) is come into possession
of these (people),' and, panic-stricken, she took to flight.

51 When the thera had made a bulwark round the country he
pronounced in the assembly the Brahmajāla(suttanta).[3]

52 Many were the people who came unto the (three) refuges
and the precepts of duty; sixty thousand were converted to

[1] I.e. 'The discourse of the setting in motion the wheel of the doctrine.' See M.V. I. 6. 17 foll. (= *Vin. Piṭ.* i, p. 10 foll.); S.V, pp. 420–431; *S.B.E.* xi, p. 146 foll.

[2] The general opinion was, until recently, that Suvaṇṇabhūmi 'the gold-land' is lower Burma with adjacent districts. But this is very doubtful, since it is a fact that Buddhism reached Burma from China in the Mahāyāna-form and not before the fourth century A.D. FLEET, *J.R.A.S.* 1910, p. 428, suggests that Suvaṇṇabhūmi might be the country in Bengal called by Hiuen-tsang 'Ka-lo-na-su-fa-la-na' = Karṇasuvarṇa, or else the country along the river Son, a river in Central India, and tributary of the Ganges on its right bank, which is also called Hiraṇyavāha 'the gold-bearer'.

[3] I.e. 'The Net of the Religious,' D. I, p. 1 foll.

the true faith. Three thousand five hundred sons of noble 53
families received the pabbajjā and one thousand five hundred
daughters of noble families received it likewise. Thenceforth 54
when a prince was born in the royal palace the kings gave to
such the name Soṇuttara.

Since they did even forbear to enter into the bliss already 55
won—(such was) also the renunciation of the all-compassionate
Conqueror—they bestowed blessing on the world,[1] (going) here
and there. Who should grow weary in (striving for) the
salvation of the world?

Here ends the twelfth chapter, called 'The Converting of Different Countries', in the Mahāvaṃsa, compiled for the serene joy and emotion of the pious.

[1] The sense is this: The theras had already attained to arahantship and were in possession of nibbāṇa. Nevertheless they forebore to pass into nibbāṇa, in order that they might first show the way salvation to the world. They thus followed the example of the Buddha who had practised the same renunciation (kaḍḍhana). See M.V. I. 5. 2 foll. (= *Vin. Piṭ.* i, p. 4 foll.).

CHAPTER XIII

THE COMING OF MAHINDA

1 THE great thera Mahinda, of lofty wisdom, who at that
time had been twelve years (a monk), charged by his teacher
2 and by the brotherhood to convert the island of Laṅkā, pon-
dered on the fitting time (for this) and thought: 'Old is the
king Muṭasiva; his son must become king.'
3 When he had resolved to visit in the meantime his kinsfolk,
he bade farewell to his teacher and the brotherhood and
4 having asked the leave of the king he took with him the four
theras [1] and also Saṃghamittā's son, the miraculously gifted
5 sāmaṇera Sumana,[2] mighty in the six supernormal powers; and
he went to Dakkhiṇāgiri [3] to confer on his kinsfolk (the) grace
(of his preaching). While he was so doing six months passed
away.
6 When he came in time to Vedisagiri [4] the city of his mother
7 Devī, he visited his mother and when Devī saw her dear son
she made him welcome, and his companions likewise, with
foods prepared by herself, and she led the thera up to the
lovely vihāra Vedisagiri.
8 When the prince Asoka, while ruling over the realm of
Avanti, that his father had bestowed on him, halted in the
9 town of Vedisa, before he came to Ujjenī, and met there a
10 lovely maiden named Devī, the daughter of a merchant, he
made her his wife; and she was (afterwards) with child by
11 him and bore in Ujjenī a beautiful boy, Mahinda, and when
two years had passed (she bore) a daughter, Saṃghamittā. At

[1] See 12. 7. [2] See 5. 170.

[3] A vihāra in Ujjenī, Skr. Ujjayinī. See note to 5. 39.

[4] Vedisa is the modern Bhilsa in Gwalior State, situated 26 miles north-east of Bhopāl. See *Imp. Gazetteer of India*, s. v.; E. MÜLLER, *J.P.T.S.* 1888, p. 87; RHYS DAVIDS, *Buddhist India*, p. 288.

that time[1] she lived in the city of Vedisa. The thera who then 12
sojourned there, perceiving (that) the time (was come), thought
thus: 'In that great festival of consecration commanded by 13
my father shall the great king Devānaṃpiyatissa take part,
and he shall know the splendour of the three things[2] when he
has heard it from the envoys. He shall climb the Missaka- 14
mountain[3] on the uposatha-day of the month Jeṭṭha.[4] On
that same day we will go to the beauteous isle of Laṅkā.'

The great Indra[5] sought out the excellent thera Mahinda 15
and said to him: 'Set forth to convert Laṅkā; by the Saṃ-
buddha also hast thou been foretold (for this) and we will be 16
those who aid thee there.'

The son of a daughter of Devī's sister, (a youth) named
Bhaṇḍuka, who had heard the doctrine preached by the thera 17
to Devī, and who had obtained the reward of one who shall
return no more unto life[6] remained with the thera.

When he had stayed there a month the thera, on the upo- 18
satha-day of the month Jeṭṭha, with the four theras and
Sumana,[7] and the lay-disciple Bhaṇḍuka also, to the end that 19
they might be known for human beings,[8] rose up in the air
(and departed) from that vihāra; and he, the (thera) of won-
drous powers, coming hither with his following alighted on 20

[1] Namely, at the time of Mahinda's visit.

[2] Cf. note to 12. 28.

[3] Now the mountain Mihintale (= 'plain of Mahinda', according to A. GUNASEKARA), 8 miles to the east of Anurādhapura.

[4] See note to 1. 12.

[5] A play upon the name Mahinda.

[6] The stage of anāgāmī is the third and last stage but one, on the path of salvation leading to nibbāṇa. Such an one will not be re-born, either in the world of gods or of men, but only in a Brahma-world, where he will attain nibbāṇa. See CHILDERS, s. v.

[7] It seems almost as if v. 18 were an interpolated verse. If we omit it 19 follows perfectly well on 17: '. . . remained with the thera; with this lay-disciple . . . he rose up, &c.' That, besides, the four theras and Sumana were Mahinda's fellow-travellers is already known from 12. 7 and 13. 4.

[8] With this cf. 14. 31, also Mah. ed., note to 13. 19b and Album Kern 205-206.

the pleasant Missaka-mountain, on the Sīla-peak on the open and fair Ambatthala.[1]

21 He who was foretold by the Sage, in the hour of death, as bringing salvation to Lankā,[2] by his merit in converting Lankā, he, who for Lankā's salvation had become like to the Master,[3] alighted there, extolled by the gods of Lankā.

Here ends the thirteenth chapter, called 'The Coming of Mahinda', in the Mahāvaṃsa, compiled for the serene joy and emotion of the pious.

[1] Cf. TENNENT, *Ceylon*, ii, p. 605 foll. The Sīlakūṭa is the northern peak of the Mihintale-mountain. Immediately below it lies the little tableland on which the Ambatthala-dagaba stands.

[2] Lit. 'For the blessing of L.'

[3] The allusion probably is to the Buddha's legendary visit to the island.

CHAPTER XIV

THE ENTRY INTO THE CAPITAL

THE king Devānampiyatissa who had arranged a water- 1
festival for the dwellers in the capital, set forth to enjoy the
pleasures of the chase. Attended by forty thousand of his 2
men he went on foot to the Missaka-mountain. The deva of 3
the mountain who desired to show the theras to him, appeared
there in the form of an elk-stag browsing in the thicket.
When the king saw him, he thought: 'It is unseemly to kill 4
an unheeding (creature)' and he struck out a sound from his
bowstring; the stag fled towards the mountain. The king 5
pursued, but the stag in his flight drew near to the thera.
When the thera came into the prince's view the (deva) himself
vanished.

Thinking: 'If he sees too many (people) he will be too 6
much afraid,' the thera let (the king) see him alone. When
the king beheld him he stood still terrified. The thera said to 7
him: 'Come hither, Tissa.' Then, from the calling him by
his name, Tissa, the king thought forthwith: '(That is) a
yakkha.' 'Samaṇas are we, O great king, disciples of the 8
King of Truth. From compassion toward thee are we come
hither from Jambudīpa,' thus said the thera. When the king 9
heard this fear left him. And remembering the message of
his friend, and persuaded that these were samaṇas, he laid bow 10
and arrow aside and approaching the sage he exchanged greeting
with the thera and sat down near him.

Then came his people and surrounded him and the great thera 11
caused the others who had come with him to become visible.
When the king beheld these too he said: 'When did these come 12
hither?' The thera answered: '(They came) with me.' And

13 he asked moreover: 'Are there in Jambudīpa other ascetics like to these?' The other said: 'Jambudīpa is gleaming with
14 yellow robes; and great is the number there of arahants learned in the three vedas, gifted with miraculous powers, skilled in reading the thoughts of others, possessing the heavenly ear:[1] the disciples of the Buddha.'

15 (The king) then asked: 'By what way are you come?' And since the answer was: 'Neither by land nor by water are we come,' he understood that they had come through the air.

16 To test him that most wise (thera) now asked a subtle question, and even as he was questioned the monarch answered the questions severally.

17 'What name does this tree bear, O king?'

'This tree is called a mango.'

'Is there yet another mango beside this?'

'There are many mango-trees.'

18 'And are there yet other trees besides this mango and the other mangoes?'

'There are many trees, sir; but those are trees that are not mangoes.'

19 'And are there, beside the other mangoes and those trees which are not mangoes, yet other trees?'

'There is this mango-tree, sir.'

'Thou hast a shrewd wit, O ruler of men!'

20 'Hast thou kinsfolk, O king?'

'They are many, sir.'

'And are there also some, O king, who are not kinsfolk of thine?'

'There are yet more[2] of those than of my kin.'

21 'Is there yet any one besides the kinsfolk and the others?'

'There is yet myself, sir.'

'Good! thou hast a shrewd wit, O ruler of men!'

22 When he had known that he was a keen-witted man, the

[1] **Iddhi**, **cetopariyañāṇa** and **dibbasota** are three of the six **abhiññā**. See note on 4. 12 (No. I, III, II).

[2] The positive **bahū**, with the abl. **ñātito**, stands instead of the comparative. See 12. 25 (with note) also Mah. ed., Introd., p. liv.

wise thera preached to the monarch the Cūlahatthipadūpama-
suttanta.[1] At the end of the discourse he, with the forty 23
thousand men, came unto the (three) refuges.[2]

In the evening they brought the king's meal to him. 24
Although the king knew that these (bhikkhus) would not eat
then he invited the sages to the meal, with the thought: 'It 25
were seemly at least to ask them.' When they told him:
'We do not eat now,' he asked concerning the time. And 26
when he was told the time, he said: 'We will go into the
city.'

'Go thou, great king, we will stay here.'

'If that be so, then must this young man[3] come with us.' 27

'This (youth) is one who has attained the goal,[4] has grasped
the doctrine and waits for the pabbajjā, (therefore) must he 28
abide near us. We wish to bestow on him the pabbajjā now;
depart then, O king.' Then, when he had taken leave of the 29
theras with the words: 'To-morrow I will send a waggon,
do you enter it and come into the city,' he took Bhaṇḍu aside
and asked him what the theras intended (to do). And he 30
told the king all. When (the king) heard the thera's name
he was full of joy and thought: 'This is blessing for me.'
And now the king, whose fear had left him because Bhaṇḍu 31
was a layman, knew that these were human beings.[5] Saying:
'Let us bestow on him the pabbajjā,' the thera bestowed on 32
young Bhaṇḍuka, within the boundaries of that village and
within that group (of bhikkhus),[6] both the pabbajjā and the

[1] I.e. 'The lesser discourse on the simile of the elephant's footprint.' M. I, pp. 175–184.

[2] See notes to 1. 32 and 62.

[3] Namely Bhaṇḍu.

[4] Āgataphala is a synonym of anāgāmiphala. See 13. 17.

[5] See the note to 13. 19. The king's remaining fears that he was in the presence of supernatural beings, were only overcome by the details communicated by Bhaṇḍu.

[6] Every monastery has its parish, the bounds of which (sīmā) are strictly fixed according to M.V. II. 11 foll., and within these the ecclesiastical proceedings take place. Since there were as yet no monasteries in Ceylon the boundaries of the village situated on Missaka served as a parish. But the chapter (gaṇa) which carried out the ordination was formed by Mahinda and his companions.

33 upasampadā-ordination, and even in the same moment he
attained to the state of arahant.
34 Then the thera ordered the sāmaṇera Sumana: 'Announce ye
the time of preaching the dhamma.' He asked: 'How far, sir,
35 shall I make the time to be heard when I announce it?' When
the thera answered: 'Over all Tambapaṇṇi,' he announced the
time of (preaching the) dhamma, making it to be heard, by
his miraculous power, over the whole of Laṅkā.
36 When the king, who was seated by the rock-basin at the
Nāgacatukka[1] and was taking his repast, heard the loud
37 summons, he sent a message to the thera asking: 'Has any
misfortune come to pass?' He answered: 'No misfortune has
come to pass; the time was proclaimed for hearing the word
of the Sambuddha.'
38 When the earth-gods heard the summons of the sāmaṇera
they echoed it and so the call rose up gradually to Brahma's
39 heaven. Because of the summons there came together a great
assembly of devas; and the thera preached before this gather-
ing the Samacitta-sutta.[2]
40 Devas without number were converted to the doctrine
and many nāgas and supaṇṇas[3] came unto the (three)
41 refuges. Even as when the thera Sāriputta uttered this
discourse so did the devas gather together to hear it from
Mahinda.
42 On the morrow the king sent a waggon. The driver came
and said: 'Mount into the waggon, we will drive to the city.'
43 'We will not mount into the waggon; go thou, we will
follow thee.' Saying this they, full of holy desires,[4] sent the
44 driver away; and they rose into the air and by their miraculous
power they descended to the east of the city in the place

[1] By this is probably meant the Nāgapokuṇa situated some distance below the Ambatthala. See GEIGER, *Ceylon*, p. 204.

[2] By Samacitta-sutta we have to understand Sutta 5–6 of the Samacitta-vagga in the Dukanipāta of A. I, pp. 63–65. The subject is spiritual calm.

[3] See note to 19. 20.

[4] In sumanorathā a play on the words ratha 'waggon' and sārathi 'driver' is intended. The ratha of the theras is sumanas 'pious feeling'.

where the first thūpa (afterwards stood). And thenceforward 45
to this day the cetiya that was built on the spot where the
theras first alighted [1] is called the Paṭhamacetiya.[2]

Since the women of the royal household, hearing from the 46
king of the virtues of the theras, desired to see them, the
monarch had a lovely pavilion built for them within the royal 47
precincts, covered with white stuffs and with flowers and
beautifully adorned.

And since he had heard from the thera that they would not 48
sit upon raised seats, he pondered doubtfully: 'Will the thera
indeed sit upon a raised seat?' In the meantime the driver 49
saw the theras standing there [3] putting on their robes and in
wonderment he came and told the king. Hearing all (this) it 50
became clear to the king that they would not sit on chairs.
And commanding: 'Let the finest carpets be spread upon the 51
ground,' he went to meet the theras, greeted them reverently,
took the almsbowl from the great thera Mahinda's hand and 52
led the thera into the city, as is the custom in hospitable
welcome and homage.

And the soothsayers, when they saw the seats prepared, 53
foretold: 'The earth is occupied by these (bhikkhus); they
will be lords upon the island.' Showing them honour the king 54
led the theras into the palace. There, according to their rank,
they took their seat on chairs covered with stuffs. The king 55
himself served them with rice-soup and with foods hard and
soft. And when the meal was finished, he himself sat down
at their feet and sent for Anulā, the consort of his younger 56
brother, the sub-king Mahānāga, who dwelt in the royal
palace. When the queen Anulā had come with five hundred 57
women and had bowed down and made offerings to the theras,
she stepped to one side. The thera preached the Petavatthu, 58

[1] Cf. the same construction in 10. 10. See also Mah. ed., Introd., p. liii.

[2] The Paṭhamacetiya 'the First cetiya' has not been found in the ruins of Anurādhapura. It stood, no doubt, outside the eastern gate of the city. Parker, *Ancient Ceylon*, p. 275.

[3] Namely at the spot where they had alighted from the air, and where the driver only arrived after them.

the Vimānavatthu[1] and the Sacca-saṃyutta.[2] The women attained to the first stage of sanctification.[3]

59 And many people from the city, hearing from persons who
had seen them the day before, of the virtues of the theras,
60 came together desirous to see the theras and made a great stir
at the palace-gates. When the king heard that and had been
told, on asking, (why it was so,) he said, thoughtful for their
61 welfare: 'Here there is not enough space for all these men;
let them cleanse the hall of the state-elephant, there shall
62 the townspeople be able to look upon the theras. When
they had cleansed the elephant's hall, and had adorned
it speedily with canopies and so forth, they prepared seats
63 there (for the theras), according to their rank. The great
thera went thither with the (other) theras and when he had
taken his seat, he, the eminent preacher, preached the Deva-
64 dūta-suttanta.[4] When the townspeople, who were come
together, heard it, they were filled with faith and a thousand
persons among them attained to the first stage of salvation.

65 When thus in the isle of Laṅkā the peerless thera, like unto the Master in the protection of Laṅkā, had preached the true doctrine in two places, in the speech of the island, he, the light of the island, thus brought to pass the descent of the true faith.

Here ends the fourteenth chapter, called 'The Entry into the Capital', in the Mahāvaṃsa, compiled for the serene joy and emotion of the pious.

[1] The Petavatthu and the Vimānavatthu are books of the Khuddaka-nikāya in the Sutta-piṭaka. The former contains stories of ghosts that dwell in the ghost-world, as a punishment for sins committed, the latter contains descriptions of the marvellous palaces that serve as dwellings for happy ghosts. Both texts have been edited by Edm. Hardy, *P.T.S.* 1889, 1886.

[2] See S. V, pp. 414–478.

[3] I. e. the sotāpatti. Cf. note to 1. 33.

[4] See note to 12. 29.

CHAPTER XV

THE ACCEPTANCE OF THE MAHĀVIHĀRA

WHEN they saw that the elephant's hall was also too small, 1
the people who had assembled there, full of pious zeal, prepared
seats for the theras outside the southern gate, in the pleasant 2
Nandana-garden[1] in the royal park, thickly shaded, cool and
covered with verdure. The thera went forth by the south gate 3
and seated himself there. Numbers of women of noble families
who came thither sat at the thera's feet filling the garden. 4
And to them the thera preached the Bālapaṇḍita-suttanta.[2] A 5
thousand of the women attained to the first stage of salvation.
So, there in the grove, evening fell.

Then the theras set forth saying: 'We will go hence to 6
the mountain.' And they told the king, and the king came
with all speed. Approaching the thera he said to him: 'It is 7
evening-time, and the mountain is far away; but here in the
Nandana-garden is a pleasant place to rest.' When they 8
answered: 'It is not fitting (for us) being too near the city,'
(he said): 'The Mahāmegha-park is neither too far nor
too near; pleasant (is it), and water and shade abound there; 9
may it please you to rest there! Thou must turn back, lord!'
Then the thera turned back.

The cetiya (afterwards) built on the spot where he turned 10
back, near the Kadamba-river, is called therefore Nivatta-cetiya.[3]

Southwards from Nandana the lord of chariots himself led 11
the thera to the Mahāmegha-park, at the east gate. When 12

[1] See note to 11. 2.

[2] I. e. 'the discourse of the fool and the wise man.' Probably the suttanta S. II, pp. 23-25, or perhaps A. I, 101-105.

[3] I. e. the turning-back cetiya. The thūpa was probably not far from the Paṭhamacetiya. See note to 14. 45.

the king had bidden them prepare fine beds and chairs in
fitting wise, in the pleasant royal dwelling, and had taken
13 leave of the theras, saying: 'Dwell here in comfort,' he
returned to the city, surrounded by his ministers; but the
theras sojourned there that night.

14 As soon as the morning came, the ruler of the land took
flowers and visited the theras, greeting them and offering
15 flowers in homage, and he asked them: 'Was (your) rest
pleasant? Is the garden fitting (for you)?'

'Pleasant was our rest, O great king, and the garden is fitting for ascetics.'

16 And he asked (moreover): 'Is an ārāma allowed to the
brotherhood, sir?' 'It is allowed,' replied the thera, who had
knowledge of that which is allowed and that which is not
17 allowed. And he related the accepting of the Veḷuvanārāma.[1]
When the other heard it, he rejoiced greatly and (all) the
people were pleased and joyful.

18 But the queen Anulā, who had come with five hundred women
to greet the theras, attained to the second stage of salvation.[2]
19 And the queen Anulā with her five hundred women said to
the king: 'We would fain receive the pabbajjā-ordination,
20 your Majesty.' The king said to the thera, 'Bestow ye on
them the pabbajjā!' But the thera made answer to the
king: 'It is not allowed (to us), O great king, to bestow the
21 pabbajjā on women. But in Pāṭaliputta there lives a nun,
my younger sister, known by the name Saṃghamittā. She,
22 who is ripe in experience, shall come hither bringing with her
the southern branch of the great Bodhi-tree of the king of
samaṇas, O king of men, and (bringing) also bhikkhunīs
23 renowned (for holiness); to this end send a message to the
king my father. When this therī is here she will confer the
pabbajjā upon these women.'

[1] The Veḷuvana 'Bamboo-grove' near Rājagaha was a present of the Māgadha-king Bimbisāra to the Buddha. M.V. I. 22. 17–18 (= *Vin. Piṭ.* i, p. 39, *S.B.E.* xiii, p. 143); *Jāt.* i, p. 85, 1 foll.

[2] I. e. the sakadāgāmiphala. A sakadāgāmī is one who will only once be reborn in the world of men before attaining to nibbāṇa.

'It is well,' said the king, and taking a splendid vase he 24
poured water (in token) of giving, over the hand of the thera
Mahinda with the words: 'This Mahāmegha-park do I give 25
to the brotherhood.'

As the water fell on the ground, the great earth quaked.
And the protector of the earth asked the (thera): 'Wherefore 26
does the earth quake?' And he replied: 'Because the
doctrine is (from henceforth) founded in the island.'

The noble (king)[1] offered jasmine-blossoms to the thera, 27
and the thera went to the royal dwelling and scattered eight
handfuls of blossoms about the picula-tree[2] standing[3] on the 28
south side of it. And then again the earth quaked and when
he was questioned he gave this reason: 'Already in the life- 29
time of three Buddhas there has been here a mālaka[4] for
carrying out the duties of the brotherhood, O king, and now
will it be so once more.'

Northward he went from the royal dwelling to the beautiful 30
bathing-tank, and there also the thera scattered as many
blossoms. And then again did the earth quake, and being 31
asked (the thera) gave this reason: 'This, O ruler of the earth,
will be the tank with the room for warm baths.'[5]

Then the wise (thera) went to the gateway of the same 32
king's dwelling and did homage to the spot with (the offering
of) as many flowers. And here again the earth quaked; and 33
quivering with joy the king asked the reason, and the thera
told him the reason: 'Here the south branch of the Bodhi- 34

[1] A play on the words jātimant 'of high birth' (jāti), and jāti 'the great flowered jasmine'.

[2] *Tamarix Indica.*

[3] I would prefer the reading ṭhite agreeing with picule instead of ṭhito. Certainly B 2 is the only one in the collated MSS. that has this reading, but it is supported by the Ṭīkā.

[4] Mālaka is a space marked off and usually terraced, within which sacred functions were carried out. In the Mahāvihāra (Tissārāma) at Anurādhapura there were 32 mālakas. Dīp. 14. 78; Mah. 15. 192. The sacred Bodhi-tree for instance was surrounded by a mālaka.

[5] On the jantāghara ('a bathing-place for hot sitting-baths', *S.B.E.* xiii, p. 157, n. 2) see M.V. I. 25. 12–13; C.V. V. 14. 3 foll.; VIII. 8. 1 foll.

tree of the three Buddhas[1] of our age was planted, when
35 they had brought it hither, O king, and the south branch of
the Bodhi-tree of our Tathāgata will likewise have its place on
this same spot, lord of the earth.'

36 Then the great thera went to the Mahāmucalamālaka and
37 scattered on that spot as many flowers. And then again the
earth quaked, and being questioned he told (the king) the
reason: 'The uposatha-hall of the brotherhood will be here,
O lord of the earth.'

38 Afterwards the wise thera went to the place of the Pañhambamālaka.

A ripe mango-tree, excellent in colour, fragrance and taste
39 and of large size, did the gardener offer to the king, and the
40 king offered the splendid (fruit) to the thera. The thera,
bringer of good to mankind, let the king know that he would
fain rest seated and forthwith the king had a fine carpet
41 spread. When the thera was seated the king gave him the
mango-fruit. When the thera had eaten it he gave the kernel
42 to the king to plant. The king himself planted it there and
43 over it, that it might grow, the thera washed his hands. In
that same moment a shoot sprouted forth from the kernel and
grew little by little to a tall tree bearing leaves and fruit.

44 When those who were present with the king beheld this miracle, they stood there doing homage to the thera, their hair raising on end (with amazement).

45 Now the thera scattered there eight handfuls of flowers and
then again the earth quaked. And being asked he gave the
46 reason: 'This place will be the place where many gifts shall
be distributed, which shall be given to the brotherhood, (the
bhikkhus) being assembled together, O ruler of men.'

47 And he went up to the place where (afterwards) the Catussālā[2] was, and there he scattered as many flowers, and then

[1] The three Buddhas who preceded the historical Buddha in the present age of the world (kappa, lasting many millions of years), are named Kakusandha, Koṇāgamana and Kassapa. According to the legend they all, like Gotama, visited Ceylon and the events always followed the same course. GEIGER, *Dīpavaṃsa and Mahāvaṃsa*, p. 8 foll., and Mah. 15. 57 foll.

[2] I. e. a quadrangular hall which served as a refectory for the monks.

again did the earth quake. And when the king asked the 48
reason of the earthquake the thera made answer: 'On the
occasion of the receipt of a royal park by the three former 49
Buddhas,[1] on this spot the gifts brought from all parts by
the dwellers in the island being laid down, the three Blessed
Ones and their communities accepted them. And now again 50
the Catussālā will stand here and here will be the refectory of
the brotherhood, O lord of men.'

From thence the great thera Mahinda, the friend [2] of the 51
island, knowing what was a fitting place, and what unfitting,
went to the spot where the Great thūpa [3] (afterwards) stood.

At that time there was within the enclosure of the royal 52
park a little pond called the Kakudha-pond; at its upper end,
on the brink of the water, was a level spot fitting for the 53
thūpa.

When the thera went thither they brought the king eight
baskets of campaka-flowers.[4] The king offered the campaka- 54
flowers to the thera and the thera did homage to the spot with
the campaka-flowers. And then again the earth quaked, the 55
king asked the reason of the earthquake and the thera gave
in due order the reasons for the earthquake.

'This place, O great king, which has been visited by four 56
Buddhas is worthy of a thūpa, to be a blessing and happiness
to beings.

'In our age of the world there lived first [5] the Conqueror 57
Kakusandha, a teacher versed in all truth, compassionate
toward all the world. At that time this Mahāmegha-grove 58
was known as Mahātittha; the capital called Abhaya lay east-
ward on the other side of the Kadamba-river,[6] there Abhaya 59
was king. This island then bore the name Ojadīpa.

'By (the power of) the demons pestilence arose here among 60

[1] See note to 15. 34.

[2] Dīpavaḍḍhana, lit. furtherer, increaser of the island.

[3] I. e. the Ruwanwæli-dagaba = pāli Hemamālī, see 15. 167.

[4] *Michelia Champaka*, Lin., belonging to the Magnoliaceae.

[5] Cf. 15. 91 foll., and 125 foll.

[6] I now prefer to refer Kadambanadiyā pāre to the preceding phrase, therefore Mah. ed. the comma after ahu (58 d.) should be deleted and placed after pāre (59 a).

the people. When Kakusandha, who was gifted with the ten
61 powers,[1] knew of this misery, then, to bring it to an end and
to achieve the converting of beings and progress of the doctrine in this island, he, urged on by the might of his compas-
62 sion, came through the air surrounded by forty thousand
63 (disciples) like to him,[2] and stood on the Devakūṭa-mountain.
By the power of the Saṃbuddha, O great king, the pestilence ceased then here over the whole island.

64 'Standing there, O king of men, the King of the Wise, the Great Sage, proclaimed his will: "All men in Ojadīpa shall
65 see me this day, and if they only desire to come (to me) all men shall draw near to me without trouble and speedily."

66 'When the king and the townsfolk saw the Prince of the Wise, shining and making the mountain to shine, they came swiftly thither.

67 'The people, who were going thither to bring offerings to the devatās, believed the Guide of the World with the brotherhood
68 to be (such) devatās. And when the king, greatly rejoicing had greeted the King of the Wise, had invited him to a repast
69 and had brought him into the city, the monarch then thinking: "This stately and pleasant place is fitting for the resting-place of the Prince of the Wise, with the brotherhood, and not too
70 small," made the Saṃbuddha and the brotherhood sit here on beautiful seats in a fine pavilion raised (by him).

71 'When the people in the island saw the Guide of the world with the brotherhood sitting here they brought gifts hither
72 from every side. And the king served the Guide of the World, together with the brotherhood with his own food, both hard and soft, and with such (foods) as were brought by sundry other folk.

73 'While the Conqueror was seated, after the meal, on this very spot,[3] the king offered him the Mahātitthaka-garden as a
74 precious gift. When the Mahātitthaka-grove, gay with

[1] See note to 3. 6.

[2] Tādī, i.e. like him, blessed like (the Buddha) himself; by extension, a synonym of arahā. Cf. Therag. 62, 205, 206; Suttanip. 86, 957, &c.

[3] Idheva, that is, 'here, just where we now are.'

blossoms at an unwonted season, was accepted by the Buddha
the great earth quaked. And sitting even here, the Master 75
preached the doctrine; forty thousand persons attained to the
fruit of the path (of salvation).

'When the Conqueror had stayed the day through in the 76
Mahātittha-grove he went in the evening to that plot of ground
which was fitting for the place of the Bodhi-tree, and after he, sit- 77
ting there, had sunk in deep meditation the Saṃbuddha, rising
from thence again, thought, mindful of the salvation of the
island-people: "Bringing the south branch of my Bodhi-tree, 78
the sirīsa,[1] with her, the bhikkhunī Rucānandā shall come
hither with (other) bhikkhunīs."

'When the therī knew his thought[2] she forthwith took the 79
king of that country[3] with her and went to the tree. Then 80
when the therī of wondrous power had drawn a line with a
pencil of red arsenic around the south branch she took the
Bodhi-tree thus separated and set it in a golden vase, and this, 81
by her miraculous power she brought hither, O great king,
with (company of her) five hundred bhikkhunīs, surrounded by
the devatās, and she placed it, with its golden vase, in the out- 82
stretched right hand of the Saṃbuddha. The Tathāgata
received the Bodhi-branch and gave it to the king Abhaya to 83
plant; the lord of the earth planted it in the Mahātittha-
garden.

'Then the Saṃbuddha went northwards from this place, and 84
sitting in the beautiful Sirīsamālaka the Tathāgata preached 85
the true doctrine to the people. Then, O prince, the conversion
of twenty thousand living beings took place.[4] Thereupon the 86
Conqueror went yet further north to that plot of ground where
(afterwards) the Thūpārāma[5] stood, and after he, sitting there,
had sunk into meditation, the Saṃbuddha rising from thence 87
again preached the doctrine to those around him, and even at
that place did ten thousand living beings attain to the fruit of
the path (of salvation).

[1] *Acacia Sirissa.* [2] By means of her omniscience.

[3] According to the Ṭīkā king Khema of Khemavatī (in Jambudīpa). See Buddhavaṃsa (ed. MORRIS, *P.T.S.* 1882) XXIII. 8.

[4] See note to 1. 32. [5] See below, note to 17. 30.

88 'Giving his own holy drinking-vessel for the homage of the
people and leaving the bhikkhunī here with her following and
89 also his disciple Mahādeva with a thousand bhikkhus, the
90 Saṃbuddha went eastward from thence, and standing on the
place of the Ratanamāla, he delivered exhortations to the people;
then rising in the air with the brotherhood the Conqueror
returned to Jambudīpa.

91 'Second[1] in our age of the world was the Lord Koṇāgamana,
the all-knowing Teacher, compassionate toward all the world.

92 'At that time this Mahāmegha-grove was known as Mahā-
noma, the capital called Vaḍḍhamāna, lay to the south.
93 Samiddha was the name of the king of that region then. This
island then bore the name Varadīpa.

94 'At that time the misery of drought prevailed here in Vara-
dīpa. When the Conqueror Koṇāgamana knew of this misery,
95 then, to bring it to an end, and afterwards to achieve the con-
verting of beings and progress of the doctrine in this island,
96 he, urged on by the might of his compassion, came through
the air, surrounded by thirty thousand (disciples) like to him-
97 self, and stood upon the Sumanakūṭaka-mountain. By the
power of the Saṃbuddha the drought came to an end, and
from the time that the decline of the doctrine ceased rainfall
in due season now began.

98 'And standing there, O king of men, the King of the Wise,
the Great Sage, proclaimed his will: "All men in Varadīpa
99 shall see me this day, and if they only desire to come (to me)
all men shall draw near to me without trouble and speedily."

100 'When the king and the townsfolk saw the Prince of the
Wise, shining and making the mountain to shine, they came
swiftly thither.

101 'The people who were going thither to bring offerings to
the devatās believed the Guide of the World with the
102 brotherhood to be (such) devatās. And when the king,
greatly rejoicing, had greeted the King of the Wise, had
103 invited him to a repast, and had brought him to the city, the
monarch then thinking: "This stately and pleasant place is

[1] Cf. 15. 57 foll., and 15. 125 foll.

fitting for the resting-place of the Prince of the Wise with
the brotherhood and not too small," made the Sambuddha and 104
the brotherhood sit here on beautiful seats in a fine pavilion
raised (by him).

'When the people of the island saw the Guide of the World 105
with the brotherhood sitting here, they brought gifts hither
from every side. And the king served the Guide of the 106
World together with the brotherhood with his own food, both
hard and soft, and with such (foods) as were brought by
sundry other folk.

'While the Conqueror was sitting, after the meal on this 107
very spot, the king offered him the Mahānoma-garden as
a precious gift. And when the Mahānoma-grove, gay with 108
blossoms at an unwonted season, was accepted by the Buddha
the great earth quaked. And sitting even here, the Master 109
preached the doctrine; then thirty thousand persons attained
to the fruit of the path (of salvation).

'When the Conqueror had stayed the day through in the 110
Mahānoma-grove, he went in the evening to that plot of
ground where the former Bodhi-tree had stood, and after 111
he, sitting there, had sunk in deep meditation, the Sambuddha,
rising from thence again, thought, mindful of the salvation of
the island-people: "Bringing the south branch of my Bodhi- 112
tree, the udumbara [1] with her, the bhikkhunī Kantakānandā
shall come hither with (other) bhikkhunīs."

'When the therī knew his thought she forthwith took the 113
king of that region [2] with her and went to the tree. Then 114
when the therī of wondrous power had drawn a line with
a pencil of red arsenic around the south branch, she took the
Bodhi-tree thus separated, and set it in a golden vase, and 115
this, by her miraculous power, she brought hither, O great
king, with (her company of) five hundred bhikkhunīs,
surrounded by the devatās, and she placed it, with its golden 116
vase, in the outstretched right hand of the Sambuddha. The
Tathāgata received it and gave it to the king Samiddha to 117

[1] *Ficus glomerata.*

[2] According to the Ṭīkā king Sobhana (Buddhavaṃsa XXIV. 16: Sobha) in the city Sobhavatī.

plant; the lord of the earth planted it there in the Mahānoma garden.

118 'Then the Saṃbuddha went northward from the Sirīsamāla and preached the doctrine to the people, sitting in the Nāga-
119 mālaka. When they heard the preaching of the doctrine, O king, the conversion of twenty thousand living beings took
120 place. When he had gone yet further northward to the place where the former Buddha had sat, and after he, sitting there,
121 had sunk into meditation, the Saṃbuddha, rising from thence again, preached the doctrine to those around him, and even at that place did ten thousand living beings attain to the fruit of the path (of salvation).

122 'Giving his girdle as a relic for the homage of the people,
123 and leaving the bhikkhuṇī here with her following and also his disciple Mahāsumba with a thousand bhikkhus, the Saṃ-
124 buddha, standing on this side of the Ratanamāla in the Sudassanamāla, delivered exhortations to the people; then rising with the brotherhood into the air, the Conqueror returned to Jambudīpa.

125 'Third [1] in our age of the world was the Conqueror of the Kassapa clan, the all-knowing Teacher, compassionate toward the whole world.

126 'The Mahāmegha-grove was called (at that time) Mahāsā-
127 gara; the capital, named Visāla, lay toward the West. Jayanta was the name of the king of that region then, and this isle bore then the name of Maṇḍadīpa.

128 'At that time a hideous and life-destroying war had broken
129 out between king Jayanta and his younger royal brother. When Kassapa, gifted with the ten powers,[2] the Sage, full of compassion, knew how great was the wretchedness caused to
130 beings by this war, then, to bring it to an end and afterwards to achieve the converting of beings and progress of the doctrine
131 in this island, he, urged on by the might of his compassion, came through the air surrounded by twenty thousand (disciples) like to himself, and he stood on the Subhakūṭa-mountain.

132 'Standing there, O king of men, the King of the Wise, the Great Sage, proclaimed his will: "All men in Maṇḍadīpa

[1] Cf. 15. 57 foll., and 91 foll.

[2] See note to 3. 6.

shall see me this day; and if they only desire to come (to me) 133
all men shall draw near to me without trouble and speedily."

'When the king and the townsfolk saw the Prince of the 134
Wise, shining and making the mountain to shine, they came
swiftly thither. The many people who were coming to the 135
mountain bringing offerings to the devatās, that their own
side might win the victory, believed the Guide of the World 136
with the brotherhood to be (such) devatās; and the king and
the prince amazed, halted in their battle. When the king, 137
greatly rejoicing, had greeted the King of the Wise, had
invited him to a repast and had brought him to the city, the
monarch then thinking: "This stately and pleasant place is 138
fitting for the resting-place of the King of the Wise with the
brotherhood and not too small," made the Saṃbuddha and 139
the brotherhood sit here on beautiful seats in a fine pavilion
raised (by him).

'When the people of the island saw the Guide of the World 140
with the brotherhood sitting here, they brought gifts hither
from every side. And the king served the Guide of the 141
World together with the brotherhood with his own food, both
hard and soft, and with such (foods) as were brought by sundry
other folk.

'While the Conqueror was sitting, after the meal, on this 142
very spot, the king offered him the Mahāsāgara-garden as
a precious gift. And when the Mahāsāgara-grove, gay with 143
blossoms at an unwonted season, was accepted by the Buddha,
the great earth quaked. And sitting even here, the Master 144
preached the doctrine; then twenty thousand persons attained
to the fruit of the path (of salvation).

'When the Blessed One had stayed the day through in the 145
Mahāsāgara-grove, he went in the evening to that plot of
ground where the former Bodhi-trees had stood, and after he, 146
sitting there, had sunk into deep meditation, the Saṃbuddha,
rising from thence again, thought, mindful of the salvation of
the island-people; "Bringing the south branch of my Bodhi- 147
tree, the nigrodha,[1] with her, the bhikkhunī Sudhammā shall
come now with (other) bhikkhunīs."

[1] *Ficus Indica*, the banyan-tree.

148 'When the therī knew his thought she forthwith took the
149 king[1] of that region with her and went to the tree. Then
when the therī of wondrous power had drawn a line with
a pencil of red arsenic around the south branch, she took the
150 Bodhi-branch thus separated and set it in a golden vase, and
this, by her miraculous power, she brought hither, O great king,
with (her company of) five hundred bhikkhunīs, surrounded by
151 the devatās; and she placed it with its golden vase, in the
out-stretched right hand of the Sambuddha; the Tathāgata
152 received it and gave it to the king Jayanta to plant; the
lord of the earth planted it there in the Mahāsāgara-garden.
153 'Then the Buddha went northward from the Nāgamālaka
and preached the doctrine to the people seated in the Asoka-
154 mālaka. When they heard the preaching of the doctrine,
O ruler of men, even there the conversion of four thousand
155 living beings took place. When he had then gone yet further
northward to the place where the former Buddhas had sat,
and after he, sitting there, had sunk into meditation, the
156 Sambuddha, rising from thence again, preached the doctrine
to those around him; and even in that place did ten thousand
living beings attain to the fruit of the path (of salvation).
157 'Giving his rain-cloak as a relic for the homage of the people,
158 and leaving the bhikkhunī here with her following, and also
his disciple Sabbananda with a thousand bhikkhus, he, stand-
159 ing on this side of the river (and) of the Sudassanamāla in
the Somanassamālaka, delivered exhortations to the people;
then rising with the brotherhood into the air, the Conqueror
returned to Jambudīpa.
160 'Fourth in our age of the world lived the Conqueror
Gotama, the teacher, knowing the whole truth, compassionate
161 toward the whole world. When he came hither the first time
he drove forth the yakkhas, when he came hither again the
162 second time he subdued the nāgas. When, besought by the
nāga Maṇiakkhi in Kalyāṇī, he returned the third time, he took
163 his meal there with the brotherhood; and when he had taken

[1] According to the Ṭīkā king Kikī in the city of Bārāṇasī (Benares). See Buddhavaṃsa XXV. 33; Therīgāthā, Comm. (Paramatthadīpanī V), p. 17^{27}, &c.

his ease [1] in the place where the former Bodhi-trees had stood and in the place here appointed for the thūpa and (also) in the place (appointed for the guarding) of those (things) used
by him (and left as) relics,[2] and when he had gone to this 164
side of the place where the former Buddhas had stood, the great Sage, the Light of the World, since there were then no
human beings in Laṅkādīpa, uttered exhortations to the host 165
of devatās, dwelling in the island, and to the nāgas; then rising into the air with the brotherhood the Conqueror returned to Jambudīpa.

'Thus was this place, O king, visited by four Buddhas; on 166
this spot, O great king, will the thūpa stand hereafter, with 167
the relic-chamber for a doṇa [3] of the relics of the Buddha's body; (it will be) a hundred and twenty cubits [4] high and (will be) known by the name Hemamālī.'

Then said the ruler of the earth: 'I myself will build it.' 168
'For thee, O king, are many other tasks to fulfil here. Do 169
thou carry them out; but one descended from thee shall build this (thūpa). A son of thy brother [5] the vice-regent
Mahānāma, one named Yaṭṭhālāyakatissa, will hereafter be 170
king, his son will be the king named Goṭhābhaya; his son 171
will be (the king) named Kākavaṇṇatissa; this king's son,
O king, will be the great king named Abhaya, renowned under 172
the title Duṭṭhagāmaṇi: he, great in glory, wondrous power and prowess, will build the thūpa here.'

Thus spoke the thera, and because of the thera's words the 173

[1] Lit. 'when he had enjoyed by sitting down (in meditation) the place, &c.'

[2] Cf. 15, 88. 122, 157. Paribhogadhātu is a relic consisting of something used by the dead Saint, in opposition to sarīradhātu 'body-relic', i. e. remains of his body.

[3] A certain measure of capacity. See CHILDERS, *P.D.*, s. v.

[4] According to the Abhidhānappadīpikā a ratana or hattha is equal to 2 vidatthi (= 8½–9 inches). See RHYS DAVIDS, *Ancient Coins and Measures of Ceylon*, p. 15. The total height of the thūpa would accordingly be nearly 180 feet. This is exactly the height of the *main body* of the Ruwanwæli-dagaba without the 'tee'. SMITHER, *Architectural Remains, Anurādhapura*, p. 27 and Plate XXIV.

[5] Cf. 22. 1 foll.

monarch set up here a pillar of stone, whereon he inscribed these sayings.

174 And as the great and most wise thera, Mahinda of wondrous power, accepted the pleasant Mahāmegha-grove, the Tissārāma,
175 he, the unshakeable caused the earth to quake in eight places;[1]
and when going his round for alms he had entered the city
176 like unto the ocean and had taken his meal in the king's
house, he left the palace, and when, sitting there in the
Nandana-grove, he had preached to the people the sutta
177 Aggikkhandhopamā[2] and had made a thousand persons par-
takers in the fruit of the path (of sanctification) he rested
(again) in the Mahāmegha-grove.

178 When the thera had eaten on the third day in the king's
house, and sitting in the Nandana-grove had preached the
179 Āsīvisūpamā,[3] and had thereby led a thousand persons to
conversion, the thera went thence to the Tissārāma.

180 But the king, who had heard the preaching, seated himself
at the thera's feet and asked: 'Does the doctrine of the
Conqueror stand, sir?' 'Not yet, O ruler of men, only,
181 O lord of nations, when the boundaries are established[4] here
for the uposatha-ceremony and the other acts (of religion),
according to the command of the Conqueror, shall the
doctrine stand.'

182 Thus spoke the great thera, and the king answered thus:
'I will abide under the Buddha's command, thou Giver of
183 light! Therefore establish the boundaries with all speed,
taking in the city.' Thus spoke the great king and the thera
184 answered thus: 'If it be so, then do thou thyself, lord of the
earth, mark out the course of the boundary; we will establish
185 it.' 'It is well,' said the lord of the earth, and even like the
king of the gods leaving the Nandana[5] (garden) he went
forth from the Mahāmeghavanārāma into his palace.

186 When the thera on the fourth day had eaten in the king's
house, he preached, sitting in the Nandana-grove, the Ana-

[1] Cf. 15. 25, 28, 31, 33, 37, 45, 47, 55.
[2] Cf. note to 12. 34.
[3] See the note to 12. 26.
[4] Cf. note to 14. 32.
[5] Nandana or Nanda (see 31. 44) is the name of a pleasure-garden in Indra's heaven.

matagga-discourse,[1] and when he had given there a thousand 187
persons to drink of the draught of immortality, the great
thera went to the Mahāmeghavanārāma. But having com- 188
manded in the morning to beat the drum and to adorn the
splendid city and the road leading to the vihāra and all around
the vihāra, the lord of chariots came upon his car to his ārāma, 189
adorned with all his ornaments, together with his ministers
and the women of the harem, with chariots, troops and beasts 190
for riders,[2] in a mighty train.

When he had here sought out the theras and paid his
respects to these to whom respect was due, he ploughed a 191
furrow in a circle, making it to begin near the ford on the
Kadamba-river, and ended it when he (again) reached the
river.[3]

When he had assigned boundary-marks on the furrow that 192
the king had ploughed and had assigned the boundaries for
thirty-two mālakas and for the Thupārāma, the great thera 193
of lofty wisdom, then fixed the inner boundary-marks like-
wise according to custom; and thus the ruler (of his senses) 194
did on one and the same day establish all the boundaries.
The great earth quaked when the fixing of the boundaries
was completed.

When on the fifth day the thera had eaten in the king's 195
house he preached, sitting in the Nandana-grove, the Khajja-
nīya-suttanta,[4] to a great multitude of people, and when he 196

[1] Note to 12. 31.

[2] The Ṭīkā explains sayoggabalavāhano so: ettha yoggaṃ ti rathasakaṭādi, balaṃ ti senā, vāhane ti hatthiassādi. Cf 25. 1.

[3] On this verse cf. Mah. ed., p. xxxvi. The ford of the Kadamba-river from which the boundary line starts and to which it returns is called in the Ṭīkā Gaṅgalatittha. Instead of the one verse 191 the Sinhalese MSS. have, in all, twenty verses which describe how the king himself guides the plough and in which the different areas marked off are designated. The passage is a later interpolation, drawn chiefly from a Sīmākathā of the Mahāvihāra.

[4] The Khajjanīyavagga from S. III, pp. 81–104. Specially, perhaps, the Sīhasuttanta (XXII. 79) on pp. 86–91.

had given to drink of the ambrosial draught to a thousand persons there, he rested (again) in the Mahāmegha-grove.

197 When also on the sixth day the thera had eaten in the
king's house he preached, sitting in the Nandana-grove, the
198 Gomayapiṇḍī-sutta,[1] and after the wise preacher had thus
brought a thousand persons to conversion he rested (again)
in the Mahāmegha-grove.

199 When on the seventh day the thera had eaten in the
king's house he preached, sitting in the Nandana-garden, the
200 Dhammacakkappavattana-suttanta,[2] and having brought a
thousand persons to conversion he rested (again) in the
201 Mahāmegha-grove, when he, the light-giver, had in this
wise brought eight thousand five hundred persons to conversion in the space of only seven days.

202 The Nandana-grove being the place where the holy one had
made the true doctrine to shine forth, is called the Jotivana.[3]
203 And in the very first days the king commanded that a pāsāda
be built for the thera in the Tissārāma, and he had the bricks
204 of clay dried speedily with fire. The dwelling-house was
dark-coloured and therefore they named it the Kālapāsāda-pariveṇa.[4]

205 Then did he set up a building for the great Bodhi-tree, the
206 Lohapāsāda,[5] a salākā-house,[6] and a seemly refectory. He
built many pariveṇas in an excellent manner, and bathing-tanks and buildings for repose, by night and by day, and so

[1] I. e. 'the discourse on the clod of cow-dung.' S. III, p. 143 foll.

[2] Cf. note to 12. 41.

[3] I. e. 'Grove of light.'

[4] I. e. 'Cell of the black house.' On pāsāda see note to 27. 14.

[5] We have here apparently a tradition according to which the Lohapāsāda was built by Devānampiyatissa and not first erected by Duṭṭhagāmaṇi. The Ṭīkā explains the passage in this way that Duṭṭhagāmaṇi built his 'House of Bronze' when the old one had been removed.

[6] Food, given as a present to the monastery collectively, is distributed to the monks by tickets or orders called salākā ('slip' of wood, bark, &c.). The building where the distribution takes place, is the salākagga 'salākā-house.' CHILDERS, *P.D.*, s. v. salākā.

forth. The pariveṇa on the brink of the bathing-tank (which 207
was allotted) to the blameless (thera) is called the Sunhāta-
pariveṇa.[1] The pariveṇa on the spot where the excellent 208
Light of the Island used to walk up and down is called Dīgha-
caṅkamana.[2] But the pariveṇa which was built where he had 209
sat sunk in the meditation[3] that brings the highest bliss is called
from this the Phalagga-pariveṇa.[4] The (pariveṇa built there) 210
where the thera had seated himself leaning against a support
is called from this the Therāpassaya-pariveṇa.[5] The (pariveṇa 211
built) where many hosts of gods had sought him out and sat
at his feet is therefore called the Marugaṇa-pariveṇa.[6] The 212
commander of the king's troops, Dīghasandana, built a
little pāsāda for the thera with eight great pillars. This 213
famed pariveṇa, the home of renowned men,[7] is called the
Dīghasandasenāpati-pariveṇa.

The wise king, whose name contains the words 'beloved of 214
the gods', patronizing the great thera Mahinda, of spotless
mind, first built here in Laṅkā this Mahāvihāra.[8]

Here ends the fifteenth chapter, called 'The Acceptance of the Mahāvihāra', in the Mahāvaṃsa, compiled for the serene joy and emotion of the pious.

[1] I. e. the cell of him who is well-bathed or purified. The nahātapāpo 'who has washed away the evil' is Mahinda, as also is the dīpadīpo in 208.

[2] I. e. the long walk or the long hall for walking. See note to 5. 226.

[3] On the eight samāpatti, i. e. the states of trance reached by samādhi 'meditation', see KERN, *Manual*, p. 57.

[4] I. e. cell of the highest reward.

[5] I. e. cell of the thera's support.

[6] I. e. cell of the hosts of gods.

[7] On this allusion to the author of the Mahāvaṃsa, Mahānāma, see GEIGER, *Dīp. and Mah.* (English ed.), p. 41.

[8] Mahāvihāra, 'the great monastery,' is henceforth the name for the Mahāmeghavanārāma.

CHAPTER XVI

THE ACCEPTANCE OF THE CETIYAPAB-BATA-VIHĀRA

1 GOING into the city for alms and showing favour to the
people (by preaching); eating in the king's house and showing
2 favour to the king (by preaching) the thera dwelt twenty-six
days in the Mahāmegha-grove. But when, on the thirteenth
day of the bright half of the month Āsāḷha,[1] the lofty-souled
3 (thera) had eaten in the great king's house and had preached
4 (to him) the Mahappamāda-suttanta,[2] he went thence, for
he would fain have a vihāra founded on the Cetiya-mountain,[3]
departing by the east gate (he went) to the Cetiya-mountain.
5 When the king heard that the thera had gone thither he
mounted his car, and taking the two queens with him he
6 followed hard after the thera. When the theras had bathed in
the Nāgacatukka-tank[4] they stood in their due order to go
7 up to the mountain-top. Then the king stepped down from the
car and stood there respectfully greeting the theras. 'Where-
fore, O king, art thou come wearied by the heat?' they said;
8 and on the reply: 'Troubled by your departure am I come,'
the theras answered: 'We are come to spend the rain-season
9 even here,' and he who was versed in the rules[5] (of the

[1] See note to 1. 12.

[2] I.e. 'Great discourse on vigilance.' There are several suttas in S., bearing the title appamādasutta. See note to 5. 68.

[3] The later name of the Missaka-mountain, given on account of the many shrines built there. See note to 13. 14.

[4] See note to 14. 36

[5] Lit. who was versed in the khandhas, i.e. the sections of the vinaya (CHILDERS, s.v. vinayo). The vassūpanāyika khandhaka is Mahāvagga III (OLDENBERG, the *Vin. Piṭ.* i, p. 137 foll.; *S.B.E.* xiii, p. 298 foll.). During the rainy season the bhikkhus were forbidden to travel, but used to live together in a vihāra. See KERN, *Manual*, p. 80 foll., on the vassavāsa.

order), expounded to the king the chapter concerning the vassa.

When the king's nephew, the chief minister Mahāriṭṭha, 10
who stood near the king with his fifty-five elder and younger
brothers, heard this, after seeking the king's leave, they 11
received the pabbajjā that very day from the thera, and all
these wise men attained to arahantship even in the shaving-hall.[1]

When the king, on that same day, had made a beginning 12
with the work of building sixty-eight rock-cells about (the
place where) the Kantaka-cetiya (afterwards stood), he 13
returned to the city; but the theras remained in that spot,
going at the appointed time, full of compassion (for the people)
to the city to beg alms there.

When the work on the rock-cells was finished, on the full- 14
moon day of the month Āsāḷha, the king came and gave the
vihāra to the theras as a consecrated offering.

When the thera, who had passed beyond the boundaries (of 15
evil) had established the boundaries for the thirty-two
mālakas[2] and the vihāra, then did he on the very same day in
the Tumbaru-mālaka, which was marked out as the first of all, 16
confer the upasampadā on all those who were weary of the
pabbajjā.[3] And these sixty-two arahants, taking up their 17
abode during the rain-season all together on the Cetiya-
mountain, showed favour to the king (by their teaching).

And, in that the hosts of gods and men drew near with 18
reverence to him, the leader of the host (of his disciples), and
to his company that had attained to wide renown for virtue,
they heaped up great merit.

Her ends the sixteenth chapter, called 'The Acceptance of the Cetiyapabbata-vihāra', in the Mahāvaṃsa, compiled for the serene joy and emotion of the pious.

[1] Where, as is the rule at the admission of bhikkhus, their hair was shaved off.

[2] See note to 15. 29.

[3] Pabbajjāpekkhānaṃ stands for pabbajjā-upekkhānaṃ. Mahāriṭṭha and his brothers have only received the pabbajjā or first ordination a few days before (see 11), but they already long for the higher ordination, the upasampadā.

CHAPTER XVII

THE ARRIVAL OF THE RELICS

1 WHEN the great thera of lofty wisdom, after spending the
rain-season (thus), had held the pavāraṇā-ceremony,[1] on the
full-moon day of the month Kattika,[2] he spoke thus to the
2 king: 'Long is the time, O lord of men, since we have seen
the Sambuddha. We lived a life without a master. There is
3 nothing here for us to worship.' And to the question: 'Yet
hast thou not told me, sir, that the Sambuddha is passed into
nibbāṇa?' he answered: 'If we behold the relics we behold the
4 Conqueror.' 'My intention to build a thūpa is known to you.
5 I will build the thūpa, and do you discover the relics.' The
thera replied to the king: 'Take counsel with Sumana'; and
the king said to the sāmaṇera: 'Whence shall we have the
6 relics?' 'O lord of men, when thou hast commanded the
adorning of the city and the road and hast taken the uposatha-
vows upon thyself[3] together with thy company, go thou, in
7 the evening, mounted on thy state-elephant, bearing the white
parasol and attended by musicians,[4] to the Mahānāga-park.
8 There, O king, wilt thou receive relics of him who knew how
to destroy the elements of existence,'[5] so said the sāmaṇera
Sumana to the (king), glad of heart.

[1] Pavāretvā. On the pavāraṇā-ceremony at the conclusion of vassa see Mahāvagga IV. *Vin. Piṭ.*, ed. OLDENBERG, i, p. 157 foll.; *S.B.E.* xiii, p. 325 foll.

[2] See note to 1. 12.

[3] Uposathī is a synonym of uposathika. The uposatha-vows as kept by laymen consist in 'fasting and abstinence from sensual pleasures' (see CHILDERS, s.v. uposatho).

[4] The Ṭīkā explains tālāvacarasaṃhito by sabbehi tālāvacarehi sahito bherimudiṅgāditurīyahatthapurisehi parivārito.

[5] A play on the word dhātu, meaning 'element' (see KERN, *Manual*, p. 51, n. 2), and dhātu 'relic'.

And now the thera went forth from the king's house to the 9
Cetiya-mountain and summoned the sāmaṇera Sumana, bent
on holy thoughts.[1] 'Go, friend Sumana, and when thou art 10
come to the fair Pupphapura,[2] deliver to the mighty king, thy
grandfather, this charge from us: "Thy friend, O great king, 11
the great king, the friend of the gods,[3] desires, being converted
to the doctrine of the Buddha, to build a thūpa; do thou give 12
him the relics of the Sage and the alms-bowl that the Master
used, for many relics of the (Buddha's) body are with thee."
When thou hast received the alms-bowl full (of relics) go to 13
the fair city of the gods and declare to Sakka, king of the
gods, this charge from us: "The relic, the right eye-tooth of 14
the (Buddha), worthy of the adoration of the three worlds, is
with thee, O king of the gods, and the relic of the right
collar-bone. Honour thou the tooth; the collar-bone of the 15
Master do thou give away. Grow not weary of thy duty
toward the isle of Laṅkā, O lord of the gods!"'

And the sāmaṇera of wondrous power, replying: 'So be it, 16
sir,' went, that very moment, to the king Dhammāsoka and 17
found him even as he stood at the foot of a sāla-tree and
honoured the beautiful and sacred Bodhi-tree with the offerings
of the Kattika-festival.

When he had delivered the thera's charge and had accepted 18
the alms-bowl full of relics received from the king he went to
the Himalaya. When, on the Himalaya, he had set down that 19
most sacred bowl with the relics, he went to the king of
the gods and delivered the thera's charge.

Sakka, the lord of the gods, took from the Cūḷāmaṇi-cetiya[4] 20
the right collar-bone (of the Buddha) and gave it to the
sāmaṇera. Thereupon the ascetic Sumana took the relic and 21
the bowl with the relics likewise and returning to the Cetiya-
mountain he handed them to the thera.

[1] Play on the name Sumana and su-manogati. Wijesinha translates the surname 'whose mind was well-disposed to the work that was to be confided to him'. For the rendering in the Ṭīkā see Mah. ed., note on this passage.

[2] See note to 4. 31.

[3] Maruppiya, a synonym of Devānampiya.

[4] A sacred shrine supposed to be erected in the heaven of gods.

22 In the evening the king, at the head of the royal troops,
went to the Mahānāga-park, in the manner (already) told.
23 The thera put all the relics down there on the mountain, and
therefore the Missaka-mountain was called the Cetiya-
mountain.

24 When the thera had put the vessel with the relics on the
Cetiya-mountain, he took the collar-bone relic and went with
his company of disciples to the appointed place.

25 'If this is a relic of the Sage then shall my parasol bow
down, of itself, my elephant shall sink upon its knees, this
26 relic-urn, coming (toward me) with the relic shall descend
upon my head.' So thought the king, and as he thought so
27 it came to pass. And as if sprinkled with ambrosia the
monarch was full of joy, and taking (the urn) from his head
he set it on the back of the elephant.

28 Then did the elephant trumpet joyfully and the earth
quaked. And the elephant turned about and having entered
29 the fair city by the east gate, together with the theras and
the troops and vehicles, and having left it again by the south
30 gate he went to the building of the Great Sacrifice set up[1]
to the west of the spot where (afterwards) the cetiya of the
Thūpārāma[2] was; and when he had turned around on the place
31 of the Bodhi-tree he remained standing, his head turned toward
the east.

But at that time the place of the thūpa was covered with
flowering kadamba-plants and ādāri-creepers.[3]

32 When the god among men had caused this holy place, pro-
tected by the gods, to be cleared and adorned, he began forth-
33 with, in seemly wise, to take the relic down from the

[1] Evidently the mahejjāghara mentioned in 10. 90. There, as here, the Sinhalese MSS. have pabheda instead of mahejjā.

[2] The thūpa of the Thūpārāma, the erection of which is described in our passage, is situated near the southern wall of the city in the Nandana-garden. Cf. note to 1. 82.

[3] This creeper is mentioned in the Mahāvaṃsa in five places, besides the above passage: 19. 73, 33. 85, 35. 104: kadambapupphagumba; 25. 48: kadambapupphavalli; 35. 116: kadambapupphaṭhāna. For ādāri I would refer to the Skt. names of plants, ādāra and ādāribimbī.

elephant's back. But this the elephant would not suffer, and
the king asked the thera what he wished. And the other 34
answered: 'He would fain have (them) put in a place that is
equal (in height) to his back; therefore will he not suffer
them to be taken down.'

Then with lumps of dry clay that he had commanded to be 35
brought[1] straightway from the dried Abhaya-tank[2] he raised
a pile even as (high as the elephant), and when the king had 36
caused this high-standing place to be adorned in manifold
ways and had caused the relic to be taken down from the
back of the elephant, he placed it there.

(Then) having entrusted the elephant with the guarding of 37
the relic and having left him there, the king, whose heart was
set on building a thūpa for the relic, and who speedily com- 38
manded many people to make bricks, went back with his minis-
ters to the city meditating (to hold) a solemn festival for the
relic. But the great thera Mahinda went with his company of 39
disciples to the beautiful Mahāmegha-grove and rested there.

During the night the elephant paced around the place with 40
the relic; through the day he stood with the relic in the
hall on the spot (destined) for the Bodhi-tree. When the 41
monarch, obedient to the thera's wish, had built up[3] the thūpa
knee-high above that (brick-)work and had caused the (festival 42
of the) laying down of the relic to be proclaimed in that same
place, he went thither and from this region and that, from
every side a multitude assembled there.

Amid this assembly the relic rose up in the air from the 43
elephant's back, and floating in the air plain to view, at the
height of seven tālas, throwing the people into amazement, 44

[1] Read ānāpetvā, as in good MSS., instead of āṇāpetvā.

[2] See note to 10. 84.

[3] According to the MSS. cināpetvā should be read, not khanāpetvā (TURNOUR). The sense is as follows: The original brickwork, as described in v. 35, remains standing. Its surface forms the base for the relic-chamber. Round about and from this the building of the thūpa is continued knee-high (jaṅghāmatta) so as to be finished in the shape of a hemisphere, after the placing of the relic in the chamber thus formed.

it wrought that miracle of the double appearances,[1] that
caused the hair (of the beholders) to stand on end, even as (did)
45 the Buddha under the Gaṇḍamba-tree. By the rays of light
and streams of water pouring down therefrom was the whole
land of Laṅkā illumined and flooded again and again.

46 When the Conqueror lay stretched upon the couch of the
great nibbāṇa the five great resolutions were formed by him,
who was endowed with the five eyes.[2]

47 'The south branch of the great Bodhi-tree, grasped by
Asoka, being detached of itself, shall place itself in a vase.
48 When it is so placed the branch, illumining all the regions of
the world, shall put forth lovely rays of six colours from its
49 fruits and leaves. Then, rising up with the golden vase, this
delightful (tree) shall abide invisible for seven days in the
50 region of snow. My right collar-bone, if it be laid in the
Thūpārāma, shall rise in the air and perform the miracle of
51 the double appearances. If my pure relics, filling a doṇa-
measure, are laid in the Hemamālika-cetiya, that ornament of
52 Laṅkā, they shall take the form of the Buddha, and rising and
floating in the air, they shall take their place after having
wrought the miracle of the double appearances.'

53 Thus did the Tathāgata form five resolutions and therefore
54 was the miracle then wrought by the relic. Coming down
from the air it rested on the head of the monarch, and full of
55 joy the king laid it in the cetiya. So soon as the relic was
laid in the cetiya a wondrous great earthquake came to pass,
56 causing a thrill (of awe). Thus are the Buddhas incompre-
hensible, and incomprehensible is the nature of the Buddhas,
and incomprehensible is the reward of those who have faith in
the incomprehensible.

[1] This yamakaṃ pāṭihāriyaṃ is mentioned again 30. 82 (ambamūle pāṭihīraṃ) and 31. 99. The reference is to the miracle performed by the Buddha in Sāvatthī, to refute the heretical teachers (cf. Samanta-pāsādika, Oldenberg, *Vin. Piṭ.* iii, p. 332[16]). It consisted in the appearance of phenomena of opposite character in pairs, as for example, streaming forth of fire and water. This same miracle was performed by the Buddha repeatedly. (Fausböll, *Jātaka*, i, p. 77[22], 88[20].)

[2] Cf. note to 3. 1.

When the people saw the miracle they had faith in the 57
Conqueror. But the prince Mattābhaya, the king's younger
brother, who had faith in the King of Sages, begged leave of 58
the king of men and received the pabbajjā of the doctrine
with a thousand of his followers.

And from Cetāvigāma and also from Dvāramaṇḍala[1] and also 59
from Vihārabīja, even as from Gallakapīṭha and from Upatis- 60
sagāma,[2] from each of these there received gladly the pabbajjā
five hundred young men in whom faith in the Tathāgata had
been awakened.

So all these who, (coming) from within the city and with- 61
out (the city), had received the pabbajjā of the Conqueror's
doctrine now numbered thirty thousand bhikkhus.

When the ruler of the earth had completed the beautiful 62
thūpa in the Thūpārāma he caused it to be worshipped per-
petually with gifts of many jewels and so forth. The women 63
of the royal household, the nobles, ministers, townspeople, and
also all the country-folk brought each their offerings.

And here the king founded a vihāra, the thūpa of which 64
had been built before; for that reason this vihāra was known
by the name Thūpārāma.

Thus by these relics of his body the Master of the World, 65
being already passed into nibbāna, truly bestowed salvation
and bliss in abundance on mankind. How can there be dis-
course (of this, as it was) when the Conqueror yet lived?

Here ends the seventeenth chapter, called 'The Arrival of the Relics', in the Mahāvaṃsa, compiled for the serene joy and emotion of the pious.

[1] See note to 10. 1.

[2] See note to 7. 44.

CHAPTER XVIII

THE RECEIVING OF THE GREAT BODHI-TREE

1 THE monarch remembered the word spoken by the thera,
that he should send for the great Bodhi-tree and the therī,
2 and when, on a certain day during the rain-season, he was
sitting in his own city with the thera and had taken counsel
3 with his ministers he entrusted his own nephew, his minister
named Ariṭṭha, with this business.

When he had pondered (on the matter) and had sum-
4 moned him he spoke to him in these words: 'Canst thou per-
chance, my dear, go to Dhammāsoka to bring hither the great
5 Bodhi-tree and the therī Saṃghamittā?' 'I can bring them
hither, your majesty, if I be allowed, when I am come back,
to receive the pabbajjā, O most exalted!'

6 'So be it,' answered the king and sent him thence. When
he had received the command of the thera and the king and
7 had taken his leave he set forth on the second day of the
bright half of the month Assayuja,[1] and having embarked,
8 filled with zeal (for his mission) at the haven Jambukola and
having passed over the great ocean he came, by the power of
the thera's will, to the pleasant Pupphapura [2] even on the day
of his departure.

9 The queen Anulā, who, with five hundred maidens and five
10 hundred women of the royal harem had accepted the ten
precepts,[3] did (meanwhile) pious as she was, (wearing) the

[1] See note to 1. 12.

[2] See note to 4. 31.

[3] Dasasīlaṃ. These are the precepts: (1) not to kill any living being, (2) to refrain from taking the property of others, (3) not to commit adultery, (4) to avoid lying, (5) to drink no intoxicating drink, (6) only to take food at certain prescribed hours, (7) to avoid worldly amusements, (8) to use neither unguents nor ornaments, (9) not to sleep on a high or decorated bed, (10) not to accept any gold or silver. There are also frequent references to the five or eight pledges which

yellow robe, waiting for the pabbajjā, in discipline, looking for
the coming of the therī, take up her abode, leading a holy life, 11
in the pleasant nunnery built by the king in a certain part of
the city. Since the nunnery was inhabited by these lay- 12
sisters it became known in Laṅkā by the name Upāsikā-
vihāra.[1]

When the nephew Mahāriṭṭha had delivered the king's 13
message to the king Dhammāsoka he gave him (also) the thera's
message: 'The spouse of the brother of thy friend, of the 14
king (Devānaṃpiya), O thou elephant among kings, lives,
longing for the pabbajjā, constantly in stern discipline. To be- 15
stow on her the pabbajjā do thou send the bhikkhunī Saṃgha-
mittā and with her the south branch of the great Bodhi-tree.'

And the same matter, even as the thera had charged him, 16
he told the therī; the therī went to her father (Asoka) and
told him the thera's purpose.

The king said: 'How shall I, when I no longer behold thee, 17
dear one, master the grief aroused by the parting with son and
grandson?'[2]

She answered: 'Weighty is the word of my brother, O 18
great king; many are they that must receive the pabbajjā;
therefore must I depart thither.' 'The great Bodhi-trees 19
must not be injured with a knife, how then can I have a
branch!' mused the king. Then when he, following the 20
counsel of his minister Mahādeva, had invited the community
of bhikkhus and had shown them hospitality the monarch
asked: 'Shall the great Bodhi-tree be sent to Laṅkā, sirs?' 21

The thera Moggaliputta answered: 'It shall be sent thither,'
and he related to the king the five great resolutions that the 22
(Buddha) gifted with the five eyes had formed.[3]

one may take on oneself. These are the first five or eight respectively of the above series. For members of the order the third precept is more rigorous, since sexual intercourse must be avoided altogether. See note on 1. 62.

[1] I.e. 'Vihāra of the lay-sisters.'

[2] That is, from Mahinda and Sumana, the son of Saṃghamittā and Aggibrahmā (5. 170; 13. 4, &c.).

[3] See 17. 46 foll.

23 When the ruler of the earth heard this he was glad, and
when he had caused the road, seven yojanas long, leading to
the great Bodhi-tree to be carefully cleaned he adorned it in
24 manifold ways, and gold he caused to be brought to make ready
a vase. Vissakamma,[1] who appeared in the semblance of
25 a goldsmith, asked: 'How large shall I make the vase?'
Then being answered: 'Thyself deciding the size do thou
26 make it,' he took the gold, and having moulded it with his
hand he made a vase in that very moment and departed
thence.

27 When the king had received the beautiful vase measuring
nine cubits[2] around and five cubits in depth and three cubits
28 across, being eight finger-breadths thick, having the upper
edge of the size of a young elephant's trunk, being in radiancy
29 equal to the young (morning) sun; when, with his army of
four divisions[3] stretching to a length of seven yojanas and
a width of three yojanas, and with a great company of
30 bhikkhus, he had gone to the great Bodhi-tree, decked with
manifold ornaments, gleaming with various jewels and gar-
31 landed with many coloured flags;[4] when he, moreover, had
ranged his troops about (the tree), bestrewn with manifold
flowers and resounding with many kinds of music and had
32 covered it round with a tent; when in seemly wise he had
surrounded himself and the great Bodhi-tree with a thousand
great theras at the head of a great company (of bhikkhus)
and with more than a thousand princes who had been
33 anointed as king, he gazed up with folded hands at the great
Bodhi-tree.

34 Then from its south bough the branches vanished, leaving
a stump four cubits long.

[1] The God of skill; Skt. Viśvakarman.

[2] See note to 15. 16.

[3] Caturaṅginī senā, consisting of foot-soldiers, cavalry, combatants in chariots, and elephants.

[4] On the world-wide custom of decking out sacred trees with gay strips of stuff see Andrée, *Ethnogr. Parallelen und Vergleiche*, p. 58 foll. Concerning such a 'Lappenbaum' on the Terrace of the Ruwanwæli-dagaba in Anurādhapura, see Geiger, *Ceylon*, p. 181.

When the ruler of the earth saw the miracle he cried out, 35
rejoicing: 'I worship the great Bodhi-tree by bestowing
kingship (thereon),' and the monarch consecrated the great 36
Bodhi-tree as king of his great realm. When he had worshipped the great Bodhi-tree with gifts of flowers and so
forth, and had passed round it three times turning to the
left[1] and had done reverence to it at eight points[2] with 37
folded hands, he had the golden vase placed upon a seat
inlaid with gold, adorned with various gems and easy to 38
mount, reaching to the height of the bough; and when, in
order to receive the sacred branch, he had mounted upon it,
grasping a pencil of red arsenic with a golden handle he drew 39
(with this) a line about the bough and uttered the solemn
declaration:[3]

'So truly as the great Bodhi-tree shall go hence to the 40
isle of Laṅkā, and so truly as I shall stand unalterably firm
in the doctrine of the Buddha, shall this fair south branch of 41
the great Bodhi-tree, severed of itself, take its place here in
this golden vase.'

Then the great Bodhi-tree severed, of itself, at the place 42
where the line was, floating above the vase filled with fragrant
earth. Above the line first (drawn) the ruler of men drew, 43
at (a distance of) three finger-breadths, round about ten
(further) pencil-strokes. And ten strong roots springing from 44
the first and ten slender from each of the other (lines) dropped
down, forming a net.

When the king saw this miracle he uttered even there, 45
greatly gladdened, a cry of joy, and with him his followers
all around and the community of bhikkhus raised, with glad 46

[1] Tipadakkhiṇaṃ katvā, i.e. had walked round it in such a manner that the thing or person worshipped is kept on the right hand.

[2] I.e. at the four cardinal points, E., N., &c., as well as the intermediate points, NE., NW., &c.

[3] The conception of the saccakiriyā, lit. 'effect of the truth,' is hardly to be rendered in a translation. Beside the declaration it includes a wish. The saccakiriyā is always given in this form: *if* or *so truly as* such and such is the case shall such and such a thing come to pass. See CHILDERS, *P. D.*, s.v.

hearts, cries of salutation and round about was a thousandfold waving of stuffs.

47 Thus with a hundred roots the great Bodhi-tree set itself
there in the fragrant earth, converting the people to the
48 faith. Ten cubits long was the stem; five lovely branches
(were thereon), each four cubits long and (each) adorned with
49 five fruits, and on these branches were a thousand twigs.
Such was the ravishing and auspicious great Bodhi-tree.

50 At the moment that the great Bodhi-tree set itself in the
vase the earth quaked and wonders of many kinds came to
51 pass. By the resounding of the instruments of music (which
gave out sound) of themselves among gods and men, by the
ringing-out of the shout of salutation from the hosts of devas
52 and brahmas,[1] by the crash of the clouds, (the voices) of
beasts and birds, of the yakkhas and so forth and by the crash
53 of the quaking of the earth all was in one tumult. Beautiful[2]
rays of six colours going forth from the fruits and leaves of
54 the Bodhi-tree made the whole universe to shine. Then
rising in the air with the vase the great Bodhi-tree stayed
for seven days invisible in the region of the snow.

55 The king came down from his seat and sojourning there
for seven days he continually brought offerings in many ways
56 to the great Bodhi-tree. When the week was gone by all
the snow-clouds and all the rays likewise entered into the
57 great Bodhi-tree, and in the clear atmosphere the glorious
great Bodhi-tree was displayed to the whole people, planted
58 in the golden vase. Whilst wonders of many kinds came to
pass the great Bodhi-tree, plunging mankind into amazement,
descended on the earth.

59 Rejoiced by the many wonders the great king worshipped
again the great Bodhi-tree by (bestowing on it) his great
60 kingdom, and, when he had consecrated the great Bodhi-tree
unto great kingship he abode, worshipping it with divers
offerings, yet another week in that same place.

61 In the bright half of the month Assayuja on the fifteenth
uposatha-day he received the great Bodhi-tree; two weeks

[1] I.e. gods of lower and higher rank.

[2] Cf. on 53-54 the prophecy in 17. 48, 49.

after in the dark half of the month Assayuja on the four- 62
teenth-uposatha day the lord of chariots brought the great
Bodhi-tree, having placed it on a beautiful car on the same 63
day, amid offerings, to his capital; and when he had built
a beautiful hall (for it) adorned in manifold ways, and there 64
on the first day of the bright half of the month Kattika had
caused the great Bodhi-tree to be placed on the east side of
the foot of a beautiful and great sāla-tree, he allotted to it 65
day by day many offerings. But on the seventeenth day
after the receiving (of the tree) new shoots appeared on it all 66
at once; therefore, rejoicing, the lord of men once more wor-
shipped the great Bodhi-tree by bestowing kingship upon it.
When the great ruler had consecrated the great Bodhi- 67
tree unto kingship he appointed a festival of offerings in
divers forms for the great Bodhi-tree.

So it came to pass that the festival of adoration of the 68
great Bodhi-tree, vivid with gay and lovely flags, great,
brilliant and splendid, in the city of flowers, opened the hearts
of gods and men (to the faith) (even as) in the lake the sun
(opens the lotuses).[1]

Here ends the eighteenth chapter, called 'The Receiving of the Great Bodhi-tree', in the Mahāvaṃsa, compiled for the serene joy and emotion of the pious.

[1] The festival of the Bodhi-tree is compared to the sun (saraṃsā), the city of flowers, i.e. Pāṭaliputta, to the lake (saras), and the hearts of gods and men to the lotus-flowers, growing in the lake.

CHAPTER XIX

THE COMING OF THE BODHI-TREE

1 WHEN the lord of chariots had appointed to watch over the
Bodhi-tree eighteen persons[1] from royal families and eight
2 from families of ministers, and moreover eight persons from
brahman families and eight from families of traders and
persons from the cowherds likewise, and from the hyena
3 and sparrowhawk-clans,[2] (from each one man), and also from
the weavers and potters and from all the handicrafts, from
4 the nāgas and the yakkhas; when then the most exalted
prince had given them eight vessels of gold and eight of
silver,[3] and had brought the great Bodhi-tree to a ship on the
5 Ganges, and likewise the therī Saṃghamittā with eleven
bhikkhunīs, and when he had caused those among whom
6 Ariṭṭha was first to embark on that same ship, he fared forth
from the city, and passing over the Viñjhā-mountains the
prince arrived, in just one week, at Tāmalittī.[4]
7 The gods also and the nāgas and men who were worshipping
the great Bodhi-tree with the most splendid offerings, arrived
8 in just one week. The ruler of the earth, who had caused
the great Bodhi-tree to be placed on the shore of the great

[1] In devakula the word deva is evidently to be taken in the sense of 'king', and merely as a synonym of khattiya. Kula means here, as below in 30 and 31, the individual belonging to a class or craft.

[2] Taraccha (= Skt. tarakṣa) 'hyena', and kuliṅga (=Skt. kuliṅga), the name of a bird of prey, the 'fork-tailed shrike', seem here to designate certain clans or crafts. Perhaps the names have a totemistic origin. FRAZER, *Totemism*, p. 3 foll.

[3] To water the tree during the journey.

[4] The king travels by land over the Vindhyā range to the mouth of the Ganges. Here he again meets the ship carrying the Bodhi-tree and its escort. On Tāmalittī, see note to 11. 38.

ocean, worshipped it once more by (bestowing upon it) the great kingship.

When the wish-fulfiller had consecrated the great Bodhi- 9
tree as a great monarch, he then, on the first day of the
bright half of the month Maggasira,[1] commanded that the
same noble persons, eight of each (of the families) appointed 10
at the foot of the great sāla-tree to escort[2] the great Bodhi-
tree, should raise up the great Bodhi-tree; and, descending 11
there into the water till it reached his neck, he caused it to
be set down in seemly wise on the ship. When he had 12
brought the great therī with the (other) therīs on to the
ship he spoke these words to the chief minister Mahāriṭṭha:
'Three times have I worshipped the great Bodhi-tree by 13
(bestowing) kingship (upon it). Even so shall the king my
friend also worship it by (bestowing) kingship (upon it).'

When the great king had spoken thus he stood with folded 14
hands on the shore, and as he gazed after the vanishing great
Bodhi-tree he shed tears. 'Sending forth a net like rays of 15
sunshine the great Bodhi-tree of the (Buddha) gifted with the
ten powers[3] departs, alas! from hence!'

Filled with sorrow at parting from the great Bodhi-tree 16
Dhammāsoka returned weeping and lamenting to his capital.

The ship, laden with the great Bodhi-tree, fared forth into 17
the sea. A yojana around the waves of the great ocean were
stilled. Lotus-flowers of the five colours blossomed all around 18
and manifold instruments of music resounded in the air.

By many devatās many offerings were provided, and the 19
nāgas practised their magic to win the great Bodhi-tree.
The great therī Saṃghamittā, who had reached the last goal 20
of supernormal powers, taking the form of a griffin[4] terrified

[1] See note to 1. 12.

[2] Uccāretuṃ mahābodhiṃ is dependent on dinnehi. The passage is related directly to 19. 1, Mahābodhirakkhaṇatthaṃ datvāna.

[3] Cf. note to 3. 6.

[4] The supaṇṇā (Skt. suparṇa) or garuḷā (Skt. garuḍa) are mythical creatures who are imagined as winged and are always considered as the sworn foes of the nāgas. See GRÜNWEDEL, *Buddhist. Kunst in Indien*, p. 47 foll.

21 the great snakes. Terrified, the great snakes betook them to
the great therī with entreaties, and when they had escorted
the great Bodhi-tree from thence to the realm of the serpents
22 and had worshipped it for a week by (bestowing on it) the
kingship of the nāgas and by manifold offerings they brought
23 it again and set it upon the ship. And on that same day
the great Bodhi-tree arrived here [1] at Jambukola.

King Devānaṃpiyatissa, thoughtful for the welfare of the
24 world, having heard before from the sāmaṇera Sumana of its
arrival, did, from the first day of the month Maggasira on-
25 wards, being always full of zeal, cause the whole of the high-
road from the north gate even to Jambukola to be made
26 ready, awaiting the arrival of the great Bodhi-tree, and
abiding on the sea-shore, in the place where the Samudda-
paṇṇasālā [2] (afterwards) was, he, by the wondrous power of
the therī, saw the great Bodhi-tree coming.

27 The hall that was built upon that spot to make known this
miracle was known here by the name Samuddapaṇṇasālā.

28 By the power of the great thera and together with the
(other) theras the king came, with his retinue, on that same
day to Jambukola.[3]

29 Then, uttering [4] an exulting cry moved by joyous agitation
at the coming of the great Bodhi-tree, he, the splendid (king),
30 descended even neck-deep into the water; and when together
with sixteen persons [5] (of noble families) he had taken the
great Bodhi-tree upon his head, had lifted it down upon the

[1] I.e. in Ceylon.

[2] I.e. the sea-hut.

[3] In the reading of the text accepted by the Colombo Editors tadahe va mahārājā, the verb is missing from the sentence. Only the text of the Burmese MSS. tadahe vāgamā rājā yields a correct construction.

[4] Udānayaṃ. By udāna is understood an utterance, mostly in metrical form, inspired by a particularly intense emotion, whether it be joyous or sorrowful. The udāna of Devānaṃpiyatissa in the circumstances described was according to the Ṭīkā: āgato vata re dasabalassa saraṃsijālavisajjanako bodhirukkho, an exact parallel to v. 15.

[5] Kulehi. Cf. on this note to 19. 1.

shore and caused it to be set in a beautiful pavilion, the king 31
of Laṅkā worshipped it by (bestowing on it) the kingship
of Laṅkā. When he had then entrusted his own govern-
ment to the sixteen persons and he himself had taken the 32
duties of a doorkeeper, the lord of men forthwith com-
manded solemn ceremonies of many kinds to be carried out
for three days.

On the tenth day he placed the great Bodhi-tree upon 33
a beautiful car and he, the king of men, accompanying this,
the king of trees, he who had knowledge of the (right) places 34
caused it to be placed on the spot where the Eastern Monastery
(afterwards) was and commanded a morning meal for the
people together with the brotherhood. Here the great thera 35
Mahinda related fully to the king the subduing of the nāgas[1]
which had been achieved by the (Buddha) gifted with the
ten powers.

When the monarch heard this from the thera he caused 36
monuments to be raised here and there in such places as had
been frequented by the Master by resting there or in other
ways. And, moreover, when he had caused the great Bodhi- 37
tree to be set down at the entrance to the village of the
brahman Tivakka and in this and that place besides, he,
(escorting it) on the road, sprinkled with white sand, bestrewn 38
with various flowers, and adorned with planted pennons and
festoons of blossoms, bringing thereto offerings unweariedly, 39
day and night, brought the great Bodhi-tree on the fourteenth
day to the neighbourhood of the city of Anurādhapura, and 40
after, at the time when the shadows increase, he had entered
the city worthily adorned by the north gate amid offerings,
and (when he then), leaving the city again by the south gate, 41
had entered the Mahāmeghavanārāma consecrated by four
Buddhas,[2] and here had brought (the tree) to the spot worthily 42
prepared by Sumana's command, to the lovely place where
the former Bodhi-trees had stood, he, with those sixteen noble 43

[1] The reference is to the second visit of the Buddha to Ceylon, and the events related in Mah. I. 44–70.

[2] The comma after pavesiya in Mah. ed. v. 41^b should be struck out and placed after catubuddhanisevitaṃ.

persons, who were wearing royal ornaments, lifted down the great Bodhi-tree and loosed his hold to set it down.

44 Hardly had he let it leave his hands but it rose up eighty
cubits into the air, and floating thus it sent forth glorious
45 rays of six colours. Spreading over the island, reaching to
46 the Brahma-world, these lovely rays lasted till sunset. Ten
thousand persons, who were filled with faith by reason of this miracle, gaining the spiritual insight and attaining to arahantship, received here the pabbajjā.

47 When the great Bodhi-tree at sunset was come down from
(its place in the air) it stood firm on the earth under the
48 constellation Rohiṇī. Then did the earth quake. The roots
growing over the brim of the vase struck down into the earth,
49 closing in the vase. When the great Bodhi-tree had taken
its place all the people who had come together from (the country) round, worshipped it with offerings of perfumes,
50 flowers and so forth. A tremendous cloud poured forth rain,
and cool and dense mists from the snow-region surrounded
51 the great Bodhi-tree on every side. Seven days did the
great Bodhi-tree abide there, awaking faith among the people
52 invisible in the region of the snow. At the end of the week
all the clouds vanished and the great Bodhi-tree became visible and the rays of six colours.

53 The great thera Mahinda and the bhikkhuṇī Saṃghamittā
went thither with their following and the king also with his
54 following. The nobles of Kājaragāma[1] and the nobles of
Candanagāma and the Brahman Tivakka and the people too
55 who dwelt in the island came thither also by the power of the
gods, (with minds) eagerly set upon a festival of the great Bodhi-tree. Amid this great assembly, plunged into amaze-
56 ment by this miracle, there grew out of the east branch, even
as they gazed, a faultless fruit.

This having fallen off the thera took it up and gave it
57 to the king to plant. In a golden vase filled with earth
mingled with perfumes, placed on the spot where the

[1] Now Kataragama on the Menik-ganga, about ten miles north of Tissamahārāma in the province of Rohaṇa. See PARKER, *Ancient Ceylon*, p. 114 foll.

Mahāāsana (afterwards) was, the ruler planted it. And while 58
they all yet gazed, there grew, springing from it, eight shoots; and they stood there, young Bodhi-trees four cubits high.

When the king saw the young Bodhi-trees he, with senses 59
all amazed, worshipped them by the gift of a white parasol[1] and bestowed royal consecration on them.

Of the eight Bodhi-saplings one was planted at the landing- 60
place Jambukola on the spot where the great Bodhi-tree had
stood, after leaving the ship, one in the village of the 61
Brahman Tivakka, one moreover in the Thūpārāma, one in the Issarasamaṇārāma,[2] one in the Court of the First thūpa,[3]
one in the ārāma of the Cetiya-mountain, one in Kājara- 62
gāma and one in Candanagāma. But the other thirty-two 63
Bodhi-saplings which sprang[4] from four (later) fruits (were planted) in a circle, at a distance of a yojana, here and there in the vihāras.

When thus, for the salvation of the people dwelling in the 64
island, by the majesty of the Sammāsambuddha, the king of
trees, the great Bodhi-tree was planted, Anulā with her 65
following having received the pabbajjā from the therī Saṃ-
ghamittā, attained to arahantship. The prince Ariṭṭha also, 66
with a retinue of five hundred men, having received the
pabbajjā from the thera, attained to arahantship. The eight 67
(persons from the) merchant-guilds who had brought the great Bodhi-tree hither were named therefrom the 'Guild of the Bodhi-bearers'.

In the nunnery, which is known as the Upāsikāvihāra[5] 68

[1] Setacchatta, as symbol of royal rank.

[2] According to the Rasavāhinī (ed. Saraṇatissatthera, Colombo, 1901, 1899), ii. 88^{32}, situated on the dam of the Tissavāpi, now Issurumunagala, about a mile south of the Mahāvihāra in Anurādhapura.

[3] Paṭhamacetiya. See note to 14. 45.

[4] This is to be taken as meaning that on four other branches of the tree the same miracle was accomplished as already described. Thus the Ṭīkā also says: pācīnasākhato avasesāsu ca catūsu sākhāsu gahitehi itarehi pakkaphalehi jātā, sambhūtā uppannā ti attho.

[5] Cf. 18. 12.

the great therī Saṃghamittā dwelt with her company (of
69 nuns). She caused twelve buildings to be erected there, of
which three buildings were important before others; in one
70 of these great buildings she caused the mast of the ship that
had come with the great Bodhi-tree to be set up, in one the
rudder, and in one the helm,[1] from these they were named.
71 Also when other sects[2] arose these twelve buildings were
always used by the Hatthāḷhaka-bhikkhunīs.

72 The king's state-elephant that was used to wander about at
73 will[3] liked to stay on one side of the city in a cool grotto, on
the border of a Kadamba-flower-thicket, when he went to feed.
Since they knew that this place was pleasing to the elephant
74 they put up a post[4] in the same spot. One day the elephant
would not take the fodder (offered to him) and the king
questioned the thera who had converted the island as to the
75 reason. 'The elephant would fain have a thūpa built in the
76 Kadamba-flower-thicket,' the great thera told the great king.
Swiftly did the king, who was ever intent on the welfare of
his people, build a thūpa, with a relic, in that very place and
a house for the thūpa.[5]

77 The great therī Saṃghamittā, who longed for a quiet
dwelling-place, because of the too great crowding of the
78 vihāra where she dwelt, she who was mindful for the progress
of the doctrine and the good of the bhikkhunīs, the wise one
79 who desired another abode for the bhikkhunīs went (once) to
the fair cetiya-house, pleasant by its remoteness, and there she

[1] Kūpayaṭṭhi, piya, aritta. According to the Ṭīkā the three agārāni bore the names Cūlagaṇāgāra, Mahāgaṇāgāra and Sirivaḍḍhāgāra. They were afterwards designated Kupayaṭṭhiṭhapitaghara (Piyaṭhapitaghara, Arittaṭhapitaghara), 'House where the mast and so forth is set up.'

[2] The Ṭīkā names as an example the sect of the Dhammarucikas. Cf. 5. 13.

[3] The episode is to explain how the dwellers in the Upāsikāvihāra came by the name Hatthāḷhaka (i.e. 'elephant-post-nuns'), mentioned by the poet in v. 71.

[4] Āḷhaka, to tether the elephant during the night.

[5] Thūpassa gharaṃ, thūpagharaṃ, or cetiyagharaṃ, as in v. 79, 82. See Appendix, s.v. thūpa.

the skilled (in choice) of dwelling-places, the blameless, stayed the day through.

When the king came to the convent for bhikkhuṇīs to 80
salute the therī, he, hearing that she had gone thither, went
also and when he had greeted her there and talked with her 81
and had heard the wish that was the cause of her going
thither, then did he, who was skilled in (perceiving) the
desires (of others), the wise, the great monarch Devānampiya- 82
tissa, order to be erected a pleasing convent for the bhik-
khuṇīs round about the thūpa-house. Since the convent for 83
the bhikkhuṇīs was built near to the elephant-post therefore
was it known by the name Hatthāḷhaka-vihāra.

The well-beloved, the great therī Saṃghamittā of lofty 84
wisdom now took up her abode in this pleasing convent for
bhikkhuṇīs.

Bringing about in such wise the good of the dwellers in 85
Laṅkā, the progress of the doctrine, the king of trees, the
great Bodhi-tree, lasted long time on the island of Laṅkā,
in the pleasant Mahāmegha-grove, endowed with many
wondrous powers.

Here ends the nineteenth chapter, called 'The Coming of the Bodhi-tree', in the Mahāvaṃsa, compiled for the serene joy and emotion of the pious.

CHAPTER XX

THE NIBBĀṆA OF THE THERA

1 In the eighteenth year (of the reign) of king Dhammāsoka,
the great Bodhi-tree was planted in the Mahāmeghavanārāma.
2 In the twelfth year afterwards died the dear consort of the
king, Asaṃdhimittā, the faithful (believer) in the Saṃbuddha.
3 In the fourth year after this the ruler of the earth Dhammā-
soka raised the treacherous Tissarakkhā to the rank of queen.
4 In the third year thereafter this fool, in the pride of her
beauty, with the thought: 'Forsooth, the king worships
5 the great Bodhi-tree to my cost!' drawn into the power of
hate and working her own harm, caused the great Bodhi-tree
6 to perish by means of a maṇḍu-thorn.[1] In the fourth year
after did Dhammāsoka of high renown fall into the power of
mortality. These make up thirty-seven years.

7 But when king Devānaṃpiyatissa, whose delight was in
the blessing of the true doctrine, had brought to completion
8 in seemly wise his undertakings in the Mahāvihāra, on the
Cetiya-mountain and also in the Thūpārāma, he asked this
question of the thera who had converted the island, who was
9 skilled in (answering) questions: 'Sir, I would fain found
many vihāras here; whence shall I get me the relics to place
in the thūpas?'

10 'There are the relics brought hither by Sumana, with which
he filled the bowl of the Saṃbuddha and which were placed
11 here on the Cetiya-mountain, O king. Have these relics placed
on the back of an elephant and brought hither.' Thus addressed
12 by the thera he brought thus the relics hither. Founding
vihāras a yojana distant from one another he caused the relics

[1] In the Dadhivāhana-jātaka (FAUSBÖLL, *Jātaka*, ii, p. 105[1]) is related how the kernel of a mango-fruit is deprived of its germinating power by being pierced with a maṇḍu-thorn.

MAP OF ANURADHAPURA

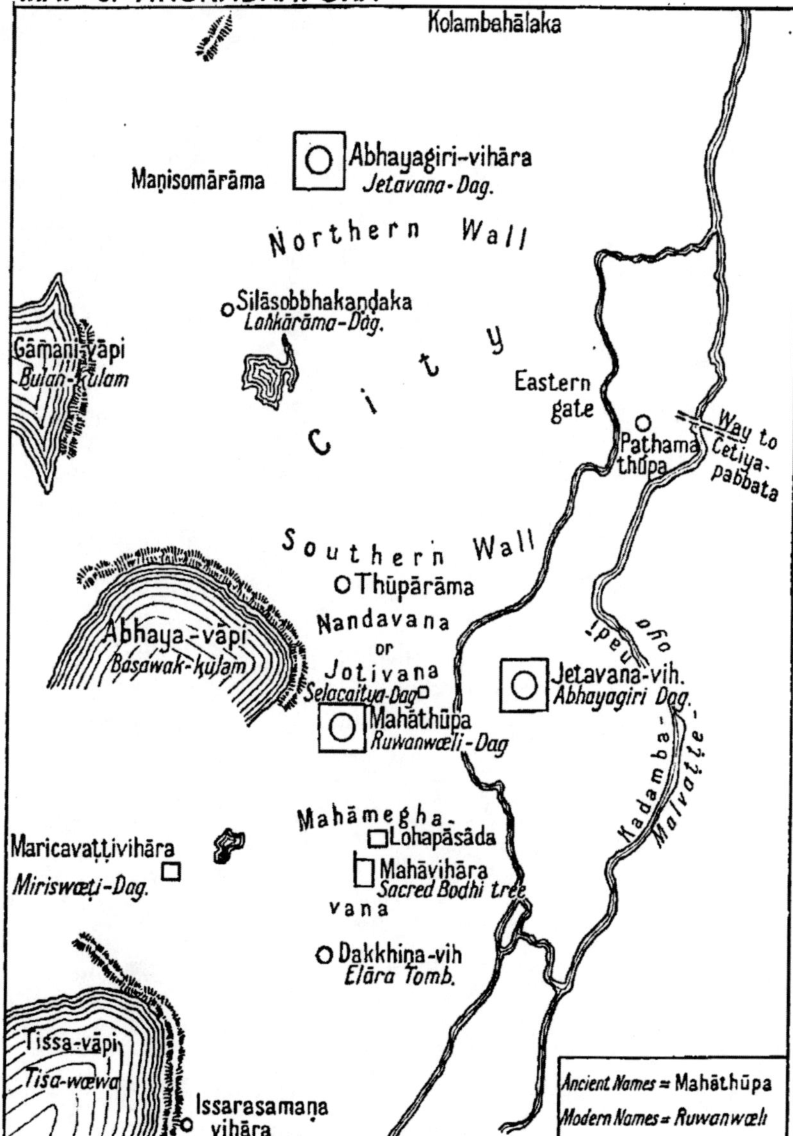

to be placed there in the thūpas, in due order. But the bowl 13
that the Saṃbuddha had used the king kept in his beautiful
palace and worshipped continually with manifold offerings.

The (vihāra that was built) in the place where the five 14
hundred nobles dwelt when they had received the pabbajjā
from the great thera,[1] was (named) Issarasamaṇaka.[2] That 15
(vihāra that was built) where five hundred vessas[3] dwelt,
when they had received the pabbajjā from the great thera,
was (called) in like manner Vessagiri. But as for the grotto 16
inhabited by the great thera Mahinda, in the vihāra built
upon the mountain,[4] it was called the 'Mahinda-grotto'.

First the Mahāvihāra,[5] then the (monastery) named Cetiya- 17
vihāra, third the beautiful Thūpārāma,[6] which the thūpa
(itself) preceded, fourth the planting of the great Bodhi-tree, 18
then fifth the (setting up) in seemly wise (of the) beautiful
stone pillar which was intended to point to the place of the
thūpa, on the place where the Great cetiya (afterwards) was, 19
and also the enshrining of the Saṃbuddha's collar-bone
relic,[7] sixth the Issarasamaṇa(vihāra), seventh the Tissa- 20
tank, eighth the Paṭhamathūpa,[8] ninth the (vihāra) called
Vessa(giri), then that pleasant (nunnery) which was known 21
as the Upāsikā(vihāra) and the (vihāra) called the Hatthāḷ-
haka, those two convents as goodly dwellings for the bhik-
khuṇīs; and (furthermore) for the accepting of food by the 22

[1] Cf. for this, 19. 66. [2] See note to 19. 61.

[3] I.e. people of the third caste (Skt. vaiśya). The Vessagiri-vihāra is situated near Anurādhapura, south of Issarasamaṇaka-vihāra, *Arch. Surv. of Ceylon*, Annual Rep. 1906 (xx. 1910), pp. 8–10; E. Müller, *Ancient Inscriptions of Ceylon*, pp. 32, 33; Wickremasinghe, *Epigraphia Zeylanica*, i, p. 10 foll.

[4] I.e. in Cetiyapabbata-vihāra on Mihintale. I would now prefer to take the words sapabbate vihāre ('in the monastery, which, or the name of which was connected with the mountain') as belonging to the relative clause yā yā &c., and to place the comma here instead of after guhā.

[5] Cf. note to 15. 214.

[6] See 17. 62–64.

[7] On this passage cf. Mah. ed., pp. xxix, xxx. On the gīvadhātu see 1. 37 foll., on the silāyūpa 15. 173.

[8] See note on 14. 45.

brotherhood of bhikkhus when they were visiting the dwell-
23 ing of the bhikkhuṇīs (called) Hatthāḷhaka(vihāra),[1] the
refectory called Mahāpāli, easy of approach, beautiful, stored
24 with all provisions and provided with service; then lavish
gifts, consisting of the needful utensils for a thousand
bhikkhus, (which things he gave) on the pavāraṇā-day, every
25 year; in Nāgadīpa the Jambukolavihāra at this landing
26 place,[2] the Tissamahāvihāra[3] and the Pācīnārāma[4]: these
works, caring for the salvation of the people of Laṅkā,
Devānampiyatissa, king of Laṅkā, rich in merit and insight,
27 caused to be carried out, even in his first year, as a friend to
virtue, and his whole life through he heaped up works of
28 merit. Our island flourished under the lordship of this king;
forty years did he hold sway as king.

29 After his death, his younger brother since there was no
son, the prince known by the name UTTIYA, held sway piously
30 as king. But the great thera, Mahinda, who had taught the
peerless doctrine of the Master, the sacred writings, the
31 precepts of righteousness and the higher perfection,[5] full

[1] The instrumental bhikkhusaṃghena belongs to the verbal noun gahaṇaṃ. Subordinate to this noun are the parallel gerunds osaritvā and gantvāna, the last being almost a pleonasm. On this subject the Ṭīkā remarks that at that time the monks in order to receive food went in order of seniority to the Hatthāḷhaka-convent. The new hall was built by Devānampiyatissa for this purpose, i.e. as refectory for the bhikkhus, separate from the nunnery.

[2] On Nāgadīpa (note to 1. 47) as the name of a district of Ceylon see 35. 124; 36. 9. On Jambukola, 11. 23, 38; 18. 7, &c.

[3] In south Ceylon, situated NE. of Hambantoṭa.

[4] I.e. 'East Monastery in Anurādhapura.' Cf. 19. 34.

[5] Pariyattiṃ paṭipattiṃ paṭivedhaṃ ca. According to the Ṭīkā pariyatti is a synonym of tipiṭaka, while paṭipatti represents the contents of the doctrines of the sacred scripture, namely, the way leading to deliverance as pointed out by the precepts of morality (Ṭīkā: pariyattisāsanassa atthabhūto sīlādikhandhattayasahito nibbāṇagāmimaggo). By paṭivedha (literally 'attainment') are meant the nine transcendental conditions (the lokuttaradhamma) which result from the observance of the paṭipatti (Ṭīkā: paṭipattisāsanassa phalabhūto navavidhalokuttaradhammo). Those nine conditions of perfection are the

excellently in the island of Laṅkā, (Mahinda) the light of
Laṅkā, the teacher of many disciples, he who, like unto the
Master, had wrought great blessing for the people, did, in 32
the eighth year of king Uttiya, while he, being sixty years
old,[1] was spending the rain season on the Cetiya-mountain,
pass, victorious over his senses, into nibbāṇa, on the eighth 33
day of the bright half of the month Assayuja. Therefore
this day received his name.

When king Uttiya heard this he went thither, stricken by 34
the dart of sorrow, and when he had paid homage to the
thera and oft and greatly had lamented (over him) he caused the 35
dead body of the thera to be laid forthwith in a golden chest
sprinkled with fragrant oil, and the well closed[2] chest to be 36
laid upon a golden, adorned bier; and when he had caused it
then to be lifted upon the bier, commanding solemn cere-
monies, he caused it to be escorted by a great multitude of 37
people,[3] that had come together from this place and that, and
by a great levy of troops; commanding due offerings (he 38
caused it to be escorted) on the adorned street to the variously
adorned capital and brought through the city in procession by
the royal highway to the Mahāvihāra. 39

When the monarch had caused the bier to be placed here
for a week in the Pañhambamālaka—with triumphal arches, 40
pennons, and flowers, and with vases filled with perfumes the
vihāra was adorned and a circle of three yojanas around, by 41
the king's decree, but the whole island was adorned in like
manner by the decree of the devas—and when the monarch 42
had commanded divers offerings throughout the week he built

four maggā 'paths' or stages of holiness, with the corresponding four phalāni 'results, effects', besides nibbāṇa as the ninth. It is, therefore, said that Mahinda had proclaimed the Buddha's doctrine and the holiness resulting therefrom.

[1] Reckoned from upasampadā-ordination onwards. Notice the play on words in vassaṃ saṭṭhivasso vasaṃ vasī.

[2] Sādhu phussitaṃ. Cf. *Jāt.* vi. 510[10]: nivāse phussitaggale 'in a safe-bolted dwelling'.

[3] I refer janoghena and baloghena to ānayitvāna in 38 c, not to kārento pūjanāvidhiṃ. This should rather stand quite independently, as does kārento sādhukīḷanaṃ in 36 d.

up, turned toward the east in the Therānambandhamālaka,
43 a funeral pyre of sweet smelling wood, leaving the (place of
the later) Great thūpa on the right, and when he had brought
44 the beautiful bier thither and caused it to be set upon the
pyre he carried out the rites of the dead.[1]

And here did he build a cetiya when he had caused the
45 relics to be gathered together. Taking the half of the relics
the monarch caused thūpas to be built on the Cetiya-mountain
46 and in all the vihāras. The place where the burial of this
sage's body had taken place is called, to do him honour,
Isibhūmaṅgaṇa.[2]

47 From that time onwards they used to bring the dead bodies of holy men from three yojanas around to this spot and there to burn them.

48 When the great therī Saṃghamittā, gifted with the great
supernormal powers and with great wisdom had fulfilled the
duties of the doctrine and had brought much blessing to the
49 people, she, being fifty-nine years old, in the ninth year of
this same king Uttiya, while she dwelt in the peaceful
50 Hatthāḷhaka-convent, passed into nibbāṇa. And for her also,
as for the thera, the king commanded supreme honours of
51 burial a week through, and the whole of Laṅkā was adorned
as for the thera.

The body of the therī laid upon a bier did he cause to be
52 brought when the week was gone by, out of the city; and to
the east of the Thūpārāma, near the Cittasālā[3] (of later
53 times) in sight of the great Bodhi-tree, on the spot pointed
out by the therī (herself), he caused the burning to take
place. And the most wise Uttiya also had a thūpa built
there.

54 The five great theras also,[4] and those theras too of whom
Ariṭṭha was the leader, and many thousand bhikkhus who
55 were freed from the āsavas, and also the twelve therīs among
whom Saṃghamittā stood highest, and many thousand bhik-

[1] Sakkāraṃ antimaṃ 'the last honours'.

[2] I.e. 'Courtyard of the sage.'

[3] I.e. 'Many-coloured hall.'

[4] Those who had come to Ceylon with Mahinda. For the following cf. 19. 66 and 19. 5.

khuṇīs who were freed from the āsavas, who, endowed with 56
great learning and deep insight had expounded the holy scripture of the Conqueror, the vinaya and the rest, fell, in time, into the power of mortality.

Ten years did king Uttiya reign; thus is mortality the 57
destroyer of the whole world.

A man who, although he knows this overmastering, over- 58
whelming, irresistible mortality, yet is not discontented with the world of existence and does not feel, in this discontent, resentment at wrong nor joy in virtue—that is the strength of the fetters of his evil delusion!—such an one is knowingly fooled.[1]

Here ends the twentieth chapter, called 'The Nibbāṇa of the Thera', in the Mahāvaṃsa, compiled for the serene joy and emotion of the pious.

[1] Wijesinha gives a wrong sense to the clause in taking it as a question. The verbs nibbindate and kurute belong to the relative sentence. The governing clause is jānaṃ pi (so) saṃmuyhati. The words tassesā atimohajālabalatā are only intelligible as a parenthesis.

CHAPTER XXI

THE FIVE KINGS

1 Uttiya's younger brother, Mahāsiva, reigned after his
2 death ten years, protecting the pious. Being devoted to the
thera Bhaddasāla, he built the noble vihāra, Nagaraṅgaṇa, in
the eastern quarter (of the city).
3 Mahāsiva's younger brother, Sūratissa, reigned after his
4 death ten years, zealously mindful of meritorious works. In
the southern quarter (of the city) he founded [1] the Nagaraṅ-
gaṇa-vihāra, in the eastern quarter the vihāra (called) Hat-
5 thikkhandha and the Goṇṇagirika(vihāra); on the Vaṅgut-
tara-mountain the (vihāra) named Pācīnapabbata and near
6 Raheraka the (vihāra) Kolambahālaka; [2] at the foot of
the Ariṭṭha(mountain) the Makulaka(vihāra), to the east [3]
the Acchagallaka(vihāra), but the Girinelavāhanaka(vihāra)
7 to the north of Kaṇḍanagara; these and other pleasing
vihāras, in number five hundred, did the lord of the earth
build on this and the further bank of the river,[4] here and
8 there in the island of Laṅkā, before and while he reigned,
during the period of sixty years, piously and justly,[5] devoted
9 to the three gems.[6] Suvaṇṇapiṇḍatissa was his name before
his reign, but he was named Sūratissa after the beginning
of the reign.
10 Two Damiḷas, Sena and Guttaka, sons of a freighter who

[1] The verb on which the accusatives in v. 4 foll. depend is *kāresi* in 8.

[2] See note to 25. 80.

[3] According to the Ṭīkā to the east of Anurādhapura near Dahegallaka.

[4] I.e. the Mahawæliganga.

[5] *Sādhukaṃ*, i.e. according to pious aims, *dhammena* without oppressing the people.

[6] See notes to 1. 62; 12. 28.

brought horses hither,[1] conquered the king Sūratissa, at the 11
head of a great army and reigned both (together) twenty-two[2]
years justly. But when ASELA had overpowered them, the
son of Muṭasiva, the ninth among his brothers, born of the 12
same mother,[3] he ruled for ten years onward from that time
in Anurādhapura.

A Damiḷa of noble descent, named EḶĀRA, who came hither 13
from the Coḷa-country[4] to seize on the kingdom, ruled when
he had overpowered king Asela, forty-four years, with even 14
justice toward friend and foe, on occasions of disputes
at law.

At the head of his bed he had a bell hung up with a long 15
rope so that those who desired a judgement at law might
ring it. The king had only one son and one daughter. 16
When once the son of the ruler was going in a car to the
Tissa-tank, he killed unintentionally a young calf lying on 17
the road with the mother cow, by driving the wheel over its
neck. The cow came and dragged at the bell in bitterness 18
of heart;[5] and the king caused his son's head to be severed
(from his body) with that same wheel.

A snake had devoured the young of a bird upon a palm- 19
tree. The hen-bird, mother of the young one, came and
rang the bell. The king caused the snake to be brought to 20
him, and when its body had been cut open and the young
bird taken out of it he caused it to be hung up upon the
tree.

[1] This is perhaps the meaning of assanāvika (lit. 'horse-seafarer'). The Sinh. Thūpavaṃsa has as-næviyakuge putvū; the Pūjāvaliya: Lak-diva-ṭa asun geṇā aśvācāri-de-bæ-kenek; the Rājāvaliya: Lak-diva-ṭa asun geṇā asuru-de-bæ-kenek.

[2] Following the reading duve dvāvīsavassāni. See the Introduction, § 8.

[3] Asela's eight brothers are enumerated in the Ṭīkā. They are named Abhaya, Devānampiyatissa, Uttiya, Mahāsiva, Mahānāga, Mattābhaya, Sūratissa, and Kīra.

[4] Southern India.

[5] Lit. 'With embittered heart.' Note the play on words in ghaṭṭesi ghaṭṭitāsayā. The Ṭīkā paraphrases the last word: puttasokena kupitacittā.

21 When the king, who was a protector of tradition, albeit
he knew not the peerless virtues of the most precious of the
22 three gems,[1] was going (once) to the Cetiya-mountain to
invite the brotherhood of bhikkhus, he caused, as he arrived
23 upon a car, with the point of the yoke on the waggon, an
injury to the thūpa of the Conqueror at a (certain) spot. The
ministers said to him: 'King, the thūpa has been injured by
24 thee.' Though this had come to pass without his intending
it, yet the king leaped from his car and flung himself down
upon the road with the words: 'Sever my head also (from
25 the trunk) with the wheel.' They answered him: 'Injury to
another does our Master in no wise allow; make thy peace
26 (with the bhikkhus) by restoring the thūpa'; and in order to
place (anew) the fifteen stones that had been broken off he
spent just fifteen thousand kahāpaṇas.[2]

27 An old woman had spread out some rice to dry it in the
sun. The heavens, pouring down rain at an unwonted season,
28 made her rice damp. She took the rice and went and dragged
at the bell. When he heard about the rain at an unwonted
29 season he dismissed the woman, and in order to decide her
cause he underwent a fast, thinking: 'A king who observes
30 justice surely obtains rain in due season.' The guardian
genius who received offerings from him, overpowered by the
fiery heat of (the penances of) the king, went and told the
31 four great kings[3] of this (matter). They took him with
them and went and told Sakka. Sakka summoned Pajjunna[4]
32 and charged him (to send) rain in due season. The guardian
genius who received his offerings told the king. From thence-
forth the heavens rained no more during the day throughout
33 his realm; only by night did the heavens give rain once every

[1] Cf. the note to 21. 8. By ratanaggassa is meant the Buddha, with whom the doctrine of the ratanattaya originates.

[2] Cf. note to 4. 13.

[3] These are the four guardians of the world, the lokapālā who usually appear near Indra in the brahmanic pantheon: Dhataraṭṭha, Virūḷhaka, Virūpakkha, and Vessavaṇa, rulers, in the above order, of the east, south, west, and north.

[4] Skt. Parjanya, the god of rain.

week, in the middle watch of the night; and even the little cisterns everywhere were full (of water).

Only because he freed himself from the guilt of walking 34
in the path of evil did this (monarch), though he had not put aside false beliefs, gain such miraculous power; how should not then an understanding man, established in pure belief, renounce here the guilt of walking in the path of evil?

Here ends the twenty-first chapter, called 'The Five Kings', in the Mahāvaṃsa, compiled for the serene joy and emotion of the pious.

CHAPTER XXII

THE BIRTH OF PRINCE GĀMAṆI

1 WHEN he had slain Eḷāra, DUṬṬHAGĀMAṆI became king.
To show clearly how this came to pass the story in due order
(of events) is this[1]:
2 King Devānampiyatissa's second brother, the vice-regent
3 named Mahānāga, was dear to his brother. The king's consort,
that foolish woman, coveted the kingship for her own son and
4 ever nursed the wish to slay the vice-regent, and while he
was making the tank called Taraccha she sent him a mango-
fruit which she had poisoned and laid uppermost among
5 (other) mango-fruits. Her little son who had gone with the
vice-regent, ate the mango-fruit, when the dish was un-
6 covered, and died therefrom. Upon this the vice-regent, with
his wives, men and horses, went, to save his life, to Rohaṇa.[2]
7 In the Yaṭṭhālaya-vihāra[3] his wife, who was with child,
8 bore a son. He gave him his brother's name.[4] Afterwards
he came to Rohaṇa and as ruler over the whole of Rohaṇa the
9 wealthy prince reigned in Mahāgāma.[5] He founded the

[1] On the insertion of the Duṭṭhagāmaṇi epic see *Dīp. and Mah.*, p. 20 (English ed.). In the Nidānakathā (*Jāt.* i. 50[8]) the story of the dream of Māyā before the birth of the Buddha is inserted with almost the same introducing words. See WINDISCH, *Buddha's Geburt und die Lehre von der Seelenwanderung*, p. 156.

[2] The south and south-east part of the island.

[3] There is certainly better authority for the form Yaṭṭhālāya. However Yaṭṭhālaya gives an appropriate meaning to the name: 'dwelling or temple of the sacrificer'. (Skt. yaṣṭar, p. yaṭṭhar and Skt. P. ālaya.) Tradition seems to identify the monastery with the Yaṭagala-vihāra to the NE. of Point de Galle. *The Ceylon National Review*, iii, p. 110.

[4] He was named (after his birthplace and Devānampiyatissa) Yaṭṭhālayakatissa.

[5] NE. of Hambantoṭa near the place where the ruins of the

Nāgamahāvihāra [1] that bore his name; he founded also many
(other) vihāras, as the Uddhakandaraka (vihāra) and so forth.
His son Yaṭṭhālayakatissa reigned after his death in that 10
same place, and in like manner also Abhaya, son of this
(last).
Goṭhābhaya's son, known by the name Kākavaṇṇatissa, 11
the prince, reigned there after his death. Vihāradevī was 12
the consort of this believing king, firm in the faith (was she),
the daughter of the king of Kalyāṇī.[2]
Now in Kalyāṇī the ruler was the king named Tissa. His 13
younger brother named Ayya-Uttika, who had roused the
wrath (of Tissa) in that he was the guilty lover of the queen,
fled thence from fear and took up his abode elsewhere. The 14
district was named after him. He sent a man wearing the 15
disguise of a bhikkhu, with a secret letter to the queen. This
man went thither, took his stand at the king's door and 16
entered the king's house with an arahant who always used to
take his meal at the palace, unnoticed by that thera. When 17
he had eaten in company with the thera, as the king was
going forth,[3] he let the letter fall to the ground when the
queen was looking.
The king turned at the (rustling) sound, and when he 18
looked down and discovered the written message he raged,
unthinking, against the thera, and in his fury he caused the 19
thera and the man to be slain and thrown into the sea.
Wroth at this the sea-gods made the sea overflow the land; 20
but the king with all speed caused his pious and beautiful
daughter named Devī to be placed in a golden vessel, whereon 21
was written 'a king's daughter', and to be launched upon
that same sea. When she had landed near to (the) Laṅkā 22

Tissamahārāma lie on the left bank of the Māgama-river. The village at the mouth of the river still bears the name Māgama.

[1] The Mahānāga-dāgaba still exists in the ruins of Mahāgāma. See PARKER, *Ancient Ceylon*, p. 324.

[2] See note to i. 63.

[3] Or 'as she (i.e. the queen) was going forth with the king', according to the reading raññā saha viniggame of the Burmese MSS.; the Ṭīkā seems also to agree with this.

(vihāra) the king Kākavaṇṇa consecrated her as queen. Therefore she received the epithet Vihāra.

23 When he had founded the Tissamahāvihāra [1] and the Citta-
lapabbata (vihāra) [2] and also the Gamiṭṭhavāli and Kūṭāli
24 (vihāra) and so forth, devoutly believing in the three gems,
he provided the brotherhood continually with the four needful
things.[3]

25 In the monastery named Koṭapabbata there lived at that time a sāmaṇera, pious in his way of life, who was ever busied with various works of merit.

26 To mount the more easily to the courtyard of the Ākāsa-
27 cetiya [4] he fixed three slabs of stone as steps. He gave (the
bhikkhus) to drink and did services to the brotherhood. Since
his body was continually wearied a grievous sickness came
28 upon him. The grateful bhikkhus, who brought him in
a litter, tended him at the Tissārāma, in the Silāpassaya-
pariveṇa.

29 Always when the self-controlled Vihāradevī had given
lavish gifts to the brotherhood in the beautifully prepared
30 royal palace, before the mid-day meal, she was used to take,
after the meal, sweet perfumes, flowers, medicines and clothing
and go to the ārāma and offer these (to the bhikkhus) according
to their dignity.

31 Now doing thus, at that time, she took her seat near the
chief thera of the community (in the vihāra) and when ex-
32 pounding the true doctrine the thera spoke thus to her: 'Thy

[1] Cf. above the note to v. 8.

[2] The ruins of the Cittalapabbata, or, in the later form, Situlpaw-vihāra lie 15 miles NE. of the Tissamahārāma near Katagamuwa. See A. JAYAWARDANA in *The Ceylon National Review*, ii, p. 23; ED. MÜLLER, *Ancient Inscriptions in Ceylon*, p. 29. The monastery is mentioned once again in 35. 81, and in the Cūlavaṃsa 45. 59 under king Dāṭhopatissa II, the first half of the seventh century A.D.

[3] See note to 3. 14.

[4] I.e. the 'Air-cetiya', which is still shown, not far from the Cittalapabbata-monastery. It is so named because it is situated on the summit of a rock. Cf. *Ceylon National Review*, ii, p. 24. See also note to 33. 68.

great happiness thou hast attained by works of merit; even
now must thou not grow weary of performing works of
merit.' But she, being thus exhorted, replied: 'What is our 33
happiness here, since we have no children? Lo, our happiness
is therefore barren!'

The thera, who, being gifted with the six (supernormal) 34
powers, foresaw that she would have children, said: 'Seek
out the sick sāmaṇera, O queen.' She went thence and said 35
to the sāmaṇera, who was near unto death: 'Utter the wish
to become my son; for that would be great happiness for us.'
And when she perceived that he would not the keen-witted 36
woman commanded, to this end, great and beautiful offerings
of flowers, and renewed her pleading.

When he was yet unwilling, she, knowing the right means, 37
gave to the brotherhood for his sake all manner of medicines
and garments and again pleaded with him. Then did he 38
desire (rebirth for himself in) the king's family, and she
caused the place to be richly adorned and taking her leave
she mounted the car and went her way. Hereupon the 39
sāmaṇera passed away, and he returned to a new life in the
womb of the queen while she was yet upon her journey;
when she perceived this she halted. She sent that message 40
to the king and returned with the king. When they two
had both fulfilled the funeral rites for the sāmaṇera they, 41
dwelling with collected minds in that very pariveṇa, ap-
pointed continually lavish gifts for the brotherhood of
bhikkhus.

And there came on the virtuous queen these longings of 42
a woman with child. (This) did she crave: that while making
a pillow for her head of a honeycomb one usabha long[1] and 43
resting on her left side in her beautiful bed, she should eat
the honey that remained when she had given twelve thousand
bhikkhus to eat of it; and then she longed to drink (the 44
water) that had served to cleanse the sword with which the

[1] A certain measure. According to Abhidhānappadīpikā = 20 yaṭṭhi ('staves') each 7 ratana ('cubits'). RHYS DAVIDS, *Ancient Coins and Measures of Ceylon*, p. 15.

head of the first warrior among king Eḷāra's warriors had
45 been struck off, (and she longed to drink it) standing on this
very head, and moreover (she longed) to adorn herself with
46 garlands of unfaded lotus-blossoms brought from the lotus-
marshes of Anurādhapura.

The queen told this to the king, and the king asked the
47 soothsayers. When the soothsayers heard it they said: 'The
queen's son, when he has vanquished the Damiḷas and built
up a united kingdom, will make the doctrine to shine forth
brightly.'

48 'Whosoever shall point out such a honeycomb, on him the
king will bestow a grace in accordance (with this service),'
49 thus did the king proclaim. A countryman who found,[1] on
the shore of the Goṭha-sea[2] a boat, which was turned upside
50 down, filled with honey, showed this to the king. The king
brought the queen thither and, in a beautifully prepared
pavilion, caused her to eat the honey as she had wished.

51 And that her other longings might also be satisfied the
king entrusted his warrior named Veḷusumana with the
52 matter. He went to Anurādhapura and became the friend
of the keeper of the king's state-horse and continually did
53 him services. When he saw that this man trusted him he,
the fearless one, laid lotus-flowers and his sword down on the
54 shore of the Kadamba-river early in the morning;[3] and
when he had led the horse out and had mounted it and had

[1] The Ṭīkā here contains a narrative, taken from the Aṭṭhakathā, of the finding of the boat; cf. *Dīp. and Mah.*, p. 37. The author of the Kamb. Mah. has versified and adopted it in his text.

[2] Goṭhasamudda (cf. 22. 85) is a designation of the sea near Ceylon. In Sinhalese the corresponding word is goḷumuhudu 'the sea not far from the land, the shallow sea' (CLOUGH, *Sinh.-Engl. Dict.*, s. v.).

[3] The Ṭīkā explains the passage thus: Anurādhapurassa uppalakkhettato gahitaṃ uppalamālaṃ ca attano khaggaratanaṃ ca gahetvā pāto va Kadambanadiyā tīraṃ netvā kassaci asaṅkito tattha ṭhapesi 'When he had taken lotus-flowers gathered from the lotus-marshes of Anurādhapura, and his own precious sword, he brought it early in the morning to the shore of the Kadamba-river and laid it there down, without being afraid of anybody'.

grasped the lotus-blossoms and the sword, he made himself known[1] and rode thence as swiftly as the horse could (go).[2]

When the king heard that he sent forth his first warrior 55
to catch him. This man mounted the horse that came second
(to the state-horse) and pursued the other.[3] He (Veḷusu- 56
mana), sitting on the horse's back, hid himself in the jungle,
drew the sword and stretched it toward his pursuer.[4] Thereby 57
was his head, as he came on, so swiftly as the horse could,
severed (from the trunk). The other took both beasts and the
head (of Eḷāra's warrior) and reached Mahāgāma in the even-
ing. And the queen satisfied her longings even as she would. 58
But the king conferred on his warrior such honours as were
in accordance (with this service).

In time the queen bore a noble son, endowed with all 59
auspicious signs,[5] and great was the rejoicing in the house of
the great monarch. By the effect of his merit there arrived 60
that very day, from this place and that, seven ships laden
with manifold gems. And in like manner, by the power of 61
his merit, an elephant of the six-tusked race[6] brought his
young one thither and left him here and went his way.
When a fisherman named Kaṇḍula saw it standing in the 62
jungle on the shore opposite the watering-place, he straight-
way told the king. The king sent his (elephant)-trainers to 63
bring the young elephant and he reared him. He was named
Kaṇḍula as he had been found by Kaṇḍula.

[1] Attānaṃ nivedayitvā as elsewhere nāmaṃ sāvayitvāna (10. 26; 33. 65).

[2] Lit. 'with the swiftness of the horse.'

[3] According to the Ṭīkā Eḷāra's man-at-arms was named Nandasārathi, his horse was called Sirigutta, the horse stolen by Veḷusumana is called Vāha.

[4] Lit. 'To him who was coming at his back or after him.'

[5] The Ṭīkā explains dhaññaṃ by paripāke gabbhe mahāpuññasampannaṃ puññatejussadaṃ ti vā attho.

[6] The chaddantā are supposed to be a particularly noble breed of elephants. Chaddanta is also a sacred lake in the Himalaya named after these elephants. Mah. 5. 27, 29. Subhūti, *Abhidhānappadīpikā-Sūci*, p. 130: Chaddanto, nāgarājā, tassa nivāsaṭṭhānasamīpattā Chaddanto saro.

64 'A ship filled with vessels of gold and so forth has arrived.' This they announced to the king. And he bade them bring (the precious things) to him.
65 As the king had invited the brotherhood of the bhikkhus, numbering twelve thousand, for the name-giving festival of his
66 son, he thought thus: 'If my son, when he has won the kingship over the whole realm of Laṅkā, shall make the doctrine of
67 the Sambuddha to shine forth (in clear brightness) then shall just one thousand and eight bhikkhus come hither and they shall wear the robe in such wise that the alms-bowl shall
68 be uppermost.[1] They shall put the right foot first inside the threshold[2] and they shall lay aside the prescribed waterpot
69 together with the umbrella (made of) one (piece).[3] A thera named Gotama shall receive my son and impart to him the confession of faith and the precepts of morality.'[4] All fell out in this manner.

[1] I.e. the alms-bowl shall not be covered by the folds of the garment. The twice repeated ca is striking. The author of the Kamb. Mahāvaṃsa also feels this; he alters ca to sa.

[2] The contrary would be an unlucky omen. This superstition still prevails among the modern Sinhalese. PARKER, *Village Folk-tales of Ceylon*, p. 14.

[3] Ekacchattayutaṃ dhammakarakaṃ nīharantu ca. My translation is based on SUBHŪTI'S interpretation (letter dated Colombo 2. I. 1911). The dhammakaraka is a pot into which the water is strained before drinking; the strainer being called parissāvana. See C.V. V. 13. 1; VI. 21. 3). 'The waterpot and the umbrella (chatta) are two principal articles used by the monks when going out.' Ekacchatta or 'single umbrella' is 'an umbrella made of leaf, having its own handle'. According to SĪLĀNANDA (letter received from H. T. de Silva, Colombo 21. I. 1911) ekacchattayutaṃ must be taken as 'provided with one handle' as an adjective belonging to dhammakarakaṃ. The waterpots are made without or with a handle or neck. In this case the neck of the waterpot would be compared to a chatta on the top of a building.

[4] WIJESIṆHA, *Mah.*, p. 87, n. 1, refers the words not to the boy but to the assembly present. He says: 'It must here be borne in mind that it is customary with the priesthood to administer the confession of faith (saraṇa) and the five precepts (pañcasīla) TO THE ASSEMBLY before the commencement of any ceremony.' But Mah. 24. 24 Gotama (cf. v. 28) is expressly designated rañño (i.e. of Duṭṭha-

When he saw all these omens the king, glad at heart, 70
bestowed rice-milk on the brotherhood; and to his son,
bringing together in one both the lordship over Mahāgāma 71
and the name of his father, he gave the name Gāmaṇi-
Abhaya.

When, on the ninth day after this, he had entered Mahā- 72
gāma, he had intercourse with the queen. She became
thereby with child. The son born in due time did the king 73
name Tissa. And both boys grew up in the midst of a great
body of retainers.

When, at the festival time of the presenting of the (first) 74
rice-foods to both (children), the king, full of pious zeal, set
rice-milk before five hundred bhikkhus, he, when the half 75
had been eaten by them, did, together with the queen, take
a little in a golden spoon and give it to them with the 76
words: 'If you, my sons, abandon the doctrine of the Saṃ-
buddha then shall this not be digested in your belly.' Both 77
princes, who understood the meaning of these words, ate the
rice-milk rejoicing as if it were ambrosia.

When they were ten and twelve years old the king, who 78
would fain put them to the test, offered hospitality in the
same way to the bhikkhus, and when he had the rice that 79
was left by them taken and placed in a dish and set before the
boys he divided it into three portions and spoke thus: 'Never, 80
dear ones, will we turn away from the bhikkhus, the guardian-
spirits of our house: with such thoughts as these eat ye this
portion here.' And furthermore: 'We two brothers will for 81
ever be without enmity one toward the other; with such
thoughts as these eat ye this portion here.' And as if it 82
were ambrosia they both ate the two portions. But when
it was said to them: 'Never will we fight with the Damiḷas;
with such thoughts eat ye this portion here,' Tissa dashed 83
the food away with his hand, but Gāmaṇi who had (in like
manner) flung away the morsel of rice, went to his bed, and 84

gāmaṇi) **sikkhāya dāyako**, with distinct reference to 22. 69. We take it then to mean that Gotama, from the very fact that he 'receives' the boy (**paṭigaṇhāti**), expresses his willingness to become his teacher in the future.

drawing in his hands and feet he lay upon his bed. The
85 queen came, and caressing Gāmaṇi spoke thus: 'Why dost
thou not lie easily upon thy bed with limbs stretched out, my
son?' 'Over there beyond the Gaṅgā[1] are the Damiḷas,
86 here on this side is the Goṭha-ocean,[2] how can I lie with out-
stretched limbs?' he answered. When the king heard his
thoughts he remained silent.

87 Growing duly Gāmaṇi came to sixteen years, vigorous, renowned, intelligent and a hero in majesty and might.

88 In this changing existence do beings indeed (only) by works of merit come to such rebirth as they desire; pondering thus the wise man will be ever filled with zeal in the heaping up of meritorious works.

Here ends the twenty-second chapter, called 'The Birth of Prince Gāmaṇi', in the Mahāvaṃsa, compiled for the serene joy and emotion of the pious.

[1] See note to 10. 44.

[2] See note to 22. 49.

CHAPTER XXIII

THE LEVYING OF THE WARRIORS

FOREMOST in strength, beauty, shape and the qualities of 1
courage and swiftness and of mighty size of body was the
elephant Kaṇḍula. Nandhimitta, Sūranimila, Mahāsoṇa, 2
Goṭhaimbara, Theraputtābhaya, Bharaṇa, and also Veḷusu-
mana, Khañjadeva, Phussadeva and Labhiyavasabha: these 3
ten were his mighty and great warriors.[1]

King Eḷāra had a general named Mitta; and he had, in 4
the village that he governed,[2] in the eastern district[3] near 5
the Citta-mountain, a (nephew, his) sister's son, named after
his uncle, whose secret parts were hidden (in his body). In 6
the years of his childhood, since he loved to creep far, they[4]
were used to bind the boy fast with a rope slung about his
body, to a great mill-stone. And since, creeping about on 7
the ground, he dragged the stone after him and in crossing
over the threshold the rope broke asunder, they called him 8
Nandhimitta. He had the strength of ten elephants. When
he was grown up he went into the city and served his uncle.
Damiḷas, who desecrated at that time thūpas and other 9
(sacred memorials), this strong man used to tear asunder,
treading one leg down with his foot while he grasped the 10
other with his hand, and then (he would) cast them out (over

[1] The story of the ten paladins of Duṭṭhagāmaṇi is treated also in the Rasavāhinī II, p. 78 foll. (Ed. by SARAṆATISSATHERA, Colombo, 1901 and 1899.)

[2] Kammantagāma, i.e. 'Village of labour' or 'activity'. 'I think the word is equivalent to the nindagama of the present day. It is a village the tenants of which are liable to render services to the landlords.' WIJESIṆHA, *Mah.*, p. 88, no. 4.

[3] Possibly the name of the village is Khaṇḍarāji. Rasav. II. 80[28] seems to bear this out.

[4] That is the boy's parents.

the walls). But the devas caused those dead bodies that he cast out to vanish.

11 When they observed the diminution of the Damiḷas they told the king; but the command 'Take him with his prey!'[1]
12 they could not carry out.[2] Nandhimitta thought: 'And if I do thus, it is but the destruction of men and brings not the
13 glory to the doctrine. In Rohaṇa[3] there are still princes who have faith in the three gems. There will I serve the
14 king, and when I have overcome all the Damiḷas and have conferred the overlordship on the princes, I shall make the doctrine of the Buddha to shine forth brightly.' Then he
15 went and told this to prince Gāmaṇi. When this latter had taken counsel with his mother he received him with honour, and with high honours the warrior Nandhimitta continued to dwell with him.

16 King Kākavaṇṇatissa caused a guard to hold the Damiḷas in check to be kept continually at all the fords of the Mahā-
17 gaṅgā. Now the king had, by another wife, a son named Dīghābhaya; and he gave the guard near the Kacchaka-
18 ford[4] into his charge. And to form the guard this (prince) commanded each noble family within a distance of two
19 yojanas round (to send) one son thither. Within the district of Koṭṭhivāla, in the village of Khaṇḍakaviṭṭhika, lived the chief of a clan the headman named Saṃgha who had seven
20 sons. To him, too, the prince sent a messenger demanding a son. His seventh son named Nimila[5] had the strength of
21 ten elephants. His six brothers who were angered at his

[1] The reading should be, without doubt, sahoḍhaṃ gaṇhathenaṃ, cf. *J.R.A.S.* 1910, p. 860; *J.P.T.S.* 1910, p. 137. Skt. sahoḍha. The Ṭīkā has hit the meaning with the paraphrase sabhaṇḍakaṃ. The Rasavāh. II, p. 80[15] makes the characteristic alteration to sahasā gaṇhathenaṃ, a proof that the phrase was no longer understood in its original sense but had fallen into a stereotyped use. Cf. also *Jāt.* iii. 59[10].

[2] Since they did not succeed in finding out the doer of the deed.

[3] See note to 22. 6. [4] See note to 10. 58.

[5] Rasavāhinī: Nimmala or Surānimmala. The first part of the latter name is derived from surā 'spirituous liquor', and must (according to II, p. 84[1-2]) refer to the drinking prowess of the hero.

bent toward idleness, wished that he might go, but not so his
mother and his father. Wroth with his other brothers he 22
went, in the early morning, a distance of three yojanas, and
sought out the prince even at sunrise. And he, to put him 23
to the test, entrusted him with a far errand: 'Near the
Cetiya-mountain in the village of Dvāramaṇḍala is a brahman 24
named Kuṇḍalī, my friend. In his possession is merchandise
from over-seas.[1] Go thou to him and bring hither the 25
merchandise that he gives thee.' When he had thus spoken
to him and had offered him a meal he sent him forth with a
letter. He travelled, yet in the forenoon, nine yojanas from 26
that place hither[2] toward Anurādhapura and sought out the
brahman. 'When thou hast bathed in the tank, my dear, 27
come to me,' said the brahman. As he had never yet come
to this place[3] he bathed in the Tissa-tank, and when he had 28
done reverence to the great Bodhi-tree and the cetiya in
the Thūpārāma he went into the city; when he had (then)
seen the whole city and had bought perfumes in the bazaar, 29
had gone forth again by the north gate and had brought
lotus-blossoms from the lotus-field he sought out the brahman, 30
and questioned by him he told him of his wayfaring. When
the brahman heard of his first march[4] and of his march
hither[5] he thought, full of amazement: 'This is a man of 31
noble race; if Eḷāra hears of him he will get him into his
power. Therefore must he not dwell near the Damiḷas, he must 32
rather take up his abode with the prince's father.' When 33
he had written in the same sense he gave the written message
into his hands, and giving him Puṇṇavaḍḍhana-garments[6]

[1] The reading samuddapārabhaṇḍāni, in a Sinhalese MS., is only a conjecture, but is probably the correct reading.

[2] Here, as frequently, taking the standpoint of the author, who lives in Anurādhapura.

[3] I.e. to Anurādhapura.

[4] I.e. the distance covered in the morning from Kacchakatittha to Dvāramaṇḍala.

[5] That is, to Anurādhapura and from there back to Dvāramaṇḍala.

[6] Ṭīkā: anagghāni evaṃnāmikāni vatthayugānīti 'precious pairs of garments bearing that name'.

34 and many gifts (to take with him), and having fed him he sent
him (back) to his friend. He came to the prince at the time
35 that the shadows grow longer and delivered up to the king's
son the letter and the gifts. Then rejoicing (the prince)
said: 'Honour this man with a thousand (pieces of money).'
36 The other servitors of the prince grew envious, then ordered
37 he to honour the youth with ten thousand (pieces). And
when (according to his charge) they had cut his hair and
bathed him in the river, and had put on him a pair of
Puṇṇavaḍḍhana-garments and a beautiful fragrant wreath,
38 and had wound a silken turban about his head, they brought
him to the prince,[1] and the latter commanded that food from
39 his own stores be given him. Moreover, the prince bade them
give his own bed worth ten thousand (pieces of money) to the
40 warrior as a couch. He gathered all these together and took
them to his mother and father and gave the ten thousand
(pieces of money) to his mother and the bed to his father.
41 The same night he came and appeared at the place of the
guard. When the prince heard this in the morning he was
42 glad at heart. When he had given him provision for the
journey and an escort and had bestowed on him (as a gift) ten
43 thousand (pieces of money) he sent him to his father. The
warrior brought the ten thousand to his mother and father,
gave it to them and went into the presence of king
44 Kākavaṇṇatissa. The king gave him (into the service of) the
prince Gāmaṇi, and with high honours the warrior Sūranimila
took up his abode with him.

45 In the Kuḷumbari-district[2] in the village Hundarīvāpi
46 lived Tissa's eighth son named Soṇa. At the time when he
was seven years old he tore up young palms; at the time
when he was ten years old the strong (boy) tore up great

[1] Veṭhayitvā, a verb common to both and governing the accusative, must be supplied to punnavaddhanayugaṃ and gandhamālaṃ.

[2] Kuḷumbarikaṇṇikāya; cf. Nakulanagakaṇṇikāyaṃ, Mah. 23. 77; Kālāyanakaṇṇikamhi, Mah. 34. 89; and Huvācakaṇṇike, Mah. 34. 90. Rasav. II. 86[19] reads Kadaḷumbarikannikāya.

palm-trees. In time Mahāsoṇa became as strong as ten 47
elephants. When the king heard that he was such a man he
took him from his father and gave him into the service of 48
the prince Gāmaṇi that he might maintain him. Receiving
honourable guerdon from him, the warrior took up his abode
with him.

In the region named Giri, in the village Niṭṭhulaviṭṭhika, 49
there lived a son of Mahānāga strong as ten elephants. By 50
reason of his dwarfish stature he was named Goṭhaka; his six
elder brothers made a merry jest of him. Once when they 51
had gone forth and were clearing the forest to lay out a bean-
field they left his share and came back and told him. Then 52
forthwith he started out, and when he had torn up the trees
called imbara and had levelled the ground he came and told
(them). His brothers went and when they had seen his 53
amazing work they returned to him praising his work.[1]
Because of this he bore the name Goṭhaimbara, and him 54
too, in like manner, the king commanded to stay with
Gāmaṇi.

A householder named Rohaṇa, who was headman in the 55
village of Kitti near the Koṭa-mountain, gave to the son who
was born to him the name of the king Goṭhābhaya.[2] At the 56
age of ten to twelve years the boy was so strong that in his 57
play he threw like balls for playing stones that could not be
lifted by four or five men. When he was sixteen years old 58
his father made him a club thirty-eight inches round and
sixteen cubits long. When, with this, he smote the stems 59
of palmyra or coco-palms, he felled them. Therefore was
he known as a warrior. And him, too, did the king in like 60
manner command to stay with Gāmaṇi. But his father was
a supporter of the thera Mahāsumma. Once when this house- 61
holder was hearing a discourse of Mahāsumma in the Koṭa-
pabbata-vihāra he attained to the fruition of (the first stage of

[1] The Rasav. II. 88 foll. tells yet another story of Goṭhaimbara, that he subdued a yakkha named Jayasena and then went among the monks. The 'dwellers in the Uttaravihāra' are mentioned as the source of this story.

[2] Samānanāmaṃ kāresi, lit. 'made of him of like name with . . .

62 salvation called) sotāpatti. With heart strongly moved[1] he
told this to the king, and when he had given over (the headship
of) his house to his son he received the pabbajjā from the
63 thera. Given up to the practice of meditation he attained
to the state of an arahant. Therefore his son was called
Theraputtābhaya.[2]

64 In the village of Kappakandara[3] a son of Kumāra[4] lived
named Bharaṇa. In time, when he was ten to twelve years
65 old, he went with the boys into the forest and chased many
hares; he struck at them with his foot and dashed them,
66 (smitten) in twain, to the ground. Then when he, at the age
of sixteen years, went with the village-folk into the forest
67 he killed antelopes, elks, and boars in like manner. Therefore
was Bharaṇa known as a great warrior. And him did the
king in like manner command to stay with Gāmaṇi.

68 In the district called Giri, in the village of Kuṭumbiyaṅ-
gaṇa there dwelt, held in honour (by the people) there, a house-
69 holder named Vasabha. His fellow-countrymen Veḷa and
Sumana, governor of Giri, came when a son was born to their
70 friend, bringing gifts, and both gave their name to the boy.
When he was grown up the governor of Giri had him to dwell
71 in his house. He had a Sindhu-horse[5] that would let no man
mount him. When he saw Veḷusumana he thought: 'Here
72 is a rider worthy of me,' and he neighed joyfully. When the
governor perceived this he said to him: 'Mount the horse.'
73 Then he mounted the horse and made him gallop in a circle;
and the animal appeared even as one single horse around the
74 whole circle, and he sat on the back of the courser seeming

[1] **Jātasaṃvego**, the conception of **saṃvega** is the negative side to the positive **pasāda**. See note to 1. 4.

[2] I.e. Abhaya, the son of the thera. The Rasav. II. 94^{7} foll. states that the son was already a sāmaṇera, then relates a story from which it appears that in strength he was even superior to Goṭhaimbara.

[3] A river of this name in Rohaṇa is also mentioned, Mah. 24. 22, besides a monastery, Rasav. II. 88^{11}, 94^{12}.

[4] Thus Rasav. II. 96^{28}: **Kumāro nāmeko kuṭumbiko.**

[5] Skt. **saindhava** 'horse from the Indus country', an excellent breed much prized in Indian literature.

to be a chain of men[1] and he loosed his mantle and girt it
about him again and again fearlessly. When the bystanders 75
saw this they broke into applauding shouts. The governor
of Giri gave him ten thousand (pieces of money) and thinking:
'he is fit for the king,' he gave him joyfully into the king's 76
service. The king made Veḷusumana dwell near him, giving 77
him honourable guerdon and favouring him greatly.

In the district of Nakulanaga in the village of Mahisa-
doṇika there lived Abhaya's last son, named Deva, endowed 78
with great strength. Since he limped a little they called him
Khañjadeva. When he went a-hunting with the village-folk, 79
he chased at those times great buffaloes, as many as rose up,
and grasped them by the leg with his hand, and when he had 80
whirled them round his head the young man dashed them to
the ground breaking their bones. When the king heard this 81
matter, having sent for Khañjadeva, he commanded him to
stay with Gāmaṇi.

Near the Cittalapabbata (vihāra)[2] in the village named 82
Gaviṭa there lived Uppala's son named Phussadeva. When 83
he went once as a boy to the vihāra with the (other) boys
he took one of the shells offered to the bodhi-tree and blew it
mightily. Powerful even as the roar at the bursting asunder 84
of a thunderbolt was his tone, and all the other boys, terrified,
were as if stunned. Therefore he was known by the name 85
Ummādaphussadeva. His father made him learn the archer's
art handed down in the family, and he was one of those who 86
hit their mark (guided) by sound, who hit by (the light of
the) lightning, and who hit a hair. A waggon laden with
sand and a hundred skins bound one upon another, a slab of 87
asana or udumbara-wood[3] eight or sixteen inches thick, or

[1] The Ṭīkā (see Mah. ed. note on this passage) explains vassa-hāraṃ va by 'like an unbroken row of men holding together'. Vassa presupposes a Skt. varṣan related to Skt. vṛṣan. The neuter gender in hāra 'string of pearls', is striking. Cf. the Greek legend of Alexander's horse Bukephalos.

[2] See Mah. 22. 23 (with note); Rasav. II. 101².

[3] Skt. asana, *Terminalia tomentosa* and udumbara, *Ficus glomerata*.

88 one of iron or copper two or four inches thick he shot
through with the arrow; an arrow shot forth by him flew
89 eight usabhas[1] over the land but one usabha through the
water. When the great king heard this thing he had him
taken away from his father and commanded him to stay
with Gāmaṇi.

90 Near the Tulādhāra-mountain in the village of Vihāravāpi
91 lived a son of the householder Matta, named Vasabha. Since
his body was nobly formed they called him Labhiyavasabha.
At the age of twenty years he was gifted with great bodily
92 strength. Taking some men with him he began, since he
would fain have some fields, (to make) a tank. Making it he,
93 being endowed with great strength, flung away masses of earth
such as only ten or twelve men had moved else, and thus in
94 a short time he finished the tank. And thereby he gained
renown, and him too did the king summon and, allotting him
honourable guerdon, he appointed him to (the service of)
95 Gāmaṇi. That field was known as Vasabha's Dam.[2] So
Labhiyavasabha abode near Gāmaṇi.

96 On these ten great warriors did the king henceforth confer
97 honours like to the honours conferred on his own son. Then
summoning the ten great warriors the king charged them:
98 'Each one find ten warriors.' They brought thither warriors
in this way and again the king commanded these hundred
99 warriors to levy (others) in like manner. They too brought
thither warriors in this way and these thousand warriors did
the king again command to levy (others) in like manner.
100 They also brought warriors thither. And they, reckoned
altogether, were then eleven thousand one hundred and ten
warriors.

101 They all continually received honourable guerdon from the
ruler of the land and abode surrounding the prince Gāmaṇi.

102 Thus when a wise man, mindful of his salvation, hears of

[1] See note to 22. 42.

[2] The Rasav. 11. 103 135 says: Kākavaṇṇatissamahārājā taṃ ānāpetva mahantaṃ sakkāraṃ katvā udakavāragāmaṃ tass' eva dāpesi; tato paṭṭhāya so Vasabhodakavāro ti pākaṭo ahosi.

the marvels wrought by the pious life, he should surely, turning aside from the evil path, evermore find pleasure in the path of piety.

Here ends the twenty-third chapter, called 'The Levying of the Warriors', in the Mahāvaṃsa, compiled for the serene joy and emotion of the pious.

CHAPTER XXIV

THE WAR OF THE TWO BROTHERS

1 SKILLED in (guiding) elephants and horses, and in (bearing) the sword and versed in archery[1] did the prince Gāmaṇi dwell
2 thenceforth in Mahāgāma. The prince Tissa, equipped with troops and chariots did the king cause to be stationed in
3 Dīghavāpi[2] in order to guard the open country. Afterwards prince Gāmaṇi, reviewing his host, sent to announce to his
4 father the king: 'I will make war upon the Damiḷas.' The king, to protect him, forbade him, saying: 'The region on this side of the river[3] is enough.' Even to three times he
5 sent to announce the same (reply). 'If my father were a man he would not speak thus: therefore shall he put this on.'
6 And therewith Gāmaṇi sent him a woman's ornament. And enraged at him the king said: 'Make a golden chain! with that will I bind him, for else he cannot be protected.'

7 Then the other fled and went, angered at his father, to Malaya,[4] and because he was wroth with his father they named him Duṭṭhagāmaṇi.[5]

8 Then the king began to build the Mahānuggala-cetiya. When the cetiya was finished the monarch summoned the
9 brotherhood. Twelve thousand bhikkhus from the Cittalapab-

[1] I believe that upāsana in katupāsana must be taken in the sense of 'archery', which is borne out by Abhidh. 390. The Ṭīkā, it is true, explains katupāsano, in a general way, by katasikkho, dassitasippo.

[2] See note to 1. 78.

[3] Cf. the note to 10. 44. The Mahāgaṅgā is considered the border between the region occupied by the Damiḷas and the provinces ruled over by the Mahāgāma dynasty.

[4] Cf. note to 7. 68.

[5] I.e. the angry Gāmaṇi. Cf. *Dīp. and Mah.*, p. 21, n. 1.

bata (vihāra) gathered together here, and from divers (other) places twelve thousand also.

When the king had celebrated the solemn festival of the 10
cetiya he brought all the (ten) warriors together and made
them take an oath in the presence of the brotherhood. They 11
all took the oath: 'We will not go to (thy) sons' battlefield';
therefore did they also not come to the war (afterwards).

When the king had built sixty-four vihāras and had lived 12
just as many years he died then in that same place.[1] The 13
queen took the king's body, brought it to the Tissamahārāma[2]
in a covered car and told this to the brotherhood. When the 14
prince Tissa heard this he came from Dīghavāpi, and when
he himself had carried out with (due) care the funeral rites
for his father, the powerful (prince) took his mother and the 15
elephant Kaṇḍula with him and for fear of his brother went
thence with all speed back to Dīghavāpi. To acquaint him 16
with these matters the whole of the ministers, who had met
together, sent a letter to Duṭṭhagāmaṇi. He repaired to 17
Guttahāla[3] and when he had placed outposts there he came
to Mahāgāma and caused himself to be consecrated king. He 18
sent a letter to his brother (asking) for his mother and the
elephant. But when after the third time he did not receive
them he set forth to make war upon him. And between 19
those two there came to pass a great battle in Cūḷaṅgaṇiya-
piṭṭhi: and there fell many thousands of the king's men.[4]
The king and his minister Tissa and the mare Dīghathūṇikā, 20
those three, took flight; the prince (Tissa) pursued them.
The bhikkhus created a mountain between the two (brothers). 21
When he (Tissa) saw it he turned about, thinking: 'This is
the work of the brotherhood of the bhikkhus.'

When he came to the Javamāla ford[5] of the river Kappa- 22

[1] In Mahāgāma.

[2] Cf. note to 22. 8.

[3] Now Buttala, situated thirty to thirty-five miles to the north of Mahāgāma, where the high-road crosses the Menik-ganga. The road from Mahāgāma to Mahiyaṅgaṇa led through Guttahālaka (cf. 25. 6). The outposts were stationed there by Duṭṭhagāmaṇi as a security against a surprise from Tissa, residing at Dīghavāpi.

[4] I.e. of Duṭṭhagāmaṇi.

[5] I think that the battle took place at some distance from Gutta-

kandara the king said to his minister Tissa: 'I am spent[1]
23 with hunger.' He offered him food that was placed in a
golden vessel. When he had set aside of the food for the
24 brotherhood and had divided it into four portions he said:
'Proclaim the meal-time.' Tissa proclaimed the time. When,
by means of his heavenly ear,[2] he who had taught the king
25 the holy precepts,[3] the thera (Gotama), dwelling in Piyaṅ-
gudīpa,[4] heard this he sent the thera Tissa the son of a house-
26 holder, thither, and he went there through the air. Tissa (the
minister) took his almsbowl from his hand and offered it to the
king. The king commanded the portion for the brotherhood
27 and his own portion to be poured into the bowl. And Tissa
poured his portion in likewise, and the mare also would not
have her portion. Therefore did Tissa pour her share too into
the bowl.

28 The king handed to the thera the bowl filled with food;
and hastening away through the air he brought it to the thera
29 Gotama. When the thera had offered their share in mor-
sels[5] to five hundred bhikkhus, who partook of the food,
30 and had (again) filled the bowl with the fragments that he
received from them, he caused it to fly through the air to the
king. (The minister) Tissa who saw it coming received it
31 and served the king. When he himself then had eaten he fed
the mare also; then the king sent the almsbowl away, making
of his own field-cloak a cushion to bear it upon.[6]

hālaka in the direction of Dīghavāpi. The site of Cūḷaṅgaṇiyapiṭṭhi may, therefore, be near Muppana, about ten miles to the north-east from Guttahālaka. On his flight the king had to cross the Kumbukkan-oya. This may be the Kappukandara-nadī. Then the Javamāla ford was near the village Kumbukkan.

[1] Chātajjhatto, in this sense also *Jāt.* i. 345[29].

[2] See note to 4. 12.

[3] See note to 22. 69 and below, v. 28.

[4] I.e. 'Panicum, or Saffron Island.' The monks living there enjoyed a reputation for particular holiness. Cf. Mah. 25. 104 foll.

[5] On ālopa see CHILDERS, *P.D.*, s. v.; literally translated it would be: 'when he had given (of it) in morsel-portions.'

[6] By cumbaṭa is meant a cloth rolled into a circular shape which serves as the support for a vessel when carried upon the head.

Arrived in Mahāgāma he assembled again a host of sixty 32
thousand men and marching into the field began the war with
his brother. The king riding on his mare and Tissa on the 33
elephant Kaṇḍula, thus did the two brothers now come at
once together, opposing each other in battle. Taking the 34
elephant in the middle the king made the mare circle round
him. When he, notwithstanding, found no unguarded place
he resolved to leap over him.[1] Leaping with the mare over 35
the elephant he shot his dart over his brother, so that he
wounded only the skin on the back (of the elephant).[2]

Many thousands of the prince's men fell there, fighting in 36
battle, and his great host was scattered. 'By reason of the 37
weakness of my rider one of the female sex has used me con-
temptuously';[3] so thought the elephant, and in wrath he
rushed upon a tree in order to throw him (Tissa). The prince 38
climbed upon the tree; the elephant went to his master
(Duṭṭhagāmaṇi). And he mounted him and pursued the
fleeing prince. The prince came to a vihāra and fleeing to the 39
cell of the chief thera, he lay down, in fear of his brother,
under the bed. The chief thera spread a cloak over the bed, 40
and the king, who followed immediately, asked: 'Where is
Tissa?' 'He is not in the bed, great king'; answered the 41
thera. Then the king perceived that he was under the bed,
and when he had gone forth he placed sentinels round about 42
the vihāra; but they laid the prince upon the bed and covered
him over with a garment and four young ascetics, grasping 43
the bed-posts, bore him out as if (they were carrying) a dead
bhikkhu. But the king, who perceived that he was being 44
carried forth, said: 'Tissa, upon the head of the guardian genii
of our house art thou carried forth; to tear away anything 45
with violence from the guardian genii of our house is not my

[1] To see whether he could perhaps attack him from above.

[2] This passage was corrupt at an early period. The Ṭīkā, too, mentions varying readings. The sense appears to me to be that Duṭṭhagāmaṇi only wishes to show his superiority without wounding either his brother or the elephant seriously. Cf. Mah. ed., Introd., p. xxii.

[3] Lit. 'Has leaped over me.' But the word 'laṅghayi' is evidently to be taken also metaphorically here.

custom. Mayst thou evermore remember the virtue of the
46 guardian genii of our house!' Hereupon the king went to
Mahāgāma, and thither did he bring his mother, whom he
47 greatly reverenced. Sixty-eight years did the king live, whose
heart stood firm in the faith, and he built sixty-eight vihāras.
48 But the prince Tissa, carried forth by the bhikkhus, went
49 thence unrecognized [1] and came to Dīghavāpi. The prince
said to the thera Godhagatta Tissa: [2] 'I have done ill, sir; I
50 will make my peace with my brother'. The thera took Tissa,
in the habit of a servitor, and five hundred bhikkhus with him
51 and sought the king out. Leaving the prince above on the
stairs the thera entered with the brotherhood. The monarch
52 invited them all to be seated and had rice-milk and other
(food) brought (to them). The thera covered his almsbowl, and
on the question: 'Wherefore this'? he answered: 'We have
53 come bringing Tissa with us.' To the question: 'Where is
the traitor?' he pointed out the place where he stood. The
Vihāradevī hurried thither and stood sheltering her young son.
54 The king said to the thera: 'It is known to you that we are
now also [3] your servants. If you had but sent a sāmaṇera of
55 seven years our strife had not taken place (and all had ended)
without loss of men.' 'O king, this is the brotherhood's guilt,
the brotherhood will do penance.'
56 'You will (first) have (to do) what is due to (guests) [4]
arriving. Take the rice-milk and the rest.' With these
words he offered the (food) to the brotherhood; and when he
57 had called his brother hither he took his seat with his

[1] According to the conjectural reading aññātako. Cf. Mah. ed., Introd., p. xlvii.

[2] We have here a surname given to the thera because of his spotted complexion, Ṭīkā: evaṃnāmikassa. TURNOUR translates, concerning the explanation of the name given in the Ṭīkā, thus: 'Who was afflicted with a cutaneous complaint which made his skin scaly like that of the godha.' (WIJESIṆHA: of an iguana.)

[3] Ñāto vo dāsabhāvo idāni no, i.e. even after I have become king; no is honorific plur.

[4] Hessat' āgatakiccaṃ vo stands briefly for āgatānaṃ kiccaṃ hessati vo kiccaṃ. With these words the king returns to the hospitality shown to the bhikkhus.

brother even there in the midst of the brotherhood; and when
he had eaten together with him he gave the brotherhood leave
to depart. And thither too[1] he sent his brother to direct the 58
work of harvest; and he too, when he had made it known by
beat of drum, directed the work of harvest.

Thus are pious men wont to appease an enmity, though 59
heaped up from many causes, even if it be great;[2] what wise
man, pondering this, shall not be of peace-loving mind toward
others?

Here ends the twenty-fourth chapter, called 'The War of the two Brothers', in the Mahāvaṃsa, compiled for the serene joy and emotion of the pious.

[1] That is, there, where he had sent the bhikkhus, i.e. to Dīghavāpi. The sassakammāni are preparations for the campaign against the Damiḷas.

[2] The Ṭīkā explains anekavikappacitaṃ by anekadhā upacitaṃ, punappunānusaraṇavasena rāsīkataṃ ti attho.

CHAPTER XXV

THE VICTORY OF DUṬṬHAGĀMAṆI

1 When the king Duṭṭhagāmaṇi had provided for his people
and had had a relic put into his spear[1] he marched, with
2 chariots, troops and beasts for riders,[2] to Tissamahārāma, and
when he had shown favour to the brotherhood he said: 'I will
go on to the land on the further side of the river[3] to bring
3 glory to the doctrine. Give us, that we may treat them with
honour, bhikkhus who shall go on with us, since the sight of
4 bhikkhus is blessing and protection for us.' As a penance[4]
the brotherhood allowed him five hundred ascetics; taking this
5 company of bhikkhus with him the king marched forth, and
when he had caused the road in Malaya leading hither[5] to be
made ready he mounted the elephant Kaṇḍula and, surrounded
6 by his warriors, he took the field with a mighty host. With
the one end yet in Mahāgāma[6] the train of the army reached
to Guttahālaka.

7 Arrived at Mahiyaṅgaṇa[7] he overpowered the Damiḷa
Chatta. When he had slain the Damiḷas in that very place
he came then to Ambatitthaka,[8] which had a trench leading
8 from the river, and (conquered) the Damiḷa Titthamba;
fighting the crafty[9] and powerful foe for four months he

[1] The spear serves as a royal standard, which is always carried before the prince.

[2] See note to 15. 189–190.

[3] See note to 24. 4.

[4] Cf. 24. 55.

[5] That is to the north of the island, towards Anurādhapura. Note to 10. 77. On Malaya see note to 7. 68.

[6] Mahāgāmena sambaddhā, lit. 'connected with Mahāgāma.'

[7] Mahiyaṅgaṇa = Bintenne (Alut-nuwara). See Appendix C.

[8] A ford of the Mahawæliganga, not far from Bintenne.

[9] Katahattha = Skt. kṛtahasta, and must be taken in the same sense.

(finally) overcame him by cunning,[1] since he placed his mother 9
in his view.

When the mighty man marching thence down (the river)
had conquered seven mighty Damiḷa princes in one day and 10
had established peace, he gave over the booty to his troops.
Therefore is (the place) called Khemārāma.

In Antarāsobbha he subdued Mahākoṭṭha, in Doṇa Gavara, 11
in Hālakola Issariya, in Nāḷisobbha Nāḷika. In Dīghābhaya- 12
gallaka he subdued, in like manner, Dīghābhaya; in Kaccha-
tittha, within four months, he subdued Kapisīsa. In Koṭana- 13
gara he subdued Koṭa, then Hālavahānaka, in Vahiṭṭha the
Damiḷa Vahiṭṭha and in Gāmaṇi (he subdued) Gāmaṇi, in Kum- 14
bagāma Kumba, in Nandigāma Nandika, Khānu in Khānugāma
but in Tamba and Unnama the two, uncle and nephew, named 15
Tamba and Unnama. Jambu also did he subdue, and each
village was named after (its commander.)

When the monarch heard (that it was said:) 'Not knowing 16
their own army they slay their own people', he made this
solemn declaration:[2] 'Not for the joy of sovereignty is this toil 17
of mine, my striving (has been) ever to establish the doctrine
of the Saṃbuddha. And even as this is truth may the armour 18
on the body of my soldiers take the colour of fire.' And now
it came to pass even thus.

All the Damiḷas on the bank of the river who had escaped 19
death threw themselves for protection into the city named
Vijitanagara.[3] In a favourable open country he pitched a 20
camp, and this became known by the name Khandhāvāra-
piṭṭhi.

Since the king, in order to take Vijitanagara, would fain 21
put Nandhimitta to the test, he let loose Kaṇḍula upon him
(once) when he saw him coming towards him. When the 22

[1] The allusion is too terse for us to make any safe conjecture as to the cunning mentioned. According to the Ṭīkā (vivāhakaraṇalesena) the reference is to Gāmaṇi's promising to his adversary marriage with his mother, and with it the expectation of government.

[2] On saccakiriyā see note to 18. 39.

[3] Near the northern bank of the Kālavāpi (Kaḷuwæwa), about 24 miles SSE. from Anurādhapura.

elephant came to overpower him, Nandhimitta seized with
his hands his two tusks and forced him on his haunches.
23 Since Nandhimitta fought with the elephant the village
built on the spot where (it came to pass) is therefore named
Hatthipora.

24 When the king had (thus) put them both to the test he
marched to Vijitanagara. Near the south gate befell a
25 fearful battle between the warriors. But near the east gate
did Veḷusumana, sitting on his horse, slay Damiḷas in great
numbers.

26 The Damiḷas shut the gate and the king sent thither his
men. Kaṇḍula and Nandhimitta and Sūranimila, at the
27 south gate, and the three, Mahāsoṇa, Goṭha and Theraputta,
28 at the three other gates did their (great) deeds. The city
had three trenches, was guarded by a high wall, furnished
with gates of wrought iron, difficult for enemies to destroy.
29 Placing himself upon his knees and battering stones, mortar
and bricks with his tusks did the elephant attack the gate of
30 iron. But the Damiḷas who stood upon the gate-tower hurled
down weapons of every kind, balls of red-hot iron and molten
31 pitch. When the smoking pitch poured on his back Kaṇḍula,
tormented with pains, betook him to a pool of water and
dived there.

32 'Here is no surā-draught[1] for thee, go forth to the destroying
of the iron gate, destroy the gate!' thus said Goṭhaimbara
33 to him. Then did the best of elephants again proudly take
heart, and trumpeting he reared himself out of the water and
stood defiantly on firm land.

34 The elephants' physician washed the pitch away and put
on balm; the king mounted the elephant and, stroking
35 his temples with his hand, he cheered him on with the
words: 'To thee I give, dear Kaṇḍula, the lordship over
the whole island of Laṅkā.' And when he had had choice
36 fodder given to him, had covered him with a cloth and had
put his armour on him and had bound upon his skin a seven

[1] Surā is an intoxicating drink. The meaning is: it is not for pleasure's sake that thou hast come here.

times folded buffalo-hide and above it had laid a hide steeped 37
in oil he set him free. Roaring like thunder he came, daring
danger, and with his tusks pierced the panels of the gate and 38
trampled the threshold with his feet; and with uproar the
gate crashed to the ground together with the arches of the
gate. The crumbling mass from the gate-tower that fell 39
upon the elephant's back did Nandhimitta dash aside, striking
it with his arms. When Kaṇḍula saw his deed, in contentment 40
of heart he ceased from the former wrath he had nursed since
he (Nandhimitta) had seized him by the tusks.

That he might enter the town close behind him Kaṇḍula 41
the best of elephants turned (to Nandhimitta) and looked at
that warrior. But Nandhimitta thought: 'I will not enter 42
(the town) by the way opened by the elephant' and with his
arm did he break down the wall. Eighteen cubits high 43
and eight usabhas long it crashed together. The (elephant)
looked on Sūranimila, but he too would not (follow in) the
track but dashed forward, leaping the wall into the town. 44
Goṭha also and Soṇa pressed forward, each one breaking down
a gate. The elephant seized a cart-wheel, Mitta a waggon- 45
frame, Goṭha a cocos-palm, Nimila his good sword, Mahāsoṇa 46
a palmyra-palm, Theraputta his great club,[1] and thus, rushing
each by himself into the streets, they shattered the Damiḷas
there.

When the king in four months had destroyed Vijitanagara 47
he went thence to Girilaka and slew the Damiḷa Giriya.
Thence he marched to Mahelanagara that had a triple trench 48
and was surrounded by an undergrowth of kadamba flowers,
possessed but one gate and was hard to come at; and staying 49
there four months the king subdued the commander of Mahela
by a cunningly planned battle.[2] Then nearing Anurādhapura 50
the king pitched his camp south of the Kāsa-mountain.[3] When
he had made a tank there in the month Jeṭṭhamūla he held 51

[1] Cf. 23. 58.

[2] Mantayuddhena. TURNOUR translates: 'By diplomatic stratagem.'

[3] On parato see note to 36. 56; on Kāsapabbata, note to 10. 27.

a water-festival. There is to be found the village named Pajjotanagara.

52 When the king Eḷāra heard that king Duṭṭhagāmaṇi was come to do battle he called together his ministers and said:
53 'This king is himself a warrior and in truth many warriors (follow him). What think the ministers, what should we
54 do?' King Eḷāra's warriors, led by Dīghajantu, resolved: 'To-
55 morrow will we give battle.' The king Duṭṭhagāmaṇi also took counsel with his mother and by her counsel formed thirty-two
56 bodies of troops. In these the king placed parasol-bearers and figures of a king;[1] the monarch himself took his place in the innermost body of troops.

57 When Eḷāra in full armour had mounted his elephant Mahāpabbata he came thither with chariots, soldiers and
58 beasts for riders. When the battle began the mighty and terrible Dīghajantu seized his sword and shield for battle,
59 and leaping eighteen cubits up into the air and cleaving the effigy of the king with his sword, he scattered the first body
60 of troops. When the mighty (warrior) had in this manner scattered also the other bodies of troops, he charged at the
61 body of troops with which king Gāmaṇi stood. But when he began to attack the king, the mighty warrior Sūranimila
62 insulted him, proclaiming his own name.[2] Dīghajantu thought: 'I will slay him,' and leaped into the air full of rage. But Sūranimila held the shield toward him as he alighted (in
63 leaping). But Dīghajantu thought: 'I will cleave him in twain, together with the shield,' and struck the shield with
64 the sword. Then Sūranimila[3] let go the shield. And as he clove (only) the shield thus released Dīghajantu fell there, and Sūranimila, springing up, slew the fallen (man) with his
65 spear. Phussadeva blew his conch shell, the army of the Damiḷas was scattered; nay, Eḷāra turned to flee and they

[1] Ṭīkā: **rañño paṭirūpakaṃ kaṭṭhamayarūpakaṃ ti**, i.e. wooden figures to represent the king.

[2] The usual form of challenge to single combat.

[3] In the original text of vv. 62, 63 there are only the pronouns **itaro, itaro, so, itaro**, instead of the names Dīghajantu, Sūranimila, Dīghajantu, Sūranimila.

slew many Damiḷas. The water in the tank there was dyed 66
red with the blood of the slain, therefore it was known by the
name Kulantavāpi.[1]

King Duṭṭhagāmaṇi proclaimed with beat of drum: 'None 67
but myself shall slay Eḷāra.' When he himself, armed, had 68
mounted the armed elephant Kaṇḍula he pursued Eḷāra and
came to the south gate (of Anurādhapura).

Near the south gate of the city the two kings fought; 69
Eḷāra hurled his dart, Gāmaṇi evaded it; he made his own 70
elephant pierce (Eḷāra's) elephant with his tusks and he
hurled his dart at Eḷāra; and this (latter) fell there, with his
elephant.

When he had thus been victorious in battle and had united 71
Laṅkā under one rule[2] he marched, with chariots, troops and
beasts for riders, into the capital. In the city he caused the 72
drum to be beaten, and when he had summoned the people
from a yojana around he celebrated the funeral rites for king
Eḷāra. On the spot where his body had fallen he burned it 73
with the catafalque, and there did he build a monument and
ordain worship. And even to this day the princes of Laṅkā, 74
when they draw near to this place, are wont to silence their
music because of this worship.

When he had thus overpowered thirty-two Damiḷa kings 75
DUṬṬHAGĀMAṆI ruled over Laṅkā in single sovereignty.

When Vijitanagara was destroyed the hero Dīghajantuka 76
had told Eḷāra of the valour of his nephew, and to this 77
nephew named Bhalluka he had sent a message to come
hither. When Bhalluka had received (the message)[3] from him 78
he landed here, on the seventh day after the day of the burning
of Eḷāra, with sixty thousand men.

Although he heard of the king's death after he had landed 79

[1] I would now like to adopt the form of this name as given in the Burmese MSS., as it gives good sense: 'End of the tribe.' The Ṭīkā ed. has Kulatthavāpi. This, however, is no guarantee for the reading of the MSS.

[2] Ekātapattaka, lit. 'Being under *one* parasol (ātapatta).' Cf. ekachattena in v. 75.

[3] The Ṭīkā adds to tassa the subst. lekhasaṃdesaṃ.

yet, from shame, with the purpose: 'I will do battle,' he
80 pressed on from Mahātittha hither.[1] He pitched his camp
near the village Kolambahālaka.[2]

When the king heard of his coming he marched forth to
81 battle in full panoply of war, mounted on the elephant
Kaṇḍula, with warriors mounted on elephants, horses and
chariots, and with foot-soldiers in great numbers.

82 Ummādaphussadeva, who was the best archer in all the
island (followed) armed with the five weapons,[3] and the rest
83 of the heroes followed him (also). While the raging battle
went forward Bhalluka in his armour came at the king
84 there; but Kaṇḍula, the king of elephants, to weaken his
onslaught, yielded his ground quite slowly and the army with
85 him drew also back quite slowly. The king said: 'Aforetime
in twenty-eight battles he has never retreated, what may this
86 be, Phussadeva?' And he answered: 'Victory lies behind
us, O king; looking to the field of victory the elephant draws
87 back, and at the place of victory he will halt.' And when
the elephant had retreated he stood firm beside (the shrine of)
the guardian god of the city within the precincts of the
Mahāvihāra.

88 When the king of elephants had halted here the Damiḷa
Bhalluka came toward the king in that place and mocked at
89 the ruler of the land. Covering his mouth with his sword the
king returned insult for insult. 'I will send (an arrow[4]) into
90 the king's mouth,' thought the other, and he let fly an arrow.
The arrow struck on the sword-blade and fell to the ground.
And Bhalluka, who thought: 'He is struck in the mouth,'
91 uttered a shout for joy. But the mighty Phussadeva sitting
behind the king, let fly an arrow into his mouth wherewith (as
92 the arrow passed) he lightly touched the king's ear-ring. And
since he made him thus to fall with his feet toward the king,
he let fly yet another arrow at the falling man and struck

[1] To Anurādhapura. Cf. note to 7. 58.

[2] It is called Kolambālaka in 33. 42, and was situated (cf. note to that passage) not far from the north gate of Anurādhapura.

[3] See note to 7. 16.

[4] After pātemi 'I let fly', understand 'kaṇḍaṃ', as in the Ṭīkā.

him in the knee; and making him (now) to turn with his 93
head toward the king, thus with swift hand he brought him
down.[1] When Bhalluka had fallen a shout of victory went up.

To make known his fault Phussadeva himself forthwith cut 94
off the lobe of his own ear and showed the king the blood
streaming down. When the king saw this he asked: 'What does 95
this mean?' 'I have carried out the royal justice upon my-
self,' he said (in answer) to the ruler of the land. And to the 96
question: 'What is thy guilt?' he answered: 'Striking thy
ear-ring.' 'Why hast thou done this, my brother, taking as
guilt that which was no guilt?' replied the great king, and 97
in gratitude he said moreover: 'Great shall be thy honourable
guerdon, even as thy arrow.'

When the king, after winning the victory, had slain all 98
the Damiḷas he went up on the terrace of the palace, and
when, in the royal chamber there in the midst of the dancers 99
and ministers, he had sent for Phussadeva's arrow and had
set it in the ground with the feathered end uppermost, he 100
covered the dart over and over with kahāpaṇas[2] poured forth
upon it, and these he forthwith caused to be given to Phussadeva.

Sitting then on the terrace of the royal palace, adorned, 101
lighted with fragrant lamps and filled with many a perfume, 102
magnificent with nymphs in the guise of dancing-girls, while he
rested on his soft and fair couch, covered with costly draperies, 103
he, looking back upon his glorious victory, great though it
was, knew no joy, remembering that thereby was wrought
the destruction of millions (of beings).

When the arahants in Piyaṅgudīpa[3] knew his thought 104
they sent eight arahants to comfort the king. And they, 105
coming in the middle watch of the night, alighted at the

[1] Pādato katvā and sīsato katvā, lit. he made him 'footwise' or 'headwise'. Rājānaṃ (Duṭṭhagāmaṇim) is dependent on pādato (sīsato). On the first shot Bhalluka fell backwards, so that he would have lain with his feet towards Duṭṭhagāmaṇi. To prevent this Phussadeva then shot a second arrow at him, which struck Bhalluka in the knee, even as he fell, so that he now fell forward on his face. From that moment he lay in the posture of one conquered and overthrown, or of a slave before the king.

[2] See note to 4. 13. [3] See note to 24 25.

palace-gate. Making known that they were come thither
through the air they mounted to the terrace of the palace.
106 The great king greeted them, and when he had invited them
to be seated and had done them reverence in many ways he
107 asked the reason of their coming. 'We are sent by the
brotherhood at Piyaṅgudīpa to comfort thee, O lord of men.'
108 And thereon the king said again to them: 'How shall there
be any comfort for me, O venerable sirs, since by me was
caused the slaughter of a great host numbering millions?'
109 'From this deed arises no hindrance in thy way to heaven.
Only one and a half human beings have been slain here by
110 thee, O lord of men. The one had come unto the (three)
refuges, the other had taken on himself the five precepts.[1]
Unbelievers and men of evil life were the rest, not more to be
111 esteemed than beasts. But as for thee, thou wilt bring glory to
the doctrine of the Buddha in manifold ways; therefore cast
away care from thy heart, O ruler of men!'
112 Thus exhorted by them the great king took comfort. When
he had bidden them farewell and had given them leave to
113 depart he lay down again and thought: 'Without the brother-
hood you shall never take a meal,' thus our mother and father
114 have caused to swear us in our boyhood at the meal. Have
I ever eaten anything whatsoever without giving to the
brotherhood of bhikkhus?' Then he saw that he had, all
115 unthinkingly, eaten pepper in the pod, at the morning meal,
leaving none for the brotherhood; and he thought: 'For this
I must do penance.'
116 Should a man think on the hosts of human beings murdered
for greed in countless myriads, and should he carefully keep
in mind the evil (arising from that), and should he also very
carefully keep in mind the mortality as being the murderer
of all, then will he, in this way, shortly win freedom from
suffering and a happy condition.

Here ends the twenty-fifth chapter, called 'The Victory of Duṭṭhagāmaṇi', in the Mahāvaṃsa, compiled for the serene joy and emotion of the pious.

[1] See notes to 1. 32 and 62.

CHAPTER XXVI

THE CONSECRATING OF THE MARICAVAṬṬI-VIHĀRA

WHEN that king of high renown had united Laṅkā in one 1
kingdom he distributed places of honour to his warriors
according to their rank. The warrior Theraputtābhaya would 2
not have that which was allotted to him, and being asked:
'Wherefore?' he answered: 'It is war.' And questioned 3
(yet again): 'When a single realm is created what war is
there?' he answered: 'I will do battle with those rebels,
the passions, (battle) wherein victory is hard to win.' Thus 4
said he, and again and again the king sought to restrain him.
When he had entreated again and again he took the pabbajjā
with the king's consent. After taking the pabbajjā he attained 5
in time to arahantship, and he lived in the midst of five
hundred (bhikkhus) who had overcome the āsavas.

When the week of the festival of kingship was gone 6
by the fearless king Abhaya,[1] who had carried out the conse-
cration with great pomp, went to the Tissa-tank, that was 7
adorned according to the festival custom, to hold festival
plays there and to observe the tradition of crowned kings.

All that had been made ready for the king and hundreds 8
of offerings did they place on the spot where the Maricavaṭṭi-
vihāra[2] (afterwards stood). There in the very place where 9
the thūpa (afterwards) stood the king's people who carried
the spear planted the splendid spear with the relic.[3] When 10
the king had disported himself in the water the whole day

[1] A play upon the words abhayo and gatabhayo.

[2] Now Miriswæṭi in the south-west part of Anurādhapura, north of Tissawæwa. SMITHER, *Architectural Remains, Anurádhapura*, p. 19 foll.; PARKER, *Ancient Ceylon*, p. 294 foll.

[3] Cf. 25. 1, with note.

through, together with the women of the harem, he said, in
the evening: 'We will go hence; carry the spear before us.'
11 And the people entrusted with (this duty) could not move
the spear from its place; and the king's soldiers came to-
12 gether and brought offerings of perfumes and flowers. When
the king saw this great miracle, glad at heart he appointed
sentinels there, and after he had returned forthwith into
13 the city he built a cetiya in such wise that it enclosed the
spear and founded a vihāra that enclosed the thūpa.
14 In three years the vihāra was finished and the ruler of
men called the brotherhood together to hold the festival (on
15 the consecration) of the monastery. A hundred thousand bhik-
khus and ninety thousand bhikkhuṇīs were gathered together
16 there. Then in this assembly the king spoke thus to the
brotherhood: 'Without a thought of the brotherhood, vener-
17 able sirs, I ate pepper in the pod. Thinking: This shall be
my act of expiation, I have built the pleasant Maricavaṭṭi-
18 vihāra, together with the cetiya. May the brotherhood
accept it!' With these words he poured forth the (ceremonial)
water of a gift and piously gave the monastery to the brother-
19 hood. When he had set up a great and beautiful hall in the
vihāra and round about it, he commanded that lavish gifts
20 should be given there to the brotherhood. The hall was so
planned that stakes were set even in the water of the Abhaya-
tank,[1] what need of further words to speak of the remaining
space (covered)?
21 When the ruler of men had given food, drink and so forth,
for a week, he offered as a gift the whole of the costly
22 necessaries for samaṇas.[2] These necessaries began with a cost
of a hundred thousand (kahāpaṇas) and ended with a cost of
23 a thousand. All this did the brotherhood receive. The
money that was spent there in gratitude by the wise king,

[1] See note to 10. 84.

[2] The most costly parikkhāra (see note to 4. 26) was allotted to the most distinguished monks (Ṭī. saṃghattherānaṃ); the value was then graduated according to the rank of the recipient. The literal translation runs thus: the parikkhāra had at first (at the beginning) the value of . . ., at the end the value of . . . .

who was a hero in battle as in largess, whose pure heart was
filled with faith in the Three Gems, who desired to raise the
(Buddha's) doctrine to glory, (that was spent) to honour the 24
Three Gems, beginning with the building of the thūpa and
ending with the festival of the vihāra, (all this money), leaving 25
aside the rest of the priceless (gifts), is reckoned as but one
less than twenty koṭis.[1]

Treasures which, in truth, bear on them the blot of the five 26
faults[2] become, if they be acquired by people who are gifted with special wisdom, possessed of the five advantages;[3] therefore let the wise man strive to have them thus.

Here ends the twenty-sixth chapter, called 'The Consecrating of the Maricavaṭṭi-vihāra', in the Mahāvaṃsa, compiled for the serene joy and emotion of the pious.

[1] The construction of the sentence in vv. 23–25 is thus: dhanāni tena kataññunā raññā pariccattāni, ratanattayaṃ pūjetuṃ—sesāni anagghāni (dānāni) vimuñciya—honti ekāya ūnavīsatikoṭiyo. The instrumental cases yuddhe dāne ca sūrena, sūrinā, ratanattaye pasannāmalacittena, sāsanujjotanatthinā are attributes of raññā, and the plural neuter thūpakārāpanādito vihāramahanantāni attribute of dhanāni.

[2] According to the Ṭīkā the five dangers which threaten the wealth are meant: loss by fire, water, living creatures, confiscation or brigandage.

[3] The construction is: bhogā . . . honti . . . gahītasārā. The five benefits are, according to the Ṭīkā: popularity among men, high esteem among pious men, fame, fidelity in fulfilment of lay-duties, and attainment of heaven after death. These advantages are possessed by a kingdom when well governed.

CHAPTER XXVII

THE CONSECRATING OF THE LOHAPĀSĀDA

1 HEREUPON the king called to mind the tradition known to
all, and duly handed down: 'The thera rich in merit, ever
intent on meritorious works, who formed his resolves in
2 wisdom, who converted the island did, as is known, speak
thus to the king, my ancestor: "Thy descendant, the king
3 Duṭṭhagāmaṇi, the wise, will hereafter found the Great
Thūpa, the splendid Soṇṇamālī[1] a hundred and twenty cubits
4 in height, and an uposatha-house, moreover, adorned with
manifold gems, making it nine stories high, namely the
Lohapāsāda."'
5 Thus thought the ruler of the land, and finding, when he
made search, a gold plate kept in a chest and laid by in the
6 palace with such a written record thereon, he commanded that
the inscription be read aloud: 'When one hundred and
7 thirty-six years have run their course, in future time will
Kākavaṇṇa's son, the ruler of men, Duṭṭhagāmaṇi, build
8 this and that in such and such wise.' When the king had
heard this read he uttered a cry of joy and clapped his hands.[2]
Then early in the morning he went to the beautiful Mahā-
9 megha-park, and when he had arranged a gathering together
of the brotherhood of the bhikkhus he said to them: 'I will
10 build for you a pāsāda[3] like to a palace of the gods. Send

[1] I.e. 'provided with golden garlands,' now Ruwanwæli. The usual designation in Mah. is Mahāthūpa.

[2] For the sense of apphoṭeti (=Skt. ā-sphoṭayati) cf. Thūpavaṃsa, 33^9–10: vāmahatthaṃ ābhujitvā dakkhiṇahatthena apphoṭesi.

[3] See note to v. 14. The building was destined to contain the cells of the bhikkhus.

to a celestial palace[1] and make me a drawing of it.' The
brotherhood of the bhikkhus sent thither eight (theras) who
had overcome the āsavas.

In the time of the sage Kassapa[2] a brahman named Asoka, 11
who had set out eight ticket-meals[3] (to be apportioned) to
the brethren, commanded his serving-woman named Bīraṇī: 12
'Give of this continually.' When she had given these gifts
faithfully her whole life long she left this (world) and was 13
reborn as a lovely maiden in a gleaming palace, floating in
the air, (and she was) continually served by a thousand
nymphs. Her gem-palace was twelve yojanas high[4] and 14
measured forty-eight yojanas round about; it was adorned 15
with a thousand jutting window-chambers, nine-storied and
provided with a thousand chambers, gleaming with light,
four-sided, with a thousand shell-garlands and with windows 16
as eyes and provided with a vedikā (adorned) with a network
of little bells. In the middle of the (building) was the 17
beautiful Ambalaṭṭhika-pāsāda, visible from every side, bright
with pennons hung out. When the theras, going to the 18
heaven of the thirty-three (gods), saw that (palace) they
made a drawing of it with red arsenic upon a linen cloth,
and they returned, and being arrived they showed the linen 19
to the brotherhood. The brotherhood took the linen and
sent it to the king. When the king full of joy saw it he went 20

[1] By vimāna are meant the palaces serving as abodes for the gods and happy spirits. Cf. the Vimānavatthu, note to 14. 58.

[2] The last Buddha before Gotama; see 1. 10; 15. 125.

[3] Salākabhatta. See note to 15. 205.

[4] Here then we have a construction of several stories, diminishing in size towards the top (navabhūmika!) after the style of the Assyro-Babylonian ziggarat (RHYS DAVIDS, *Buddhist India*, p. 70 foll.; PERROT et CHIPIEZ, *Histoire de l'Art dans l'antiquité*, ii, p. 390 foll.). Such a building is the Sat-mahal-prāsāda at Polannaruwa, although belonging to a later time. See TENNENT, *Ceylon*, ii, p. 588; BURROWS, *Archaeological Report*, x, 1886, p. 8; FERGUSSON, *History of Indian and Eastern Architecture*, 1910, i, p. 245; *Arch. Survey of Ceylon, Annual Report*, 1903 (lxv, 1908), p. 14 foll. The word pāsāda serves now to designate the graduated galleries which form the base of thūpas. See SMITHER, *Anurádhapura*, p. 20, &c.

to the splendid ārāma and caused the noble Lohapāsāda to be
built after the drawing.
21 At the time that the work was begun the generous (king)
commanded that eight hundred thousand gold pieces should be
22 placed at each of the four gates; moreover, at each gate he com-
manded them to lay a thousand bundles of garments and many
23 pitchers filled with ball-sugar, oil, sugar-dust, and honey, and
proclaiming, 'No work is to be done here without reward,' he
had the work done (by the people), appraised, and their wage
given to them.
24 The pāsāda was four-sided, (measuring) on each side a
25 hundred cubits, and even so much in height. In this most
beautiful of palaces there were nine stories, and in each story
26 a hundred window-chambers. All the chambers were overlaid
with silver and their coral vedikās[1] were adorned with mani-
27 fold precious stones, gay with various gems were the lotus-
flowers[2] on the (vedikās) and they (the vedikās) were sur-
rounded with rows of little silver bells.
28 A thousand well-arranged chambers were in the pāsāda,
29 overlaid with various gems and adorned with windows. And
since he heard of Vessavaṇa's[3] chariot which served as a car
for the women, he had a gem-pavilion set up in the middle
30 (of the palace) fashioned in like manner. It was adorned
with pillars consisting of precious stones, on which were
figures of lions, tigers, and so forth, and shapes of devatās;
31 a bordering of pearl network ran round the edge of the
pavilion and thereon was a coral vedikā of the kind that has
been described above.
32 Within the pavilion, gaily adorned with the seven gems,
stood a shining beauteous throne of ivory with a seat of
33 mountain-crystal, and in the ivory back (was fashioned) a sun

[1] On the balustrades of the projecting windows, cf. the descriptions in FOUCHER, *L'Art Gréco-Bouddhique du Gandhāra*, fig. 100; GRÜNWEDEL, *Buddhist. Kunst*, fig. 27. See Appendix D, no. 30.

[2] For lotus-blossoms as a frequent ornament: FOUCHER, in the same work, fig. 97, 98; GRÜNWEDEL, fig. 3; balustrade with leaf-ornaments on cornices: FOUCHER, fig. 99.

[3] See note to 10. 89.

in gold, a moon in silver, and stars in pearls, and lotus-blossoms 34
made of various gems were fitly placed here and there and
Jātaka-tales in the same place[1] within a festoon of gold.

On the exceedingly beautiful throne covered with costly 35
cushions was placed a beautiful fan of ivory, gleaming
(magnificently), and a white parasol with a coral foot, resting 36
on mountain-crystal and having a silver staff, shone forth
over the throne. On it, depicted in the seven gems, were 37
the eight auspicious figures[2] and rows of figures of beasts
with jewels and pearls in between; and rows of little silver 38
bells were hung upon the edge of the parasol. Palace,
parasol, throne, and pavilion were beyond price.

Costly beds and chairs, according to rank, and carpets and 39
coverlets of great price did he command them to spread about.
The rinsing-vessel and the ladle (belonging thereto) were even 40
of gold;[3] what need then to speak of the other utensils in
the palace? Surrounded by a beautiful enclosure and provided 41
with four gateways the pāsāda gleamed in its magnificence
like the hall in the heaven of the thirty-three (gods). The 42
pāsāda was covered over with plates of copper, and thence
came its name 'Brazen palace'.

When the Lohapāsāda was ready the king assembled the 43
brotherhood, and the brotherhood came together as at the
consecration-festival of the Maricavaṭṭi (vihāra). Those 44
bhikkhus who were yet simple folk stood on the first story,
those learned in the tipiṭaka on the second, but those who
had entered on the path of salvation and the others (stood) 45

[1] On events in the former existences of the Buddha as a motive for decorative scenes see particularly FOUCHER, *l. l.*, p. 270 foll. For arrangements in the manner described here, see CUNNINGHAM, *Bharhut*, plate xl foll.

[2] WIJESIṆHA enumerates the aṭṭha maṅgalikāni: lion, bull, elephant, water-pitcher, fan, standard, conch-shell, lamp. The Thūpavaṃsa, 64^{25}, mentions sirivaccha as the first (cf. 30. 65).

[3] Ācāmakumbhī or ācamanakumbhī—thus the Thūpavaṃsa 54^{2}—is a vessel to hold water for washing the feet and hands, and is placed at the entrance of the temple (WIJESIṆHA). See M.V. I. 25. 19; C.V. V. 35. 4.

each on one of the third and higher stories,[1] but the arahants stood on those four stories that were highest of all.

46 When the king had bestowed the pāsāda on the brotherhood, after pouring forth the (ceremonial) water of presentation, he commanded, as before, a lavish gift of alms for
47 a week. That which was spent by the generous king for the pāsāda, leaving aside all that which was beyond price, is reckoned at thirty koṭis.

48 The wise who consider how marvellously precious is the giving of alms, while the gathering together of treasures (for oneself) is worthless, give alms lavishly, with a mind freed from the fetters (of lust), mindful of the good of beings.

Here ends the twenty-seventh chapter, called 'the Consecrating of the Lohapāsāda', in the Mahāvaṃsa, compiled for the serene joy and emotion of the pious.

[1] That is, on the 3rd, 4th, and 5th stories stood those who had attained to the first three stages of the path: the sotāpannā, the sakadāgāmino, and the anāgāmino. See notes to 1. 33, 15. 18 and 13. 17. 'Simple folk' in verse 44 is puthujjanā, the unconverted, those who had not even entered on the path.

CHAPTER XXVIII

THE OBTAINING OF THE WHEREWITHAL TO BUILD THE GREAT THŪPA

SPENDING a hundred thousand (pieces of money) the king 1
hereupon commanded a great and splendid ceremony of gifts
for the great Bodhi-tree. As he then, when entering the 2
city, saw the pillar of stone raised upon the place of the (future)
thūpa and remembered the old tradition, he became glad,
thinking: 'I will build the Great Thūpa.' Then he mounted 3
the high terrace (of his palace), and when he had taken his
repast and had lain down he thought thus: 'At the conquer- 4
ing of the Damiḷas this people was oppressed by me. It is
not possible to levy a tax; yet if without a tax I build the 5
Great Thūpa how shall I be able to have bricks duly made?'

As he thus reflected the devatā of the parasol observed his 6
thought, and thereupon arose a tumult among the gods;
when Sakka was aware of this he said to Vissakamma:[1]
'King Gāmaṇi has been pondering over the bricks for the 7
cetiya: Go thou a yojana from the city near the Gambhīra-
river and prepare the bricks there.'[2] 8

Thus commanded by Sakka, Vissakamma came hither[3] and
prepared the bricks in that very place.

In the morning a huntsman there went into the forest with 9
his dogs; the devatā of the place appeared to the huntsman
in the form of an iguana. The hunter pursued it, and 10
when he came (to the place) and saw the bricks, and when
the iguana vanished there, he thought: 'Our king intends to 11
build the Great Thūpa;[4] here is an aid thereto!' Thereupon
he went and told (this thing). When the king, to whom his 12

[1] See note to 18. 24.

[2] See note to 7. 44.

[3] To Laṅkā or to Anurādhapura.

[4] Or 'a great thūpa'.

people's good was dear, heard his welcome words he, glad at heart, bestowed on him a rich guerdon.

13 In a north-easterly direction from the city, at a distance of three yojanas and near Ācāraviṭṭhigāma, on a plain covering
14 sixteen karīsas (of land) there appeared nuggets of gold of different sizes; the greatest measured a span, the least were
15 of a finger's measure. When the dwellers in the village saw the earth full of gold, they put some of it into a gold vessel and went and told the king of this matter.

16 On the east side of the city, at a distance of seven yojanas, on the further bank of the river and near Tambapiṭṭha, copper
17 appeared. And the dwellers in the village there put the nuggets of copper into a vessel, and when they had sought the king they told him this matter.

18 In a south-easterly direction from the city, four yojanas distant, near the village of Sumanavāpi many precious stones
19 appeared. The dwellers in the village put them, mingled with sapphires and rubies, into a vessel and went and showed them to the king.

20 In a southerly direction from the city, at a distance of eight yojanas, silver appeared in the Ambaṭṭhakola-cave.[1]
21 A merchant from the city, taking many waggons with him, in order to bring ginger and so forth from Malaya, had set
22 out for Malaya. Not far from the cave he brought the waggons to a halt and since he had need of wood for whips
23 he went up that mountain. As he saw here a branch of a bread-fruit-tree, bearing one single fruit as large as a water-pitcher, and dragged down by the weight of the fruit, he cut
24 the (fruit) which was lying on a stone away from the stalk with his knife, and thinking: 'I will give the first (produce as alms),' with faith he announced the (meal) time. And there came thither four (theras) who were free

[1] Where the Rajatalena-vihāra (Mah. 35. 4) was afterwards built, now the Ridi-vihāra (Silver Monastery), to the north-east of Kurunægala, cf. E. MÜLLER, *Ancient Inscriptions in Ceylon*, p. 39; TURNOUR, *Mah. Index*, s. v. Ambaṭṭhakola; RHYS DAVIDS, *Ancient Coins*, &c., p. 17. The distance between Anurādhapura and Ridi-vihāra is 55 miles = 95 km. as the crow flies.

from the āsavas. When he had greeted them gladly and 25
had invited them with all reverence to be seated, he cut away
the rind around the stalk with his knife and tore out the 26
bottom (of the fruit), and pouring the juice which filled the
hollow forth into their bowls he offered them the four bowls
filled with fruit-juice. They accepted them and went their way. 27
Then he yet again[1] announced the (meal) time. Four other
theras, free from the āsavas, appeared before him. He took their 28
alms-bowls and when he had filled them with the kernels of
the bread-fruit he gave them back. Three went their way,
but one did not depart. In order to show him the silver he 29
went further down and seating himself near the cave he ate
the kernels. When the merchant also had eaten as he wished 30
of the kernels that were left, and had put the rest in a bundle, he
went on, following the track of the thera, and when he saw the 31
thera he showed him the (usual) attentions. The thera opened
a path for him to the mouth of the cavern: 'Go thou now 32
also on this path, lay brother!' When he had done reverence
to the thera he went that way and saw the cave. Standing 33
by the mouth of the cave and seeing the silver he struck upon
it with his axe, and when he knew it to be silver he took 34
a lump of the silver and went to his freight-waggons. Then
leaving the waggons behind and taking the lump of silver
with him the excellent merchant went in haste to Anurādha- 35
pura and told the king of this matter, showing him the
silver.

In a westerly direction from the city, at a distance of five 36
yojanas, near the landing-place Uruvelā,[2] pearls in size like
to great myrobalan fruits, mingled with coral, six waggon- 37
loads, came forth to the dry land. Fishermen who saw them
piled them together in a heap, and taking the pearls together 38
with coral in a vessel they went to the king and told him of
this matter.

In a northerly direction from the city, at a distance of 39

[1] Pana should probably be altered to puna.

[2] According to our passage the site of Uruvelā seems to be near the mouth of the Kala-oya, which is distant about 40 miles, as the crow flies, from Anurādhapura.

seven yojanas, in a cave opening on the Peḷivāpikagāma-[1]
40 tank, above on the sand, four splendid gems had formed in
size like to a small mill-stone, in colour like flax-flowers,
41 (radiantly) beautiful. When a hunter with his dogs saw
these he came to the king and told him: 'I have seen
precious stones of such and such a kind.'

42 The lord of the land, rich in merit, heard, on one and the
same day, that the bricks and the other (treasures) had
43 appeared for the Great Thūpa. Glad at heart he bestowed
due reward upon those people, and appointing them forthwith
as watchers he had the treasures all brought to him.

44 Merit, that a man has thus heaped up with believing heart, careless of insupportable ills of the body, brings to pass hundreds of results which are a mine of happiness; therefore one must do works of merit with believing heart.

Here ends the twenty-eighth chapter, called 'the Obtaining of the wherewithal to build the Great Thūpa', in the Mahāvaṃsa, compiled for the serene joy and emotion of the pious.

[1] The Peḷivāpi is the present Vavunik-kulam, a little over 50 miles north of Anurādhapura. The river, of which the damming-up has formed the tank, is called Pāli-āru. PARKER, *Ancient Ceylon*, pp. 256, 365-366.

CHAPTER XXIX

THE BEGINNING OF THE GREAT THŪPA

WHEN the wherewithal to build was thus brought together 1
he began the work of the Great Thūpa on the full-moon day
of the month Vesākha,[1] when the Visākha-constellation had
appeared. When he had ordered to take away the stone pillar 2
the lord of the land had the place for the thūpa dug out to
a depth of seven cubits[2] to make it firm in every way.
Round stones that he commanded his soldiers to bring hither 3
did he cause to be broken with hammers, and then did he,
having knowledge of the right and the wrong ways, command 4
that the crushed stone, to make the ground firmer, be stamped
down by great elephants whose feet were bound with leather.

The fine clay that is to be found on the spot, for ever 5
moist, where the heavenly Gaṅgā falls down (upon the earth[3])
(on a space) thirty yojanas around, is called because of its fine- 6
ness, 'butter-clay.' Sāmaṇeras who had overcome the āsavas,
brought the clay hither from that place. The king commanded 7
that the clay be spread over the layer of stones and that bricks
then be laid over the clay, over these a rough cement and over 8
this cinnabar,[4] and over this a network of iron, and over this
sweet-scented marumba[5] that was brought by the sāmaṇeras 9

[1] See note to 1. 12.

[2] The reading sattahatthe is undoubtedly the correct one. WIJESIṆHA (note to this passage) says: the Ṭīkā has sata. That, however, is not the case. It also reads satta.

[3] The idea is that the Gaṅgā flows through the atmosphere, the earth and underworld.

[4] Kuruvinda is 'ruby' or 'cinnabar'.

[5] Marumba is used (C.V. V. 14. 5; 35.4; VI. 3. 8) for besprinkling a damp pariveṇa (living-cell). At Pācittiya X. 2 (*Vin. Piṭ.* iv, p. 33) pāsāṇā, sakkharā, kaṭhalā, marumbā, vālikā follow one upon another.

from the Himalaya. Over this did the lord of the land com-
10 mand them to lay mountain-crystal. Over the layer of moun-
tain-crystal he had stones spread; everywhere throughout the
11 work did the clay called butter-clay serve (as cement). With
resin of the kapittha-tree,[1] dissolved in sweetened water,[2]
12 the lord of chariots laid over the stones a sheet of copper
eight inches thick, and over this, with arsenic dissolved in
sesamum-oil, (he laid) a sheet of silver seven inches thick.

13 When the king, glad at heart, had thus had preparation
made upon the spot where the Great Thūpa was to be built,
14 he arranged, on the fourteenth day of the bright half of the
month Āsāḷha, an assembly of the brotherhood of the
15 bhikkhus, and spoke thus: 'To-morrow, venerable sirs, I shall
lay the foundation-stone of the Great Cetiya. Then let our
16 whole brotherhood assemble here, to the end that a festival
may be held for the Buddha, mindful of the weal of the people;
and let the people in festal array, with fragrant flowers and
17 so forth, come to-morrow to the place where the Great Thūpa
will be built.'

He entrusted ministers[3] with the adorning of the place of
18 the cetiya. Commanded by the lord of men, they, filled
with deep reverence for the Sage (Buddha), adorned the
19 place in manifold ways. The whole city also and the streets
leading thither did the king command to be adorned in
20 manifold ways. On the following morning he placed at the
four gates of the city many barbers and servants for the
21 bath and for cutting the hair, clothes likewise and fragrant
flowers and sweet foods (did) the king (place there) for his
22 people's good, he who rejoiced in the people's welfare. Taking,
according to their wish, the things thus put before them,
townsfolk and country-people went to the place of the thūpa.

23 The king supported, in order of their rank, by many
24 ministers, richly clothed as befitted their office, surrounded

[1] *Feronia Elephantum.*

[2] Rasodaka is translated by TURNOUR 'water of the small red cocoanut'. The Ṭīkā gives no explanation.

[3] The Ṭīkā, following the Aṭṭhakathā, gives their names, Visākha and Sirideva.

by many dancers richly clothed like to celestial nymphs,
(he himself) being clad in his state-raiment, attended by 25
forty thousand men, while around him crashed the music
(he being) glorious as the king of the gods; in the evening 26
he who had knowledge of fit and unfit places went to the
place of the Great Thūpa,[1] delighting the people (with the
sight). A thousand and eight waggon-loads of clothes rolled 27
in bundles did the king place in the midst, and on the four
sides he had clothes heaped up in abundance; and moreover 28
he had honey, clarified butter, sugar and so forth set (there)
for the festival.

From various (foreign) countries also did many bhikkhus 29
come hither; what need to speak of the coming of the
brotherhood living here upon the island? With eighty thou- 30
sand bhikkhus from the region of Rājagaha[2] came the thera
Indagutta, the head of a great school. From Isipatana[3] 31
came the great thera Dhammasena with twelve thousand
bhikkhus to the place of the cetiya.

With sixty thousand bhikkhus came hither the great thera 32
Piyadassi from the Jetārāma-vihāra.[4] From the Mahāvana 33
(monastery) in Vesālī[5] came the thera Urubuddharakkhita[6]
with eighteen thousand bhikkhus. From the Ghositārāma in 34
Kosambī[7] came the thera Urudhammarakkhita with thirty
thousand bhikkhus. From the Dakkhiṇāgiri in Ujjenī[8] came 35
the thera Urusaṃgharakkhita with forty thousand ascetics.

With a hundred and sixty thousand bhikkhus came the 36

[1] We should rather expect Mahāthūpapatiṭṭhānaṭṭhānaṃ ṭhānavicakkhaṇo: 'he went to the place where the Great Thūpa should be built, having knowledge of (fitting) places.'

[2] Cf. note to 2. 6.

[3] A park and afterwards a monastery near Bārāṇasī (Benares) where the Buddha had preached his first sermon. M.V. I. 6. 6 foll.

[4] I. e. Jetavana. See note to 1. 44.

[5] See note to 4. 9. Also M.V. VI. 30. 6; C.V. V. 13. 3, and in many other places.

[6] I. e. Mahābuddharakkhita.

[7] See note to 4. 17; M.V. X. 1. 1; C.V. I. 25. 1, and often.

[8] See note to 5. 39; 13. 5. Notice that the names of the three theras in 33, 34, 35, contain the words buddha, dhamma, saṃgha.

thera named Mittiṇṇa from the Asokārāma in Pupphapura.[1]
37 From the Kasmīra country came the thera Uttiṇṇa bringing
38 with him two hundred and eighty thousand bhikkhus. The
wise Mahādeva came from Pallavabhogga[2] with four hundred
39 and sixty thousand bhikkhus, and from Alasanda[3] the city
of the Yonas came the thera Yonamahādhammarakkhita with
40 thirty thousand bhikkhus. From his dwelling by the road
through the Viñjhā forest mountains,[4] came the thera Uttara
with sixty thousand bhikkhus.

41 The great thera Cittagutta came hither from the Bodhi-
42 maṇḍa-vihāra[5] with thirty thousand bhikkhus. The great
thera Candagutta came hither from the Vanavāsa[6] country
43 with eighty thousand ascetics. The great thera Suriyagutta
came from the great Kelāsa-vihāra with ninety-six thousand
44 bhikkhus. As for the number of the bhikkhus dwelling in
the island who met together from every side, no strict account
45 has been handed down by the ancients. Among all these
bhikkhus who were met in that assembly those alone who had
overcome the āsavas, as it is told, were ninety-six koṭis.

46 These bhikkhus stood according to their rank around the
place of the Great Thūpa, leaving in the midst an open space
47 for the king. As the king stepped into this (space) and saw[7]

[1] I.e. Pāṭaliputta; see note to 4. 31. For Asokārāma, cf. 5. 80.

[2] Pallava is the name of the Persians = Skt. Pallava or Pahlava. Bhoggaṃ is perhaps 'fief'; cf. rājabhoggaṃ in D. I. 87[9] and often elsewhere.

[3] Alexandria in the land of the Yonas, i.e. the Greeks, probably the town founded by the Macedonian king in the country of the Paropanisadae near Kābul. See ARRIAN, *Anabasis* iii. 28, iv. 22.

[4] I.e. Vindhyā. See 19. 6 with note.

[5] A monastery built near the bodhimaṇḍa at Bodhgayā, the place where Gotama attained to Buddhaship.

[6] See note to 12. 31.

[7] The Ṭīkā gives here (from the Aṭṭhakathā) the following peculiar explanation: 'As the king steps into the middle of the circle he expresses the following wish: if his work is to come to a happy issue then, as a sign thereof, may theras who bear the name of the Buddha, his doctrine and his order, take their places on the east, south, and west sides; but on the north side a thera with the name of Ānanda, the Buddha's beloved disciple. Each bhikkhu shall be surrounded by

the brotherhood of bhikkhus standing thus he greeted them
joyfully, with believing heart; when he had then duly offered 48
them fragrant flowers and had passed round them three times,
turning to the left,[1] he went into the midst, to the consecrated
place of the 'filled pitcher'. Then forthwith uplifted by the 49
power of pure gladness he, devoted to the welfare of the
beings, commanded that the pure turning staff (for tracing
the circular boundary), made of silver and secured (by means 50
of a rope) to a post of gold, be grasped by a minister of
noble birth, well attired and in festival array,[2] and, being 51
resolved to allot a great space for the cetiya, he ordered him
to walk round (with the turning staff in his hands) along the
ground already prepared.[3] But the great thera of wondrous 52
power named Siddhattha, the far-seeing, prevented the king
as he did this. Reflecting: 'If our king shall begin to build 53
so great a thūpa death will come upon him, ere the thūpa be
finished; moreover, so great a thūpa will be hard to repair,' 54
he, looking to the future, prevented (the measuring of) that
great dimension. In agreement with the brotherhood and 55
from reverence toward the thera, the king, though he would
fain have made (the thūpa) great, hearkened to the thera's
word and did, according to the thera's instruction, allot a 56
moderate space for the cetiya, that the (foundation) stones
might be laid.

Eight vases of silver and eight (vases) of gold did he, with 57
tireless zeal, place in the midst, and in a circle around these he 58
placed a thousand and eight new vases, and likewise (around

a troop of companions of the same name. The king's wish is fulfilled.' The theras in question and their companions are called (cf. Ṭīkā, pp. 383–384 and above v. 33 foll.) Mahābuddharakkhita, Mahādhammarakkhita, Mahāsaṃgharakkhita, and Mahānanda.

[1] Katvāna tipadakkhiṇaṃ. See note to 18. 36.

[2] Ṭīkā: Abhimaṅgalabhūtenā ti, janehi pīṇitattā abhimaṅgalasammatehi ahatavatthādihi alaṃkārehi patimaṇḍitattā ca samaṅgaliko ti 'he was samaṅgalika because he was liked by the people and because he was adorned with ornaments that were believed to be festival, as new garments (not washed before) and so forth'.

[3] And to draw, in this way, the circular outline of the thūpa.

59 each of these) a hundred and eight garments.[1] Eight splendid
bricks did he lay, each one apart by itself.[2] When he then had
60 commanded an official chosen for this and adorned in every way
to take one of them, he laid on the east side, which had been
61 prepared with many ceremonies, the first foundation stone,[3]
solemnly, upon the sweet-smelling clay.

When jasmine-flowers[4] had been offered on that spot an
62 earthquake came to pass. And he caused the other seven
(stones) to be laid by seven (other) ministers and ceremonies (of
63 consecration) to be carried out. Thus he caused the stones
to be laid on the day appointed, the fifteenth uposatha day
in the bright half of the month Āsāḷha.

64 When he had reverentially greeted the four great theras
who were free from the āsavas, who stood there at the
four heavenly quarters, and when he had honoured them
65 with gifts he came in due course, greatly rejoicing, to the
north-east side, and when he (here) had greeted the great
thera Piyadassi, who was free from the āsavas, he took his
66 place near him. Exalting the festival ceremony there this
thera preached the true doctrine to him; the preaching of the
67 thera was rich in blessing for the people. The conversion of
forty thousand to the true doctrine took place, and (yet) forty
thousand (more) became partakers in the fruit of entering
68 into the path of salvation.[5] A thousand lay-folk became even

[1] According to the Ṭīkā from aṭṭhuttare aṭṭhuttare to visuṃ visuṃ is to be read as ONE sentence, so that the stop after panā (in 58 d) in the edition should be deleted. In this case we must add in 58 c, d a second parivāriya with the meaning: 'laying around (them),' and the translation would be 'and in a circle around these he placed a thousand and eight new vases, and eight splendid bricks did he lay, each one apart by itself, (laying in a circle around) each of them a hundred and eight garments'.

[2] Namely East, NE., N., and so forth. The stones are called pavarā as they were of gold.

[3] According to the Ṭīkā the thera Mittasena had mixed the clay (gandhapiṇḍa), the thera Jayasena had poured the water on it.

[4] Jāti and sumanā are both names for *Jasminum grandiflorum*.

[5] They attained to the first stage of sanctification. See notes to 1. 32 and 33.

such as have but one (earthly) existence before them, a thou-
sand became such as have no other (earthly) existence (to
come), and a thousand also became arahants.[1] Eighteen 69
thousand bhikkhus and fourteen thousand bhikkhuṇīs attained
to arahantship.

Even so may every one whose heart is inclined to (faith in) 70
the Three Gems, knowing that by a benefactor of mankind,
whose heart is set on generous giving, the highest blessing is
brought to pass for the world, strive toward the attainment
of many virtues, as faith and so forth.

Here ends the twenty-ninth chapter, called 'The beginning of the Great Thūpa', in the Mahāvaṃsa, compiled for the serene joy and emotion of the pious.

[1] They attained to the second and third, and to the last and highest stage of sanctification. See notes to 15. 18 and 13. 17.

CHAPTER XXX

THE MAKING OF THE RELIC-CHAMBER

1 When the great king had reverentially greeted the whole
brotherhood he invited them, saying: 'Even till the cetiya is
2 finished accept ye alms from me.' The brotherhood would
not consent; when he then by degrees[1] prayed (them to
3 accept) for a week he won acceptance, for one week, by the
half of the bhikkhus. When he had obtained this from them
4 he, satisfied, had pavilions set up in eighteen places around
the place of the thūpa and commanded there, for one week,
lavish gifts to the brotherhood. Then he gave the brotherhood
leave to depart.

5 Thereupon commanding that the drums be beaten he called
the master-builders together with all speed; in number they
6 were five hundred. And one of them answered the king, on
his asking: 'How wilt thou make (the thūpa)?' 'Taking a
7 hundred workmen I will use one waggon-load of sand in
one day.'

The king rejected him.[2] Thereon they offered (to work
with) one half less and yet one half less again, and (at last
8 with) two ammaṇas[3] of sand. These four master-builders also
did the king reject. Then an experienced and shrewd master-
9 builder said to the king: 'I shall pound (the sand) in a
mortar, and then, when it is sifted, have it crushed in the
mill and (thus will use) one ammaṇa (only) of sand.'

[1] I.e. limiting his invitation more and more.

[2] The use of too much sand would tell against the durability of the thūpa. Therefore the Ṭīkā makes the king say to the master-builder: 'Shouldst thou do so the cetiya would be like a heap of pure sand and would be covered with grass and bushes.'

[3] As a measure of capacity. The Abhidhānappadīpikā 484 defines the ammaṇa as 11 doṇā. The doṇa is 64 pasatā, i.e. handfuls. Cf. Rhys Davids, *Ancient Coins and Measures of Ceylon*, pp. 17–18.

And on these words the lord of the land, whose courage 10
was like to Indra's, consented, with the thought: 'There will
be no grass nor any such thing on our cetiya,' and he 11
questioned him saying: 'In what form wilt thou make the
cetiya?' At that moment Vissakamma[1] entered into (and
possessed) him. When the master-builder had had a golden 12
bowl filled with water, he took water in his hand and let
it fall on the surface of the water. A great bubble rose up 13
like unto a half-globe of crystal. He said: 'Thus will
I make it.' And well-pleased the king bestowed on him 14
a pair of garments worth a thousand (pieces of money) and
ornamented shoes and twelve thousand kahāpaṇas.

'How shall I have the bricks transported without laying 15
burdens on the people?' Thus pondered the king in the
night-time; when the gods were aware of this they brought 16
night after night bricks to the four gates of the cetiya and
laid them down there, always as many as sufficed for one day.
When the king heard this, glad at heart, he began work on 17
the thūpa. And he made it known: 'Work shall not be done
here without wage.' At every gate he commanded to place 18
sixteen hundred thousand kahāpaṇas, very many garments,
different ornaments, solid and liquid foods and drink withal, 19
fragrant flowers, sugar and so forth, as well as the five
perfumes for the mouth.

'Let them take of these as they will when they have 20
laboured as they will.' Observing this command the king's
work-people allotted (the wages).

A bhikkhu who wished to take part in the building of the 21
thūpa took a lump of clay which he himself had prepared,[2]
went to the place of the cetiya, and deceiving the king's 22
work-people, he gave it to a workman. So soon as he received
it he knew what it was,[3] perceiving the bhikkhu's design. 23

[1] Cf. the note to 18. 24. Thus it is the god who acts and speaks through the medium of the master-builder.

[2] I.e. had kneaded and mixed. As he received no wage for this he hoped to have a share in the meritorious work of building the thūpa.

[3] He recognized the brick by the difference in the composition.

A dispute arose there. When the king afterwards heard this
he came and questioned the workman.
24 'Sire, with flowers in the one hand the bhikkhus are used
25 to give me a piece of clay with the other; but I can only
know (just so much) whether he be a bhikkhu from another
land or of this country, Sire.'[1]
26 When the king heard this word he appointed an overseer
to show him the ascetic who had offered the lump of clay.
The other showed him to the overseer and he told the king.
27 The king had three pitchers with jasmine-blossoms placed in the
courtyard of the sacred Bodhi-tree and bade the overseer give
28 them to the bhikkhu.[2] When the bhikkhu, observing nothing,
had offered them, the overseer told him this while he yet stood
there. Then did the ascetic understand.
29 A thera living in Piyaṅgalla in the Koṭṭhivāla district, who
also wished to take part in the work of building the cetiya
30 and who was a kinsman of that brick-worker, came hither and
when he had made a brick in the size (such as was used there)
31 after having learned (the exact measure) he, deceiving the
work-people, gave it to the workman. This man laid it on
its place (in the thūpa), and a quarrel arose (on this matter).
32 When the king knew this he asked: 'Is it possible to
recognize the brick?' Although the workman knew it, he
33 answered the king: 'It is impossible.' To the question:
'Dost thou know the thera?' he answered: 'Yes.' So that
he might be made known the king placed an overseer near
34 him. When the overseer had thereby come to know him he
went, with the king's consent, and visited the thera in the
35 Kaṭṭhahāla-pariveṇa and spoke with him; and when he had
learned the day of the thera's departure and the place whither

[1] The workman means by this that a more exact description of the personage was impossible to him. The conjectural reading of the Colombo edition nevā ti instead of devāti is unnecessary. The Thūpavaṃsa has also (p. 61[35]): ayaṃ pana āgantuko ayaṃ nevāsiko ti ettakaṃ jānāmi. See Mah. ed., note to this passage.

[2] So that the bhikkhu might be rewarded in this way for his work on the thūpa.

he was going, and had said to him: 'I am going with thee to
thy village,' he told the king all. The king commanded that 36
a pair of garments, worth a thousand (pieces of money), and a
costly red coverlet be given to him, and when he had (also) 37
commanded to give him many things used by samaṇas, and
sugar and a nāḷī[1] of fragrant oil withal, he laid his command
upon him.

He went with the thera, and when Piyaṅgallaka was in 38
sight he made the thera sit down in a cool shady place where
there was water, and when he had given him sugar-water and 39
had rubbed his feet with fragrant oil and put sandals upon
them, he gave him the necessaries (saying): 'For the thera 40
who visits my house[2] have I brought these with me, but the
two garments for my son. All this do I give to thee now.'
When with these words he had given those (necessaries)[3] to 41
the thera who, after receiving them, set out again upon his
journey, he, taking leave of (the thera), told him, in the king's
words, the king's command.

While the Great Thūpa was built, people in great numbers 42
who laboured for wages, being converted to the faith, went to
heaven. A wise man who perceives that only by inner faith 43
in the Holy One is the way to heaven found, will therefore
bring offerings to the thūpa.[4]

Two women, who since they had also laboured here for hire, 44
were re-born in the heaven of the thirty-three (gods), pondered
when the thūpa was finished, upon what they had formerly 45

[1] A measure of capacity (Abhidh. 1057), Sinh. næliya, according to CLOUGH 'about three pints wine-measure'.

[2] Kulūpaka or -aga is the name given in a family to a bhikkhu who continually frequents the house to receive alms, and enters thus into confidential relations with the family.

[3] After te must be understood parikkhāre.

[4] It is significant that in the Ṭīkā there is no explanation of verses 42–50. These have indeed the look of a monastic legend (cf. particularly the practical application in verse 43), which may have been interpolated at a later period. In any case the interpolation must be old. It is found in all the groups of MSS. and also in the Kambodian Mahāvaṃsa, and the story appears again in the Thūpavaṃsa.

done, and when they both became aware of the reward of
their deeds, they took fragrant flowers and came to do
46 reverence to the thūpa with offerings. When they had
offered the fragrant flowers they did homage to the cetiya.
At this moment came the thera Mahāsiva who dwelt in
47 Bhātivaṅka (with the thought): 'I will pay homage by
night to the Great Thūpa.' As he, leaning against a great
48 sattapaṇṇa-tree,[1] saw those women and without letting him-
self be seen stood there gazing at their marvellous splen-
dour, he, when their adoration was ended asked them:
49 'Here the whole island shines with the brightness of your
bodies; what works have ye done that ye have passed from
50 this world into the world of gods?' The devatās told him of
the work done by them in the (building of the) Great Thūpa;
thus does faith in the Tathāgata bring a rich reward.

51 The three terraces for the flower-offerings to the thūpa[2]
did the theras of miraculous power cause to sink down so soon
as they were laid with bricks, making them equal to the
52 surface of the soil. Nine times did they cause them to sink
down when they were laid. Then the king called together an
53 assembly of the brotherhood of bhikkhus. Eighty thousand
bhikkhus assembled there. The king sought out the brother-
hood, and when he had paid homage to them with gifts and had
54 reverentially greeted them he asked the reason of the sinking
down of the bricks. The brotherhood answered: 'In order
that the thūpa may not sink down of itself was this thing
55 done by the bhikkhus of miraculous power, O great king;
they will do it no more, make no alteration and finish the
Great Thūpa.'

56 When the king heard this, glad at heart he caused the work
on the thūpa to be continued. For the ten flower-terraces[3]

[1] Skt. saptaparṇa, *Alstonia scholaris.*

[2] It seems that pupphādhāna means the three concentric galleries (the so-called pāsāda) which form the base of the thūpa proper. SMITHER, *Architectural Remains, Anurādhapura*, p. 27; PARKER, *Ancient Ceylon*, p. 286.

[3] I.e. for the nine pupphādhānattayāni which had sunk and the tenth that remained on the surface.

ten koṭis of bricks (were used). The brotherhood of 57
bhikkhus charged the two sāmaṇeras, Uttara and Sumana,
saying: 'Bring hither, to (make) the relic-chamber in the
cetiya, fat-coloured stones.'[1] And they set out for (the land 58
of) the Northern Kurus[2] and brought from thence six massive
fat-coloured stones measuring eighty cubits in length and 59
breadth, bright as the sun, eight inches thick and like to
gaṇṭhi blossoms.[3] When they had laid one on the flower- 60
terrace in the middle and had disposed four (others) on the
four sides, in the fashion of a chest, the (theras) of wondrous 61
might placed the sixth, to serve (afterwards) as a lid, upon the
east side, making it invisible.

In the midst of the relic-chamber the king placed a bodhi- 62
tree made of jewels, splendid in every way. It had a stem 63
eighteen cubits high and five branches; the root, made of
coral, rested on sapphire. The stem made of perfectly pure 64
silver was adorned with leaves made of gems, had withered
leaves and fruits of gold and young shoots made of coral.
The eight auspicious figures[4] were on the stem and festoons 65
of flowers and beautiful rows of fourfooted beasts and rows of
geese. Over it, on the border of a beautiful canopy, was 66
a network of pearl bells and chains of little golden bells and
bands here and there. From the four corners of the canopy 67
hung bundles of pearl strings each worth nine hundred
thousand (pieces of money). The figures of sun, moon and 68
stars and different lotus-flowers, made of jewels, were
fastened to the canopy. A thousand and eight pieces of 69
divers stuffs, precious and of varied colours, were hung to the
canopy. Around the bodhi-tree ran a vedikā made of all manner 70
of jewels; the pavement within was made of great myrobalan-
pearls.[5]

Rows of vases (some) empty and (some) filled with flowers 71

[1] See note to 1. 39. [2] See note to 1. 18.

[3] The Ṭīkā explains gaṇṭhipuppha by bandhujīvaka-puppha. Cf. B.R., *Skt.-Wtb.*, s.v. bandhujīva: *Pentapetes phoenicea* (hat eine schöne rote Blume . . .).

[4] Cf. note to 27. 37.

[5] See 11. 14; cf. 28. 36.

made of all kinds of jewels and filled with four kinds of
fragrant water were placed at the foot of the bodhi-tree.
72 On a throne, the cost whereof was one koṭi, erected to the
east of the bodhi-tree, he placed a shining golden Buddha-
73 image seated. The body and members of this image were duly[1]
made of jewels of different colours, beautifully shining. Mahā-
74 brahmā stood there holding a silver parasol and Sakka carry-
75 ing out the consecration with the Vijayuttara shell, Pañcasikha
with his lute in his hand,[2] and Kālanāga with the dancing-girls,
and the thousand-handed Māra with his elephants and train
76 of followers. Even like the throne to the east (other) thrones
were erected, the cost of each being a koṭi, facing the other
77 seven regions of the heavens. And even thus, so that the
bodhi-tree was at the head, a couch[3] was placed, also worth
one koṭi, adorned with jewels of every kind.

78 The events[4] during the seven weeks[5] he commanded them
to depict duly here and there in the relic chamber, and also the
79 prayer of Brahmā,[6] the setting in motion the wheel of the

[1] According to the Ṭīkā the finger-nails and the whites of the eyes were made of mountain-crystal, the palms of the hands, soles of the feet, and the lips of red coral, the eyebrows and pupils of sapphire, the teeth of diamonds, &c.

[2] Pañcasikho gandhabbaputto (D. II. 265[12] foll.; Jāt. IV. 69[1]) is the poet and minstrel of the gods. He appears in attendance on Sakka in Jāt. III. 222[10], &c.; IV. 63[7], &c., and often. The gandhabbā (Skt. gandharva) are the heavenly musicians.

[3] To represent the death-bed of the Buddha, the parinibbāṇa-mañca, and intended as a receptacle for the relics.

[4] In the vv. 78-87 scenes from the Buddha's life, from the sambodhi to his death and obsequies, are enumerated. Cf. for this especially M.V. I. 1–23 (Oldenberg, *Vin. Piṭ.* i, p. 1 foll.); the Jātakanidāna (Fausböll, *Jātakas*, i, p. 77 foll.); and for 84[d] foll. the Mahāparinibbāṇasutta (D. II. p. 106 foll.; Rhys Davids, *S.B.E.* xi, p. 44 foll., and *S.B.B.* iii, p. 71 foll.). Kern, *Manual of Indian Buddhism*, p. 21 foll. On such scenes as the subject of bas-reliefs in buddhistic monuments see Foucher, *L'Art Gréco-Bouddhique*, i, p. 414 foll.; Grünwedel, *Buddh. Kunst*, pp. 61 foll., 118 foll.

[5] The time immediately after the sambodhi which the Buddha spent near the bodhi-tree.

[6] Brahmā and the other gods entreat the Buddha to preach the discovered truth to the world.

doctrine, the admission of Yasa into the order, the pabbajjā of
the Bhaddavaggiyas and the subduing of the jaṭilas; the visit 80
of Bimbisāra and the entry into Rājagaha, the accepting of the
Veḷuvana, the eighty disciples,[1] the journey to Kapilavatthu 81
and the (miracle of the) jewelled path in that place,[2] the pab-
bajjā of Rāhula and Nanda,[3] the accepting of the Jetavana, the 82
miracle at the foot of the mango-tree, the preaching in the
heaven of the gods, the miracle of the descent of the gods,[4] and
the assembly with the questioning of the thera,[5] the Mahāsa- 83
mayasuttanta,[6] and the exhortation to Rāhula,[7] the Mahāmaṅ-
galasutta,[8] and the encounter with (the elephant) Dhanapāla;[9]
the subduing of the (yakkha) Āḷavaka, of the (robber) Aṅguli- 84

[1] The smaller circle of the disciples after the admission of Sāriputta and Moggallāna.

[2] The miracle of the ratanacaṅkama consisted in this that the Buddha created a path of gems in the air, pacing upon which he preached to the Sakyas. According to *Jāt.* i, p. 88, the Buddha performed in Kapilavatthu the yamakapāṭihāriya (also called in v. 82 ambamūle pāṭihīra). Cf. note to 17. 44.

[3] Mah. ed. read Rāhulananda° instead of Rāhulān°.

[4] On these legends see SPENCE HARDY, *Manual of Buddhism*, pp. 295 foll., 298 foll., 301. Cf. FOUCHER, *l. l.*, pp. 473 foll., 483 foll., 537 foll.

[5] The allusion is to the assembly before the gates of Saṅkapura, where the Buddha appears, after his return from the heaven of the gods, and Sāriputta's intellectual superiority to the other disciples is demonstrated. SPENCE HARDY, *l. l.*, p. 302.

[6] = Sutta 20 of the Dīghanikāya (D. II. p. 253 foll.) preached in Kapilavatthu.

[7] In Majjhima-Nik. I. p. 414 foll. is an Ambalaṭṭhikā-Rāhulovādasutta preached in Veḷuvana near Rājagaha; and at III. p. 277 foll. a Cūla-Rāhulovādasutta preached at Jetavana. Cf. also Saṃyutta-Nik. III. 135–136; IV. 105–107.

[8] = Sutta-nipāta II. 4 (ed. FAUSBÖLL, p. 45).

[9] A later name of the elephant which Devadatta lets loose upon the Buddha to crush him and whom the Buddha subdues by the power of his gentleness. SPENCE HARDY (*l. l.*, p. 320 foll.) mentions Nālāgiri or Mālāgiri as his original name. The Milindapañha (ed. TRENCKNER), p. 207[25], has Dhanapālaka. In Sanskrit Buddhist sources Vasupāla also occurs. KERN, *Buddhismus*, transl. by Jacobi, i, p. 251; FOUCHER, *l. l.*, p. 542 foll.

māla and the (nāga-king) Apalāla,[1] the meeting with the
85 Pārāyanakas,[2] the giving-up of life,[3] the accepting of the dish
of pork,[4] and of the two gold-coloured garments,[5] the drinking
86 of the pure water,[6] and the Parinibbāṇa itself; the lamentation
of gods and men, the revering of the feet by the thera,[7] the
burning (of the body[8]), the quenching of the fire,[9] the funeral
87 rites in that very place and the distributing of the relics by
Doṇa.[10] Jātakas[11] also which are fitted to awaken faith did the
88 noble (king) place here in abundance. The Vessantarajātaka[12]

[1] SPENCE HARDY, *l. l.*, pp. 261 foll., 249 foll.; BURNOUF, *Introduction à l'histoire du Bouddhisme Indien*, p. 377; FOUCHER, *l. l.*, pp. 507 foll., 544 foll.

[2] TURNOUR: 'the Pārāyana brahman tribe (at Rājagaha).'

[3] Three months before his death the Buddha resolves to enter into the nibbāṇa at the end of that appointed time. An earthquake accompanies his resolve.

[4] The dish set before the Buddha by the smith Cunda—the sūkaramaddava—brought on the illness which finally caused his death.

[5] The garments were presented to the Buddha by the Malla Pukkusa. As Ānanda put them on him his body radiated unearthly brightness, as a sign of approaching death.

[6] The turgid waters of the Kakutthā-river become clear by a miracle when Ānanda takes from it a draught for the Master.

[7] None can succeed in setting light to the funeral pyre on which the body of the Buddha is lying, for the thera Mahākassapa is still on his way from Pāvā to pay the last honours to the dead Master.

[8] After Mahākassapa has passed round the funeral pyre three times, and has then uncovered the master's feet and done homage to them, the pyre breaks into flame of itself.

[9] Streams of water fall from heaven and extinguish the fire.

[10] In order to settle the dispute that threatens to burn fiercely over the remains of the Buddha the brahman Doṇa divides them into eight parts.

[11] On pictorial representations of the Buddha's former existences (jātaka-stories) see FOUCHER, *l. l.*, p. 270 foll.

[12] *The Jātaka*, ed. FAUSBÖLL, vi, p. 479 foll. The existence as Vessantara is the Buddha's last earthly existence. He passes from this into the Tusita-heaven. Hence this jātaka has a particular significance. See FOUCHER, *l. l.*, pp. 283–285. On a fresco representing this jātaka in a series of detached single scenes, in the Degaldoruwa monastery in Ceylon, see COOMARASWAMY, *Open Letter to the Kandyan Chiefs*, p. 6 foll. (reprinted from *Ceylon Observer*, Feb. 17, 1905).

he commanded them to depict fully, and in like manner
(that which befell beginning at the descent) from the Tusita-
heaven even to the Bodhi-throne.[1]

At the four quarters of the heaven stood the (figures of) 89
the four Great kings,[2] and the thirty-three gods and the
thirty-two (celestial) maidens and the twenty-eight chiefs of 90
the yakkhas; but above these[3] devas raising their folded
hands, vases filled with flowers likewise, dancing devatās and 91
devatās playing instruments of music, devas with mirrors in
their hands, and devas also bearing flowers and branches,
devas with lotus-blossoms and so forth in their hands and 92
other devas of many kinds, rows of arches made of gems and
(rows) of dhammacakkas;[4] rows of sword-bearing devas and 93
also devas bearing pitchers. Above their heads were pitchers
five cubits high, filled with fragrant oil, with wicks made of 94
dukūla fibres continually alight. In an arch of crystal there
was in each of the four corners a great gem and (moreover) 95
in the four corners four glimmering heaps of gold, precious
stones and pearls and of diamonds were placed. On the wall 96
made of fat-coloured stones sparkling zig-zag lines[5] were
traced, serving as adornment for the relic-chamber. The king 97
commanded them to make all the figures here in the en-
chanting relic-chamber of massive wrought gold.[6]

[1] FOUCHER, *l. l.*, pp. 285-289, 290 foll. The tusitā are a class of gods, Skt. tuṣita.

[2] The four guardians of the world (lokapālā): Dhataraṭṭha in the N., Virūḷha in the S., Virūpakkha in the W., and Vessavaṇa in the E.

[3] According to the Ṭīkā's interpretation this tatopari belongs to añjalipaggahā devā. The comma in Mah. ed. should then be moved accordingly.

[4] The 'wheel of the doctrine', a sacred symbol of the Buddhists. Originally perhaps a sun-symbol. See SEWELL, *J.R.A.S.* 1886, p. 392.

[5] Vijjulatā, literally 'lightnings'. The Ṭīkā explains vijjulatā by meghalatā nāma vijjukumāriyo, and quotes from the Porāṇā (cf. GEIGER, *Dīp. and Mah.*, p. 45) the following verse: meghalatā vijjukumārī medapiṇḍikabhittiyā | samantā caturo passe dhātugabbhe parikkhipi.

[6] The Ṭīkā goes into fuller details, to refute those who may perhaps doubt the truth of the description. GEIGER, *l. l.*, p. 35.

98 The great thera Indagutta, who was gifted with the six
supernormal faculties, the most wise, directed here all this,
99 being set over the work. All this was completed without
hindrance by reason of the wondrous power of the king, the
wondrous power of the devatās, and the wondrous power of
the holy (theras).

100 If the wise man who is adorned with the good gifts of faith, has done homage to the blessed (Buddha) the supremely venerable, the highest of the world, who is freed from darkness, while he was yet living, and then to his relics, that were dispersed abroad by him who had in view the salvation of mankind; and if he then understands: herein is equal merit; then indeed will he reverence the relics of the Sage even as the blessed (Buddha himself) in his lifetime.

Here ends the thirtieth chapter, called 'The Making of the Relic-Chamber', in the Mahāvaṃsa, compiled for the serene joy and emotion of the pious.

CHAPTER XXXI

THE ENSHRINING OF THE RELICS

WHEN the subduer of foes had completed the work on the 1
relic-chamber he brought about an assembly of the brotherhood
and spoke thus: 'The work on the relic-chamber has been com- 2
pleted by me; to-morrow I will enshrine the relics; do you,
venerable sirs, take thought for the relics.' When the great 3
king had spoken thus he went thence into the city; but the
assembly of bhikkhus sought out a bhikkhu who should bring
relics hither; and they charged the ascetic named Soṇuttara, 4
gifted with the six supernormal faculties, who dwelt in the
Pūjā-pariveṇa, with the task of bringing the relics.

Now once, when the Master was wandering about (on the 5
earth) for the salvation of the world, on the shore of the
Ganges a brahman named Nanduttara invited the Saṃ- 6
buddha and offered him hospitality together with the
brotherhood. Near the landing-place Payāga [1] the Master,
with the brotherhood, embarked on a ship. As then the 7
thera Bhaddaji of wondrous might, endowed with the six
supernormal faculties, saw there a place where the water
whirled in eddies, he said to the bhikkhus: 'The golden 8
palace measuring twenty-five yojanas wherein I dwelt, when
I was (the king) Mahāpanāda,[2] is sunk here. When the 9
water of the Ganges comes to it here it whirls in eddies.'

The bhikkhus, who did not believe him, told this to the
Master. The Master said: 'Banish the doubts of the 10
bhikkhus.' Then to show his power to command even in
the Brahma-world he rose, by his wondrous might, into the 11

[1] Skt. Prayāga, the holy place where Gaṅgā and Yamunā unite.

[2] Cf. Mah. 2. 4; Dīp. 3. 7. There is also mention of M.'s palace, Mah. 37. 62 (= Cūlavaṃsa 37. 12, ed. Col., p. 7; TURNOUR, *Mah.*, p. 239).

air and when he, floating at a height even of seven tālas,
had taken the Dussa-thūpa[1] in the Brahma-world upon his
12 outstretched hand, and had brought it hither and shown it to
the people, he put it again in the place to which it belonged.
13 Thereon he dived, by his wondrous power, into the Ganges,
and seizing the palace by its spire[2] with his toe he raised it
high up, and when he had shown it to the people he let it
14 fall again there (to its place). When the brahman Nand-
uttara saw this wonder he uttered the wish: 'May I (at
some time) have the power to procure relics that others
15 hold in their possession.' Therefore did the brotherhood
lay this charge upon the ascetic Soṇuttara[3] although he
16 was but sixteen years old. 'Whence shall I bring a relic?'
he asked the brotherhood, and thereupon the brotherhood
described the relics thus:

17 'Lying on his deathbed the Master of the world, that with
his relics he might bring to pass salvation for the world,
18 spoke thus to (Sakka) the king of the gods: O king of the
gods, of the eight doṇas[4] of my bodily relics one doṇa, adored
19 (first) by the Koḷiyas in Rāmagāma,[5] shall be borne thence
into the kingdom of the nāgas and when it will be adored
even there by the nāgas it (at the last) shall come to be
20 enshrined in the Great Thūpa on the island of Laṅkā. The
far-seeing and most wise thera Mahākassapa[6] then, mindful
of the (coming) division of the relics by king Dhammāsoka,

[1] Dāṭhāvaṃsa 35 (*J.P.T.S.* 1884, p. 113).

[2] For the meaning of thūpikā see Attanagaluvaṃsa, ed. ALWIS, IX. 7 (p. 32[24]): cetiyasīse kirīṭaṃ viya kanakamayaṃ thūpikaṃ ca yojetvā 'having fastened a golden thūpikā on the summit of the cetiya like a diadem'.

[3] Who had in fact been that same Nanduttara in a former existence.

[4] A certain measure of capacity. See 17. 51. For the passage following cf. D. II. pp. 165–168.

[5] The Koḷiyas were a tribe related to the Sakyas. The Rohiṇī was the boundary river between them. In the Sumaṅgala-Vilāsinī (ed. RHYS DAVIDS and CARPENTER, i, p. 262) the capital of the Koḷiyas is called Vyagghapajja.

[6] The saṃghathera after the Buddha's death and head of the First Council.

had a great and well-guarded treasure of relics placed[1] near 21
Rājagaha (the capital) of king Ajātasattu as he brought 22
thither the seven doṇas of relics; but the doṇa in Rāmagāma
he did not take, knowing the Master's intention. When the 23
king Dhammāsoka saw the great treasure of relics he thought
to have the eighth doṇa also brought thither. But, bethinking 24
them that it was destined by the Conqueror to be enshrined
in the Great Thūpa, the ascetics[2] of that time who had
overcome the āsavas prevented Dhammāsoka from (doing)
this. The thūpa in Rājagāma, that was built on the shore 25
of the Ganges, was destroyed by the overflowing of the
Ganges, but the urn with the relics reached the ocean and 26
stayed there in the twofold divided waters[3] on a throne made
of many-coloured gems surrounded by rays of light. When 27
the nāgas saw the urn they went to the nāga palace
Mañjerika of the king Kālanāga and told him. And he went 28
thither with ten thousand koṭis of nāgas, and when he
had brought the relics to his palace, (adoring them) with
offerings meanwhile, and had built over them a thūpa made 29
of all kinds of jewels and a temple above the (thūpa) also,
he, filled with zeal, brought offerings continually, together
with the (other) nāgas. There a strong guard is set; go thou 30
and bring the relics hither. To-morrow will the lord of the
land set about enshrining the relics.'

When he had heard these words of the brotherhood he, 31
answering 'Yes (I shall do so)', withdrew to his cell pondering
over the time when he must set forth. 'To-morrow the 32
enshrining of the relics shall take place,' thus proclaimed
the king by beat of drums in the city, by which all that

[1] Kārāpento at 21 c seems to be employed pleonastically. The construction of the sentence may be explained, as I have indicated by the punctuation in the edition, thus: Mahākassapathero ... mahādhātunidhānaṃ ... kārayi, Rājagahassa rañño Ajātasattuno sāmante (taṃ nidhānaṃ) kārāpento.

[2] Ṭīkā: tattha khīṇāsavā yatī ti tasmiṃ Dhammāsokakāle khīṇāsavā bhikkhū.

[3] The waters of the sea divide to receive the urn. TURNOUR's translation: 'Where the stream of the Ganges spreads in two opposite directions,' certainly does not give the right sense.

33 must be done is set forth. He commanded that the whole
city and the road leading hither[1] be carefully adorned and
34 that the burghers be clad in festal garments. Sakka, the king
of the gods, summoning Vissakamma (for this task), caused
the whole island of Laṅkā to be adorned in manifold ways.
35 At the four gates of the city the ruler of men had garments, food and so forth placed for the use of the people.
36 On the fifteenth uposatha-day in the evening, (the king)
glad at heart, well versed in the duties of kings, arrayed in all
37 his ornaments, surrounded on every side by all his dancing-
women and his warriors in complete armour, by a great body
38 of troops, as well as by variously adorned elephants, horses
and chariots, mounted his car of state[2] that was drawn by
39 four pure white Sindhu-horses[3] and stood there, making the
(sumptuously) adorned and beautiful elephant Kaṇḍula pace
before him, holding a golden casket[4] under the white parasol.
40 A thousand and eight beautiful women from the city, with
the adornment of well-filled pitchers, surrounded the car and,
41 even as many women bearing baskets (filled) with various
42 flowers, and as many again bearing lamps on staves. A thou-
sand and eight boys in festal array surrounded him, bearing
43 beautiful many-coloured flags. While the earth seemed as it
were rent[5] asunder by all manner of sounds from various
instruments of music, by the (thundering) noise of elephants,
44 horses and chariots, the renowned king shone forth, as he
went to the Mahāmeghavana, in glory like to the king of
the gods when he goes to Nandavana.[6]
45 When the ascetic Soṇuttara, sitting in his cell, heard the
noise of the music in the city[7] as the king began to

[1] I.e. to the Mahāvihāra.

[2] Suratha, according to the Ṭīkā, is used here as maṅgalaratha elsewhere.

[3] See note to 23. 71.

[4] To receive the relics.

[5] The loc. absol. bhijjante viya bhūtale does not belong to the whole sentence but especially to the pres. part. yanto.

[6] See note to 15. 185.

[7] Pure is not 'for the first time' (TURNOUR) but = nagaramhi (Ṭīkā).

set out, he went, plunging into the earth to the palace of the 46
nāgas and appeared there in a short time before the nāga-
king. When the king of the nāgas had risen up and had 47
greeted him and invited him to be seated on a throne, he
paid him the honours due to a guest and questioned him as
to the country whence he had come. When this was told he 48
asked the reason of the thera's coming. And he told him
the whole matter and gave him the message of the brother-
hood: 'The relics that are here in thy hands are appointed 49
by the Buddha to be enshrined in the Great Thūpa; do thou
then give them to me.' When the nāga-king heard this, he 50
was sorely troubled and thought: 'This samaṇa might have
the power to take them from me by force; therefore must the 51
relics be carried elsewhere,' and he made this known by a sign
to his nephew, who was present there. And he, who was 52
named Vāsuladatta, understanding the hint, went to the
temple of the cetiya, and when he had swallowed the urn
(with the relics) he went to the foot of Mount Sineru[1] and 53
lay there coiled in a circle. Three hundred yojanas long
was the ring and one yojana was his measure around.[2] When 54
the (nāga) of wondrous might had created many thousand
(heads with puffed-up) hoods he belched forth, as he lay
there, smoke and fire. When he (then) had created many 55
thousand snakes like to himself, he made them lie about him
in a circle.

Many nāgas and devas came thither then with the thought: 56
'We will behold the combat of the two nāgas.'[3]

[1] Name of the mythical mountain Meru which is the central point of the universe.

[2] That is, the nāga's body was a yojana in circumference. The Ṭīkā gives another sense to the passage. According to it **bhogo** is equal to **bhogavā**, i.e. snake, and **yojanavaṭṭavā** equal to **yojanasatavaṭṭavā**, **sata** being understood from what precedes. That is certainly too artificial. TURNOUR translates, 'with a hood forty yojanas broad'; WIJESIṆHA: 'one yojana broad.' But none of this appears in the text.

[3] A double meaning. Read one way **nāga** 'snake-demon', refers to Vāsuladatta; the other way, referring to the thera, it means, 'hero, great or mighty man.'

57 When the uncle perceived that the relics had been taken
thence by his nephew, he said to the thera: 'There are no
58 relics with me.' The thera told him the story of the coming
of the relics from the beginning, and said then to the nāga-
king: 'Give thou the relics.'
59 And to content him by some other means the serpent-king
took the thera with him and went to the temple with the
60 cetiya and described it to him: 'See, O bhikkhu, this cetiya
adorned with many gems in many ways and the nobly built
61 temple for the cetiya. Nay, but all the jewels in the whole
island of Laṅkā are not of so great worth as the stone-slab[1] at
the foot of the steps; what shall be said of the other (treasures)?
62 Truly it beseems thee not, O bhikkhu, to bear away the relics
from a place of high honour to a place of lesser honour.'
63 'Verily, there is no understanding of the truth[2] among
you nāgas. It were fitting indeed to bear away the relics to
64 a place where there is understanding of the truth. The
Tathāgatas are born for deliverance from the saṃsāra, and
thereon is the Buddha intent, therefore I will bear away the
65 relics. This very day the king will set about enshrining
the relics; swiftly then give me the relics without delay.'
66 The nāga said: 'If thou shalt see the relics, venerable sir,
take them and go.' Three times the thera made him repeat
67 this (word), then did the thera standing on that very spot
create a (long) slender arm, and stretching the hand straight-
68 way down the throat of the nephew he took the urn with
the relics, and crying: 'Stay, nāga!' he plunged into the
earth and rose up (out of it) in his cell.
69 The nāga-king thought: 'The bhikkhu is gone hence,

[1] At the lower end of the stairway of buildings in Ceylon lie semi-circular stones with gracefully executed ornaments, the so-called 'Moonstones'. SMITHER, *Anurádhapura*, p. 58, with Plate LVII, fig. 3.

[2] Certainly to be taken in the concrete sense of the four holy Truths (ariyasaccāni) which form the foundation of Buddhist doctrine: the Truths concerning sorrow, the cause of sorrow, the cessation of sorrow, and the way leading to the cessation of sorrow. Saṃyutta, v. 420.

deceived by us,' and he sent to his nephew to bring the relics
(again). But when the nephew could not find the urn in his 70
belly he came lamenting and told his uncle. Then the nāga- 71
king also lamented: 'We are betrayed,' and all the nāgas who
came in crowds lamented likewise. But rejoicing in the victory 72
of the mighty bhikkhu [1] the gods assembled, and adoring the
relics with offerings they came together with the (thera).

Lamenting, the nāgas came to the brotherhood and made 73
right woful plaint sorrowful over the carrying away of the
relics. From compassion the brotherhood left them a few of 74
the relics; rejoicing at this they went and brought treasures
as offerings.

Sakka came to the spot with the gods bringing a throne 75
set with jewels and a casket of gold. In a beautiful pavilion 76
made of jewels that was built by Vissakamma on the spot,
where the thera had emerged (from the earth), he set up the
throne and when he had received the urn with the relics from 77
the hand of the thera, and had put them in the casket he
placed it on the throne.

Brahmā held the parasol, Saṃtusita the yak-tail whisk, 78
Suyāma [2] held the jewelled fan, Sakka the shell with water.
The four great kings [3] stood with swords in their grip and the 79
thirty-three gods of wondrous power with baskets in their
hands. When they had gone thither offering pāricchattaka- 80
flowers [4] the thirty-two celestial maidens stood there bearing
lamps on staves. Moreover, to ward off the evil yakkhas the 81
twenty-eight yakkha-chieftains stood holding guard. Pañca- 82
sikha stood there playing the lute, and Timbaru who had set
up a stage, making music to sound forth.[5] Many devas (stood 83
there) singing sweet songs and the nāga-king Mahākāla

[1] Lit. 'Of the nāga among bhikkhus.' See note to v. 56.

[2] Saṃtusita and Suyāma also appear as devaputtā at A. IV. 242^{26}, 243^{1}, and S. IV. 280^{23}. Cf. also Jāt. I. 48^{16}, 53^{17}, 81^{10-11}; IV. 266^{3}.

[3] See note to 30. 89.

[4] Blossoms of a tree growing in the Tāvatiṃsa-heaven. M.V. I. 20. 10; Jāt. I. 202^{14}, IV. 265^{18}.

[5] On Pañcasikha see note to 30. 75; Timbaru is called in D. II. 268^{2-3} G a n d h a b b a - r ā j a. With raṅgabhūmi cf. Sinh. raṅgabim (= raṅgamaḍulu) 'place for acting, theatre'.

84 chanting praises in manifold ways. Celestial instruments of
music resounded, a celestial chorus pealed forth, the devatās
85 let fall a rain of heavenly perfumes and so forth. But the
thera Indagutta created, to ward off Māra, a parasol of copper
86 that he made great as the universe. On the east side of the
relics and here and there in the five regions[1] the bhikkhus
raised their song in chorus.

87 Thither, glad at heart, went the great king Duṭṭhagāmaṇi,
and when he had laid the casket with the relics in the golden
88 casket that he had brought upon his head, and had placed it
upon a throne, he stood there with folded hands, offering
gifts to the relics and adoring them.

89 When the prince saw the celestial parasol, the celestial
perfumes, and the rest, and heard the sound of celestial in-
90 struments of music and so forth, albeit he did not see the
Brahma-gods he, rejoicing and amazed at the miracle, wor-
shipped the relics, with the offering of a parasol and investing
them with the kingship over Laṅkā.

91 'To the Master of the world, to the Teacher who bears the
threefold parasol, the heavenly parasol and the earthly and
92 the parasol of deliverance I consecrate three times my kingly
rank.' With these words he, with joyful heart, thrice con-
ferred on the relics the kingship of Laṅkā.

93 Thus, together with gods and men, worshipping the relics
with offerings, the prince placed them, with the caskets, upon
94 his head, and when he, surrounded by the brotherhood of the
bhikkhus, had passed three times, going toward the left,
around the thūpa, he ascended it on the east side and
95 descended into the relic-chamber. Ninety-six koṭis of ara-
hants stood with folded hands surrounding the magnificent
96 thūpa. While the king, filled with joy, when he had mounted
into the relic-chamber, thought: 'I will lay them on the
97 costly and beautiful couch,' the relic-casket, together with
the relics, rose up from his head, and, floating at a height of
98 seven tālas in the air, the casket forthwith opened of itself;

[1] By this is meant east, west, south, and north, and north-east, also cf. 29. 64 and 65. In Skt. the north-east is called aparājitā diś, Manu VI. 31.

the relics rose up out of it and taking the form of the Buddha,
gleaming with the greater and lesser signs,[1] they performed, 99
even as the Buddha (himself) at the foot of the gaṇḍamba-
tree that miracle of the double appearances, that was brought
to pass by the Blessed One during his lifetime.[2] As they 100
beheld this miracle, with believing and joyous heart, twelve
koṭis of devas and men attained to arahantship; those 101
who attained the three other fruits (of salvation)[3] were past
reckoning.

Quitting the form of the Buddha those (relics) returned to
their place in the casket; but the casket sank down again 102
and rested on the head of the king. Then passing round[4]
the relic-chamber in procession with the thera Indagutta and 103
the dancing-women, the glorious king coming even to the
beautiful couch laid the casket on the jewelled throne. And 104
when he, filled with zeal, had washed again his hands in
water fragrant with perfumes, and had rubbed them with the
five kinds of perfumes, he opened the casket, and taking out 105
the relics the ruler of the land, who was intent on the
welfare of his people, thought thus:[5] 'If these relics shall 106
abide undisturbed by any man soever, and if the relics,
serving as a refuge for the people, shall endure continually,
then may they rest, in the form of the Master as he lay upon 107
his deathbed, upon this well-ordered and precious couch.'

Thinking thus he laid the relics upon the splendid couch; 108
the relics lay there upon the splendid couch even in such
a shape. On the fifteenth uposatha-day in the bright half 109
of the month Āsāḷha, under the constellation Uttarāsāḷha,
were the relics enshrined in this way. At the enshrining of 110
the relics the great earth quaked and many wonders came to
pass in divers ways.

[1] See note to 5. 92.

[2] Cf. 17. 44, also the note to 30. 81.

[3] I.e. the state of a sotāpanno, of a sakadāgāmī or of an anāgāmī. See notes to 1. 33; 15. 18; 13. 17.

[4] Pariharaṃ (part. pres.). The subst. parihāra=Sinh. pæra-hæra means a solemn procession.

[5] A saccakiriyā, cf. note to 18. 39.

111 With believing heart did the king worship the relics by (offering) a white parasol, and conferred on them the entire overlordship of Laṅkā for seven days.

112 All the adornments on his body he offered in the relic-chamber, and so likewise (did) the dancing-women, the
113 ministers, the retinue and the devatās. When the king had distributed garments, sugar, clarified butter and so forth among the brotherhood, and had caused the bhikkhus to recite
114 in chorus the whole night, then, when it was again day, he had the drum beaten in the city, being mindful of the welfare of the people: 'All the people shall adore the relics
115 throughout this week.' The great thera Indagutta, of wondrous might, commanded: 'Those men of the island
116 of Laṅkā who would fain adore the relics shall arrive hither at the same moment, and when they have adored the relics here shall return each one to his house.' This came to pass as he had commanded.

117 When the great king of great renown had commanded great offerings of alms to the great brotherhood of the
118 bhikkhus for the week uninterruptedly, he proclaimed: 'All that was to be done in the relic-chamber has been carried out by me; now let the brotherhood take the charge of closing the relic-chamber.'

119 The brotherhood charged the two sāmaṇeras with this task. They closed up the relic-chamber with the fat-coloured stone that they had brought.[1]

120 'The flowers here shall not wither, these perfumes shall not dry up; the lamps shall not be extinguished; nothing
121 whatsoever shall perish; the six fat-coloured stones shall hold together for evermore.' All this did the (theras) who had overcome the āsavas command at that time.

122 The great king, mindful of the welfare (of the people), issued the command: 'So far as they are able (to do so) the
123 people shall enshrine relics.' And above the great relic-treasure did the people, so far as they could, carry out the
124 enshrining of thousands of relics. Enclosing all together

[1] Cf. with this 30. 61. The two novices are Uttara and Sumana, mentioned in 30. 57.

the king completed the thūpa and, moreover, he completed the four-sided building [1] on the cetiya.

Thus are the Buddhas incomprehensible, and incompre- 125
hensible is the nature of the Buddhas, and incomprehensible
is the reward of those who have faith in the incomprehensible.[2]

Thus do the pious themselves perform pure deeds of merit, 126
in order to obtain the most glorious of all blessings; and
they, with pure heart, make also others to perform them in
order to win a following of eminent people of many kinds.[3]

Here ends the thirty-first chapter, called 'The Enshrining of the Relics', in the Mahāvaṃsa, compiled for the serene joy and emotion of the pious.

[1] A dāgaba consists essentially of three elements. The dome, usually hemispherical, and ordinarily raised on a cylindrical base, forms the principal part. In the upper part of this is the relic chamber. The second part is a square block of brickwork now mostly known by the Burmese term 'tee'. This is the caturassacaya of our passage. Finally the 'tee' forms the base for the conical spire (chatta = parasol) that crowns the whole. PARKER, *Ancient Ceylon*, p. 263. In 32. 5 is evidently muddhavedī 'top or upper-terrace' or 'rail', a designation of the 'tee'. Cf. Appendix D, s. v. vedī.

[2] Cf. 17. 56.

[3] Ṭīkā: khattiyabrāhmaṇādivividhavisesajanaparivāra-hetubhūtāni puññāni pi pare ca kārentīti attho 'they make also others to perform meritorious works which are the cause of (obtaining) a following of eminent people of various kinds as khattiyas, brāhmaṇas and so forth.'

CHAPTER XXXII

THE ENTRANCE INTO THE TUSITA-HEAVEN

1 ERE yet the making of the chatta and the plaster-work[1]
on the cetiya was finished the king fell sick with a sickness
2 that was (fated) to be mortal. He sent for his younger
brother Tissa from Dīghavāpi and said to him: 'Complete
3 thou the work of the thūpa that is not yet finished.' Because
of his brother's weakness he had a covering made of
white cloths by seamsters and therewith was the cetiya
4 covered, and thereon did he command painters to make on it a
vedikā duly and rows of filled vases likewise and the row with
5 the five-finger ornament.[2] And he had a chatta made of
bamboo-reeds by plaiters of reeds and on the upper vedikā
6 a sun and moon of kharapatta.[3] And when he had had this
(thūpa) painted cunningly with lacquer and kaṅkuṭṭhaka[4] he
declared to the king: 'That which was yet to do to the thūpa
is completed.'

7 Lying on a palanquin the king went thither, and when on

[1] On chatta see note to 31. 124. By sudhākamma is meant covering with stucco the dome of the cetiya which was made of brick.

[2] The vedikā (rail) seems, as it was counterfeited in painting, to have been merely an ornament. 'Buddhist railings' occur in low-relief as ornament on the cornice of the first pāsāda of the Ruwanwæli-dagaba (SMITHER, *Anurádhapura*, p. 26) as also, which may be taken into account here, on the 'tee' of the Abhayagiri and the Jetavana-dagaba (SMITHER, pp. 47 and 52). We also frequently meet with 'urns' as ornaments. But it is not clear what ornament is meant by pañcaṅgulikapantikā.

[3] Muddhavedī='tee', see note to 31. 124. The picture of the sun on the four sides of the 'tee' is an emblem constantly found. Kharapatta=Skt. kharapatra is a name of different plants.

[4] On kaṅkuṭṭhaka 'a kind of soil or mould of a golden or silver colour'=Skt. kaṅkuṣṭha, see Mah. ed., p. 355.

his palanquin he had passed round the cetiya, going toward
the left, he paid homage to it at the south entrance, and as he 8
then, lying on his right side on his couch spread upon the
ground, beheld the splendid Great Thūpa, and lying on his 9
left side the splendid Lohapāsāda, he became glad at heart,
surrounded by the brotherhood of bhikkhus.

Since they had come from here and there to have news of the 10
sick (king), there were (present) in that assembly ninety-six
koṭis of bhikkhus. The bhikkhus, group by group, recited in 11
chorus. When the king did not see the thera Theraputtābhaya
among them he thought: 'The great warrior, who fought 12
victoriously through twenty-eight great battles with me nor
ever yielded his ground, the thera Therasutābhaya comes not 13
now to help me, now that the death-struggle is begun, for
methinks he (fore)sees my defeat.'

When the thera, who dwelt by the source of the Karinda- 14
river[1] on the Pañjali-mountain, knew his thought he came 15
with a company of five hundred (bhikkhus) who had over-
come the āsavas, passing through the air by his miraculous
power, and he stood among those who surrounded the king.
When the king saw him he was glad at heart and he bade him 16
be seated before him and said: 'Formerly I fought with you,
the ten great warriors, by my side; now have I entered alone 17
upon the battle with death, and the foe death I cannot conquer.'

The thera answered: 'O great king, fear not, ruler of men. 18
Without conquering the foe sin the foe death is unconquer-
able. All that has come into (this transitory) existence 19
must necessarily perish also, perishable is all that exists;[2]

[1] The Kirindu-oya or Māgama-ganga of which the mouth is in the Southern Province, east of Hambantoṭa, and the source in the mountains south of Badulla. Consequently the Pañjali-pabbata must be sought here also.

[2] The thera alludes to the oft-quoted verse that is put into Sakka's mouth after the Buddha's death in the Mahāparinibbāṇasutta (D. II. 157[8]):

anicca vata saṃkhārā uppādavayadhammino
uppajjitvā nirujjhanti tesaṃ vūpasamo sukho ·

'Transient are, alas! the saṃkhāras, having the nature of growth and

20 thus did the Master teach. Mortality overcomes even the
Buddhas, untouched by shame or fear; therefore think
thou: all that exists is perishable, full of sorrow, and unreal.
21 In thy last mortal existence[1] thy love for the true doctrine
was indeed great. Albeit the world of gods was within thy
22 sight, yet didst thou, renouncing heavenly bliss, return to
this world and didst many works of merit in manifold ways.
Moreover, the setting up of sole sovereignty by thee did serve
23 to bring glory to the doctrine. Oh thou who art rich in
merit, think on all those works of merit accomplished by thee
even to this present day, then will all be well with thee
straightway!'

24 When the king heard the thera's words he was glad at
heart and said: 'In single combat also thou art my help.'

25 And rejoicing he forthwith commanded that the book of
meritorious deeds be brought, and he bade the scribe read it
aloud, and he read the book aloud:

26 'Ninety-nine vihāras have been built by the great king,
and, with (the spending of) nineteen koṭis,[2] the Maricavaṭṭi-
27 vihāra; the splendid Lohapāsāda was built for thirty koṭis.[3]
But those precious things[4] that have been made for the Great
28 Thūpa were worth twenty koṭis; the rest that was made for
the Great Thūpa by the wise (king was worth) a thousand
29 koṭis, O great king.' Thus did he read. As he read further:[5]
'In the mountain-region called Koṭṭa, at the time of the famine
called the Akkhakhāyika[6] famine, two precious ear-rings were
30 given (by the king), and thus a goodly dish of sour millet-

decay; having been produced they are dissolved again; blissful is their subjection.' The meaning of saṃkhārā is by no means fully rendered by 'existence'. Rhys Davids, *S.B.E.* xi, p. 117; *S.B.B.* iii, pp. 175–176, translates it with 'each being's parts and powers'.

[1] This refers to the story told in 22. 25–41.

[2] Cf. 26. 25.

[3] Cf. 27. 47.

[4] According to the Ṭīkā the adorning of the relic-chamber is meant here.

[5] Translation of the words ti vutte in 32.

[6] Lit. famine during which the nuts called akkha (*Terminalia Bellerica*) were eaten, which at other times are used as dice. In the Aṭṭhakathā, according to the Ṭīkā, the famine is called Pāsāṇachātaka.

gruel was gotten for five great theras who had overcome the
āsavas, and offered[1] to them with a believing heart; when, 31
vanquished in the battle of Cūḷaṅgaṇiya, he was fleeing[2] he
proclaimed the hour (of the meal) and to the ascetic (Tissa), 32
free from the āsavas, who came thither through the air he,
without thought for himself, gave the food from his bowl'—
then did the king take up the tale:

'In the week of the consecration-festival of the (Mari- 33
cavaṭṭi) vihāra as at the consecration of the (Loha) pāsāda, in
the week when the (Great) Thūpa was begun even as when
the relics[3] were enshrined, a general, great and costly giving 34
of alms was arranged by me to the great community of both
(sexes) from the four quarters.[4] I held twenty-four great 35
Vesākha-festivals;[5] three times did I bestow the three
garments on the brotherhood of the island.

Five times, each time for seven days, have I bestowed (glad 36
at heart) the rank of ruler of this island upon the doctrine.[6]
I have had a thousand lamps with oil and white wicks 37
burning perpetually in twelve places, adoring the Blessed
(Buddha) with this offering. Constantly in eighteen places 38
have I bestowed on the sick the foods for the sick and
remedies, as ordered by the physicians.

In forty-four places have I commanded the perpetual giving 39
of rice-foods prepared with honey;[7] and in as many places

[1] Ṭīkā: kaṅgutaṇḍulaṃ gahetvā ambilayāguṃ pacāpetvā attano santikaṃ āgatānaṃ Malayamahādevattherādīnaṃ pañcannaṃ khīṇāsavamahātherānaṃ adāsi.

[2] Cf. with this 24. 22–31.

[3] Cf. 26. 21; 27. 46; 30. 4; 31. 117.

[4] Ubhato-saṃgha is bhikkhusaṃgha and bhikkhunīsaṃgha. We meet with the epithet cātuddisa 'of the four quarters', frequently in the oldest cave-inscriptions of Ceylon. Cf. E. MÜLLER, *Ancient Inscriptions in Ceylon*, p. 73; WICKREMASINGHE, *Epigraphia Zeylanica*, i, p. 144 foll.

[5] Tradition makes the Buddha's nibbāṇa fall on the full-moon day of the month Vesākha (at that time March–April), Sum. I, p. 2; Smp., p. 283; Mah. 3. 2. See FLEET, *J.R.A.S.* 1909, p. 6 foll.

[6] Cf. 31. 90–92; 111.

[7] Ṭīkā: saṃkhataṃ madhupāyasaṃ, sakkharamadhusappitelehi saṃyojitaṃ madhupāyāsaṃ.

40 lumps of rice with oil,[1] and in even as many places
great jāla-cakes,[2] baked in butter and also therewith the
41 ordinary rice. For the uposatha-festivals I have had oil for
the lamps distributed one day in every month in eight
42 vihāras on the island of Laṅkā. And since I heard that
a gift (by preaching) of the doctrine is more than a gift
of worldly wealth I said: At the foot of the Lohapāsāda, in
43 the (preacher's) chair in the midst of the brotherhood, I will
preach the Maṅgalasutta to the brotherhood;[3] but when
I was seated there I could not preach it, from reverence for
44 the brotherhood. Since then I have commanded the preaching of the doctrine everywhere, in the vihāras of Laṅkā,
45 giving rewards to the preachers. To each preacher of the
doctrine did I order to give a nāḷi[4] of butter, molasses and
46 sugar; moreover, I bestowed on them a handful of liquorice,[5]
four inches long, and I gave them, moreover, a pair of
garments. But all this giving while that I reigned, rejoices
47 not my heart; only the two gifts that I gave, without care
for my life, the while I was in adversity, those gladden my
heart.'

48 When the thera Abhaya heard this he described those two
gifts, to rejoice the king's heart withal, in manifold ways:
49 'When (the one) of those five theras[6] the thera Malayamahādeva, who received the sour millet-gruel, had given thereof
50 to nine hundred bhikkhus on the Sumanakūṭa-mountain[7]
he ate of it himself. But the thera Dhammagutta who
51 could cause the earth to quake shared it with the bhikkhus
in the Kalyāṇika-vihāra,[8] (who were) five hundred in num-
52 ber, and then ate of it himself. The thera Dhammadinna,

[1] Ṭīkā: telullopakam eva cāti, telaussadakhīrasappimaṇḍasaṃkhātaṃ ālopadānaṃ ca adāpayiṃ.

[2] What jālapūva is I do not know. Nor does the Ṭīkā give any explanation.

[3] Sutta-nipāta, ed. FAUSBÖLL, p. 45. See note to 30. 83.

[4] See note to 30. 37.

[5] Yaṭṭhimadhukā (= Skt. yaṣṭimadhukā) the same as madhulaṭṭhikā in CHILDERS, *P.D.*, s. v.

[6] A detailed narration of the story alluded to in 32. 30.

[7] See note to 1. 33.

[8] See note to 1. 63.

dwelling in Talaṅga, gave to twelve thousand (bhikkhus) in
Piyaṅgudīpa[1] and then ate of it. The thera Khuddatissa of 53
wondrous power, who dwelt in Maṅgaṇa, divided it among
sixty thousand (bhikkhus) in the Kelāsa (vihāra) and then
ate of it himself. The thera Mahāvyaggha gave thereof 54
to seven hundred (bhikkhus) in the Ukkanagara-vihāra and
then ate of it himself.[2]

The thera[3] who received the food in his dish divided it 55
among twelve thousand bhikkhus in Piyaṅgudīpa and then
ate of it himself.'

With such words as these the thera Abhaya gladdened the 56
king's mood, and the king, rejoicing in his heart, spoke thus
to the thera:

'Twenty-four years have I been a patron of the brother- 57
hood, and my body shall also be a patron of the brotherhood.
In a place whence the Great Thūpa may be seen, in the 58
mālaka[4] (bounded about) for the ceremonial acts of the
brotherhood, do ye burn the body of me the servant of
the brotherhood.'

To his younger brother he said: 'All the work of the 59
Great Thūpa which is still unfinished, do thou complete, my
dear Tissa, caring duly for it. Evening and morning offer 60
thou flowers at the Great Thūpa and three times (in the day)
command a solemn oblation at the Great Thūpa. All the 61
ceremonies introduced by me in honour of the doctrine of the
Blessed (Buddha) do thou carry on, my dear, stinting nothing.
Never grow weary, my dear, in duty toward the brother- 62
hood.' When he had thus exhorted him, the king fell into
silence.

At this moment the brotherhood of bhikkhus began the 63
chanting in chorus, and the devatās led thither six cars with

[1] See note to 24. 25. We cannot establish the identity of Talaṅga. TURNOUR (*Mah.*, p. 25) says: 'Singh. Talaguru-wiháre in Róhaṇa not identified.'

[2] The geographical names in 53 and 54 cannot be identified. Kelāsa according to 29. 43 was a monastery in India.

[3] The allusion in this verse is to the story in 24. 22-31; 32. 31-32.

[4] See note to 15. 29.

64 six gods, and severally the gods implored the king as they
stood in their cars: 'Enter into our delightful celestial world,
O king.'

65 When the king heard their words he stayed them with
a gesture of his hand: 'Wait ye as long as I listen to the
66 dhamma.' Then the bhikkhus thinking: 'He would fain
stop the chanting in chorus,' ceased from their recitations;
67 the king asked the reason of the interruption. 'Because the
sign (to bid us) "be still" was given,' they answered. But
the king said: 'It is not so, venerable sirs,' and he told them
what had passed.

68 When they heard this, certain of the people thought:
'Seized by the fear of death, he wanders in his speech.' And
69 to banish their doubts the thera Abhaya spoke thus to the
king: 'How would it be possible to make known (the presence
70 of) the cars that have been brought hither?' The wise
king commanded that garlands of flowers be flung into the
air, these severally wound themselves around the poles of
the cars and hung loose from them.

71 When the people saw them floating free in the air, they
conquered their doubts; but the king said to the thera:
72 'Which of the celestial worlds is the most beautiful, venerable
sir?' And the other answered: 'The city of the Tusitas,[1]
73 O king, is the fairest; so think the pious. Awaiting the
time when he shall become a Buddha, the compassionate
Bodhisatta Metteyya[2] dwells in the Tusita-city.'

74 When the most wise king heard these words of the thera,
he, casting a glance at the Great Thūpa, closed his eyes as
he lay.

75 And when he, even at that moment, had passed away, he
was seen, reborn and standing in celestial form in the car
76 that had come from Tusita-heaven. And to make manifest
the reward of the works of merit performed by him he drove,
77 showing himself in all his glory to the people, standing
on the same car, three times around the Great Thūpa,

[1] See note to 30. 88.

[2] Metteyya = Skt. Maitreya is the name of the future Buddha, successor of the historic Buddha Gotama.

going to the left, and then, when he had done homage to the thūpa and the brotherhood he passed into the Tusita-heaven.

Even where the dancing-women who had come thither laid 78
off their head-ornaments there was a hall built called Makuṭamuttasālā. Even where the people, when the body of the 79
king was laid on the funeral pyre, broke into wailing there was the so-called Ravivaṭṭisālā built.

The mālaka outside the precincts (of the monastery), in 80
which they burned the body of the king here bears the name Rājamālaka.

The great king Duṭṭhagāmaṇi, he who is worthy of the 81
name of king, will be the first disciple of the sublime
Metteyya, the king's father (will be) his father[1] and the 82
mother his mother.[1] The younger brother Saddhātissa will
be his second disciple, but Sālirājakumāra, the king's son, 83
will be the son of the sublime Metteyya.

He who, holding the good life to be the greatest (good), 84
does works of merit, passes, covering over much that perchance is evil-doing,[2] into heaven as into his own house; therefore will the wise man continually take delight in works of merit.

Here ends the thirty-second chapter, called 'The Entrance into the Tusita-heaven', in the Mahāvaṃsa, compiled for the serene joy and emotion of the pious.

[1] That is, Metteyya's.

[2] Niyatapāpakaṃ is that which is certainly or without doubt evil; aniyatapāpakaṃ that which is possibly evil. Here there is an allusion to the scruples of conscience which the king himself felt at the close of his warlike career. See 25. 103 foll.

CHAPTER XXXIII

THE TEN KINGS

1 UNDER the rule of the king Duṭṭhagāmaṇi the subjects in the kingdom lived happily; Sālirājakumāra was his famous son.

2 Greatly gifted was he and ever took delight in works of
merit; he tenderly loved a caṇḍāla woman of exceedingly
3 great beauty. Since he was greatly enamoured of the Aso-
kamālādevī, who already in a former birth had been his
consort,[1] because of her loveliness, he cared nothing for
4 kingly rule. Therefore Duṭṭhagāmaṇi's brother, SADDHĀ-
TISSA, anointed king after his death, ruled, a peerless (prince),
5 for eighteen years. He finished the work on the parasol,
and the plaster-work and the elephant-wall[2] of the Great
6 Thūpa, he who won his name by his faith.[3] The magnificent
Lohapāsāda caught fire from a lamp; he built the Lohapāsāda
7 anew, seven stories high. And now was the pāsāda worth
(only) ninety times a hundred thousand. He built the Dak-
8 khiṇāgiri-vihāra[4] and the (vihāra) Kallakālena, the Kalam-
baka-vihāra, and the (vihāra) Pettaṅgavālika, (the vihāras)

[1] The story is told at length in the Ṭīkā. Cf. GEIGER, *Dīp. and Mah.*, p. 37.

[2] Hatthipākāra: according to PARKER (*Ancient Ceylon*, p. 284), who bases his conjecture on the dimensions of the tiles, the sustaining-wall of the upper 'pāsāda' on which are figures of elephants in relief. The sustaining-wall of the great terrace on which the Ruwanwæli-dagaba stands is also ornamented with similar figures of elephants in relief, the forepart of the body jutting out from the wall (SMITHER, *Anurádhapura*, p. 40). But this hatthipākāra seems to be of later origin.

[3] A play on the name Saddhātissa from saddhā = faith.

[4] A monastery of this name appears also in the Cūlavaṃsa, 52. 60.

Velaṅgāviṭṭhika,[1] Dubbalavāpitissaka and Dūratissakavāpi,[2] 9
and the Mātuvihāraka. He also built vihāras (from Anurā-
dhapura) to Dīghavāpi, one for every yojana (of the way).

Moreover, he founded the Dīghavāpi-vihāra[3] together 10
with the cetiya; for this cetiya he had a covering of net-
work[4] made set with gems, and in every mesh thereof was 11
hung a splendid flower of gold, large as a waggon-wheel,
that he had commanded them to fashion. (In honour) of 12
the eighty-four thousand sections of the dhamma the ruler
commanded also eighty-four thousand offerings. When the 13
king had thus accomplished many works of merit he was
reborn, after his death, among the Tusita gods.

While the great king Saddhātissa lived yet in Dīghavāpi 14
his eldest son Lañjatissa[5] built the beautiful vihāra called
Girikumbhila; and Thūlathana, a younger son of this same 15
(king), built the vihāra called Kandara. When his father 16
(Saddhātissa) went to his brother (Duṭṭhagāmaṇi at Anurā-
dhapura) Thūlathanaka went with him, to bestow land for the
use of the brotherhood upon his vihāra.

When Saddhātissa died all the counsellors assembled, and 17
when they had summoned together the whole brotherhood of
bhikkhus in the Thūpārāma, they, with the consent of the 18
brotherhood consecrated the prince THŪLATHANA as king, that
he might take the kingdom under his protection. When
LAÑJATISSA heard this he came hither,[6] overpowered[7] him, 19
and took the government upon himself. Only for one month
and ten days had Thūlathana been king.

During three years did Lañjatissa use the brotherhood 20
slightingly and neglect them, with the thought: 'They did
not decide according to age.' When, afterwards, he was 21

[1] See 37. 48.

[2] The tank Dūratissa is situated in Rohaṇa not far from Mahāgāma. PARKER, *l. l.*, p. 393 foll.

[3] See note to 1. 78.

[4] The Ṭīkā explains nānāratanakacchannaṃ by sattaratanakhacitajālaṃ.

[5] Lajjitissa or Lañjitissa are variants of this name.

[6] That is, to Anurādhapura.

[7] Gahetvā is, without doubt, an euphemism for '(having) killed'.

reconciled with the brotherhood, the king built, in atonement,
22 spending three hundred thousand (pieces of money), three
stone terraces for offerings of flowers [1] to the Great Cetiya,
and then did the lord of the land, with (the expense of)
23 a hundred thousand, have the earth heaped up between the
Great Thūpa and the Thūpārāma [2] so that it was level. More-
over, he made a splendid stone mantling to the thūpa in the
24 Thūpārāma, and to the east of the Thūpārāma a little thūpa
built of stones,[3] and the Lañjakāsana hall for the brotherhood
25 of bhikkhus. Moreover, he had a mantling made of stone
for the Khandhakathūpa. When he had spent a hundred
26 thousand for the Cetiya-vihāra [4] he commanded that at the
(consecration) festival of the vihāra called Girikumbhila the
six garments [5] be distributed to sixty thousand bhikkhus.
27 He built the Ariṭṭha-vihāra [6] and the (vihāra) Kuñjarahī-
naka, and to the bhikkhus in the villages he distributed
28 medicines. To the bhikkhunīs he ordered to give rice as
much as they wanted. Nine years and one half-month did
he reign here.

29 When Lañjakatissa was dead his younger brother named
30 KHALLĀṬANĀGA reigned six years. Round about the Loha-

[1] See note to 30. 51.

[2] The Thūpārāma is situated 400 yards north of the Ruwanwæli-dagaba.

[3] PARKER, *Ancient Ceylon*, p. 297, identifies the thūpa called Dīghathūpa in the Dīp., with the so-called Khujjatissārāma or Sela-dagaba. But this is not situated to the east (the Mah. has purato just as the Dīp. 20. 11 describes the position of the Dīghathūpa by Thūpārāma-puratthato) but to the south-east of the Thūpārāma, and it is twice as far from this latter as from the Ruwanwæli-dagaba, so that orientation by the last-named, would be much more to the purpose. SMITHER (*Anurādhapura*, p. 55) is probably right in the conjecture that there is a reference in silāthūpaka to a little stone dagaba, a sort of model, similar to one that stands on the platform of the Ruwanwæli-dagaba.

[4] The monastery on the Cetiyapabbata or Missaka-mountain. Cf. note to 20. 16.

[5] That is, to each one a pair of the three articles of clothing (ticīvara), the antaravāsaka 'under-garment, shirt', the uttarāsaṅga 'robe', and the saṃghāṭī 'mantle'.

[6] On the Ariṭṭhapabbata, now Riṭigala. See note to 10. 63.

pāsāda he built thirty-two exceedingly beautiful (other)
pāsādās[1] to make the Lohapāsāda yet more splendid. Round 31
the Great Thūpa, the beautiful Hemamālī,[2] he made as a
border a court[3] (strewn) with sand and a wall. Moreover, he 32
built the Kurundavāsoka-vihāra, and yet other works of merit
did the king carry out.

A commander of troops named Kammahārattaka, over- 33
powered the ruler, king Khallāṭanāga, in the capital itself.
But the king's younger brother named VAṬṬAGĀMAṆI killed 34
the villainous commander and took on himself the govern-
ment. The little son of his brother, king Khallāṭanāga, 35
whose name was Mahācūḷika, he took as his son; and the 36
(child's) mother, Anulādevī, he made his queen. Since
he had thus taken the place of a father they called him
Pitirāja.[4]

In the fifth month after he was thus anointed king, a young 37
brahman named Tissa, in Rohaṇa, in the city (that was the
seat) of his clan,[5] hearkened, fool that he was, to the pro- 38
phesying of a brahman and became a rebel, and his following
waxed great. Seven Damiḷas landed (at the same time) 39
with their troops in Mahātittha.[6] Then Tissa the brahman
and the seven Damiḷas also sent the king a written message 40
concerning the (handing over of the) parasol.[7] The sagacious
king sent a written message to Tissa the brahman: 'The 41
kingdom is now thine, conquer thou the Damiḷas.' He
answered: 'So be it,' and fought a battle with the Damiḷas,
but they conquered him.

Thereupon the Damiḷas made war upon the king; in 42

[1] Perhaps dwellings of smaller dimensions, for the bhikkhus.

[2] See 15. 167; 17. 51 and 27. 3.

[3] Literally, a 'sandcourt-boundary'. The allusion is to the so-called elephant-path that runs all round the terrace of the Ruwanwæli-dagaba and is bounded on the outside by a wall. On the east, south, and north it is 97 feet wide, on the west, i.e. at the back, $88\frac{1}{2}$ feet, SMITHER, *l. l.*, p. 41.

[4] I.e. 'King father.'

[5] I read kulanagare and understand by this Mahāgāma the town from which the dynasty of Duṭṭhagāmaṇi came.

[6] See note to 7. 58.

[7] As the symbol of kingly rank.

a battle near Kolambālaka[1] the king was vanquished. (Near
the gate of the Titthārāma he mounted into his car and fled.
But the Titthārāma was built by king Paṇḍukābhaya and it
43 had been constantly inhabited under twenty-one kings.)[2] As
a nigaṇṭha[3] named Giri saw him take flight he cried out
44 loudly: 'The great black lion is fleeing.'[4] When the great
king heard that he thought thus: 'If my wish be fulfilled
I will build a vihāra here.'

45 He took Anulādevī with him, who was with child,
thinking: 'She must be protected,' and Mahācūḷa also and
(his son) the prince Mahānāga, also thinking: 'They must be
46 protected.' But, to lighten the car the king gave to Soma-
devī[5] his splendid diadem-jewel and let her, with her own
consent, descend from the car.

47 When going forth to battle he had set out, full of fears,
taking his little son and his two queens with him. Being
48 vanquished he took flight and, unable to take with him the
almsbowl used by the Conqueror,[6] he hid in the Vessagiri-
49 forest.[7] When the thera Mahātissa from Kupikkala (vihāra)
saw him there, he gave him food, avoiding thereby the giving
50 of an untouched alms.[8] Thereon the king, glad at heart,

[1] Evidently identical with the Kolambahālaka, mentioned in 25. 80. See the note thereon.

[2] The passage enclosed in brackets occurs in all the groups of MSS. and is also referred to in the Ṭīkā. I have omitted the three lines of verse from the edition, chiefly for reasons of form (see Introduction, p. xxi) as being a later gloss. The battle took place not far from the north gate of the city. See also 25. 80 foll. and the note to 33. 81.

[3] See note to 10. 97. The name Titthārāma alone indicates that the monastery was inhabited by non-Buddhist monks (tittha=sect).

[4] Mahākālasīhala is a play on the word sīha 'lion' and the name sīhala (Mah. 7. 42).

[5] His second wife.

[6] According to Mah. 17. 12 foll. it had come to Ceylon as a relic in the time of king Devānampiyatissa.

[7] South of Anurādhapura. See note to 20. 15 on the Vessagiri-vihāra.

[8] The bhikkhu is not allowed to share with a layman before he himself has eaten of the food that he has received as alms. So Mahātissa first ate of the food and then offered some to the king. SUBHŪTI, communication in a letter of Feb. 27, 1903.

recording it upon a ketaka-leaf,[1] allotted lands to his vihāra
for the use of the brotherhood. From thence, he went to 51
Silāsobbhakaṇḍaka[2] and sojourned there; then he went to
Mātuvelaṅga near Sāmagalla and there met the thera (Kupik- 52
kalamahātissa) whom he had already seen before. The thera
entrusted the king with due carefulness to Tanasīva, who was
his attendant. Then in the house of this Tanasīva, his subject, 53
the king lived[3] fourteen years, maintained by him.

Of the seven Damiḷas one, fired with passion for the lovely 54
Somadevī, made her his own and forthwith returned again
to the further coast.[4] Another took the almsbowl of the 55
(Master) endowed with the ten miraculous powers, that was
in Anurādhapura, and returned straightway, well contented,
to the other coast.

But the Damiḷa PUḶAHATTHA reigned three years, making 56
the Damiḷa named Bāhiya commander of his troops. BĀHIYA 57
slew[5] Puḷahattha and reigned two years; his commander-in-
chief was Panayamāra. PANAYAMĀRAKA slew Bāhiya and was 58
king for seven years; his commander-in-chief was Piḷayamāra.
PIḶAYAMĀRAKA slew Panayamāra and was king for seven 59
months; his commander-in-chief was Dāṭhika. And the 60
Damiḷa DĀṬHIKA slew Piḷayamāra and reigned two years in
Anurādhapura. Thus the time of these five Damiḷa-kings 61
was fourteen years and seven months.

When one day, in Malaya, Anulādevī went to seek 62
her (daily) portion the wife of Tanasīva struck against her
basket with her foot. And she was wroth and came weeping 63
to the king. When Tanasīva heard this he hastened forth
(from the house) grasping his bow. When the king had 64
heard what the queen said, he, ere yet the other came, took

[1] *Pandanus odoratissimus.* As a rule royal donations were recorded on copper plates or might be on silver and gold plates. GEIGER, *Litteratur und Sprache der Singhalesen*, pp. 24-25.

[2] Cf. note to 33. 87; judging from the Ṭīkā we should probably read °kaṇḍakamhi rather than °kaṭakamhi.

[3] Tahiṃ = in Malaya, according to 33. 62.

[4] That is, he returned oversea to India.

[5] Gahetvā. Cf. note to 33. 19.

65 the two boys and his consort and hastened out also. Putting
the arrow to his bow[1] the glorious (hero) transfixed Sīva[2] as he
came on. The king proclaimed (then) his name and gathered
66 followers around him. He obtained as ministers eight famous
warriors, and great was the following of the king and his
equipment (for war).

67 The famous (king) sought out the thera Mahātissa of
Kupikkala and commanded that a festival in honour of the
68 Buddha be held in the Acchagalla-vihāra.[3] At the very time
when the minister Kapisīsa, having gone up to the courtyard
of the Ākāsa-cetiya to sweep the building, had come down
69 from thence, the king, who was going up with the queen,
saw him sitting by the road, and being wroth with him that
he had not flung himself down (before him) he slew Kapisīsa.
70 Then in anger against the king the other seven ministers
withdrew themselves from him, and going whither it seemed
71 good to them, they were stripped of their possessions by
robbers on the way, and they took refuge in the vihāra
Hambugallaka where they sought out the learned thera Tissa.
72 The thera, who was versed in the four nikāyas,[4] gave them,
as he had received it (as alms), clothing, sugar and oil, and
rice, too, in sufficing measure.

73 When he had refreshed them the thera asked them:
'Whither are you going?' They made themselves known
74 to him, and told him this matter. But when they were asked
afterwards: 'With whom will it be possible to further the
doctrine of the Buddha? With the Damiḷas or with the
75 king?' they answered: 'By the king will this be possible.'
And when they had thus convinced them the two theras,

[1] Cf. the Skt. dhanuḥ saṃdhā in the same sense B.R., *Skt. Wtb.*, s. v. dhā with sam.

[2] A play on the words Sīvaṃ and mahāsivo.

[3] See note to 21. 6. If the Ṭīkā is right in placing the Acchagalla-vihāra to the east of Anurādhapura, the ākāsacetiya mentioned in verse 68 cannot be identical with that mentioned in 22. 26 (see the note). The site of the latter is, no doubt, in Rohaṇa.

[4] I.e. in the four oldest collections of the Sutta-piṭaka: Dīgha-, Majjhima-, Saṃyutta- and Aṅguttara-nikāya.

Tissa and Mahātissa, took them forth from thence and brought 76
them to the king and reconciled them one to another. The
king and the ministers besought the theras saying: 'If our 77
undertaking has prospered then must ye come to us, when
a message is sent to you.' The theras agreed and returned
each one to his place.

When the renowned king had come to Anurādhapura and 78
had slain the Damiḷa Dāṭhika he himself assumed the government.
And forthwith the king destroyed the ārāma of the 79
nigaṇṭhas and built there a vihāra with twelve cells. When 80
two hundred and seventeen years ten months and ten days
had passed since the founding of the Mahāvihāra the king, 81
filled with pious zeal, built the Abhayagiri-vihāra.[1] He sent 82
for the (two) theras, and to the thera Mahātissa, who had
first assisted him of the two, he gave the vihāra, to do him
honour. Since the king Abhaya built it[2] on the place of the 83
ārāma of (the nigaṇṭha) Giri, the vihāra received the name
Abhayagiri.

When he had sent for Somadevī he raised her again to her 84
rank and built, in her honour, the Somārāma,[3] bearing her
name. For this fair woman, who had alighted from the car 85
at this spot and had concealed herself in a thicket of flowering
Kadambas, saw in that very place a sāmaṇera who was relieving 86

[1] According to 33. 42–44 the monastery of the nigaṇṭhas, the Titthārāma stood outside the north gate of Anurādhapura. Since, on its place the Abhayagiri-vihāra was built, it cannot be identical with the vihāra of the dagaba, which is now called the Abhayagiri-dagaba, but it must be that of the now so-called Jetavana-dagaba. On the other hand, as we will see below (cf. note to 37. 33), the site of the Jetavana-vihāra must be looked for south of the city where now the so-called Abhayagiri-dagaba stands. Tradition appears to have confounded one name with the other. PARKER, *Ancient Ceylon*, p. 299 foll.

[2] The king's full name was Vaṭṭagāmaṇi Abhaya.

[3] The Somārāma or Maṇisomārāma, as the monastery is called 36. 8, 106, 107 (in allusion to the story in 33. 46) after the culāmaṇi entrusted to Somadevī, must be sought near the Abhayagiri-vihāra, perhaps in the place of the building described by SMITHER, *Anurádhapura*, p. 61, which is popularly designated the 'Queen's Pavilion'.

his need, using (decently) his hand for concealment. When the king heard her story he built a vihāra there.

87 To the north of the Mahāthūpa this same king founded upon a lofty spot the cetiya called Silāsobbhakaṇḍaka.[1]

88 One of the seven warriors (of the king), Uttiya, built, to
89 the south of the city, the so-called Dakkhiṇa-vihāra.[2] In the
same place the minister named Mūla built the Mūlavokāsa-
90 vihāra, which was, therefore, called after him. The minister
named Sāliya built the Sāliyārāma, and the minister named
91 Pabbata built the Pabbatārāma; but the minister Tissa founded
the Uttaratissārāma. When the beautiful vihāras were com-
pleted they sought out the thera Tissa and gave them to him
92 with these words: 'In gratitude for thy kindness we give
thee these vihāras built by us.'

93 The thera established sundry bhikkhus everywhere (in these
vihāras), according to their rank, and the ministers bestowed
upon the brotherhood the different (things) useful to a samaṇa.
94 The king provided those (bhikkhus) living in his vihāra with
the (needful) things for use, so that nothing was lacking:
therefore were they many in number.

95 A thera known by the name Mahātissa, who had frequented
the families of laymen, was expelled by the brotherhood from
our monastery[3] for this fault, the frequenting of lay-families.
96 His disciple, the thera who was known as Bahalamassutissa,
went in anger to the Abhayagiri (vihāra) and abode there,
97 forming a (separate) faction. And thenceforward these
bhikkhus came no more to the Mahāvihāra: thus did the
bhikkhus of the Abhayagiri (vihāra) secede from the Thera-

[1] The statement as to locality, given in our verse, points, as PARKER, *Ancient Ceylon*, p. 311, rightly insists, to the Laṅkārāmadagaba, which is situated about a mile north of the Ruwanwælidagaba. It received this name in remembrance of the place where Vaṭṭagāmaṇi had found refuge, according to 33. 51.

[2] I.e. 'South Monastery.' PARKER, *l. l.*, p. 312, identifies the remains of the thūpa belonging to this monastery with the building south of the Mahāvihāra, which is called by the people, 'Eḷāra's sepulchre.' See also note to 35. 5.

[3] Ito 'from here' is from the standpoint of the author, 'out of the Mahāvihāra.'

vāda. From the monks of the Abhayagiri-vihāra those of the 98
Dakkhiṇa-vihāra separated (afterwards); in this wise those bhikkhus (who had seceded) from the adherents of the Theravāda were divided into two (groups).[1]

He (the king) built the cells of the vihāra so that a greater 99
number were joined together, for he reflected: 'In this way it will be possible to restore them.'

The text of the three piṭakas and the aṭṭhakathā thereon 100
did the most wise bhikkhus hand down in former times orally,
but since they saw that the people were falling away (from 101
religion) the bhikkhus came together, and in order that the true doctrine might endure, they wrote them down in books.

Thus did the king Vaṭṭagāmaṇi-Abhaya reign twelve 102
years, and, at the beginning,[2] five months beside.

Thus does the wise man labour, when he comes to rule, for 103
the bliss of others and for his own bliss, but a man without understanding does not render the possessions which he has won,[3] however great they are, blissful for both, being greedy of (more) possessions.

Here ends the thirty-third chapter, called 'The Ten Kings', in the Mahāvaṃsa, compiled for the serene joy and emotion of the pious.

[1] After 98 a spurious verse is interpolated: 'To bring prosperity to the bhikkhus dwelling on the island, who belonged to the great Abhaya-(giri-community), the lord of the land, Vaṭṭagāmaṇi, made over to them the so-called patti.' In 35. 48 patti simply means 'revenue'.

[2] That is, before the Damiḷas dethroned him.

[3] Laddhabhogaṃ, according to the Ṭīkā stands (*metri causâ*) for laddhā (=labhitvā, Skt. labdhvā) bhogaṃ. But, I think, this is not necessary. We have to take laddhabhogaṃ=laddhaṃ bhogaṃ and ubhayahitaṃ as predicative object.

CHAPTER XXXIV

THE ELEVEN KINGS

1 AFTER his death MAHĀCŪḶĪ MAHĀTISSA reigned fourteen years with piety and justice.

2 Since he heard that a gift brought about by the work of
a man's own hand is full of merit, the king, in the very first
3 year (of his reign), went in disguise and laboured in the rice-
harvest, and with the wage that he received for this he gave
4 food as alms to the thera Mahāsumma. When the king had
laboured also in Soṇṇagiri[1] three years in a sugar-mill, and
5 had received lumps of sugar as wage for this, he took the
lumps of sugar, and being returned to the capital he, the ruler
of the earth, appointed great almsgiving to the brotherhood of
6 bhikkhus. He bestowed clothing on thirty thousand bhikkhus
and the same on twelve thousand bhikkhuṇīs.

7 When the protector of the earth had built a well-planned
vihāra, he gave the six garments[2] to sixty thousand bhikkhus
8 and to bhikkhuṇīs likewise, in number thirty thousand. The
same king built the Maṇḍavāpi-vihāra, the Abhayagallaka
9 (vihāra), the (vihāras) Vaṅkāvaṭṭakagalla and Dīghabāhu-
gallaka and the Jālagāma-vihāra.

10 When the king (inspired) by faith had done works of merit in many ways he passed into heaven, at the end of the fourteen years.

[1] I.e. 'Gold mountain,' according to the Ṭīkā situated near Ambaṭṭhakola. On this see note to 28. 20. The rocky mountain that rises on the east of Ambaṭṭhakola bounding the valley of Nālanda-Dambul on the west is called Rangala. GEIGER, *Ceylon*, p. 155; ED. MÜLLER, *Ancient Inscriptions*, p. 36. The Dambulla-caves are also called Suvaṇṇagiri-guhā in king Nissaṅka Malla's inscription, ED. MÜLLER, *l. l.*, pp. 92, 126.

[2] See note to 33. 26.

Vaṭṭagāmaṇi's son known as CORANĀGA lived as a rebel 11
under the rule of Mahācūḷa. When Mahācūḷa had departed 12
he came and reigned. Those places, where he had found
no refuge during the time of his rebellion, eighteen vihāras, 13
did this fool destroy. Twelve years did Coranāga reign.
And eating poisoned (food) that his consort gave him the 14
evildoer died and was reborn in the Lokantarika-hell.

After his death king Mahācūḷa's son ruled three years as 15
king, being known by name TISSA. But Coranāga's spouse, 16
the infamous Anulā, had done her infamous (consort) to death,
giving him poison, because she was enamoured of one of the
palace-guards. And for love of this same palace-guard Anulā 17
now killed Tissa also by poison and gave the government
into the hands of that other.

When the palace-guard, whose name was SIVA, and who 18
(had been) the first of the gate-watchmen, had made Anulā
his queen he reigned a year and two months in the city; but 19
Anulā, who was enamoured of the Damiḷa Vaṭuka, did him
to death with poison and gave the reign to Vaṭuka. The 20
Damiḷa VAṬUKA, who had been a city-carpenter in the capital,
made Anulā his queen and then reigned a year and two 21
months in the city.

But when Anulā (one day) saw a wood-carrier, who had come
to the house, she fell in love with him, and when she had 22
killed Vaṭuka with poison she gave the government into his
hands. TISSA, the wood-carrier, when he had made Anulā
his queen, ruled one year and one month in the city. In haste 23
he had a bathing-tank made in the Mahāmeghavana. But 24
Anulā, enslaved by passion for a Damiḷa named Niliya, a
brahman who was the palace-priest, and eager to be united
with him, did Tissa the wood-carrier to death giving him 25
poison and gave the government into (Niliya's) hands. And
the brahman NILIYA also made her his queen and reigned, 26
upheld constantly by her, six months here in Anurādhapura.
When the princess Anulā (who desired to take her pleasure 27
even as she listed with thirty-two of the palace-guards)[1] had

[1] The passage enclosed in brackets occurs in all the groups of MSS., but seems, as it interferes with the division of the ślokas,

put to death Niliya also with poison, the queen ANULĀ herself,
reigned four months.
28 But king Mahācūḷika's second son, named KUṬAKAṆṆA-
29 TISSA, who had fled from fear of Anulā and had taken the
pabbajjā returned hither when, in time, he had gathered an
30 army together, and when he had slain the wicked Anulā he,
the ruler of men, reigned twenty-two years. He built upon
the Cetiya-mountain a great building for the uposatha-
31 festival and to the east of this building he raised a thūpa of
stone, and in that same place on the Cetiya-mountain he
planted a bodhi-tree.
32 In the region between the rivers he founded the Peḷagāma-
vihāra and in the same place (he made) a great canal called
33 Vaṇṇaka and the great Ambadugga-tank and the Bhayo-
luppala,[1] and moreover (he made) around the city a wall seven
34 cubits high and a trench. When he had burned the licen-
tious Anulā in the palace (upon the funeral pyre), he, with-
drawing a little (distance) from thence, built a new palace.
35 In the city itself he laid out the Padumassara-park. His
mother entered the order of the doctrine of the Conqueror
36 when she had just cleansed her teeth. On a plot for building[2]
belonging to his family he founded a nunnery for his mother:
and this was therefore known by name Dantageha.[3]
37 After his death his son, the prince named BHĀTIKĀBHAYA,
38 reigned twenty-eight years. Since he, the pious ruler of the
earth, was the brother of king Mahādāṭhika he was known
39 on the island by the name Bhātikarāja. Here[4] did he carry
out the work of repairing the Lohapāsāda and built two

to be a later addition. (See Mah. ed., Introduction, p. xxi.) kattuṃ in kattukāmā is a pregnant expression for saṃvāsaṃ kattuṃ.

[1] We fail to establish the names here because we do not know what is meant by antaragaṅgāya. The expression hardly denotes the delta of a river, but perhaps rather the region between Ambanganga and Mahawæliganga.

[2] Lit. 'place for a house.' I read kulasante. The Ṭīkā, too, renders its kulāyatte by kulasantake.

[3] Lit. 'Tooth-house.'

[4] I.e. in Anurādhapura.

vedikās for the Mahāthūpa, and the (hall) called the Uposatha
(-hall) in the (vihāra) named after the thūpa.[1]
And doing away with the tax appointed for himself he 40
planted sumana and ujjuka-flowers[2] over a yojana of land
round the city. And when the king had commanded that 41
the Great Cetiya, from the vedikā at the foot to the parasol at
the top, be plastered with (a paste of) sweet-smelling unguent 42
four fingers thick and that flowers be carefully embedded
therein by their stalks, he made the thūpa even as a globe of
flowers. Another time he commanded them to plaster the 43
cetiya with (a paste of) minium eight fingers thick, and thus
he changed it into a heap of flowers. Yet another time 44
he commanded that the cetiya be strewn with flowers from
the steps[3] to the parasol on the top, and thus he covered it
over with a mass of blossoms. Then when he had raised 45
water by means of machines from the Abhaya-tank he, by
pouring (masses of) water over the thūpa, carried out a water-
offering. From a hundred waggon-loads of pearls, he, 46
bidding that the mass of plaster be carefully kneaded together
with oil, made a plaster-covering (for the Great Thūpa). He 47
had a net of coral prepared and cast over the cetiya, and
when he had commanded them to fasten in the meshes thereof
lotus-flowers of gold large as waggon-wheels, and to hang 48
clusters of pearls on these that reached to the lotus-flower
beneath, he worshipped the Great Thūpa with this offering.

When he heard one day in the relic-chamber the sound of 49
the arahants[4] chanting in chorus he made the resolve: 'I will
not rise up till I have seen it,' and fasting he lay down at 50
the foot of the stone-pillar on the east side.[5] The theras
created a door for him and brought him into the relic-

[1] I.e. in the Thūpārāma.

[2] Ṭīkā: mahāsumanāni ca ujjakasumanāni ca, namely two kinds of jasmine.

[3] The steps form the ascent from the 'elephant-path' (cf. note to 33. 31) to the great terrace, on which the cetiya stands.

[4] Tādī is a synonym of arahā.

[5] The Ṭīkā paraphrases pācīnaddikamūlamhi with pācīnaaddikassa samīpe, pācīnadisāya silātthambhaussāpitaṭṭhāne.

51 chamber. When the ruler of the earth had beheld all the adornment of the relic-chamber he went forth and made an offering of figures modelled with clay in close likeness to those (within).

52 With honeycombs, with perfumes, with vases (filled with flowers), and with essences, with auri-pigment (prepared) as
53 unguent and minium; with lotus-flowers arrayed in minium that lay ankle-deep in the courtyard of the cetiya, where they
54 had poured it molten; with lotus-flowers that were fastened in the holes of mattings, spread on fragrant earth, wherewith
55 the whole courtyard of the cetiya was filled; with many lighted lamps, prepared with wicks made of strips of stuff in clarified butter, which had likewise been poured (into the
56 courtyard) when the ways for the outflow had been closed up; and in like manner with many lamps with stuff-wicks in
57 madhuka-oil[1] and sesamum-oil besides; with these things, as they were named, the prince commanded severally with each seven times offerings for the Great Thūpa.

58 And moreover, urged by faith, he ordered year by year perpetually a great festival (for the renewing) of the plaster-work; and festivals also of the great Bodhi-tree (in honour)
59 of the watering of the Bodhi-tree, and furthermore twenty-eight great Vesākha-festivals[2] and eighty-four thousand lesser
60 festivals, and also divers mimic dances and concerts, with the playing of all kinds of instruments of music (in honour) of
61 the Great Thūpa. Three times a day he went to do homage to the Buddha and he commanded (them to give) twice (a day) continually (the offering known as) the 'flower-drum'.[3]

62 And he continually gave alms at the preaching[4] and alms at the pavāraṇā-ceremony, and (distributed) also, in abundance, the things needed for the ascetic, such as oil, molasses,

[1] Oil pressed from the seeds of the *Bassia Latifolia*. The MSS. all have madhuka, and this should be the reading. In Skt. also the form madhuka exists beside madhūka.

[2] See note to 32. 35.

[3] Ṭīkā: divasassa dvīsu vāresu niyataṃ pupphapūjaṃ ca akārayi.

[4] Very doubtful. The MSS. support the reading chandadānaṃ. Perhaps chanda is here a synonym of sajjhāya.

garments and so forth among the brotherhood. Moreover, 63
the prince bestowed everywhere land for the cetiyas, to the end
that the cetiyas might be kept in repair. And constantly the 64
king bestowed food (as alms allotted) by tickets[1] to a thousand
bhikkhus in the vihāra (of the) Cetiya-pabbata. At five spots, 65
namely, the three receiving-places,[2] called Citta, Maṇi, and
Mucala, as also in the Paduma-house and the beautiful Chatta-
pāsāda, offering hospitality to the bhikkhus who were harnessed 66
to the yoke of the sacred word he provided them always with
all that was needful, being filled with reverence for the
religion. Moreover, all those works of merit which had been 67
ordered by the kings of old regarding the doctrine, all these
did king Bhātika carry out.

After the death of Bhātikarāja his younger brother named 68
MAHĀDĀṬHIKAMAHĀNĀGA reigned twelve years, intent on 69
works of merit of many kinds. He had kiñcikkha-stones[3] laid
as plaster on (the square of) the Great Thūpa and he turned 70
the sand-pathway round (the thūpa)[4] into a wide court; in
all the vihāras he had (raised) chairs put up for the preachers.
The king built the great Ambatthala-thūpa;[5] since the 71
building was not firm he lay down in that place, bethinking
him of the merit of the Sage (Buddha), risking his own life.[6] 72
When he had thus made the building firm and had completed
the cetiya he set up at the four entrances four bejewelled 73
arches that had been well planned by artists and shone with

[1] Salākavaṭṭabhatta, see note to 15. 205.

[2] Upaṭṭhāna is 'attendance, service'. Thus the allusion is to a place where people waited on the monks to offer gifts. The Ṭīkā calls the three places which are said to have been in the interior of the royal palace, Cittupaṭṭhānapāsāda, Maṇiupaṭṭhānapāsāda, and Mucalupaṭṭhānapāsāda.

[3] Cf. Skt. kiñjalka 'stamens of the lotus-blossom'. CHILDERS, *P.D.*, s. v. 'Kiñjakkhapāsāṇo appears to be some sort of marble or other ornamental stone'.

[4] On the vālikāmariyādā see note to 33. 31.

[5] On the Cetiya-pabbata (Mihintale). See PARKER, *Ancient Ceylon*, pp. 320–322. Cf. 13. 20.

[6] He ran a risk of being killed by falling stones during his meditation.

74 gems of every kind. To be fastened to the cetiya he spent
a cover (for it) of red stuff and golden balls thereto and
festoons of pearls.'

75 When he had made ready around the Cetiya-mountain a
(tract of land measuring a) yojana, and had made four gateways
76 and a beautiful road round about (the mountain), and when
he had then set up (traders') shops on both sides of the road
and had adorned (the road) here and there with flags, arches,
77 and triumphal gates, and had illuminated all with chains of
78 lamps, he commanded mimic dances, songs, and music. That
the people might go with clean feet on the road from the
Kadamba-river to the Cetiya-mountain he had it laid with
79 carpets—the gods themselves might hold a festival assembly[1]
there with dance and music—and he gave great largess at the
80 four gates of the capital. Over the whole island he put up
chains of lamps without a break, nay over the waters of the
81 ocean within a distance of a yojana around. At the festival
of (consecrating of) the cetiya these beautiful offerings were
appointed by him: the splendid feast is called here (in the
country) the great Giribhaṇḍa-offering.

82 When the lord of the earth had commanded almsgiving in
eight places to the bhikkhus who were come together in the
83 festal assembly, he, with the beating of eight golden drums
that were set up even there, allotted lavish gifts to twenty-four
84 thousand (bhikkhus). He distributed the six garments, commanded
the remission of the prison-penalties and he ordered
the barbers to carry on their trade continually at the four
85 gates. Moreover, all those works of merit that had been
decreed by the kings of old and that had also been decreed by
his brother, those did he carry out without neglecting any-
86 thing. He gave himself and the queen, his two sons,[2] his
state-elephant and his state horse to the brotherhood as their
own, albeit the brotherhood forbade him.

87 To the brotherhood of the bhikkhus he gave gifts worth
six hundred thousand, but to the company of bhikkhunīs
88 (such gifts) worth a hundred thousand, and in giving them,

[1] On samajjā see HARDY in *Album Kern*, p. 61 foll.

[2] Āmaṇḍagāmaṇi Abhaya and Tissa.

with knowledge of the custom, various possessions suited (to their needs) he redeemed (again) himself and the rest from
the brotherhood. In Kālāyanakaṇṇika the ruler of men built 89
the (vihāra) called Maṇināgapabbata and the vihāra which was
called Kalanda, furthermore on the bank of the Kubukanda- 90
river the Samudda-vihāra and in Huvācakaṇṇika[1] the
vihāra that bore the name Cūlanāgapabbata. Delighted with 91
the service rendered him in the vihāra that he himself had
built, called Pāsāṇadīpaka, by a sāmaṇera who had given him
a draught of water, the king bestowed on that vihāra (a tract 92
of land) in measure half a yojana round about, for the use of
the brotherhood. And rejoicing likewise at (the behaviour of) 93
a sāmaṇera in the Maṇḍavāpi-vihāra the prince gave land for the use of the brotherhood to this vihāra.

Thus men of good understanding, who have conquered 94
pride and indolence, and have freed themselves from the attachment to lust, when they have attained to great power, without working harm to the people, delighting in deeds of merit, rejoicing in faith, do many and various pious works.

Here ends the thirty-fourth chapter, called 'The Eleven Kings', in the Mahāvaṃsa, compiled for the serene joy and emotion of the pious.

[1] According to the Ṭīkā a district in Rohaṇa.

CHAPTER XXXV

THE TWELVE KINGS

1 AFTER Mahādāṭhika's death ĀMAṆḌAGĀMAṆI ABHAYA, his
son, reigned nine years and eight months. On the splendid
2 Great Thūpa he caused to be made a parasol above the parasol,[1]
and he built even there a vedī at the base and at the top.
3 And in like manner he made an inner courtyard and an inner
verandah[2] to the Lohapāsāda and to the (building) called the
4 Uposatha (house) of the Thūpārāma. Moreover, for both he
built a beautiful pavilion adorned with precious stones; and
5 the ruler of men also built the Rajatalena-vihāra.[3] When he
had made the Mahāgāmeṇḍi-tank on the south side (of Anurā-
dhapura), he, who was clever in works of merit, bestowed it
6 on the Dakkhiṇa-vihāra.[4] On the whole island the ruler of
men commanded not to kill. All kinds of vine-fruits did he
7 plant in divers places, and the king Āmaṇḍiya, filling the
almsbowls with the fruit called 'flesh-melons',[5] and bestowing
8 garments as a support (for the bowls) he gave of these, with
believing heart, to the whole brotherhood; because he had

[1] I. e. he heightened the cone crowning the thūpa at the top.

[2] For ājira cf. Abhidhānappadīpikā 218 (ajira = Skt. ajira 'courtyard'). Ālinda is the terrace before the house-door, as is evident from D. I. 89[30], [34]. See also the passages M.V. VI. 36. 4, and C.V. VI. 3. 5 and 14. 1. (*Vin. Piṭ.*, ed. OLDENBERG, i. 248[2], ii. 153[3], 169[25].)

[3] Now Ridi-vihāra, see note to 28. 20.

[4] Cf. note to 33. 88. The Mahāgāmeṇḍi-vāpi will probably be the smaller tank which is in the immediate neighbourhood of the ruins of the monastery. Note the play on the words puññadakkhiṇo and dakkhiṇassa vihārassa.

[5] Kumbhaṇḍaka is, according to Abhidh. 1030, a creeping-plant which (according to SUBHŪTI) is now called in Sinh. puhul 'pumpkin gourd'. Evidently maṃsak° is a particular variety. Since our text connects the king's name with it, āmaṇḍa, which elsewhere means the ricinus plant, seems to be a synonym of the above-mentioned.

filled the almsbowls (with them) he received the name Āmaṇḍagāmaṇi.

His younger brother, the prince KAṆIRAJĀNUTISSA, reigned 9
three years in the city, when he had slain his brother. He 10
decided the lawsuit concerning the uposatha-house in the
(vihāra) named after the cetiya,[1] but sixty bhikkhus who were
involved in the crime of high treason did the king order to be 11
taken captive, with all that was theirs,[2] upon the Cetiyapabbata, and he commanded these evildoers to be flung into the caves called Kaṇira.

After Kaṇirajānu's death Āmaṇḍagāmaṇi's son, the prince 12
CŪLĀBHAYA, reigned a year. The king built the Cūlagallaka- 13
vihāra on the bank of the Goṇaka-river[3] to the south of the capital.

After the death of Cūlābhaya his younger sister SĪVALĪ, 14
the daughter of Āmaṇḍa, reigned four months. But Āmaṇḍa's 15
nephew named IḶANĀGA dethroned Sīvalī and raised the
parasol (of sovereignty) in the capital. When, one day, in the 16
first year (of his reign), the king went to the Tissa-tank, many
of the Lambakaṇṇas[4] deserted him and went back to the capital.
When the king saw them not he was wroth and (in punishment) 17
he ordered that they, even they themselves, should make
a road to the Mahāthūpa, commanding to stamp it down
firmly, where it ran beside the tank, and he set caṇḍālas 18
to be their overseers. And full of anger because of this the
Lambakaṇṇas came together, and when they had taken the 19
king captive and imprisoned him in his palace they themselves
administered the government; but the king's consort put
festal garments on her little son the prince Candamukhasiva, 20
gave him into the hands of the serving-women and sent him
to the state-elephant, charging (the attendants) with a message. 21

[1] Judging from the expression used (cf. 34. 39) the Thūpārāma must be meant. Cetiya = thūpa.

[2] See note to 23. 11.

[3] This is, no doubt, the correct reading. The Goṇa-nadī is the river now called Kaḷu-oya. By banking it up king Dhātusena constructed the Kāla-vāpi (Kaḷuwæwa), Cūlavaṃsa 38. 42.

[4] An important clan in Laṅkā.

The serving-women conveyed him thither and gave the state-
22 elephant the queen's whole message: 'This is thy lord's son;
thy lord is in prison; better is it for this (boy) to meet his
23 death by thee than by the enemies; then slay thou him: that
is the queen's command.' With these words they laid him
24 down at the elephant's feet. And for grief the elephant
began to shed tears, and breaking to pieces the posts (to
which he was chained) he pressed forward into the palace and
25 dashed against the gate with fury, and when he had broken
down the door[1] in the room where the king sat, he made him
26 mount upon his back and went towards Mahātittha. There the
elephant made the king embark on a ship (that brought him)
to the western shore of the sea; he himself went toward Malaya.
27 When the king had stayed three years on the other coast he
28 raised an army and went by ship to Rohaṇa. Having landed
at the haven Sakkharasobbha the king assembled there in
29 Rohaṇa a mighty force. Then came the king's state-elephant
forthwith out of the southern Malaya to Rohaṇa to do him
30 service. As he had heard there the Kapi-jātaka[2] from the
great thera, the preacher of jātakas, named Mahāpaduma, who
31 dwelt in the (vihāra) called Tulādhāra, he, being won to faith
in the Bodhisatta, restored the Nāgamahāvihāra and gave it
32 the extension of a hundred unbent bows in length,[3] and he
enlarged the thūpa even to what it has been (since then);
moreover, he made the Tissa-tank[4] and the tank called Dūra.[5]
33 When the king had raised an army he marched to battle;
when the Lambakaṇṇas heard this they also prepared them-
34 selves for battle. Near the gate of Kapallakkhaṇḍa on the

[1] While dvāra means the principal gate of a building, kavāṭāni are the doors of the separate rooms in the interior. See *S.B.E.* xx. p. 160, n. 3.

[2] Two jātakas bear this title, in Fausböll's edition, ii, pp. 268-270 and iii, pp. 355-358.

[3] Dhanu is a measure of length equal to about 8 feet. Parker, *Ancient Ceylon*, p. 274.

[4] In the neighbourhood of Mahāgāma, Parker, *l. l.*, p. 388 foll.

[5] Probably the Dūratissa-vāpi, to which Saddhātissa, according to Mah. 33. 8, built a monastery. Kāresi here means, I presume, 'to restore' not 'to build'.

field of Haṅkārapiṭṭhi was waged the battle between the two (armies) that brought destruction to both.

Since their bodies were exhausted by the sea-journey, the 35
king's men yielded their ground, therefore the king pro-
claimed his name and pressed forward. Terrified thereat 36
the Lambakaṇṇas threw themselves down upon their belly,
and they hewed off their heads and heaped them up high as
the nave of the (king's) waggon-wheel, and when this had 37
come to pass three times the king, from pity, said: 'Slay them
not, but take them captive living.'

When then the king had come into the capital as victor in 38
battle and had raised the parasol (of sovereignty) he went to
a festival at the Tissa-tank.[1] And when he, fully arrayed in 39
his ornaments and armour, had withdrawn from the water-
sports and reflected on the good-fortune that he had attained,
and thought of the Lambakaṇṇas who had opposed his progress, 40
he was wroth and commanded that they be yoked two and
two behind one another to his car, and thus did he enter
the city in front of them. Halting on the threshold of the 41
palace the king gave the command: 'Here on this threshold,
soldiers, strike off their heads.' 'These are but oxen yoked to 42
thy chariot, O lord of chariots; therefore let their horns
and hoofs be struck off,' thus admonished by his mother the 43
king recalled (the order) to behead them and commanded that
their nose and toes be cut off. The district where the elephant 44
had stayed the prince allotted to the elephant; and therefore
the tract is called Hatthibhoga.[2]

So Iḷanāga, ruler of the earth, reigned full six years as king 45
in Anurādhapura.

After the death of Iḷanāga his son CANDAMUKHA SIVA 46
reigned eight years and seven months as king.

When the lord of the earth had constructed a tank near 47
Maṇikāragāmaka he gave it to the vihāra called Issara-
samaṇa. This king's consort who was known by the name 48
Damiḷādevī, allotted her own revenues from that village to the
same vihāra.

[1] Cf. with this 26. 6-7.

[2] I.e. 'the elephant's usufruct, the elephant's fief.'

49 Having slain Candamukha Siva in the festival-sports at
the Tissa-tank his younger brother, known by the name
50 YASALĀLAKATISSA, reigned as king in delightful Anurādhapura,
the fair face of Laṅkā, seven years and eight months.

51 Now a son of Datta the gate-watchman, named Subha,
who was himself a gate-watchman, bore a close likeness to
52 the king. And this palace-guard Subha did the king Yasalā-
laka, in jest, bedeck with the royal ornaments and place upon
53 the throne and binding the guard's turban about his own head,
and taking himself his place, staff in hand, at the gate,
54 he made merry over the ministers as they paid homage to
(Subha) sitting on the throne. Thus was he wont to do,
from time to time.

55 Now one day the guard cried out to the king, who was
laughing: 'Why does this guard laugh in my presence?'
56 And SUBHA the guard ordered to slay the king, and he him-
self reigned here six years under the name Subharāja.

57 In both the great vihāras [1] Subharāja built a noble row of
58 cells called Subharāja after him. Near Uruvelā (he built)
the Vallī-vihāra, to the east the (vihāra) Ekadvāra and at the
mouth of the Gaṅgā [2] the (vihāra) Nandigāmaka.

59 One sprung of the Lambakaṇṇa (clan), named Vasabha,
whose home was in the northern province, served under his
60 uncle, a commander of troops. Since it was declared: [3] 'One
named Vasabha shall be king,' the king at that time com-
manded that all in the island who bore the name of Vasabha
61 should be slain. The commander, thinking: 'We must
deliver up our Vasabha to the king,' and having taken
counsel with his wife (upon the matter) set out early in the
62 morning to go to the king's residence. And the wife, to
guard Vasabha carefully who went with him, put betel into
his hand but without powdered chalk.[4]

[1] According to the Ṭīkā Abhayagiri and Mahāvihāra.

[2] Gangante, by Gaṅgā we should probably understand the Mahawæliganga. The Ṭīkā has *Kacchakanadītīre*. Kacchaka is the name of a ford in the Mahawæliganga (see note to 10. 58).

[3] According to the Ṭīkā Yasalālaka was said to have uttered a similar prophecy publicly.

[4] Betel is chewed with powdered chalk (cuṇṇa, Sinh. huṇu).

Now when the commander, at the gate of the palace, saw 63
the betel without chalk, he sent him back for chalk. When 64
Vasabha came for the chalk the commander's wife spoke with
him secretly, gave him a thousand (pieces of money) and aided
him to take flight. Vasabha went to the Mahāvihāra and by 65
the theras there was provided with milk, food and clothes, and 66
when he had again heard from a leper the certain prophecy
that he would be king, rejoicing he resolved: 'I will be a
rebel.' And when he had found men suited (to his purpose) 67
he went, seizing in his further course village by village,
according to the instruction (in the story) of the cake,[1] to
Rohaṇa, and gradually winning the kingdom to himself he 68
advanced, after two years, with the needful army and train,
towards the capital. When the mighty VASABHA had con- 69
quered Subharāja in battle he raised the parasol (of sovereignty)
in the capital. His uncle had fallen in battle. But his 70
uncle's wife, named Potthā, who had first helped him, did
king Vasabha raise to be queen.

Once he questioned a soothsayer concerning the length of 71
his life, and he told him secretly (that he should live) just
twelve years. And when he had given him a thousand 72
(pieces of money) to keep the secret the king assembled the
brotherhood and greeted them reverently and asked them:
'Is there perchance, venerable sirs, a means to lengthen life?' 73
'There is,' so did the brotherhood teach him, 'a way to do
away with the hindrances (to long life); gifts of strainers[2] 74
must be given and gifts of dwellings and gifts for main-
tenance of the sick, O ruler of men, and in like manner the 75
restoring of ruined buildings must be carried out; one should
take the five precepts on himself and keep them carefully,

[1] The story of Candagutta and the kapallapūva is to be found in Mah. Ṭīkā, p. 123[4] foll.: cf. GEIGER, *Dīp. and Mah.*, pp. 39-40; RHYS DAVIDS, *Buddhist India*, p. 269; JACOBI, *Hemacandra's Pariśiṣṭaparvan*, viii. 290-296; preface, p. 58.

[2] The parissāvana is among the requisites of the bhikkhu: its use is for straining water so that he who is drinking shall not swallow some living creature who may perhaps be in it.

76 and one should also keep the solemn fast on the uposatha-
day.' The king said: 'It is well,' and went thence and
carried out all these (duties).

77 Every three years that went by the king bestowed the
78 three garments on the whole brotherhood in the island; and
to those theras that lived far away he sent them. In thirty-
two places he ordered milk-rice with honey to be distributed,
79 but in sixty-four places a lavish gift of mixed alms.

He had a thousand lamps lighted in four places; that is,
80 on the Cetiya-pabbata, about the cetiya in the Thūpārāma,
about the Great Thūpa and in the temple of the great
Bodhi-tree.

81 In the Cittalakūṭa (vihāra) [1] he built ten beautiful thūpas
82 and over the whole island he restored ruined buildings. From
pious trust in a thera in the Valliyera-vihāra he built the vihāra
83 called Mahāvalligotta. And (moreover) he built the Anurā-
rāma (vihāra) near Mahāgāma and bestowed on it a thousand
84 and eight karīsa [2] (of land) of (the village) Heḷigāma. When
he had built the Mucela-vihāra [3] in Tissavaḍḍhamānaka [4] he
allotted to the vihāra a share in the water of the (canal) Āḷisāra.
85 To the thūpa in Galambatittha he added a mantling of bricks,
and he built an uposatha-house too, and to provide oil for
86 the lamps he constructed a pond (yielding water to) a thousand
karīsa (of land) [5] and gave it to the (vihāra). In the Kumbhi-
87 gallaka-vihāra he built an uposatha-house. In like manner
the king built an uposatha-house in the Issarasamaṇaka
88 (vihāra) [6] here and in the Thūpārāma a thūpa-temple. In
the Mahāvihāra he built a row of cells facing the west, and
89 he restored the ruined Catussālā (hall). In like manner the
same king made four beautiful Buddha-images and a temple
for the images in the fair courtyard of the great Bodhi-tree.

90 The king's consort, named Potthā, built in that same

[1] The same as Cittalapabbata, see note to 22. 23.

[2] Ṭīkā: aṭṭhuttaraṃ karīsasahassakaṃ.

[3] According to the Ṭīkā situated puratthimadisābhāge.

[4] Cf. 37. 48.

[5] In TURNOUR'S view sahassakarīsa is the name of the pond.

[6] Cf. note to 19. 61.

place a splendid thūpa and a beautiful temple for the thūpa.
When the king had completed the thūpa-temple in the 91
Thūpārāma he commanded lavish almsgiving for the festival
of its completion. Among those bhikkhus who were busied 92
with (the learning of) the word of the Buddha he distributed
the things needed (by bhikkhus), and among the bhikkhus
who explained the doctrine butter and sugar-molasses. At 93
the four gates of the city he had food given away to the poor
and, to such bhikkhus who were sick, food suited to the sick.
The Cayantī[1] and the Rājuppala-tank, the Vaha and the 94
Kolambagāmaka, the Mahānikkhavaṭṭi-tank and the Mahārā-
metti, the Kohāla[2] and the Kāli-tank,[3] the Cambuṭi, the 95
Cāthamaṅgaṇa and the Aggivaḍḍhamānaka:[4] these twelve
tanks and twelve canals he constructed, to make (the land) 96
fruitful. For safety he built up the city wall even so high
(as it now is)[5] and he built fortress-towers at the four gates 97
and a palace besides; in the garden he made a tank and put
geese therein.[6]

When the king had constructed many bathing-tanks here 98
and there in the capital he brought water to them by subter-
ranean canals. And in this way carrying out various works 99
of merit king Vasabha did away with the hindrances (to
long life), and delighting perpetually in well doing he reigned 100
forty-four years in the capital. He appointed also forty-
four Vesākha-festivals.[7]

Subharāja while he yet lived had anxiously, for fear of 101
Vasabha, entrusted his daughter to a brick-worker and had 102

[1] The names are extraordinarily erratic in the MSS. This adds greatly to the difficulty of identifying the separate tanks.

[2] The Ṭīkā has Kehāḷa and places the tank near Titthapaṭṭana.

[3] The Ṭīkā reads Keḷivāsaṃ ca instead of Kālivāpiṃ ca.

[4] See WICKREMASINGHE, *Epigraphia Zeylanica*, i, p. 211.

[5] The Ṭīkā gives the height of 18 cubits (aṭṭhārasahatthappamāṇaṃ) = about 25-27 feet.

[6] I do not believe that we need have recourse to the translation 'swan' or 'flamingo'. The goose is a sacred bird to the Buddhists and appears frequently on the monuments of Ceylon.

[7] See 1. 12 and 32. 35 with note.

at the same time given into his care his mantle and the royal insignia. When he was killed by Vasabha the brick-worker
103 took her with him, put her in the place of a daughter, and brought her up in his own house. When he was at work the girl used to bring him his food.

104 When (one day) in a thicket of flowering kadambas, she saw an (ascetic) who was in the seventh day of the state of
105 nirodha,[1] she the wise (maiden) gave him the food. When she had then prepared food afresh she carried the food to her father, and when she was asked the cause of the delay she
106 told her father this matter. And full of joy he bade (her) offer food repeatedly to the thera. When the thera had come out (of his trance) he said to the maiden, looking into
107 the future: 'When royal rank has fallen to thy lot then bethink thee, O maiden, of this place.' And forthwith the thera died.

108 Now did king Vasabha when his son Vaṅkanāsikatissa had
109 come to (full) age seek a fitting wife for him. When those people who understood the (auspicious) signs in women saw
110 the maiden in the brick-worker's village they told the king; the king thereon was about to send for her. And now the
111 brick-worker told him that she was a king's daughter, but that she was the daughter of Subharāja he showed by the mantle and so forth. Rejoiced the king gave her (in marriage) to his son when all had been duly provided.[2]

112 After Vasabha's death his son VAṄKANĀSIKATISSAKA reigned
113 three years in Anurādhapura. On the bank of the Goṇa-river the king Vaṅkanāsikatissaka built the vihāra called
114 Mahāmaṅgala. But his consort Mahāmattā collected money to build a vihāra, bethinking her of the thera's words.

115 After Vaṅkanāsikatissa's death his son GAJABĀHUKAGĀMAṆI

[1] Nirodha or saṃñāvedayitanirodha is a state of trance, cessation of consciousness. KERN, *Manual*, pp. 55, 57. If the state lasts over seven days it ends in death.

[2] Skt. kṛtamaṅgala (f. ā) means a person over whom prayers have been pronounced or who is arrayed with the auspicious things for some undertaking. B.R., *Skt. Wtb.*, s.v. maṅgala. The pāli katamaṅgala must be taken in the same sense.

reigned twenty-two years. Hearkening to his mother's word 116
the king founded the Mātuvihāra on the place of the thicket
of flowering kadambas, in honour of his mother. His wise 117
mother gave to the great vihāra a hundred thousand (pieces
of money) for the plot of land and built the vihāra;[1] he 118
himself built a thūpa of stone there and gave (land) for the
use of the brotherhood, when he had bought it from various
owners.

He erected the great Abhayuttara-thūpa, making it greater, 119
and to the four gates thereof he made vestibules. When the 120
king had made the Gāmaṇitissa-tank he bestowed it on the
Abhayagiri-vihāra for maintenance in food. He made a mant- 121
ling to the Maricavaṭṭi-thūpa and gave (land) thereto for
the use of the brotherhood, having bought it for a hundred
thousand (pieces of money). In the last year he founded the 122
vihāra called Rāmuka and built in the city the Mahejāsana-
sālā (hall).

After Gajabāhu's death the king's father-in-law MAHAL- 123
LAKA NĀGA reigned six years. (The vihāras) Sejalaka in 124
the east, Goṭapabbata in the south, Dakapāsāṇa in the west,
in Nāgadīpa Sālipabbata, in Bījagāma Tanaveli, in the 125
country of Rohaṇa Tobbalanāgapabbata, in the inland country
Girihālika: these seven vihāras did the king Mahallanāga, 126
ruler of the earth, build in the time (of his reign), short
though it was.

In this way do the wise, doing many works of merit, gain 127
with worthless riches that which is precious, but fools in
their blindness, for the sake of pleasures, do much evil.

Here ends the thirty-fifth chapter, called 'The Twelve Kings', in the Mahāvaṃsa, compiled for the serene joy and emotion of the pious.

[1] The meaning plainly is that the mother and son jointly founded the vihāra. In 116 it is said, in a general way, that the king together with his mother, founded the Mātuvihāra. How the undertaking was shared is explained in 117 and 118. The mother buys the plot of land and constructs the monastery buildings; the son builds the thūpa and presents the necessary lands for the maintenance of the inmates of the monastery.

CHAPTER XXXVI

THE THIRTEEN KINGS

1 After the death of Mahallanāga his son Bhātikatissaka
2 reigned twenty-four years in Laṅkā. He built a wall around
the Mahāvihāra. When the king had built the Gavaratissa-
3 vihāra he made the Mahāmaṇi-tank and gave it to the vihāra.
4 Moreover, he built the vihāra called Bhātikatissa. He built
an uposatha-house in the beautiful Thūpārāma; the king
5 also made the Randhakaṇḍaka-tank. Filled with tenderness
towards beings and zealous in reverencing the brotherhood
the protector of the earth commanded lavish almsgiving to
the community of both sexes.
6 After the death of Bhātikatissa (his younger brother)
Kaniṭṭhatissaka[1] reigned eighteen years in the island of
7 Laṅkā. Since he was well pleased with the thera Mahānāga
in the Bhūtārāma he built for him in splendid fashion the
8 Ratanapāsāda in the Abhayagiri. Moreover, he built in the
Abhayagiri a wall and a great pariveṇa and a great pariveṇa
9 besides in the (vihāra) called Maṇisoma.[2] In that place he
built a temple for the cetiya and in like manner for the
Ambatthala-thūpa; and (he ordered) the restoration of the
10 temple in Nāgadīpa. Doing away with the boundary of the
Mahāvihāra, the king built there the row of cells (called)
11 Kukkuṭagiri with all things provided. In the Mahāvihāra
the ruler of men built twelve great four-sided pāsādas,
12 admirable to see and beautiful, and he added a mantling to
the thūpa of the Dakkhiṇavihāra, and a refectory besides,
13 doing away with the boundary of the Mahāmeghavana. And
moving the wall of the Mahāvihāra to the side, he also made
14 a road leading to the Dakkhiṇavihāra. He built the Bhūtā-

[1] The name means 'the younger brother Tissa'.
[2] Cf. note to 33. 84.

rāmavihāra and the Rāmagoṇaka, and the ārāma of Nandatissa besides.

In the east the king built the Anulatissapabbata (vihāra) 15
in Gaṅgarājī, the Niyelatissārāma and the Pīlapiṭṭhivihāra
as well as the Rājamahāvihāra. In like manner he built in 16
three places an uposatha-house, in the three following vihāras, 17
the Kalyāṇikavihāra,[1] the Maṇḍalagirika, also the (vihāra)
called Dubbalavāpitissa.

After Kaniṭṭhatissa's death his son, who was known as 18
KHUJJANĀGA, reigned one year. The younger brother of 19
Khujjanāga KUÑCANĀGA, when he had slain the king his
brother, reigned two years in Laṅkā. During the great 20
Ekanāḷika[2] famine the king maintained without interruption
a great almsgiving[3] appointed for five hundred bhikkhus.

But the brother of Kuñcanāga's consort, the commander of 21
troops, SIRINĀGA, became a rebel against the king, and when 22
he was equipped with troops and horses he moved on to the
capital and when he, in battle with the king's army, had put 23
king Kuñcanāga to flight, victorious he reigned over Laṅkā
nineteen years in splendid Anurādhapura. When the king had 24
placed a parasol on the stately Great Thūpa, he had it gilded
in admirable and splendid fashion. He built the Lohapāsāda, 25
keeping it within five stories (height), and he restored the steps
to the four entrances leading to the great Bodhi-tree. When 26
he had completed the parasol and the pāsāda[4] he commanded
offerings at the festival (of the consecration); great in compassion, he remitted the tribute of families[5] throughout the island.

[1] Cf. 32. 51 and note to 1. 63.

[2] Nālī is a certain measure = 4 pasata 'handfuls'. RHYS DAVIDS, *Ancient Coins and Measures of Ceylon*, p. 17. To so small a quantity of food were the people reduced in that famine. Thence the designation.

[3] Mahāpeḷā, lit. 'great basket,' in contrast to ekanāḷikā.

[4] The reading is, I think, chattapāsādam. Still Chattapāsāda may also be understood as the name of a building. Thus TURNOUR, WIJESIṆHA and my edition.

[5] Kulambaṇa is obscure. Perhaps it means a certain tribute in kind (ambaṇa is a measure of capacity, used as a corn-measure), which was levied from single families (kula).

27 After the death of Sirināga his son TISSA reigned twenty-
two years, with knowledge of (the) law and (the) tradition.
28 Because he first in this country made a law that set aside
(bodily) injury (as penalty) he received the name king Vohārika-
29 tissa. When he had heard the (preaching of the) doctrine by
the thera Deva, who dwelt in Kappukagāma, he restored five
30 buildings. Moreover, contented with the thera Mahātissa, who
dwelt in Anurārāma,[1] he commanded almsgiving in Mucela-
31 paṭṭana.[2] When the king Tissa[3] had set up a pavilion in the
two great vihāras[4] and in the eastern temple of the great
32 Bodhi-tree two bronze images, and had built also the Satta-
paṇṇakapāsāda, goodly to dwell in, he appointed every month
33 a thousand (pieces of money)[5] for the Mahāvihāra. In the
Abhayagiri-vihāra and in the (vihāra) called Dakkhiṇamūla,
in the Maricavaṭṭi-vihāra and the (vihāra) called Kulālitissa,
34 in the Mahiyaṅgaṇa-vihāra, in the (vihāra) called Mahāgā-
manāga, in the (vihāras) called Mahānāgatissa, and Kalyāṇika
35 he put parasols to their eight thūpas. In the Mūlanāgasenā-
36 pati-vihāra and in the Dakkhiṇa(vihāra), in the Maricavaṭṭi-
vihāra and in the (vihāra) called Puttabhāga, in the (vihāra)
called Issarasamaṇa and the (vihāra) named Tissa in Nāga-
37 dīpaka; in these six vihāras he put up a wall, and he also
built an uposatha-house in the (vihāra) called Anurārāma.
38 For the occasions when the Ariyavaṃsa[6] was read he decreed
over the whole island a regular giving of alms, from reverence
39 for the true doctrine. With the spending of three hundred

[1] According to 35. 83 near Mahāgāma in the province of Rohaṇa.

[2] According to the Ṭīkā mucelapaṭṭana is the name of a 'ship' made of bronze in which offerings were placed. Such 'canoes' but of stone, which evidently served the same purpose, are, in fact, found in the ruins of Anurādhapura. (BURROWS, *Buried Cities of Ceylon*, pp. 38, 43-44.)

[3] Following the reading Tissarājā maṇḍapaṃ. If we read Tissarājamaṇḍapaṃ we must translate 'a pavilion (called) Tissarāja (after him)'.

[4] I.e. the Mahāvihāra and Abhayagiri-vihāra.

[5] According to the Ṭīkā, articles of clothing.

[6] Lit. 'book of the holy ones,' probably the life-histories of men eminent in the Buddhist Church, which were read aloud publicly for the edification of the people.

thousand (pieces of money) this king, who was a friend to the
doctrine, freed from their indebtedness such bhikkhus as were
in debt. When he had decreed a great Vesākha-festival,[1] 40
he bestowed the three garments on all the bhikkhus dwelling
in the island. Suppressing the Vetulya-doctrine[2] and keeping 41
heretics in check by his minister Kapila, he made the true
doctrine to shine forth in glory.

This king's younger brother, known as ABHAYANĀGA, who 42
was the queen's lover, being discovered (in his guilt) took
flight for fear of his brother and went with his serving-men 43
to Bhallatittha and as if wroth with him, he had his uncle's
hands and feet cut off. And that he might bring about 44
division in the kingdom, he left him behind here and took his
most faithful followers with him, showing them the example
of the dog,[3] and he himself took ship at the same place and 45
went to the other shore. But the uncle, Subhadeva, went to
the king and making as if he were his friend he wrought 46
division in the kingdom. And that he might have knowledge
of this, Abhaya sent a messenger thither. When Subhadeva 47
saw him he loosened (the earth) round about an areca-palm,
with the shaft of his spear, as he walked round (the tree), and
when he had made it thus (to hold) but feebly by the roots,
he struck it down with his arm; then did he threaten the 48
(messenger), and drove him forth. The messenger went and
told this matter to Abhaya. And when he knew this, Abhaya 49
took many Damiḷas with him and marched from there against
the city to do battle with his brother. On news of this the king 50

[1] See note to 32. 35.

[2] Cf. the Vaipulya-sūtras, sometimes also called Vaitulya-sūtras, which form part of the Northern Mahāyānist Canon. KERN, *Manual*, p. 5; idem, *Verslagen en Mededeelingen van de K. Ak. van Wetenschapen*, Afd. Letterk., 4e R., D. VIII, p. 312 foll., Amsterdam, 1907 (see L. DE LA VALLÉE POUSSIN, *J.R.A.S.* 1907, p. 432 foll.; WINDISCH, *Abh. d. k. Sächs. Gesellsch. d. W.*, xxvii, p. 472; OLDENBERG, *Archiv für Religionswissenschaft*, xiii, 1910, p. 614).

[3] According to the Ṭīkā, when he was about to embark on the ship, he had chided and punished a dog that he had with him. Nevertheless the animal followed him, wagging his tail. Then he said to his followers, 'Even as this dog, you must stand by me with unchangeable fidelity.'

took flight, and, with his consort, mounting a horse he came to
51 Malaya. The younger brother pursued him, and when he
had slain the king in Malaya, he returned with the queen and
reigned eight years in the capital as king.
52 The king set up a vedī of stone round about the great
Bodhi-tree, and a pavilion in the courtyard of the Lohapā-
53 sāda. And obtaining garments of every kind for twice a
hundred thousand (pieces of money), he distributed gifts of
clothing among the brotherhood of bhikkhus on the island.
54 After Abhaya's death, SIRINĀGA, the son of his brother
55 Tissa, reigned two years in Laṅkā. When he had restored the
wall round about the great Bodhi-tree, then did this king also
56 build in the sand-court[1] of the temple of the great Bodhi-
tree, to the south of the Mucela-tree,[2] the beautiful Haṃ-
savaṭṭa and a great pavilion besides.
57 Sirināga's son named VIJAYA-KUMĀRAKA reigned for one
year after his father's death.
58 (At that time) three Lambakaṇṇas lived in friendship at
Mahiyaṅgaṇa: Saṃghatissa and Saṃghabodhi, the third
59 being Goṭhakābhaya. When they were coming (to Anurā-
dhapura) to do service to the king, a blind man who had
the gift of prophecy, being by the edge of the Tissa-tank,
60 cried out at the sound of their footsteps: 'The ground bears
here three rulers of the earth!' As Abhaya, who was walking
last, heard this he asked (the meaning of the saying). The
61 other uttered yet again (the prophecy). 'Whose race will
endure?' then asked again the other, and he answered:
'That of the last.' When he had heard that he went (on)
62 with the two (others). When they were come into the capital
the three, being the close and trusted (counsellors) of the
king, remained in the royal service about the king.
63 When they together had slain king Vijaya in his royal
palace the two (others) consecrated SAṂGHATISSA, the com-
64 mander of the troops, as king. Thus crowned did Saṃgha-

[1] Vālikātala is employed here in the same way as vāli-kaṅgaṇa in 33. 31.

[2] Parato is paraphrased in the Ṭīkā by dakkhiṇadisābhāge, cf. Mah. 25. 50.

tissa reign four years in stately Anurādhapura. He set up 65
a parasol on the Great Thūpa and gilded it, and moreover the
king put four great gems, each worth a hundred thousand
(pieces of money), in the middle of the four suns,[1] and put 66
upon the spire of the thūpa a precious ring of crystal. At 67
the festival of (consecrating) the chatta the ruler of men dis-
tributed the six garments to the brotherhood (in number) forty
thousand. As he (one day) when listening to the khandhakas[2] 68
heard from the thera Mahādeva, dwelling in Dāmahālaka,
the sutta that sets forth the merit of (a gift of) rice-gruel,[3] 69
he, joyfully believing, distributed to the brotherhood at the
four gates of the city an abundant and well-prepared gift of
rice-gruel.

From time to time the king, with the women of the royal 70
household and the ministers, used to go to Pācīnadīpaka[4] to eat
jambu-fruits. Vexed by his coming the people dwelling in 71
Pācīnadīpa poisoned the fruit of the jambu-tree from which
the king was to eat. When he had eaten the jambu-fruits he 72
died forthwith even there. And Abhaya consecrated as king
Saṃghabodhi who was charged with the (command of) the
army.

The king, who was known by the name SIRISAṂGHABODHI, 73
reigned two years in Anurādhapura, keeping the five precepts.[5]

In the Mahāvihāra he set up a beautiful salākā-house.[6] 74
When the king heard that the people of the island were
come to want by reason of a drought he himself, his heart 75
shaken with pity, lay down on the ground in the courtyard
of the Great Thūpa, forming the resolve: 'Unless I be raised 76

[1] Which were placed on the four sides of the 'Tee'.

[2] The sections of the M.V. and C.V. in the Vinaya-piṭaka.

[3] See M.V. VI. 24. Cf. particularly 5 and 6. The scene of the exhortation is Andhakavinda.

[4] I.e. 'East-Island.' The Ṭīkā says: Mahātitthapaṭṭane parato samuddamajjhe sambhūtaṃ Pācīnadīpaṃ agamāsi. According to this Pācīnadīpa is one of the islands between the north point of Ceylon and the Indian continent.

[5] See note to 1. 62.

[6] On salākagga see note to 15. 205.

up by the water that the god shall rain down I will nevermore
77 rise up from hence, even though I die here.' As the ruler of
the earth lay there thus the god poured down rain forthwith on
78 the whole island of Laṅkā, reviving the wide earth. And even
then he did not yet rise up because he was not swimming
in the water. Then his counsellors closed up the pipes by
79 which the water flowed away. And as he now swam in the
water the pious king rose up. By his compassion did he in
this way avert the fear of a famine in the island.

80 At the news: 'Rebels are risen here and there,' the king
had the rebels brought before him, but he released them again
81 secretly; then did he send secretly for bodies of dead men, and
causing terror to the people by the burning[1] of these he did
away with the fear from rebels.

82 A yakkha known as Ratakkhi,[2] who had come hither, made
83 red the eyes of the people here and there. If the people did
but see one another and did but speak of the redness of the
eyes they died forthwith, and the yakkha devoured them
without fear.

84 When the king heard of their distress he lay down with
sorrowful heart alone in the chamber of fasting, keeping the
85 eight uposatha vows,[3] (and said): 'Till I have seen the
yakkha I will not rise up.' By the (magic) power of his
86 piety the yakkha came to him. To the king's (question):
'Who art thou?' he answered: 'It is I, (the yakkha).' 'Why
87 dost thou devour my subjects? Swallow them not!' 'Give
up to me then only the people of one region,' said the other.
And being answered: 'That is impossible,' he came gradually
88 (demanding ever less and less) to one (man) only. The (king)
spoke: 'No other can I give up to thee; take thou me and
devour me.' With the words: 'That is impossible,' the other

[1] He had the corpses burnt in place of the rebels and thus inspired the belief that he had condemned them to death by fire. Cf. also sūle uttāseti 'to impale'. Jāt. I. 500[11] and frequently.

[2] I.e. 'Red-eye.' Perhaps scarlatina? The Attanagaluvaṃsa which relates this episode in chap. VI (ed. Alwis, p. 16 foll.), speaks of a fever (jararoga) beginning with inflammation of the eyes.

[3] Cf. with this SPENCE HARDY, *Eastern Monachism*, p. 237.

prayed him (at last) to give him an offering in every village.
'It is well,' said the king, and over the whole island he 89
decreed that offerings[1] be brought to the entrance of the
villages, and these he gave up to him. Thus by the great 90
man,[2] compassionate to all beings, by the torch of the island
was the fear pestilence brought to an end.

The king's treasurer, the minister Goṭhakābhaya, who had 91
become a rebel, marched from the north against the capital.
Taking his water-strainer with him the king fled alone by 92
the south gate, since he would not bring harm to others.

A man who came, bearing his food in a basket, along that 93
road entreated the king again and again to eat of his food.
When he, rich in compassion, had strained the water and had 94
eaten he spoke these words, to show kindness to the other:
'I am the king Saṃghabodhi; take thou my head and show 95
it to Goṭhābhaya, he will give thee much gold.' This he 96
would not do, and the king to render him service gave up the
ghost even as he sat. And the other took the head and 97
showed it to Goṭhābhaya and he, in amazement of spirit,
gave him gold and carried out the funeral rites of the king
with due care.

Thus GOṬHĀBHAYA, also known as Meghavaṇṇābhaya, ruled 98
thirteen years over Laṅkā.

He built a palace, and when he had built a pavilion at the 99
entrance to the palace and had adorned it, even there did
he daily invite a thousand and eight bhikkhus of the brother- 100
hood to be seated, and rejoicing them with rice-gruel and
with foods excellent and of many kinds, both hard and soft,
together with garments, he bestowed alms lavishly upon them. 101
Twenty-one days did he continue (to give) thus.

In the Mahāvihāra he built a splendid pavilion of stone; 102
he renewed[3] the pillars of the Lohapāsāda. He set up a vedī 103

[1] By bali are understood particularly the offerings brought to the subordinate divinities, devatās, tutelary genii, local sprites, &c.

[2] Mahāsatta is used elsewhere as designation of a Bodhisatta.

[3] Lit. 'He set them up when he had changed them.' In Skt. parivartayati (B.R. s. v. vart with pari) has the same meaning.

of stone for the great Bodhi-tree and an arched gateway
at the northern entrance, and likewise at the four corners (of
the courtyard) pillars with wheel-symbols.[1]
104 At three entrances he made three statues of stone and at
105 the south gate he set up a throne of stone. To the west
of the Mahāvihāra he laid out a tract of land for exercises
of meditation,[2] and over the island he restored all ruined
106 buildings. In the Thūpārāma he ordered the thūpa-temple to
be restored and also in the Ambatthala-monastery of the thera
107 (Mahinda);[3] and in the ārāma called Maṇisoma, and in the
Thūpārāma, in the Maṇisomārāma and in the Maricavaṭṭi
(vihāra), and moreover in the vihāra called Dakkhiṇa (he
108 restored) the uposatha-houses. And he founded also a new
vihāra called Meghavaṇṇābhaya and at the (time of) festal
109 offerings at the consecration of the vihāra he distributed the
six garments to thirty thousand bhikkhus dwelling on the
island, whom he had assembled.

In like manner he appointed then a great Vesākha-festival,[4]
110 and yearly did he distribute the six garments to the brother-
111 hood. Purifying the doctrine by suppression of heresy he
seized bhikkhus dwelling in the Abhayagiri (vihāra), sixty in
number, who had turned to the Vetulya-doctrine[5] and were
112 like a thorn in the doctrine of the Buddha, and when he had
excommunicated them,[6] he banished them to the further
coast. A bhikkhu from the Coḷa people, named Saṃghamitta,
113 who was versed in the teachings concerning the exorcism of
spirits, and so forth, had attached himself[7] to a thera banished

[1] See note to 30. 92.

[2] Childers, *P.D.* s.v. padhānam, says: 'padhānabhūmi, a cloister in a monastery for monks to walk in who are striving to attain arhatship.'

[3] The Therambatthalaka is without doubt the Ambatthala-thūpa built in memory of Mahinda on the Cetiya-mountain. See note to 34. 71.

[4] Cf. note to 32. 35.

[5] Cf. note to 36. 41.

[6] Katvāna niggahaṃ tesaṃ, lit. 'having suppressed them.' See pāpakānam niggahena in v. 110.

[7] Nissito, the term for one who stands to an older monk in the relation of pupil to teacher (nissaya).

thither, and he came hither embittered against the bhikkhus of the Mahāvihāra.

When this lawless (bhikkhu) had thrust himself into an 114
assembly in the Thūpārāma and had refuted there the words
of the thera living in the pariveṇa of Saṃghapāla, namely the 115
thera Goṭhābhaya, uncle of the king on the mother's side,
who had addressed the king with his (old) name, he became a 116
constant guest in the king's house.[1] The king who was well
pleased with him entrusted his eldest son Jeṭṭhatissa and his
younger son Mahāsena, to the bhikkhu. And he made the 117
second his favourite, therefore prince Jeṭṭhatissa bore ill-will
to the bhikkhu.

After his father's death Jeṭṭhatissa became king. To 118
punish the hostile ministers who would not go in procession
with him, at the performing of the king's funeral rites, the 119
king himself proceeded forth, and placing his younger brother
at the head and then the body following close behind, and 120
then the ministers whilst he himself was at the end (of the
procession), he, when his younger brother and the body were
gone forth, had the gate closed immediately behind them, and 121
he commanded that the treasonous ministers be slain and (their
bodies) impaled on stakes round about his father's pyre.

Because of this deed he came by the surname 'the Cruel'. 122
But the bhikkhu Saṃghamitta, for fear of the king, went hence 123

[1] The passage is very obscure as the course of events in the Thūpārāma is too briefly described. I believe that we must supply the object rājānaṃ to rañño nāmenālapato, and that we have to understand the passage in the following way. A solemn assembly of the brotherhood was held in the Thūpārāma to settle the dissensions between the various parties. The king himself was present. In this assembly Saṃghamitta exposed his heretical doctrine, speaking against the monks of the Mahāvihāra, and he succeeded in convincing the king. The thera Goṭhābhaya, the king's uncle, after whom the king himself was named, tried to bring the king round to the orthodox party. But although he spoke urgently to him, even addressing him tenderly, not with his royal title Meghavaṇṇābhaya, but with his familiar name Goṭhābhaya (Ṭīkā: tāta Goṭhābhaya Goṭhābhayā ti...), he did not succeed, and Saṃghamitta even became the king's kulūpaka. On this see note to 30. 40.

at the time of his coronation, when he had taken counsel with Mahāsena, to the further coast awaiting the time of (Mahāsena's) consecrating.

124 He (Jeṭṭhatissa) built up to seven stories the splendid Lohapāsāda, that had been left unfinished[1] by his father, so
125 that it was now worth a koṭi (pieces) of money. When he had offered there a jewel worth sixty thousand, Jeṭṭhatissa named it the Maṇipāsāda.

126 He offered two precious gems to the Great Thūpa, and he built three gateways to the temple of the great Bodhi-tree.
127 When he had built the vihāra Pācīnatissapabbata the ruler gave it to the brotherhood in the five settlements.

128 The great and beautiful stone image that was placed of old
129 by Devānampiyatissa in the Thūpārāma did king Jeṭṭhatissa take away from the Thūpārāma, and set up in the ārāma
130 Pācīnatissapabbata. He bestowed the Kālamattika-tank on the Cetiyapabbata (vihāra), and when he celebrated the consecrating festival of the vihāra and the pāsāda and (held)
131 a great Vesākha-ceremony he distributed the six garments among the brotherhood, in number thirty thousand. Jeṭṭha-
132 tissa also made the Ālambagāma-tank. Accomplishing thus many works of merit, beginning with the building of the pāsāda, the king reigned ten years.

133 Thus, reflecting that sovereignty, being the source of manifold works of merit, is at the same time the source of many an injustice, a man of pious heart will never enjoy it as if it were sweet food mixed with poison.

Here ends the thirty-sixth chapter, called 'The Thirteen Kings', in the Mahāvaṃsa, compiled for the serene joy and emotion of the pious.

[1] **Vippakata** is used (e.g. D.I. 2^{26}) of an interrupted discourse. Here we have the interrupting of building (cf. 36. 102 cd.). The Ṭīkā renders the word correctly **niṭṭhānaṃ agataṃ apariniṭṭhāpitaṃ**.

CHAPTER XXXVII

KING MAHĀSENA[1]

AFTER king Jeṭṭhatissa's death, his younger brother MAHĀ- 1
SENA ruled twenty-seven years as king. And to consecrate him 2
as king, the thera Saṃghamitta came thither from the further
coast, when he heard the time (of Jeṭṭhatissa's death).[2]
When he had carried out the consecration and the other 3
ceremonies of various kind, the lawless (bhikkhu) who would
fain bring about the destruction of the Mahāvihāra won the 4
king to himself with the words:—'The dwellers in the
Mahāvihāra do not teach the (true) vinaya, we are those who
teach the (true) vinaya, O king', and he established a royal 5
penalty: 'Whosoever gives food to a bhikkhu dwelling in
the Mahāvihāra is liable to a fine of a hundred (pieces of
money).'

The bhikkhus dwelling in the Mahāvihāra, who thereby 6
fell into want, abandoned the Mahāvihāra, and went to
Malaya and Rohaṇa. Thus was our Mahāvihāra desolate for 7
nine years and empty of those bhikkhus who (else) had dwelt
in the Mahāvihāra. And the unwise thera persuaded the 8

[1] After verse 50 in chapter 37 the old Mahāvaṃsa breaks off. But the later author, who continued the work, carried on this chapter and added 198 verses, giving to the whole the subscription Sattarājako ='the Seven Kings'. (However, there are in reality six:—Mahāsena, Kittisiri-Meghavaṇṇa, Jeṭṭhatissa II, Buddhadāsa, Upatissa II, and Mahānāma.) Our section (verses 1–50) has thus no conclusion, neither the usual memorial verse, nor a subscription. The substance of the former ought to have corresponded to that of the closing verses of the Dīp., but was clothed in a more artistic form. The writer who continued the Mah. put the last two verses of the Dīp. at the head of his own work and thus connected the new part of the poem with the old one. On the whole process, cf. GEIGER, *Dīp. and Mah.*, pp. 18-19.

[2] Ṭīkā: kālaṃ ñatvā, Jeṭṭhatissassa matakālaṃ jānitvā.

9 unwise king :—'Ownerless land belongs to the king,'[1] and
when he had gained leave from the king to destroy the
Mahāvihāra, this (bhikkhu), in the enmity of his heart, set on
people to do so.
10 An adherent of the thera Saṃghamitta, the ruthless
minister Soṇa, a favourite servant of the king, and (with
11 him) shameless bhikkhus, destroyed the splendid Lohapāsāda
seven stories high, and carried away the (material of the)
12 various buildings from hence to the Abhayagiri (vihāra), and
by means of the many buildings[2] that were borne away from
the Mahāvihāra the Abhayagiri-vihāra became rich in build-
13 ings. Holding fast to his evil friend, the thera Saṃghamitta,
and to his servant Soṇa, the king wrought many a deed of wrong.
14 The king sent for the great stone image from the Pācīna-
tissapabbata (vihāra) and set it up in the Abhayagiri (vihāra).
15 He set up a building for the image, a temple for the Bodhi-
tree, a beautiful relic-hall and a four-sided hall,[3] and he
16 restored the (pariveṇa) called Kukkuṭa.[4] Then by the ruthless
thera Saṃghamitta was the Abhayagiri-vihāra made stately
to see.

17 The minister named Meghavaṇṇābhaya, the friend of the
king, who was busied with all his affairs, was wroth with him
18 for destroying the Mahāvihāra; he became a rebel, and when
he had gone to Malaya and had raised a great force, he
pitched a camp by the Dūratissaka-tank.[5]

19 When the king heard that his friend was come thither, he

[1] A play on the words assāmiko and pathavīsāmī 'owner (ruler) of the earth'.

[2] Pāsāda means here, in quite a general sense, the habitations of the bhikkhus in the Mahāvihāra, which were demolished here and the material of which was conveyed to the Abhayagiri-vihāra.

[3] Catu(s)sālā. A certain building of this name in Anurādhapura is mentioned, Mah. 15. 47, 50; and 35. 88. In our passage the word is evidently an *appellativum*.

[4] By this is probably meant the Kukkuṭagiri-pariveṇa erected by Kaniṭṭhatissa. See 36. 10.

[5] See note to 33. 9. Meghavaṇṇābhaya evidently marches from the central mountain-district of Malaya to secure the province of Rohaṇa.

marched forth to do battle with him, and he also pitched a camp.

The other had good drink and meat, that he had brought 20
with him from Malaya and thinking: 'I will not enjoy it
without my friend the king,' he took some, and he himself 21
went forth alone by night, and coming to the king he told him
this thing. When the king had eaten with him, in perfect 22
trust, that which he had brought, he asked him: 'Why hast
thou become a rebel?' 'Because the Mahāvihāra has been 23
destroyed by thee' he answered. 'I will make the vihāra to
be dwelt in yet again; forgive me my fault,' thus spoke 24
the king, and the other was reconciled with the king.
Following his counsel the king returned to the capital. But 25
Meghavaṇṇābhaya, who persuaded the king (that it was
fitting to do this), did not go with the king that he might
collect in the meantime the wherewithal to build.

One of the king's wives, who was exceedingly dear to him, 26
the daughter of a scribe, grieved over the destruction of the
Mahāvihāra, and when she, in bitterness of heart, had won over 27
a labourer to kill the thera who had destroyed it, she caused the
violent thera Saṃghamitta to be done to death as he came to 28
the Thūpārāma to destroy it. And they slew likewise the
violent and lawless minister Soṇa. But when Meghavaṇṇā- 29
bhaya had brought the building-materials (that he had
collected), he built several pariveṇas in the Mahāvihāra. When 30
this fear had (thus) been calmed by Abhaya the bhikkhus
coming from here and there again inhabited the Mahāvihāra.
But the king made two bronze images and set them up on 31
the west side of the temple of the great Bodhi-tree.

Being well-pleased with the hypocrite, the plotter, the 32
lawless thera Tissa, his evil friend, who dwelt in the Dakkhi-
ṇārāma, he, although he was warned, built within the 33
boundaries of the Mahāvihāra, in the garden called Joti,
the Jetavana-vihāra.[1] Then he called upon the brotherhood 34

[1] According to 15. 202, Jotivana is a name for the Nandana park which, according to 15. 1, 7–8, was situated immediately before the south gate of Anurādhapura. From this and from our passage it appears quite certain that the Jetavana-vihāra must be the monastery

of monks to do away with their boundaries, and since the bhikkhus would not do this, they abandoned the vihāra.
35 But now, to make the shifting of the boundary void of effect, if others should seek to do this, certain bhikkhus hid themselves in various places.[1]

36 Thus was the Mahāvihāra abandoned for nine months by the bhikkhus, and the other bhikkhus thought: 'We will
37 begin to shift (the boundaries).' Then, when this attempt to shift the boundary was given up,[2] the bhikkhus
38 came back hither and dwelt again in the Mahāvihāra. But within the brotherhood of bhikkhus a complaint touching an offence of the gravest kind[3] was raised against the thera
39 Tissa, who had received the (Jetavana) vihāra. The high minister, known to be just, who decided (the matter) excluded him, according to right and law, from the order, albeit against the king's wishes.

40 The king built also the Maṇihīra-vihāra[4] and founded three
41 vihāras, destroying temples of the (brahmanical) gods:—the Gokaṇṇa (vihāra), (and another vihāra) in Erakāvilla, (and a third) in the village of the Brahman Kalanda;[5] (moreover

the thūpa of which was mistakenly (called) the Abhayagiri Dagaba. On the other hand the present Jetavana Dagaba to the north of the city belonged to the Abhayagiri. Cf. note 33. 81.

[1] Namely, within the old boundaries of the Mahāvihāra, possession of which was thus formally maintained. Ṭīkā: antosimāya eva aññattha agantvā tasmiṃ tasmiṃ ṭhāne paticchannā hutvā nilīyiṃsu.

[2] Evidently since the bhikkhus remaining behind raised a protest.

[3] Antimavatthu is a matter that involves expulsion from the order. Cf. M.V. II. 22. 3; 36. 1; *S.B.E.* xiii, p. 276, note 1.

[4] Now Minneriya, the name of a tank (see below, v. 47) not far from Poḷonnaruwa.

[5] According to the Ṭīkā the Gokaṇṇa-vihāra is situated on the coast of the 'Eastern Sea', the two other vihāras in Rohaṇa. The Ṭīkā then adds: evaṃ sabbattha Laṅkadīpamhi kudiṭṭhikānaṃ ālayaṃ viddhaṃsetvā, Sivaliṅgādayo nāsetvā buddhasāsanaṃ eva patiṭṭhapesi 'everywhere in the island of Laṅkā he established the doctrine of the Buddha, having destroyed the temples of the unbelievers, i.e. having abolished the phallic symbols of Siva and so forth'.

he built) the Migagāma-vihāra and the Gaṅgāsenakapabbata
(vihāra). To the west, he built the Dhātusenapabbata 42
(vihāra); the king founded also the great vihāra in Kokavāta.
He built the Thūpārāma-vihāra and the Huḷapiṭṭhi (vihāra) 43
and the two nunneries, called Uttara and Abhaya. At the place 44
of the yakkha Kālavela[1] he built a thūpa, and on the island
he restored many ruined buildings. To one thousand saṃ- 45
ghattheras[2] he distributed alms for theras, at a cost of a
thousand (pieces of money), and to all (the bhikkhus he dis-
tributed) yearly a garment. There is no record of his gifts 46
of food and drink.

To make (the land) more fertile, he made sixteen tanks, the 47
Maṇihīra,[3] the Mahāgāma, the Challūra, and the (tank) named
Khānu,[4] the Mahāmaṇi,[5] the Kokavāta[6] and the Dhamma- 48
ramma-tank, the Kumbālaka and the Vāhana, besides the
Rattamālakaṇḍaka,[7] the tank Tissavaḍḍhamānaka,[8] that of
Velaṅgaviṭṭhi,[9] that of Mahāgallaka, the Cīra-tank and the 49
Mahādāragallaka and the Kālapāsāṇa-tank. These are the
sixteen tanks. On the Gaṅgā he built the great canal named 50
Pabbatanta.

Thus did he gather to himself much merit and much guilt.

The Mahāvaṃsa is ended.

[1] Cf. 10. 84.

[2] I.e. superiors of the communities of bhikkhus. Cf. 3. 4; 4. 56.

[3] See above note to 37. 40.

[4] A Khānugāma is mentioned 25. 14.

[5] In 36. 3 the construction of a Mahāmaṇi-tank is ascribed to Bhātikatissa.

[6] Cf. the Kokavāta-vihāra in 37. 42.

[7] Maharatmala is the older name of the great Padaviya-lake in the North Central Province, 25 miles north of Anurādhapura. Arch. Survey of Ceylon, XIII, 1896, p. 40. There is, however, also a Ratmala-tank $2\frac{1}{2}$ miles south of Anurādhapura. ED. MÜLLER, *Ancient Inscriptions of Ceylon*, p. 27.

[8] A village or district of this name is mentioned in 35. 84.

[9] A vihāra of the same name, see 33. 8.

APPENDIX A

THE DYNASTY OF MAHĀSAṂMATA

ON Mah. 2 = Dīp. 3 = Sum. T. p. 258 = Rājāv. p. 4 foll. (Engl. transl. by B. GUṆASEKARA) I should like to give a reference to two parallel passages in northern Buddhist literature, the *Mahāvastu*[1] which belongs to the Vinaya of the Mahāsaṃghikas and, moreover, of the Lokottaravāda-school, and to the *Dulva*,[2] the Tibetan translation of the Vinaya of the Sarvāstivādins.

The names handed down in both these sources may be compared with those of the D. and M. in the following list:—

Dīp. Mah.	Mahāvastu	Dulva
Mahāsaṃmata	Mahāsaṃmata	Mahāsaṃmata
Roja	—	Rōkha
Vararoja	—	—
Kalyāṇa	Kalyāṇa	Kalyāṇa
Varakalyāṇa	Rava?	Varakalyāṇa
Uposatha	Upoṣadha	Utpoṣadha
Mandhātar	Māndhāta	Māndhātā
Caraka	—	Kāru
Upacara	—	Upakāru
&c.	&c.	Kārumat, &c.
|	|	|
Okkāka (Dīp.: surnamed Sujāta)	Ikṣvāku (surnamed Sujāta)	Ikṣvāku (Gotama)
Okkāmukha, Nipuṇa and three other sons	Ulkāmukha,[3] Nipura and three other sons	Ulkāmukha, Nūpura and two other sons

[1] Ed. SENART, i, p. 348.

[2] See ROCKHILL, *Life of the Buddha* (1907), p. 11 foll.

[3] In the Mahāvastu tradition not Ulkāmukha but Opura is said to be the eldest son; but in the Dulva again the former is so.

In the Mahāvastu I. 348[3]–352[8] and in the Dulva (ROCKHILL, p. 11 foll.) there follows a story about the rise of the Śākya and the founding of Kapilavastu. Ikṣvāku banishes his legitimate sons from the country as he wishes to hand on the throne to Jenta the son of a concubine. He is thus fulfilling a promise into which the mother of Jenta has beguiled him. Ikṣvāku's sons withdraw into the wilderness and there take to wife their sisters who have accompanied them. Afterwards Kapilavastu is built by them. Their descendants are the Śākyas.

This story was also known to the Theravādins. It occurs in Sum. T. p. 258 foll. and in the Ṭīkā to the Mahāvaṃsa, p. 84.[1] In agreement with the Dulva the M. Ṭ. mentions only four sons of Okkāka who were banished from the country; the fifth is Jantu to whom the brothers have to give way.

Further on (I. p. 352[16] foll.) the Mahāvastu relates the story of a Śākya king's daughter who is a leper and therefore banished to the forest. Here she is cured and is found by a hermit named Kola. Kola had formerly been king of Benares and had withdrawn into the forest because he too suffered from leprosy. He married the Śākya princess and from these two sprang the Koliya clan.

This legend too was known in Ceylon, we come across it in Sum. T. p. 260 foll. and in the (Sinhalese) Rājāvali immediately following on the story of the sons of Ikṣvāku.[2]

The Mahāvastu and Dulva speak of Siṃhahanu (= Sīhahanu in Dīp. Mah.) as the Buddha's grandfather. He has four sons: (1) Suddhodana the Buddha's father, (2) Dhautodana, (3) Śuklodana and (4) Amṛtodana. These are the Suddhodana, Dhotodana, Sukkodana and Amitodana of the Dīp. and Mah., which add yet another, Sakkodana.

According to the Dīp. Mah. the Buddha's genealogical tree[3] is this:—

[1] *Mahāvaṃsa-Ṭīkā*, ed. BAṬUWANTUḌĀWE and ÑĀNISSARA BHIKSHU, Colombo, 1895. GEIGER, *Dīp. and Mah.*, p. 38.

[2] The *Rājāvaliya*, ed. (in English) by B. GUṆASEKARA, Colombo, 1900, pp. 11–13. GEIGER, *l. l.*, p. 95.

[3] See also RHYS DAVIDS, *Buddhism* (1910), p. 52.

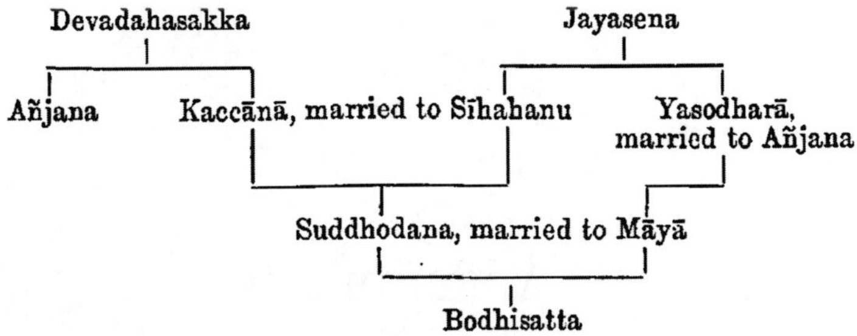

The Mahāvastu I. 355[15] foll. names as Māyā's father Subhūti who was married to a Koliya princess and lived in Devadaha. Plainly this is the Añjana of the Mah., and the Suprabuddha of the Dulva (p. 14), while the Mah. (2. 18–19) takes Suppabuddha to be the son of Añjana and brother of Māyā. Perhaps Suprabuddha was a surname borne by the father and son.[1]

[1] For the whole subject cf. also SPENCE HARDY, *Manual of Buddhism*, p. 125 foll.

APPENDIX B

THE BUDDHIST SECTS

(On Mah. 5. 1–13)

RHYS DAVIDS. 'The Sects of the Buddhists,' *J.R.A.S.*, 1891, p. 409 foll.; the same, 'Schools of Buddhist Belief,' *J.R.A.S.* 1892, p. 1 foll.; MINAYEFF, *Recherches sur le Bouddhisme*, p. 187 foll.

SOUTHERN BUDDHIST LISTS (SB.) occur besides *Mah.* 5 in the *Dīp.* 5. 39 foll.; also in the *Mahābodhivaṃsa* (ed. STRONG, *P.T.S.* 1891), pp. 96–97, in the *Sāsanavaṃsa* (ed. M. BODE, *P.T.S.* 1897), p. 14, 24–25; in the Sinhalese *Nikāya-Saṃgraha* (ed. WICKREMASINGHE), pp. 6–9. Special mention should be made of the Commentary on the *Kathāvatthu*, the *Kathāvatthuppakaraṇa-Aṭṭhakathā* (ed. MINAYEFF, *J.P.T.S.* 1889, pp. 2–3, 5 and *passim*). The Kathāvatthuppakaraṇa is ascribed to Tissa Moggaliputta,[1] who is said to have composed it after the holding of the Third Council in order to refute the views held by sectaries. The names of the sects are not mentioned in the Kathāvatthu but are in the commentary thereon, mentioned above, which was composed by Buddhaghosa.[2]

All the Southern Buddhist lists are in complete agreement with one another.

[1] I adhere to this assertion (Mah. 5. 278) as a statement of fact. That the objection raised by MINAYEFF (*Recherches*, p. 200) to the age of the work is based upon an error has been already demonstrated by OLDENBERG, *Z.D.M.G.*, 52, p. 633, and RHYS DAVIDS, *Dialogues*, i, p. xviii.

[2] Quoted by me as Kvu. Co.

I will mention, when occasion arises, certain trifling variations in the *Nik. Saṃgr.* The ground for the agreement is that all the southern sources are based, in the last resort, upon the old-sinhalese Aṭṭhakathā.

NORTHERN BUDDHIST LISTS (NB.) occur in the Dulva, the Tibetan Vinaya of the Sarvāstivādins according to a work of Bhavya, see ROCKHILL, *Life of the Buddha* (1907), p. 182 foll. (R.), and according to a work of Vasumitra, see WASSILJEW, *Der Buddhismus* (1860), i, p. 224 foll. (W.), also BEAL, 'The Eighteen Schools of Buddhism' (*Ind. Ant.*, ix, p. 299 foll.) (VB.).[1]

Besides we have lists in Tāranātha. See SCHIEFNER, *Tāranātha's History of Buddhism in India* (1869), pp. 270–274 (Tār.).

ST. JULIEN gives five Chinese lists based, for the most part, upon Vasumitra: 'Listes diverses des noms de dix-huit écoles schismatiques qui sont sorties du Bouddhisme,' *Journ. As.*, v. série, t. xiv (1859), p. 327 foll. (St. J.). To these may be added the statements of the Chinese pilgrims Fa-hian, Hiuen-thsang[2] and I-tsing.[3]

The number of the sects is unanimously given as 18. Evidently we again have to do with one of those established numbers which form the backbone of tradition.

The individual names vary and the dividing-up of the sects also shows certain variations. This is shown by the following survey:—

1. SB. THERAVĀDA = NB. STHAVIRAVĀDA is one of the two original schools into which the united church was divided at the first schism. It was so according to Mah. Dīp., &c., also according to St. J., p. 343 (list V), 100 years after the Nirvāṇa. On the other hand the number is 116 in St. J. 333 (list II); and 160 in R. 182, St. J. 336 (list V).

[1] BEAL gives two lists following Vasumitra, as ROCKHILL gives two following Bhavya.

[2] I call them Ch. 1, 2, and quote Fa-hian and Hiuen-thsang according to BEAL (B.), *Buddhist Records of the Western Worlds*.

[3] *A record of the Buddhist religion by I-tsing*, transl. by TAKAKUSU, Ch. 3.

We may consider as a synonymous designation :—

1[a]. SB. Hemavata = NB. Haimavata in W. 253, VB. 300, R. 184. Still in R. 190 distinctions are made between the Sthaviras and the Haimavatas. In Dīp. and Mah., &c., they are considered as separate sects. Probably the Haimavatas were a local school of the Sthaviras of continental India.

2. SB. Mahāsaṃghika = NB. Mahāsaṃghika.[1] For their particular doctrine see W. 258 foll. They are the second school of the first great schism.

3. SB. Gokulika = NB. Gokulika (R. 186, 187; Tār. 271; VB. 301; St. J. 330, 334, 337, 341 = lists I–IV). The name is missing in Ch. 1, 2, 3 as also in W. In its place here appears :—

3[a]. Kukkuṭika (W. 252, 258) or Kukkulika (W. 249; VB. 300). Similarly in St. J. 344 (list V), the Kaukkuṭikas are put in instead of the Gokulikas and the two are expressly said 341 (list IV) to be identical.

Very closely related to the Gokulikas are :—

3[b]. Lokottaravādin who do not appear in the tradition of the Southern Buddhists. They are mentioned immediately beside the Gokulikas (or Kukkuṭikas). (W. 249, 252, 258; VB. 301; St. J. 334, 337, 341, 343 = lists II–V.) In R. 182 they are to be found just in the place where we should expect the Gokulikas. Cf. St. J. 330 = list I and Tār. 271, where the Gokulikas appear in the list, whilst, on the other hand, the Lokottaravādins are missing. Lastly, Tār. says, 273, that Lokottaravādins and Kaukkuṭapādas are the same. Ch. 2 mentions the L. in Bāmiān (Beal, i. 50).

4. SB. Ekavyohārika = NB. Ekavyavahārika (W. 249, 252; VB. 300, 301; R. 182, 187; Tār. 271; St. J. 330, 334, 337, 341, 344 = lists I–V). According to Tār. 273 the name is employed as a general designation of the Mahāsaṃghikas. Their doctrines according to W. 258 are the same as those of 2, 3[a] and 3[b].

[1] In St. J. 340 (list II) the Kārmikas, besides the Yogācāras and Aiśvarikas, are reckoned as belonging to the Mahāsaṃghikas.

5. SB. PAṆṆATTIVĀDIN = NB. PRAJÑAPTIVĀDIN (W. 251; R. 182; Tār. 271; St. J. 341 = list IV; missing in VB. 300; St. J. lists I–III, V, also in R. 185). They are the Si-chi in VB. 301. For their particular doctrines see W. 268, R. 189.

6. SB. BAHULIKA = NB. BAHUŚRUTĪYA (W. 250; VB. 300, 301; R. 182; Tār. 250, 252; St. J. 330, 334, 338, 341, 345 = lists I–V). For their doctrines see W. 268; R. 189.

7. SB. CETIYAVĀDA = NB. CAITIKA or CAITYIKA (W. 251, 252; VB. 300, 301; R. 182, 186). They are said to be a branch of the Gokulikas, R. 189; Tār. 252. In Tār. 273 they are said to be identical with the Pūrvaśailas. Corresponding to them in the lists I–III, V = St. J. 330, 334, 338, 345 are the Jetikas or Jetavaniyās or Jetaśailas.

8. SB. MAHIṂSĀSAKA = NB. MAHĪŚĀSAKA. They are, according to R. 186; Tār. 271, to be reckoned as belonging to the Vibhajyavādins (cf. 14[a]) and are said to be a branch of the Sarvāstivādins in W. 254; VB. 300, 301; St. J. 335, 339, 342, 345 = lists II–V. For their doctrines see R. 185, 191; W. 280 foll. Ch. 2 mentions them in Swāt (BEAL, i, p. 121). According to the same authority (BEAL, i, p. 226) the Bodhisattva Asaṅga professed himself to be of the school of the M., but went over to the Mahāyāna.

9. SB. VAJJIPUTTAKA = NB. VATSĪPUTRĪYA or VĀSAPUTRĪYA (W. 253, 256; VB. 300, 301; R. 182, 184, 186, 193; Tār. 271, 272, 273; St. J. 331, 335, 339, 342 = lists I–IV). They are said to be a branch of the Sarvāstivādins in W. 253, VB. 301, St. J. 335 (list II), while according to the southern Buddhist tradition the relation is reversed; and they are said, R. 186, to be a principal branch of the Sthaviras beside the Sarvāstivādins. The Kvu. Co., however, mentions them very slightly. The Pāli form of the name must be understood as an assimilation to the name of the Vajjiputtaka monks, the sectaries of Vesālī.

10. SB. DHAMMUTTARIYA = NB. DHARMOTTARĪYA the Dharmakārikas of the Nik. S., are said, as also in the southern

tradition, to be a branch of the Vatsīputrīya (W. 253; VB. 300, 301; R. 182, 186; Tār. 271; St. J. 331, 335, 339, 342, 345 = lists I–V).

11. SB. Bhadrayānika = Bhadrāyanīya are also a branch of the Vatsīputrīyas (W. 253; VB. 300, 301; R. 186; Tār. 271, 273; St. J. 335, 339, 342, 345 = lists II–V), and stand in especially close relation (R. 194) to the Dharmottarīyas from whom, according to St. J. 331 (list I), they had taken their rise.[1] For 10 and 11, R. gives the common designation Mahāgiriya.

12. SB. Chandāgārika = NB. Ṣaṇṇagarika 'those from the 6 cities', also a branch of the Vatsīputrīyas (W. 254; VB. 300; R. 186, cf. 194; Tār. 271; St. J. 335, 342 = lists II, IV) and are but slightly distinguished from 11 (W. 279). In the lists I, III, V in St. J. 337, 339, 345 there appear, instead of them, the Abhayagirivāsins.

13. SB. Saṃmitīya = NB. Saṃmatīya, taking their rise like 10–12, from 9 (W. 254; R. 186; Tār. 271, 272; St. J. 331, 335, 339, 342, 345 = lists I–V). According to R. 182 they are also called (13[a]) Avantaka or (13[b]) Kurukullaka, and Tār. 272 relates that according to the view of the Sarvāstivādins, the Kaurukullakas, the Avantakas, and the Vatsīputrīyas are the three kinds of the Saṃmatīyas. They are the Mi-li in VB. 301. They must have been a widely spread sect; Ch. 2 mentions them repeatedly as a school of the Hīnayāna (see Beal, ii. 14, 44, 45, 186, &c.); according to Ch. 3 (Takakusu, p. xxiv) they fall into four subdivisions and are spread over Western India and in Campā (Cochin-China) especially. The Kvu. Co. in a whole series of passages is occupied with their doctrines. On those see R. 194.

14. SB. Sabbatthavādin = NB. Sarvāstivādin. According to W. 253, VB. 301, St. J. 339 (list III) and 342 (list IV), they are also called (14[a]) Hetuvāda or Hetuvidya, and according to R. 182, also Muruntaka, and they are said (W. 253, R. 182, Tār. 271) to be, beside the Vatsīputrīyas,

[1] It should be observed, however, that in the list I, in St. J., each school is made to take its rise from the one mentioned before it.

one of the principal schools of the Sthaviras. The statements of the Chinese pilgrims agree with this.

Ch. 1 (Beal, i, p. lxx) states that the Vinaya of the S. is held to be particularly correct and agrees in essentials with that which is observed in China. Ch. 2 (Beal, i, pp. 18, 19, 49, &c., ii, pp. 182, 270, &c.) mentions them frequently as a branch of the Hīnayāna; the Bodhisattva Vasubandhu (Beal, i. 226) professed himself of this school. According to Ch. 3 (Takakusu, p. xxiv) the S. were (beside the Sthaviras, Mahāsaṃghikas and Saṃmatīyas) one of the four principal Buddhist schools; they themselves fell into four groups (Mūlasarvāstivādins, Dharmaguptas, Mahīśāsakas and Kāśyapīyas), and had spread mostly in Magadha and Eastern India. On their doctrines see W. 270 foll.; R. 184, 185, 190. See also Takakusu, *J.P.T.S.* 1904–1905, pp. 67 foll.

Here I will mention :—

14[b]. SB. Vibhajjavādin = NB. Vibhajyavādin. These are mentioned Mah. 5. 271. It is said here that the Buddha professed himself belonging to the V. From this as from the relation of the list in Tār. 271, 272 to the Ceylonese list (Dīp. 5. 45 foll.; Mah. 5. 6–9), Oldenberg[1] has concluded that V. is another name for the Theravādins. In the Mahābodhivaṃsa, besides, this is said in plain terms.[2] However, according to Tār. 272, the V. are reckoned as belonging to the Sarvāstivādins, beside which they appear in R. 182 as a Sthavira school. According to R. 186, 191, Tār. 271 they embrace the sects of the Mahīśāsakas, Kāśyapīyas, Dharmaguptakas and (14[c]) Tāmraśāṭīyas. The last named are in Tār. 272, 274 counted as belonging to the Sarvāstivādins and identified with the Saṃkrāntikas and (14[d]) the Uttarīyas.

If we resume these data it appears that Vibhajjavādin denotes not so much a particular sect but rather a philosophical tendency, which, for the Theravādins, was bound up

[1] *Vin. Piṭ.*, i, p. xli foll.

[2] P. 95[17]: *therānaṃ sambandhavacanattā theravādo ti, vibhajjavādinā munindena desitattā vibhajjavādo ti vuccati.* The same conclusion may be drawn from *Mah. Ṭīkā*, 94[8], 99[2].

with their conception of orthodoxy[1] and to which their different schools thenceforward laid claim.[2]

15. SB. Dhammaguttika = NB. Dharmaguptaka. They are, as we have just seen, reckoned as belonging to the Vibhajyavādins and are said (W. 254; VB. 300, 301; St. J. 335, 339, 342, 345 = lists II–V) to be a branch of the Mahīśāsaka. On their doctrines see W. 283, R. 192.

16. SB. Kassapiya = NB. Kāśyapīya, belonging also to the Vibhajyavādins. They took their rise in the Sarvāstivādins (W. 255; VB. 300, 301; St. J. 335, 340, 342, 346 = lists II–V) and are also called (16[a]) Suvarṣaka (W. and St. J. as above; cf. Tār. 271). For their doctrines see W. 283–284, R. 193.

17. SB. Saṃkantika = NB. Saṃkrāntivādin, a branch of the Sarvāstivādins (W. 255; BV. 300, 301; Tār. 271, 272; R. 193; St. J. 336, 340, 342 = lists II–IV). Their other name is said to be Uttarīya (R. 183; Tar. 273), also Tāmraśāṭīya (see under 14[b]). In W. 256, St. J. 336, 342 = lists II–IV they are identified with the Sautrāntika.

18. SB. Suttavāda = NB. Sautrāntika. The accounts of this school are far from clear. In the SB. sources no further mention is made of it. Its identity with 17 seems also to be evident from R. 186 where in the list the Sautrāntikas are introduced as a branch of the Sarvāstivādins, but the Saṃkrāntivādins are missing.

In Ch. 2 also the former (see Beal, i, pp. 139, 226; ii, p. 302) are mentioned, but not the latter. Besides, in list I, St. J. 332 the Sautrāntika evidently appear in the place of 17, being a branch of the Kāśyapīya. On the other hand, according to St. J. 340, 346 (lists III, V) the Sautrāntika would seem to be identical with the Prajñaptivādins (5), thus would belong not to the Sthaviras at all but to the Mahāsaṃghikas.

[1] Only thus can we understand how the Buddha himself can be called a Vibhajjavādī. He could never be called a Theravādī.

[2] Cf. Kathāvatthu (ed. Taylor), ii, p. 578, with the Co., pp. 177–178.

It seems that this last conclusion may also be drawn from R. 186 (n. 1) and Tār. 271.

Besides these eighteen schools the SB. sources mention the following branches:—

19. SB. HEMAVATA = NB. HAIMAVATA. See above 1[a].

20. SB. RĀJAGIRIYA = NB. RĀJAGIRIYA. They are counted (R. 186) as belonging to the Mahāsaṃghikas, but are missing entirely from the other list, R. 182. In Tār. 271, too, they only appear in the list belonging to the Mahāsaṃghikas. In the Chinese lists in St. J. they appear just as little as in Ch. 1, 2, 3.

21. SB. SIDDHATTHIKA. They are not mentioned in the NB. lists.

22. SB. PUBBASELIYA = NB. PŪRVAŚAILA. It is clear and beyond doubt, from all the data, that these are most closely related to the Caityika. They are mentioned beside them (R. 182, 186; Tār. 271) or positively in place of them (W. 251, 252). In Ch. 2 they are mentioned only once as the Avaraśaila (BEAL, ii, p. 221); Ch. 1 and 3 do not mention them. In St. J. 331, 334, 338, 342, 345 (lists I–V) the (22[a]) UTTARAŚAILA are also mentioned, always beside the Jetikas; in list I, VB. 300, also beside the Pūrvaśailas; and in list V, VB. 301 beside the Aparaśailas.

23. SB. APARASELIYA = NB. APARAŚAILA or AVARAŚAILA, introduced as a school of the Mahāsaṃghikas in W. 254, 255; R. 182, 186; Tār. 271.

24. SB. VĀJIRIYA (Dīp. 5. 54 = Aparарājagiriya). They are not mentioned in the northern sources, and the same may be said of the 23. DHAMMARUCI and 24. SĀGALIYA which are expressly called (Mah. 5. 13) Ceylonese sects.[1] Lastly, we may refer to the 25. VETULYA mentioned Mah. 36. 41, 111, also KERN's ingenious combination by which they are brought into relation with the Mahāyāna.

---

[1] On their origin see the interesting passage in the *Mah. Ṭīkā*, p. 115, l. 31 foll., translated by TURNOUR, *Mah.*, p. liii.

The different opinions as to the relation of the different sects to one another and their rise of one from another may be given in the form of a genealogical tree.

1. Vasumitra (W. 249; VB. 301) divides them after the separation of 1 and 2 thus—

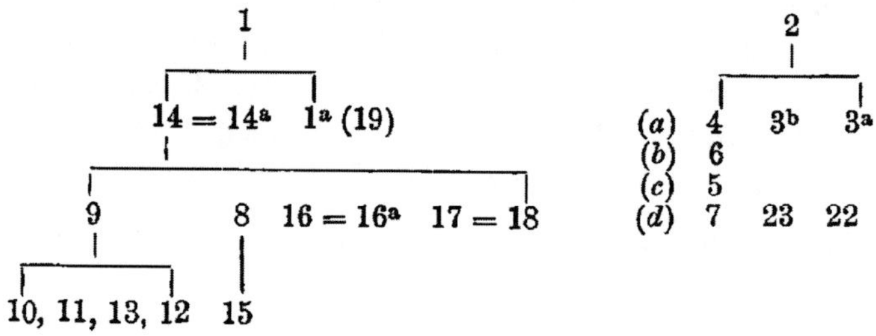

2. Bhavya (R. 182, 186) represents two views of which the one is based on the same division as in Vasumitra's list, but the second on an original division into three, where the Vibhajyavādins form the third group.

I.

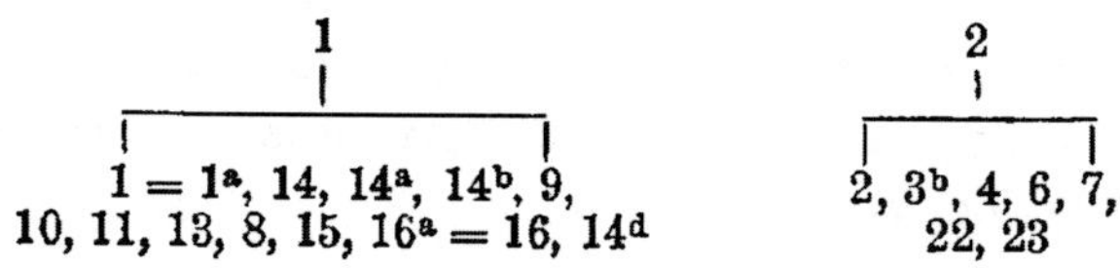

II.

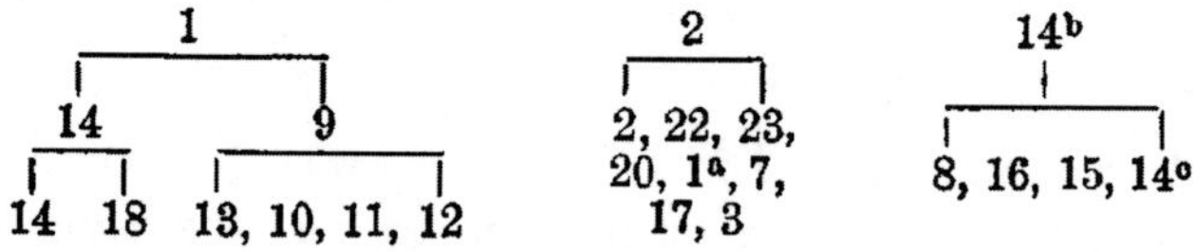

3. Tāranātha (270–271) gives four different lists: I, according to the Sthaviras; II, according to the Mahāsaṃghikas; III, according to the Saṃmatīyas; and IV, according to the Sarvāstivādins. The first is based on a division into two principal groups, the second on a similar division into three, the third and fourth on a division into four. The first two lists coincide with those of Bhavya.

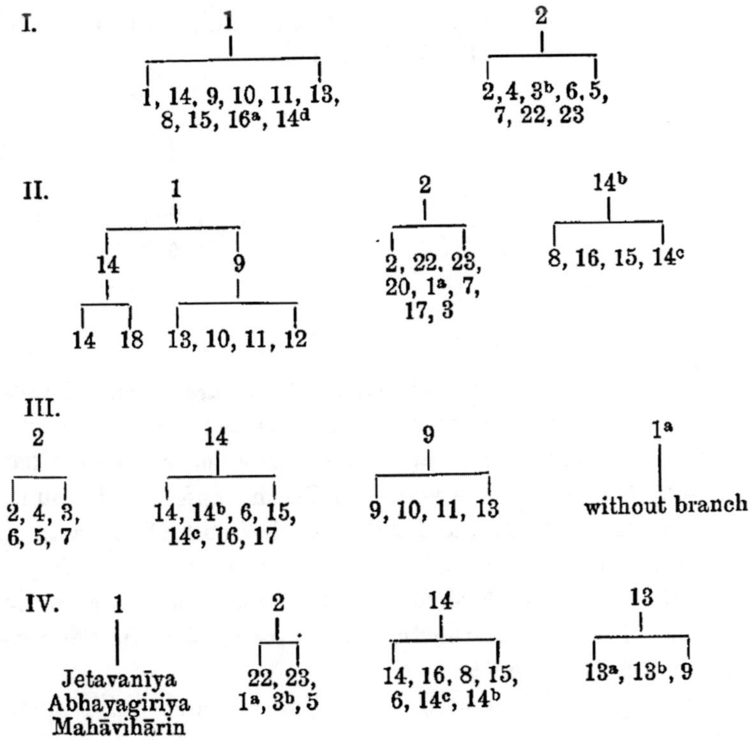

4. Of the Chinese lists in St. Julien the lists II–V are in agreement with each other and agree with Vasumitra's list with quite trifling variations. List I is connected with Bhavya's first list and Vasumitra's also (in BEAL), but makes each sect branch off from the preceding one within the two great groups. The series is as follows:—

1. : 14 : 1^a : 9 : 10 : 11 : 13 : 13^a[1] : 15 : 16 : 18.
2. : 4 : 3 : 6 : 7 : 22 : 22^a.

5. I-TSING admits four principal groups: (*a*) Mahāsaṃghika (with seven subdivisions); (*b*) Sthavira (with three subdivisions); (*c*) Sarvāstivāda (with Mūlasarvāstivāda, Dharmagupta, Mahīśāsaka, and Kāśyapīya as subdivisions); and (*d*) Saṃmitīya (with four subdivisions). Here, too, eighteen is given as the sum-total of the schools.

[1] The sect of the Abhayagirivāsins is inserted between 13 and 13^a.

6. According to Dīp. and Mah. the relation of the schools takes this shape (cf. list I of Tār.):—

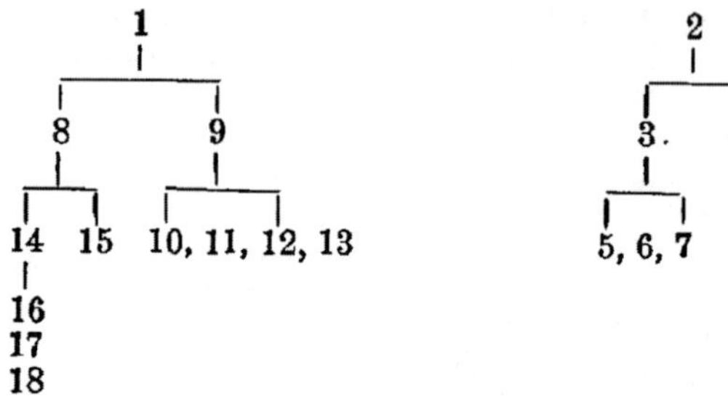

As regards the time at which the separate schools arose, according to the Ceylonese sources the first schism took place 100 years after the Nirvāṇa. The remaining sects must have arisen in the time between the Second and Third Council, i.e. between 100 A.B. and 247 A.B., the most of them in the second century after the Nirvāṇa, but the last six (19, 20, 21, 22, 23, 24) in the third century, the Dhammarucis, according to the Mah. Ṭīkā at the time of Vaṭṭagāmaṇi, the Sāgaliyas at that of Mahāsena.[1]

Among the Northern Buddhists we find quite similar traditions.

According to Vasumitra (W. 249 foll., VB. 301) the sects 4, 3^b, and 3^a, as also 6 and 5, were formed in the course of the second century A.B., that is, after the first schism. By the end of the second century 7, 22, and 22^a had arisen. In the third century arose 14 (14^a), and 1^a, later 9, and then 10, 11, 13, 12, also 8, and from this last 15. Only the rise of 17 (=18) is placed in the fourth century. These dates are transferred from Vasumitra into the Chinese lists (St. Julien).

The information given by I-tsing on the spread of the schools at his time, i.e. towards the end of the seventh century A.D.,[2] is of great interest. At that time the Sarvāstivādins prevailed in Magadha, the Saṃmitīyas in North-west India, the Sarvāstivādins in the North, and in the South the Sthaviras. In the East the four great groups, i.e. the three above mentioned and the Mahāsaṃghikas, were mixed.

[1] See p. 283, n. 1.

[2] Takakusu, *I-tsing*, pp. 8-9.

In the polemics of the Kathāvatthu[1] the most prominent schools, according to the commentator Buddhaghosa, are the Theravādins, the Saṃmitīyas, the Mahiṃsāsakas, the Sabbatthavādins, and the Mahāsaṃghikas. But more frequently than these the names Andhaka and Uttarapathaka are employed, in which Buddhaghosa evidently comprises the South Indian and North Indian sects.

[1] See Rhys Davids, *J.R.A.S.* 1891, p. 413.

APPENDIX C

CAMPAIGNS OF PAṆḌUKĀBHAYA (Mah. 10. 27 foll.) AND DUṬṬHAGĀMAṆI (Mah. 25. 1 foll.)

PAṆḌUKĀBHAYA takes refuge from the persecution of his uncles in Paṇḍulagāmaka.

The place is unknown. In our inquiry, therefore, we must take as starting-point Paṇa, where he gathers together his first followers, to engage in battle with his uncles.

Paṇa is situated near Kāsapabbata. This name has been, I believe, preserved in the modern Kahagala-gama,[1] the name of a village situated about ten miles to the north of Kaḷuwæwa and fifteen miles to the south-west of Anurādhapura.

From Paṇa he does not direct his march northward on the then capital of the country Upatissagāma.[2] He is not strong enough for this. Rather he is obliged to follow the tactics of all rebels, to bring first the border-districts, the *paccantagāmā*, into his power.[3] Therefore he marches first towards the south-east, more or less along the line which Duṭṭhagāmaṇi followed, in the opposite direction in his march against Anurādhapura. Probably the old military road ran along here. So he comes first into the district of Girikaṇḍasiva. This name is, we may conjecture, connected with that of Girilaka, which is mentioned Mah. 25. 47 with reference to Duṭṭhagāmaṇi's campaign. We must look for this district between the Kaḷuwæwa and the Riṭigala.

[1] On the map of Ceylon, four miles to an inch.

[2] Upatissagāma is situated on the Gambhīranadī (Mah. 7. 44) to the north of Anurādhapura. From here to the Gambhīranadī (Mah. 28. 7) is a distance of a yojana = 7–8 miles. By this we arrive at a general notion of the position of Upatissagāma.

[3] GEIGER, *Dīp. and Mah.*, pp. 39–40.

P. now marches on southward of Riṭigala to the spot where the Ambanganga and Mahawæliganga unite. To the south of the Mineri-tank the people of Girikaṇḍasiva come up with him. The result is the battle of Kalaha-nagara. This is the Kalahagala[1] of the present day, situated 7–8 miles distant from the lake mentioned. Not far from here we must look for the scene of the second battle of Lohitavāhakhaṇḍa (Mah. 10. 43).

Although the victory in both battles is attributed to P., he does not yet venture to attack Upatissagāma directly. On the contrary, he continues his march in the direction followed hitherto, and crosses the Mahawæliganga (*pāragaṅgaṃ*, Mah. 10. 44).

The place where he crossed over must have been the Kacchaka-ford, which I take to be the Mahagantoṭa[2] below the spot where the Ambanganga flows into the Mahawæliganga.

As the base of further operations P. chooses a region on the right bank of the Mahāgaṅgā (Mahawæliganga), the Doḷa-mountain. This name survives in that of the village Dolagalawela[3] in the Bintenne district, twenty miles to the north of the place so named, which is now called Alutnuwara.

During the four years that P. spends near the Doḷa-mountain he is said to have been making preparations for the really decisive battle. This is made possible for him by the fact that he has now the whole province of Rohaṇa, with all its resources, behind him. By his position he has also the key to the most important or the only ford of the Mahawæliganga.

In the meantime P.'s uncles have also completed their preparations. They march against the rebels and entrench themselves on the Dhūmarakkha-mountain. Its position is shown clearly by Mah. 10. 53, 57, 58. We must look for it

[1] See *Census of Ceylon*, 1901, iv, p. 468.

[2] *Itinerary of Roads in Ceylon*, i (1909), p. 39, no. 68.

[3] *Census*, 1901, iv, p. 262. The Doḷukaṇḍa which PARKER (*Ancient Ceylon*, p. 192) mentions cannot be the Doḷa-pabbata of the Mah., since it is situated (PARKER, in a letter dated July 17, 1910) about ten miles to the north of Kurunægala.

on the left bank of the Mahawæliganga, not far from the Kacchaka-ford. The chief object of the uncles was evidently to prevent P. from crossing the river.

However, to be beforehand with them, P. risks the crossing. He defeats the enemy in flight, and takes possession of their camp. He then proceeds on the direct road to the capital.

On the Ariṭṭha-pabbata (Riṭigala) he pitches an entrenched camp which is to serve as a base for his final operations. The uncles once more march against him with fresh troops. The decisive battle takes place near Lābu-gāmaka (Mah. 10. 72), the Labunoruwa [1] of the present day, on the north-west slope of the Riṭigala. P. carries off the victory.

The road to the capital now lies open to him. He takes possession of it and afterwards, having assumed sole sovereignty, he removes the royal residence to Anurādhapura.

We see that the information given by the Mahāvaṃsa on Paṇḍukābhaya's campaigns, if rightly understood, is quite adequate. The military measures taken seem thoroughly methodical; their aim can be clearly understood.

On quite similar lines is the advance of Duṭṭhagāmaṇi on Anurādhapura, a proof that we have to do in both cases with old connecting roads between the regions left and right of the Mahawæliganga. P. was obliged to secure these in order to carry out successfully his operations against Upatissagāma. D. used them for bringing up his troops.

Duṭṭhagāmaṇi starts (Mah. 25. 5) from Mahāgāma in Rohaṇa, the site of which is indicated by the ruins of Tissa-Mahārāma in the South Province, sixteen miles north-east of Hambantoṭa. Taking a northerly direction, he marches through Guttahālaka, [2] now Buttala, towards Mahiyaṅgaṇa. This, according to the local tradition, is the modern Bintenne or Alutnuwara.

[1] *Census*, 1901, iv, p. 464.

[2] The evidence for this site is chiefly Mah. 24. 17. D. stations outposts in G. on the look-out for his brother Tissa, whose advance from Dīghavāpi is expected here.

D. is here on the bank of the Mahawæliganga. Now follows the enumeration of a whole series of forts which were occupied by Damiḷas and taken by D.

Among these, too, appears Kaccha-tittha (now Mahagantoṭa), to take which required a four months' siege (Mah. 25. 12). I think, therefore, that the places mentioned are mere frontier-outposts or forts which had been placed along the Mahawæliganga[1] from the bend of the river above Bintenne to the neighbourhood of the mouth. The individual names cannot now be settled.

The remains of the vanquished Damiḷa-divisions retreat towards Vijita-nagara. It still seems to me most probable that we should look for this city in the neighbourhood of Kaḷuwæwa, where the Vijitapura-vihāra is now situated, and ruins in the jungle testify to the former existence of a larger settlement.[2]

In all probability D. will have crossed the Mahāgaṅgā near Kacchaka-tittha. On the advance against Vijita he first followed the same road that Paṇḍukābhaya used when he marched from the Kāsa-pabbata to the Doḷa-pabbata. It must have run somewhere between Sīgiri and the Mineri-tank.

The siege and storming of Vijita are described with great clearness and vivacity. The further stations, Girilaka, Mahela-nagara, and Kāsa-pabbata lay far along the road which leads from Dambul to Anurādhapura. On the Kāsa-pabbata D. entrenched himself, evidently in order to await in a favourable position his adversary Eḷāra. Here again in fact it comes to a decisive battle, the fortunate issue of which opens to D. the road to the capital. The conquered foe was pursued up to the immediate vicinity of Anurādhapura. In a last attempt to bring the fleeing troops to a halt beneath the walls of the city Eḷāra falls by the hand of D. in heroic single combat.

[1] Cf. Mah. 25. 19, where this seems to be plainly said.

[2] Burrows, *Buried Cities of Ceylon*, p. 75. Parker certainly (*Ancient Ceylon*, p. 237 foll.) looks for Vijita in the region of the later Poḷonnaruwa.

APPENDIX D

LIST OF PĀLI TERMS OCCURRING IN THE TRANSLATION

1. Ācariya, 'teacher, master.' See p. 31, n. 4.

2. Arahant. Literally 'able, worthy', a person who has reached the ideal. In an Arahant the *āsavā*, the deadly drugs of delusion, are brought to an end; he is no longer subject to re-birth, but lives in Nirvāṇa, the final liberation. Rhys Davids, *Buddhism*, 110; *Early Buddhism*, 72–74.

3. Ārāma, 'park, garden.' Designation of a Buddhist convent = *vihāra*, Childers, *Pāli Dictionary*, s.v.

4. Āsava. The term is hardly translatable. It has been first explained by Rhys Davids, *Dialogues*, i, p. 92, ii, p. 28 (= SBB. ii, iii). According to Buddhaghosa, Asl. 48[15], well-matured spirituous liquors are called *āsavā*. Jāt. IV. 222[19] we read: *āsavo tāta lokasmiṃ surā nāma pavuccati.* The underlying idea is, therefore, that of 'overwhelming intoxication', not that of a deadly flood. There are four *āsavā*: (1) *kāma* 'lust, desire', (2) *bhava* '(desire of a future) existence', (3) *avijjā* 'ignorance (of the four holy truths)', and (4) *diṭṭhi* 'false belief'. D. I. 84; II. 81; M. I. 7, &c., *khīṇāsava* 'one who has overcome the āsavas', and *anāsava* 'one who is free from the āsavas', are epithets of the *arahant.*

5. Bhikkhu, Bhikkhuṇī, mendicant monk, nun. Member of the Buddhist order.

6. Buddha (*Saṃbuddha, Sammā-Saṃbuddha* convey the same notion in a heightened degree) denotes a being who by his own force has attained to possession of the highest knowledge. He is neither man nor god. He is able to perform certain wonders in accord with the laws of nature. In an endless

series of existences the Buddha prepares himself for his state of Buddhahood. During the whole of this time he is called a *bodhisatta* (Skt. *bodhisattva*) till in his last existence as a man—the last but one he generally spends in a heaven of the gods—he attains to knowledge (*bodhi, sambodhi, abhisambodhi*). In the ancient texts *sambodhi* is always the insight of an Arahant.[1] Since this event comes to pass for the historical Buddha under an *assattha* tree (*Ficus religiosa*), this is the sacred tree of the Buddhists, and the 'Bodhi-tree' (Sinh. *bōgaha*) is not lacking in any Buddhist sanctuary in Ceylon.

A Paccekabuddha has also reached Nirvāṇa (see below) by his own force, but does not come forward as a teacher. The historical Buddha is called, after his family, Gotama Buddha or Sakyamuni, 'the sage of the house of the Sakyas.' See Kern, p. 62 foll.

7. Cetiya. See under Thūpa.

8. Devatā, divinity, genius, particularly applied to the spirits which, according to popular belief, inhabit trees, wells, hills, and in fact every place. In Mah. 28. 6 a *devatā* of the royal parasol is mentioned.

9. Dhamma, truth, religion, the sum-total of Buddhist doctrine. Opposed to *vinaya*, 'Discipline, the monastic rule,' Dhamma in the more restricted sense denotes the second part of the tipiṭaka (which see).

10. Karīsa, first a measure of capacity; in another sense an area of about 4 acres, i.e. as much ground as can be sown with a *karīsa* of seed-corn. See Rhys Davids, *Ancient Coins and Measures of Ceylon*, p. 18.

11. Khattiya (Skt. *kṣatriya*), the class of nobles or warriors. This was one of the four ancient *vaṇṇā*, or social grades. The Buddhists and Jainas put them first in the list, the Brahmans put themselves first. The Khattiyas have been sometimes called a caste; but they never formed an organized community, like the modern castes, with connubium and commensality between all Khattiyas. See Rhys Davids, *Dialogues*, i. 96–107; *Buddhist India*, 52 ff.

[1] Rhys Davids, *Dialogues*, i, pp. 190–192.

12. Manta, formula, sacred formula, charm, spell, designation of the Vedic hymns. Cf. Mah. 5. 109.

13. Nāga, designation of supernatural beings, snake-demons, sometimes represented in human form with a snake's hood in the neck, sometimes as mixed forms, half man half snake. They are distinguished by devout reverence toward the Buddha. Their sworn enemies are the Garuḍa, winged beings resembling the griffin (cf. p. 129, n. 4). See Grünwedel, *Buddhist. Kunst*, p. 42 foll.

14. Nibbāṇa (Skt. *nirvāṇa*). One of the terms for Arahantship. At Saṃyutta IV. 251, 261 it is defined as the destruction (in the heart) of *rāga*, *dosa*, and *moha* (lust, illwill, and stupidity); and is stated to be attainable by the eightfold Path. See also de la Vallée Poussin, *Bouddhisme*, p. 57 ff.

15. Pabbajjā. Literally 'going forth'; the technical term for giving up the household life and becoming a *religieux*, entering an order. The rules for the reception of candidates for membership varied in the various orders. The Buddhist rules are now translated by Rhys Davids and H. Oldenberg, *Vinaya Texts*, vol. i. When a candidate is first admitted he is called a *Sāmaṇera*, novice.

16. Paccekabuddha. See under Buddha.

17. Pariveṇa, monk's cell, the private dwelling of a bhikkhu within the monastery.

18. Pavāraṇā, 'invitation,' name of a festival held by the bhikkhus at the close of the *vassa*, i.e. the rainy season, spent in the monastery. See *Vinaya Texts*, i, pp. 335–353.

19. Samaṇa, 'ascetic,' designation of the Buddhist priests as opposed to the Brāhmaṇa.

20. Sāmaṇera. See under Pabbajjā.

21. Saṃghatthera. See under Thera.

22. Sudda (Skt. *Śūdra*), a man of the fourth, non-Aryan caste.

23. Tāla. Lit. 'palm,' a measure of length. Rhys Davids, *Ancient Coins, &c.*, p. 18.

24. Tathāgata, one of the terms of veneration applied to the Buddhas. The Buddha usually speaks of himself thus. The meaning is a matter of controversy. The native commentators explain the word in quite different ways. See Burnouf, *Introduction à l'histoire du Bouddhisme indien*, p. 75.

25. Thera, Therī (Skt. *sthavira*, °*rā*), term of respect applied to monks and nuns, especially to those of venerable age. *Saṃghatthera* is the denotion of the senior priest in any assembly of bhikkhus, or in the whole community. See *J.P.T.S.* 1908, p. 19.

26. Thūpa (Skt. *stūpa*, tope), name of edifices which serve as receptacle for a relic or as monument. They are hemispherical or bell-shaped, and rest upon a base of three concentric stories which form ambulatories round the tope; they sustain a cubical erection, the so-called *tee* from which rises the spire (*chatta*) which crowns the whole. The relic-chamber (*dhātugabbha*, whence the name 'Dagaba', used in Ceylon for the whole edifice) is in the interior, below the *tee*.

The expression *cetiya* (Skt. *caitya*), originally the most general term for 'sanctuary'—a tree, too, can be a *cetiya*—is used in the Mah. mostly as a synonym for *thūpa*. Cf., for instance, *Mahācetiya* or *Mahāthūpa* as the name of the Ruwanwæli-Dagaba in Anurādhapura.

There is frequent mention in the Mah. of a *thūpaghara* or *cetiyaghara*, 'house of the thūpa or cetiya.'

There can be no doubt, from Mah. 31. 29, that sometimes a sort of roof or temple was built over the tope. In Anurādhapura the Thūpārāma-Dagaba is surrounded by four concentric rows of pillars. It appears as if the two inner rows, where the capitals of the pillars have tenons, were intended to bear the roof of a thūpaghara. Parker (*Ancient Ceylon*, p. 270) considers it altogether possible, differing in this from Smither (*Anurádhapura*, p. 7). Of course such temples could only be constructed over the smaller thūpas, and, as far as I can see, are only mentioned in this case. If mention is made of a *bodhighara*, i.e. of a temple for the bodhi-tree, then it is naturally only a question of building round and not over the sacred tree.

27. TIPIṬAKA (Skt. *tripiṭaka*). Lit. 'three baskets,' collective name for the canonical scriptures of the Buddhists. They fall into three main divisions, Vinaya-piṭaka, Sutta-p. (or Dhamma), and Abhidhamma-p. See CHILDERS, s.v.; KERN, p. 1 foll.

28. UPASAMPADĀ, the solemn ordination of the monk who is a novice until that time, by a chapter of the order; the higher consecration of the priesthood. See CHILDERS, s.v.; KERN, p. 77 foll.; SP. HARDY, *Eastern Monachism*, p. 44 foll.

29. UPOSATHA (Skt. *upavasatha*). The Buddhist sabbath which is considered a holy day both for priests and laymen. It occurs four times in the month: on the full- and new-moon day, and on the eighth day following full- and new-moon. On two of these four days the recitation of the Pātimokkha-precepts (*pātimokkhuddesa*) takes place, i.e. the priestly ceremony of confession, in which every member of the order is to acknowledge the faults he has committed. CHILDERS, s.v.; KERN, p. 99.

Uposathāgāra, or *uposathaghara*, is a building belonging to the monastery used for the performance of the uposatha ceremonies.

30. VEDĪ or VEDIKĀ (Skt. the same), means first 'terrace, altar'. When in Mah. 36. 52 a *pāsāṇavedī* around the bodhi-tree is mentioned, it means a stone terrace, on which such sacred trees usually stand. Cf. in the same sense *silāvedī*, Mah. 36. 103.

Further, this word has the sense of 'terrace with balustrade'. It is to be understood thus in D. II. pp. 182–183 in the description of Sudassana's palace. Exactly in the same manner, D. II. pp. 181–182, by *sopāna* a 'staircase with balustrade' is meant, and in both passages an accurate description follows, not of the terrace or of the staircase, but especially of the rail.

When a *muddhavedī* and *pādavedī* of a thūpa are mentioned (Mah. 35. 2) the former is the so-called *tee*, the latter the storied base (see no. 26). Railings in relief are frequently added to both. SMITHER, p. 52, 27. Finally the meaning 'balustrade, railing' supersedes the others. Thus by the coral-vedikās to the *kūṭāgāra*, the 'window-chambers' of the Lohapāsāda, the parapet-balustrade to the windows is evidently meant. Cf. *vedikā-vātapāna,* C.V. VI. 2. 2. Plainly in the same way *vedikā,* C.V. V. 14. 2, means a balustrade. See *S.B.E.* xx, p. 104, n. 3; p. 162, n. 4.

31. VESSA (Skt. *vaiśya*), a man of the third social grade.

32. VIHĀRA, dwelling, habitation for gods as also for monks, therefore temple or convent (FERGUSSON, *History of Indian and Eastern Architecture,* 1910, i, p. 170). In the Mah. the latter meaning prevails.

33. YAKKHA (f. *yakkhiṇī*; Skt. *yakṣa, yakṣiṇī*), designation of certain supernatural beings who are under the rule of Vessavaṇa (Skt. *Vaiśravaṇa,* name of the god Kubera). In the Mah. the aboriginal inhabitants of Ceylon are frequently called Yakkha.

34. YOJANA, a measure of length. According to the system of the Abhidhānappadīpikā 196, 1 *yojana* is = 4 *gāvuta* = 80 *usabha* = 20 *yaṭṭhi* = 7 *ratana* (or *hattha* 'ell') = 2 *vidatthi* (span) = 12 *aṅgula*. According to RHYS DAVIDS, *Ancient Coins* &c., p. 15 foll., the native tables of linear measures make the yojana between 12 and 12½ miles, but in actual practice it must have been reckoned as 7–8 miles.

INDEXES

(The numbers refer to pages and notes)

A. LIST OF GEOGRAPHICAL AND TOPOGRAPHICAL NAMES

B. LIST OF TERMS EXPLAINED IN THE NOTES

ADDENDA

v. 132. The meaning is as follows: The words *gacchāti* are a polite form of refusing a mendicant friar: 'go on (to the next house).' Therefore Siggava could say that he had received something (i. e. a polite answer), without telling a lie. Formerly he had received nothing at all, no alms, nor even an answer, but had been entirely disregarded. See *Milinda-pañha* 8; Rhys Davids, *S.B.E.* xxxv, p. 15, and note.

xxix. 40. Translate: From his dwelling-place, the Vattaniya (ārāma) in the Viñjhā forest hills came the thera Uttara &c.

PALI TEXT SOCIETY

Translation Series.

The Pali Text Society having published almost all the original texts of the canonical Pali scriptures has now undertaken a series of translations in order to make these important historical texts better known. The series will include versions of texts not in the Canon, if such texts are either themselves of historical importance or throw light on the interpretation or history of the texts or of the doctrine they contain.

At present there have appeared the following :—

1. **Psalms of the Early Buddhists**, Part I, Psalms of the Sisters, translated from the *Therī-gāthā*. By Mrs. Rhys Davids, M.A., Lecturer on Indian Philosophy at Manchester University, Fellow of University College, London. Price 5*s*. net.

'We conclude with best thanks to Mrs. Rhys Davids for the capital work she has given us . . . and the hope that the psalms of the brethren will follow soon.'—*Journal of the Royal Asiatic Society.*

'Are of much interest as a contribution to the history of women under Monasticism and as an expression of the Buddhist view of life.'—*The Times.*

'Next to her learned husband, the distinguished Professor of Comparative Religion at the Manchester University, there is probably no more authoritative exponent of Pali Buddhistic literature in this country than Mrs. Rhys Davids, the author of this interesting work, issued in an elegant and attractive form by the Pali Text Society.'—*The Manchester Guardian.*

'The verses give us many exceedingly interesting glimpses of the religious spirit of the East in its redeeming work. . . . The present work is intended for serious students, and not for those in search of simplified versions of the world's religions. It is published for the Pali Text Society, and will be welcomed by those who are interested in the East.'—*The Daily News.*

'A baffling sense of the futility of much that we so desperately busy ourselves about comes into the mind in reading these pages. A strange and elusive influence seems to haunt them—an influence that does not age nor change. It speaks with a voice that echoes in many a volume of modern poetry. We read, and seem to be striving in some inexplicable way to remember, and to be groping after the forgotten vicissitudes of our own countless lives.'—*The Westminster Gazette.*

'Mrs. Rhys Davids's rendering is masterly—in places it reflects what seems to be very fine poetry—and her notes and introduction sustain her high reputation as a scholar.'—*The New York Nation.*

'Dass der Übersetzerin die vortrefflichsten Hilfsmittel der Pālilexikographie zur Hand sind, wird der fachkundige Leser an mehr als einer Stelle bemerken. Weit aber über den Kreis der Fachgenossen hinaus wird dieses Buch geschätzt und genossen werden können als ein seltenes Specimen philologischer und ästhetischer Durchbildung.'—*Deutsche Literaturzeitung.*

'The English reading public is in a position, thanks to her accomplished hand, to study these ancient testimonies to the power of Buddhist doctrine in a complete and satisfactory form. . . . It has long been recognized, in the study of Sanskrit literature, that it is vain to attempt to dispense with the help of native light, and to interpret texts solely by means of grammar and lexicon. No doubt much may be explained without the vernacular commentators, and the student must always exercise his critical faculty in using them, but, with all reserves made, these commentators do stand closer to their texts than occidentals can stand, and point out many things that, without their help, would be overlooked or only half understood. "Chaque pays a sa pensée" says the French poet, and the greater German poet bids us go to the poet's country if we would understand the poet's word. Of all this Mrs. Rhys Davids has been duly mindful, and her version has gained much in point of trustworthiness on this account. But the flow and spontaneity of the verse has by no means suffered through this accuracy and rigid adherence to the tradition. The metrical form moves lightly withal, and this freedom of movement is a witness to the sympathy of the translator with the thoughts of the ancient Therīs.—*The Buddhist Review.*

2. **Compendium of Philosophy**, being a translation of the *Abhidhammattha-sangaha*. By Shwe Zan Aung, B.A., revised and edited by Mrs. Rhys Davids. Price 5*s*. net.

'The translation now before us is, in the best and fullest sense of the words, the result of Eastern and Western effort combined. The most intrinsically interesting part of the book, the Appendix (pp. 220–85), which contains Mr. Aung's extensive notes on some of the most important technical terms of Buddhist philosophy, will be found extremely useful by all students of Buddhism. More especially I would point out the very lucid and highly instructive discussions on the vexed question of the Paṭiccasamuppāda and on the true meaning of the term Saṃkhārā. Three useful indexes add to the usefulness of the volume, for which both the English editor and the Burmese author deserve our best thanks, and on the publication of which the Pali Text Society is to be heartily congratulated.'—*Journal of the Royal Asiatic Society.*

'Ein entscheidender Grund für die Unzulänglichkeit unserer bezüglichen Kenntnisse ist aber wohl darin zu suchen, dass die Gedankenkreise, in denen die buddhistische Weltanschauung sich bewegt, so wenig mit okzidentalischen Begriffen in Einklang zu bringen sind, dass eine wesentliche Förderung in der angedeuteten Richtung vielleicht nur dann zu erhoffen ist, wenn es gelingen sollte, die berufenen Vertreter der buddhistischen Gelehrsamkeit in den in Frage kommenden Ländern—vor allem Japan, Birma, Ceylon—für die Übersetzung und Bearbeitung der massgebenden Werke zu interessieren. Dass eine derartige Teilnahme an der wissenschaftlichen Erforschung des Buddhismus, namentlich soweit dessen jüngere Entwicklungszustände in Betracht kommen, nur von dem vorteilhaftesten Einfluss sein könnte, wird vor allem auch durch die hier vorliegende Übersetzung eines der wichtigsten neu-buddhistischen Texte der "südlichen" Schule, der "Zusammenfassung des Sinnes des Abhidhamma", durch den Birmesen Shwe Zan Aung nahegelegt. Der Name des Mitherausgebers, Mrs. Rhys Davids, bietet für die Zuverlässigkeit der Übersetzung sowohl wie für die in Anhängen und Bemerkungen gebotene Bearbeitung der verschiedenartigen Probleme, vor allem auch philosophiegeschichtlichen Inhalts, die beste Gewähr.'—*Deutsche Literaturzeitung.*

'Here, for the first time in the history of modern research into the ancient Buddhist lore, we have a work produced by a Buddhist scholar, working in a Buddhist land with all the immense advantage which a life-long training, the actual religion, and free access to the living tradition of the monasteries confer; himself also a deep student of the western philosophical systems; and his work is rendered, if possible, of still greater value, by the revision and collaboration of one who may justly be admitted to be the foremost living occidental authority on the subject. . . . The editor has, with characteristic acumen and appreciation of their high value, considerably augmented the usefulness of the work before us by the inclusion, in an appendix of some 60 pp., of a number of notes written by the author in the course of the correspondence which the work involved. Here, once more, we have Buddhist psychology as the born and instructed Buddhist student sees it, and many an occidental Buddhist student will find in these important notes much matter for deep study as well as great enlightenment.'—*The Rangoon Gazette.*